CW00549881

The Wasikadars of Awadh

The Wasikadars of Awadh

A History of Certain Nineteenth Century Families of Lucknow

MALCOLM SPEIRS

Rupa & Co

Typeset in Aldine by
Mindways Design
1410 Chiranjiv Tower
43 Nehru Place
New Delhi 110 019

Printed in India by
Rekha Printers Pvt. Ltd.
A-102/1 Okhla Industrial Area, Phase-II
New Delhi-110 020

Dedication

To my late father, Lawrence Speirs, who inspired me with all his memories of his childhood in India, fostered my interest in the land that had been home to four generations of our family, and provided me with an excellent basis for my subsequent detailed research about our family history

Dedication

CONTENTS

ACKNOWLEDGEMENT

I would like to acknowledge with thanks the help and assistance given to me in England by the staff of the 'Asia, Pacific and African Collections' Department of the British Library on my many visits there; by the staff of King's College, London, Archives Department and by the staff of the Norfolk Records Office in Norwich. In Scotland, I would similarly like to thank the staff of the Mitchell Library, Glasgow; the staff of the Strathclyde Records Office (in the Mitchell Library); and Mark Crichton Maitland, for permitting me to research the private records of the Speirs family held at Houston House, Houston. In India, I warmly thank for their help the staff of the National Archives, New Delhi; the staff of the Uttar Pradesh State Archives, Lucknow; Mr D'Souza, the Principal of La Martiniere College, Lucknow; the Principal of Oak Grove School, Mussourie; Father Robert Pinto, parish priest of St Joseph's Cathedral, Lucknow; and most particularly Dr Yadendra Yadav and the staff of the Wasika Office, Lucknow, for giving permission and assisting me in searching the records.

My very special thanks must go to Dr Rosie Llewellyn-Jones, who very kindly looked through early drafts of this book and gave me a great deal of guidance and many hints on improving my style of writing. Also, of course, her well-researched books on Lucknow have assisted me immensely whilst writing the book. I am likewise greatly indebted to Cherry Armstrong, who gave me a vast amount of information on the Pogson family (see Chapter 8) and much assistance in writing this section. I am grateful to Annette Moriarty for providing information and photographs of my great-uncle William and to Caroline Laing for recent information on the Duhan family. I thank Dr Lindsay Gethin for providing a lot of information on the La Frenais family.

I am particularly grateful to Rizwan Rahman of Delhi, to Nurul Abidin and Ehtishan-ul-Dahma of Aligarh, to Asma Manan of Bhopal and Tayyaba Qidwai of Muscat for their help. They are all descendents of Maulvi Syed Zain-ul-Abidin, and without their assistance the chapter on Wahidunnisa Begum could not have been written. They warmly welcomed me to their homes and helped me solve this mystery.

I sincerely believe that I could not have completed my work in Lucknow without the assistance of my good friend Ram Advani. From the first time that I set foot in his bookshop, Ram has helped and encouraged me immensely. He brought me in contact with many people of Lucknow who have helped in my research. Through Ram I met Professor Nayyur Massood, Dr Ahsan-ul-Zafar, Professor Shah Abdus Salam, Anwar Abbas, Austin Lobo, Mrs Nandini Shepherd and many others who have all helped with my research.

I thank my publishers, Rupa & Co, for having faith in my work. I have a special debt of gratitude to Milee Ashwarya, the editor of the book, who has made innumerable improvements to the original text—transforming my inelegant prose into a readable book. Thank you so much for your hard work and patience.

And finally I offer my grateful thanks to my wife, Doreen, who has assisted and encouraged me through all the years of research, and has patiently read through and commented on each of my drafts. Doreen has never complained when I neglected household matters, burying myself in my study, or spending long days at the British Library, or long periods of research in India. Thank you for being so understanding.

PROLOGUE

Letter from Alexander Speirs to Walter Logan, Canal Office, Glasgow, NB

Marlow College,
29 May 1803

Sir,

I am now settled in the Military College in expectation of which I waited so long in London. I find now if I had been detained one week less I should not have been admitted which I am certain I would if it had not been by accident I met a gentleman who was going down to see his son at the College; for the most part of the way there was no person in the coach but himself, a friend of his and myself. He was from Scotland and seeing that I was from Scotland likewise he asked me if I knew old Mrs Spiers. I told him I did; he said he was very intimately acquainted with her and asked me if I was going to the Academy. I told him I was. He asked me who I was recommended to there and if I had any letter of introduction. I told him I had not but I showed him the papers that I received at the India House. He told me that it would admit me but it was very curious that Mr Elphinstone had given me no other; but he said he should do everything that lay in his power. He was acquainted with some of the officers who command us and by that means he got me easily admitted into the College until such time as a Collegiate Board should assemble to examine me which was in the latter end of the week. The regulations that you gave me were wrong in several places. There were several things that I was obliged to have that were not mentioned in it. We only get one shilling per week allowed (to) us instead of half a crown, but all the cadets either get money sent them from their friends or some other persons in London are ordered by their friends to advance it for them to purchase any necessaries they may want. I want some things at present such as drawers. I got some when I came to the College but they were so slight that they are all going to pieces already. I have very good flannel drawers which I got in Glasgow but they won't allow us to wear them. I would apply to Mr Elphinstone but I do not know whether he is allowed to advance any more or not. He paid my accounts in London (on) the money he drew out of the hands of the bankers to whom I had the letter of Credit which I am afraid was wrong as the sum specified was 45£ to pay for my board at the College. If you would write (to) Mr Spiers and let him know of it and as we are to get two months leave in winter namely Dec and Jan I wish you would let me know what I am to do as no Cadets are allowed to stay during that time at the College. I am sorry to trouble you any longer about the watch but as it is almost absolutely necessary here as we are so much confined to hours and as almost all the Cadets have them I wish you would mention it and the money as I receive some letters from Scotland which come up to a deal more than my week's allowance and likewise we are obliged to purchase a great parts of our pens as the College only allows three per week and when (I need) paper. I should have wrote Mr Spiers himself as Mr Elphinstone particularly desired me but I did not know his address. If you would favour me with an answer as soon as possible it would much oblige.

Your most obed. &c
Alexr Spiers

By Direct
Royal Military College,
Great Marlow, Bucks[1]

My father traced the above letter during a research visit to Scotland in 1987, from a perusal of an index of private family papers held at the Scottish National Register of Archives. When he subsequently visited Houston House, the ancestral home of the Speirs family, and was kindly shown the letter, he was delighted to realise that the letter proved what had been passed down our family for four generations, but which we had never previously been able to provide evidence for.

The letter establishes beyond any reasonable doubt that our ancestor, Alexander Speirs (who went to India as an Officer in the EIC army following his training at the Royal Military College), was the illegitimate son of Archibald Speirs, a rich tobacco merchant, and the grandson of Alexander Speirs, one of the most successful tobacco merchants of Glasgow. And the proof is simply that this letter was found amongst Archibald Speirs' papers.

Recently, however, the majority of the Speirs family papers from Houston House have been purchased by the Glasgow City Archives— so it is now possible to study these papers in much greater detail. An in-depth study has now revealed a further forty-three letters from Alexander Speirs, written whilst he was a Cadet at Marlow, together with several draft replies, accounts and bills covering his expenses both before and during his stay at Marlow. Let us now continue the story of his days at Marlow and before.

One major discovery from reading Alexander's letters was that in order to gain admittance to the Royal Military College, both he and his father had lied on oath about his age on admittance! Having found the following sworn certificates in the Cadet papers of the India Office Collections at the British Library, our family had naturally accepted these statements as they stood:

> I Alexr Spiers presented for the Appointment of Cadet by the Honourable Wm Elphinstone, do make oath & swear that I have caused search to be made for a Parish Register, whereby to ascertain my age, but am unable to produce the same, there being none to be found, & further I make oath & swear that from the information of my parents (& other relations) which information I believe to be true, that I was born in the Parish of Paisley in

Scotland on the 17th of Dec 1788 & that I am not at this time under the age of fourteen or above twenty-two years.

Witness my hand
The 30th day of March 1803
Alexander Spiers

Sworn at the Mansion House
London 30th March 1803
before Notary Crice Mayon[2]

I do certify that Alexander Spiers my son was fourteen years of age in the month of December last.

Witness my hand at Glasgow
This 3rd day of February 1803
Archd Spiers[2]

Alexander revealed the truth about his age in a letter dated 1 March 1804, when he was expressing anxiety over a new college rule that Cadets could not take up their appointments in the Honorable Company until they were eighteen, or were qualified as Officers. In the letter he says: 'I am now eighteen by right but by the College certificate I am only fifteen and by that means if I stay the proper time I shall be twenty before I go to India...'[3] It is not clear why Alexander or his father thought it necessary to lie about his age on entry, as the College rules state that Cadets must be between the ages of fourteen and twenty two on entry—but presumably it was thought that he would have stood less chance if his real age was disclosed, as the majority of Cadets gained admission to the College at the age of fourteen. However, the result of this lie was that for the rest of his long career with the Honorable Company, Alexander could never disclose his real age. Even the memorial inscription on his tomb states that he died in his 60th year, whereas at his death on the 9 March 1847 he would have been in his 62nd year (assuming that he was actually born on 18 Dec 1785).

It appears that Walter Logan, to whom Alexander was writing the above letter and many others, was not strictly Alexander's guardian, but was responsible for funding his education and acted as an intermediary in dealings with his father (who had married after Alexander's birth and presumably wished to keep the existence of this illegitimate son a secret from his wife). Walter Logan was a close friend of Archibald Speirs and evidently dealt with a large proportion of his business affairs, sending annual accounts of all such transactions, often totalling as much as £9000 p.a. The Logan family had in fact been closely associated with the Speirs family for many years, as Walter's father (another Walter Logan) had been Chamberlain of Glasgow City Council at the time when Alexander Speirs (the Tobacco merchant) had served on the Council as Baillie. The fact that Walter Logan (senior) was a close friend can be easily gathered by the following excerpts from Alexander Speirs' diary for 1782:

Tu 19th February	Mr Logan supd & dined with me
Th 21st	Mr Logan dined & supd, also his 2 sons
Su 24th	Mr Logan & family supd
Tu 26th	By ourselve–Mr Logan came

But Alexander (the Tobacco merchant) had died in 1782, and we are now dealing with events that took place over twenty years later. By now, Walter Logan (junior) had for some years been a merchant, firstly working as a clerk for Provost Colquhoun, but more recently he had set up his own business, based at the Canal Office in Buchanan Street, Glasgow. At first, all of Alexander's letters were addressed to him, but evidently Walter got tired of dealing directly with his young charge, and from mid-November 1803 onwards, Alexander wrote to Andrew Virtue, who was clearly a lowly clerk in Walter's business.

In the following amusing excerpt from a letter from Andrew Virtue to Alexander, in which he is complaining about the latter's writing (which appears to me to be quite legible and reasonably grammatical), it is clear that, though illegitimate, Alexander is treated as a young gentleman, above a clerk's status:

…The excuse you make for not writing your letters so well as it appears…is quite inadmissible, being a mere commonplace one—and when you consider that to any person skilled in holography it is readily seen from the inspection of any piece whether proper pains has been taken by the penman and also what allowance is to be made for badness of the paper, as well as the pen & ink you will then see this to be a slight cover for some other cause that is wished to be concealed. No doubt there may be circumstances proper to mention as an excuse for a desultory letter, such as being unwell, much fatigued, writing aboard a ship in a storm or on the top of a hat on the butt of a musket in the field for want of a better accommodation any of which would be necessary to mention; as by the diction, and even the writing of a letter from a person with whom you are in the habit of corresponding, some idea may be formed of the state of his mind at the time he wrote, which when it appears to have been confused if not properly accounted for may readily be attributed to a lead cause as carelessness—which is only another term for laziness...***You may think I make too free with a gentleman of your cloth but recollect I am out of the reach of your side arms*** and I hope you will not take it amiss as I only mean to expose the impropriety of the above excuse in order that you...(illegible).

However, let us retrace our steps somewhat, as Walter Logan's invoices to Alexander's father give a reasonable idea of what Alexander had been doing before gaining entry to Marlow College. It is clear that after leaving school he was given training as a weaver. In March 1803, William Norval presented his bill amounting to £5 for 'teaching him the weaving trade for a considerable time'. Probably this training started in November 1802, when Walter Logan's bills commence, with an entry for 'carriage of trunk and apron' followed by 'candle at the weaving'. It is interesting to note from these bills how fragile footwear must have been in those days. In November 1802, Alexander bought a new pair of shoes and had a pair repaired. In each following month his shoes are repaired (at a cost of 6d), and in February 1803 he buys another pair. He also received pocket money, the monthly amounts varying between 3s/8d and 4s/4d.

Returning now to Alexander's stay at Marlow, it is painfully clear that he faced severe difficulties with finances throughout his time there, simply because he could not directly approach his father for money, but had to write to Walter Logan or Andrew Virtue and then wait until they had contacted his father, who often had further questions before sending funds. Only a month after his first letter, he had to write that he had 'received an order from the Commandant of the College to pay my half year's subscription on pain of being expelled from the College. I wrote to Mr Elphinstone & he was so kind as to give an order on his banker for the money, from which I supposed that there was not money enough left in the banker's hands for that purpose.'

The 'Mr Elphinstone' mentioned by Alexander frequently in his letters was the Honorable William Elphinstone, a director of the East India Company and a member of an aristocratic Scottish family. All cadets training for entry to the Honorable Company had to be sponsored by a director, and William Elphinstone was acting as Alexander's sponsor. (He also sponsored five of his own nephews, including Mountstuart Elphinstone, who had an illustrious career in India, becoming Governor of Bombay).

As a temporary measure, Alexander was asked to borrow two guineas from 'a friend of Mr Selbie's', but this had been refused as the latter had not received any orders to that effect. He was also advised not to ask for anything other than his immediate needs and so he promptly confirmed that these comprised 'four pair of cotton drawers which are six shillings a pair & a small writing desk which I don't know the exact price of'. He added that he only received one shilling as weekly pocket money 'out of which I am obliged to purchase soap for my own use, paper, pens, ink &c &c, including postage of letters; you may see from which that I am very much straightened. The other cadets have no more allowed them from the College, but the most of them as I mentioned to you in my former letter have money advanced them from their friends which the College has nothing to do with unless we have in our profession more than one guinea, which a great many of them have often. The reason I ask for a writing desk is that we have only one small drawer for to hold our books in and that every other day the officer of our division rummages to see if we have anything else in it but our books and it is only as he pleases that we keep anything else in it which makes the most of the cadets keep them.'

Alexander continued to press his case for more funds in each subsequent letter. Writing in late September he points out that. 'The cold weather is fast approaching & we being obliged to get up so soon in the morning which at this season is particularly cold, we are all under the necessity of wearing gloves, which all the cadets do. You will perceive that it is out of my power to purchase them & likewise my leg begins to trouble me sometimes in the morning. I have spoke to the Surgeon & he tells me to keep it warm which is impossible for me to do with the drawers I have at present. My pantaloons which the College provides me with are none of the warmest.' And, to emphasise his plight, he dramatically states in a post-script: 'Please write me soon & transmit me the money as soon as convenient in case I should be put in gaol for my debts!'

Alexander's next concern, of which he had given Walter Logan warning in his first letter, was to know where he was to stay during the winter vacation—which commenced on 1 December. Initially, he was simply told to remain at the college, until he explained that this was impossible as the college was closed for the whole two month holiday period. He discovered that one of the professors, Mr Ticken, provided lodging and tuition for those cadets who were unable to return home during the holidays, at a cost of one guinea a week for lodging and four guineas for the instruction over the two months. But Alexander became less keen when he asked another cadet who had stayed there the previous year, 'if he was going to stay with him this holiday. He told me not for the world as he was so much huffed about & talked to about it afterwards by the cadets. If Mr Spiers could think on any other place for me to stay during the vacation wherever it should be I should prefer it before this as it is such a dull place during the winter & few or none of the cadets staying here (that) I shall have no one to associate with.'

On being instructed to stay with the professor, Alexander again tried to dissuade his father with the following argument:

I beg you will explain to him that we stay with one of the writing masters as none of the others do keep lodgers & he knows nothing more than his profession which is to teach writing & is reckoned the most vulgar fellow imaginable by the whole of us & there is none but two or three little fellows whose friends stay at a great distance such as at the East Indies or Ireland stay with him. When I mentioned to some of the cadets my thoughts of staying with him they laughed at me & could not believe me & when I mentioned to himself that I thought I should be under the necessity of staying with him he said, 'do you think of stopping? I am sure I do not care of whether you do so or not'. You may see from that what kind of a man he is. I beg you will mention this to Mr Spiers & I hope he will see what a disagreeable situation I would be in & likewise I do not know if any will be allowed to stay as there is a putrid fever raging in this village just now & we are all confined to the College at present on that account.

But Alexander's father was not swayed by such arguments, replying through Walter Logan that he would not hear of him returning to Scotland and 'that you cannot be better employed during the vacation than in improving yourself in writing and spelling—as you are very deficient in both'. So, having run out of excuses and with only a few days left before the holidays, Alexander admitted defeat and went to stay with Mr Ticken. Evidently, apart from overcrowding, Alexander found the situation there not quite so bad as he had been warned, as he reported:

I don't think this is a good place for improvement as the few who are left are so much straightened for room that one part of us are obliged to study one day & the other part to go out. I don't mean from this to appear discontented for if it were not that we are so straightened for room I should like this place [tolerably well] though we are dull. For though (we do) but little it is just the same as if (we do) it at College which would not be the case anywhere else as we would be obliged to do it all over again so that this puts me a little forward in my studies at College.

In fact, after he had been at Mr Ticken's house for three weeks, Alexander received an invitation from Sir William Clayton (who had a son in Alexander's year at Marlow) to spend the rest of the holiday at his house near Marlow. He was told to bring along any books and trunks that he wished, and was given a room to himself and the use of an extensive library. Unfortunately, though, this pleasant stay was cut short after only a few days, when Alexander discovered that there was to be a ball at the house and he felt embarrassed by his lack of suitable clothes: 'I made a feint that I was going to London so on that account went home because that I had no clothes proper to appear in. I won't return again until I hear from you as Mr Spiers won't wish me to go again as there may be some more dances & it would seem so very curious to refuse going again. I wish you would show this letter to Mr Spiers & write me his opinion or Mr Logan's.'

It is easy to picture his feelings of unease and frustration at not being adequately provided for by his father. But he was careful to show gratitude for what he did receive, commenting to Walter Logan when his annual report was received: 'I have all along endeavoured to profit by Mr Spiers's goodness towards me to the utmost of my power & I trust he will find his goodness has not been abused.'

Alexander benefited from his short stay at Sir William Clayton's house though, as he says: 'They have introduced me to several genteel families in this neighbourhood. I am very glad of their acquaintance. A great number of the cadets are allowed to spend the Sunday afternoon with some neighbouring gentlemen.' But, although he had to leave due to lack of clothes for the ball, this did not deter him from buying more clothes—both for his stay there and for his next year at the college. He ordered these clothes through a merchant whilst staying at Mr Ticken's house, and at the end of the holidays the professor presented the following bill to Alexander's father.

Vacation Royal Military College	
Board and Studies	13.13.0
Extra washing	1.1.0
Draper's bill	14.1.9
Stationers	12.10
Advanced him at different times	5.0.0
Pocket money for next 43 weeks at College 2/6	5.7.6
To put in his pocket the day he joins	1.1.0
Making stockings &c	1.6
Shoemaker's Bill	1.6.7
	£42.15.2

Alexander made sure he apologised in advance for spending so much on clothes (the draper's bill exceeds the amount for board and study for two months), but in the event his father simply paid the bill without demur.

Although in his earlier letter, Alexander had been quite scathing in his criticism of Professor Ticken (describing him as the most vulgar fellow imaginable), these feelings do not seem to have been reciprocated, and the professor reported as follows to his father at the end of the holiday: 'I have a satisfaction in saying that his conduct has been uniformly manly and good and he has been much noticed by Sir Wm Clayton a very respectable character in this neighbourhood.' However, Alexander evidently had little faith in Mr Ticken, giving the following intriguing comment in a letter to Walter Logan: 'I shall give you the professor's proper address but I hope you will not tell him who I am on any account as he is by no means a proper person to be entrusted with this secret—this I have found by experience. Excuse me to Mr Spiers for giving his address to the professor when he desired me to give him my father's address.'

So evidently, Alexander had been sworn to secrecy over the identity of his father—presumably to avoid any embarrassment to Archibald if the fact that he had an illegitimate son became known. It is probably significant that although Alexander was obviously obliged to give his father's address to Mr Ticken, when the latter wrote to his father, his letter was addressed to Alexander Spiers, instead of Archibald Speirs. So, it seems that Alexander did manage to protect his father by giving the wrong Christian name. Alexander was certainly worried over the possibility of exposure, as he commented in another letter:

If you would be so obliging as to let him (ie. Walter Logan) know I should take it very kind of him if he would not mention that secret I spoke of to him in my last to the professor, as this very day he exposed one of the cadets though not in the same predicament yet it was a thing that was just as bad.' And he went on to apologise once again for his recent spending spree: 'I beg you will let me know if Mr Spiers was offended at the expensiveness of my acct. I should be extremely sorry if I should have offended him but I really could not help expending more money than I wished amongst so many extravagant young men. There was some of them squandered pretty nigh one hundred pounds but I hope Mr Spiers won't think I have squandered away that I have spent.

Shortly after Alexander returned to the college, the College Superintendent announced in class that the East India Company were amending the rules so that cadets must stay at the college either until they were eighteen or until they were given a certificate that they were qualified as officers. Previously, the Company would accept cadets who had been made non-commissioned officers, which normally occurred in their second year at Marlow. It was at this point that Alexander revealed in his letter that he was actually eighteen, but was shown as fifteen on the college records. He was obviously impatient to complete his studies and commence his military career. But he was now concerned that he would have to remain at the college for a further two and a half years, as he clearly could not reveal the deception over his true age. He had expected to have been made a non-commissioned officer already, but 'some favourites of our Colonel's step'd in before me'. A week or so later, the situation was clarified to the cadets after the Professor of Eastern languages visited India house to obtain the true facts. It appeared that the Company had always intended for cadets to have a minimum of four years' training, but that this rule had been relaxed as there was no upper school at Marlow. However, the upper school was now about to be formed—and once this had happened, cadets would have to stay for the full four years. So, Alexander now offered the following plea:

> If the Commandant will give anyone a certificate that I have been in no scrapes & have an irreproachable character & studies equal to the time employed which certificate being laid before the Directors at the India House may procure me my discharge from College. I am certain that Colonel Butler our Commandant will have no objections to give me such a certificate which may be had by writing him & enquiring if I may have the certificate requisite for East India Cadets previous to their leaving College. His address is Colonel Butler, Royal Military College, Marlow. Write me soon or I shall think you have forgotten me.

A week or so later the Captain of the Company said to Alexander: 'Spiers, I have recommended you to Col Butler to be made Corporal for your irreproachable conduct & forwardness in study & I hope you will do your duty when a Corporal as well as when a private.' However, before Alexander received his promotion, he was dismayed to learn that another cadet in a similar position had applied for a discharge certificate, but this had been refused until he had completed his regular course of study—i.e for another 2 ½ years. But Alexander was not one to take such a fate without trying every alternative way of obtaining his discharge so he suggested:

> If Mr Speirs, in case of the Company refusing to allow me to go out this season, if he would offer to refund the Company their expenses that they have been at on my account (which is £45 exactly) I do not doubt in the least they would allow me to leave the College immediately. There is no time to be lost now as the season is very far advanced for the sailing of East India ships & Mr Elphinstone being President at the India House he has more interest on that account & he only keeps his seat I believe ½ year. The paying of the half yearly money to the College likewise being so near if great expedition is not used I won't perhaps leave the College this 2½ years yet which would cost Mr Speirs for board alone at the College pretty nigh £135 which is befar too much.

Then, in early May 1804, Alexander at last was promoted to a Corporal. This he took to be a great compliment as the College had departed from the established rule of promoting initially to Lance Corporal. The Captain in fact informed him that it had been a mistake that he had not been promoted earlier. In usual form, Alexander took the opportunity to press his case for more funds:

> Now I am to stay so long at College & being made a Non Com Officer I have great need for a watch as I have both to be up betimes in the Morning & to see that my Division is up which I cannot possibly do without one & besides it looks as curious to see a great fellow almost 6 feet without one. I have got the present of a very nice seal—the impression you will see on the back of my letter. I got it from a well wisher for my good conduct along with another present of a different sort but what is the use of a seal without a watch? You ask me if my pay is advanced with my promotion. It is for the most part with Non Com Officers as we have to provide news papers for the supply of a room appropriated for our own use & we have to advance a small sum of money for keeping that room in repairs & keeping it clean &c. I suppose for the extra pay &c £4 will pay all & if Mr Speirs is so good as to allow me a watch 4 or 5£ will purchase as good as I can wish.

The reason that Alexander referred in the above letter to staying so long in College was that he had just been informed that his father preferred that he should stay for a further three years at the College. A few days later, Alexander was awarded the silver reward of Merit, for his good conduct and application to his studies. In passing on this good news, he naturally took the opportunity of giving a further hint of how necessary a watch was to him: 'I have got into several scrapes for the want of one such as letting my Division sleep too long in the morning & not coming too late to parade and our Commanding Officer will admit of no excuse whatever besides all the Non Com Officers have watches myself excepted.' And there shortly followed more pleas for cash:

I have been asked for my subscription money for the orderly room, a room which is entirely appropriated to the use of Officers & Non Com Officers which we are obliged to furnish & keep in repair at our own expense in consequence of which we are obliged to advance each of us to the senior officers a certain sum more or less as the room requires it. In this room we make out all our reports &c. and I suppose the Captain expects me to advance my pay. You may see from this that I am in great need for the cash at present. I do suppose that the senior officers think I am a very scrubbish fellow for not paying it before this; however I cannot help or hinder his thoughts.

Alexander generally hit the mark with such requests, and this was no exception. A few days later, he received ten pounds and so he went to see the watchmaker, a skilled craftsman, who promised to make a watch for him. This took a few weeks to make, but was worth waiting for, being an ornate silver hunting watch which kept very good time.

For the remainder of Alexander's time at Marlow, he relentlessly pursued his objective of gaining early release from the college, even though he knew his father preferred that he stay for the full course. Early in June he wrote to Mr Elphinstone, asking whether he would be allowed to proceed to India if he obtained a certificate of release from the college. William Elphinstone replied, 'As soon as you get your certificate, you will be allowed to proceed to India, but I must own I am surprised at your impatience when you may be employed so usefully for your own good...' Similarly, when Alexander mentioned his approach to Mr Elphinstone in a letter to Mr Virtue, he was informed that his father 'thought with Mr Elphinstone that it was strange you should be so impatient to go out to India—especially as he was certain you must be very deficient in many parts of your education and that if you leave the College without finishing your studies you will probably never get forward—and therefore he begged you would give every attention to your learning and not trouble yourself any more about getting away till such time as the College shall think fit to appoint you'. Along with this advice, Alexander also received a strong rebuke (second-hand) from his father for his poor handwriting and for making excuses: 'Tell him to make no more excuses about his writing but to pay more attention to it and try to improve his hand'.

Then, on 2 July, Alexander received a further promotion to the rank of a Sergeant. Naturally, though, he did not miss this opportunity of pressing his case for extra funds, supposedly needed on account of his latest advancement:

> I find so much trouble in being a Sergeant that I could almost dispense with the honour if I did not live in hopes of preferment. There are some things which I want very much viz: a dressing gown. You must not think from this that I am effeminate—it is quite the contrary, the Sergeant being obliged to go round the rooms himself every night after he is undressed to see that every Cadet is in bed & that his cloth's are put in the place appointed for them there is an order that every Cadet should have a flannel dressing gown but this order is not attended to except by the Sergeants who are obliged to do it for their own sakes. Three night shirts, four pairs stocking web'd drawers, paper & quills—the last two articles I use a great deal of as I have to make so many returns. I have spent all the little money I had to purchase as much as serve me till I hear from you. The purchase of my watch has cost me 15s more than I thought it would & I have to pay 10s 6d for the mending of my writing desk. The Sergeants ought always to have a little money by them as they have always some little thing to pay.

Not immediately receiving a reply to this request, Alexander then swiftly followed it with the following (which includes further interesting comments on his dilemma over naming his father):

The articles I mentioned in my last I am in great want of especially the drawers. I wear them out so much fencing—the fencing Master makes us lounge so far. I have been thinking the best way of getting these things if you think Mr Speirs would agree to it, to let Mr Ticking get such things as I stood most in need of which I think he would certainly do as he does the same to several others who staid (sic) with him during the vacation & the most of the cadets have some friend or other either here or in London who will send them anything in an exigency. If Mr Speirs will allow it you had better write one side of the letter for him, but say nothing about Mr Speirs because in the letter you wrote to him about my board enclosing the money he asked me who Mr Speirs was or if you meant my father. I put him of (f) the best way I could. I hope you will write to me soon as the House Keeper has spoken to me more than once about my drawers.

Andrew Virtue replied that, without the above warning, he would have mentioned Archibald Speirs, as Alexander had already given Mr Ticken his address but he would now try to avoid all further mention of Mr Speirs. He also told Alexander that Mr Elphinstone had advised his father, 'that you have every opportunity that could be wished for at the College to make an improvement in your studies—and thinks if your inclination was as eager as it ought to be for pushing yourself forward in useful knowledge that you would not be wishing to get away from the College. Mr Elphinstone I understand considers your expenses to be high. I observe you mention about some of the cadets spending nearly £200 pounds, but this is no rule for you to go by altho' I must allow that it is a strong temptation to be placed among such company. But unless you set yourself to act in opposition to the common & prevailing views of the world about extravagance, inattentiveness and intemperance of every kind you cannot expect to acquire opulence or acquire renown for there is no possibility of arriving at great & true honour without suffering every privation that stands in the way of duty—to attend to which you will always find your best interest and truest enjoyment in the end, whatever may be the whispers of your own inclination on the examples of others at the time'.

It might be expected that the foregoing little homily on extravagance would have been accompanied by a refusal to fund any more of

Alexander's expenses. But, once again, Alexander seems to have won the argument, as Andrew Virtue also wrote to Mr Ticker on exactly the same lines Alexander had suggested—namely to request that he would equip Alexander with clothes and other items as he deemed necessary and to confirm that Walter Logan would settle any accounts promptly.

Moreover, Alexander did not take the implied criticism by Mr Elphinstone of his performance at his studies lying down. He contested it saying:

> I cannot comprehend how Mr Elphinstone could think of stirring up Mr Speirs against me by telling him I do not pay attention to my studies. I should have written to Mr E requesting him to be so good as to let me know from whom he received that information (for I have enquired of most of the professors if they had; on the contrary they assured me if any such information had been requested of them they would have given me quite a different character) if it had not been I was afraid of putting (sic) him in a passion by requesting an explanation from him & thereby incurring both his & Mr Speirs displeasure.

And he went on to confirm that Mr Elphinstone really had no knowledge of the costs of living at Marlow as a cadet. In fact, the proof that Alexander was not exaggerating his dire need of drawers is shown by the following letter, which the reader will note is addressed to his father:

Archd Speirs Esqr
Elderslie House
Renfrew
Glasgow

R.M. College August 12th 1804

Sir,

Upon inspecting the necessaries of Cadet Speirs it appears that the following articles are unserviceable or wanting viz:

    7 handkerchiefs
    4 pair drawers

I am directed by Lt Col Butler Commandant of the Junior Department to request you will cause them to be replaced or supplied without loss of time marked A. No 91 & forwarded to this place addressed to cadet Speirs. I have the honour to be

Sir

Your most obedt humble servant

James McDermott

Capt RMC

Alexander had to write to Andrew Virtue apologising for the fact that he had given his father's name and address to the Captain. He explained that he had been forced to do so, because the letter was a standard one which the Captain insisted must be addressed to his father or mother. So gradually, unintentionally, the truth about Alexander's parentage was emerging—because Alexander obviously had difficulty in answering such direct questions with a convincing bluff. But he was rebuked by Andrew Virtue for doing so:

It was surely very improper for you to give the Capt Mr Speirs' address after I had desired Mr Ticken by your orders (?) to apply to Mr Logan for payt of his acct. The rule of College which you say in this case cannot be departed from can be nothing more than that when the cadets are in need of any pecuniaries (?) their parents, friends, tutors or whoever has the management of their affairs should be requested to furnish them without delay—and of course had you informed the Capt that Mr Logan acted as Manager of your affairs he could have required nothing further.

Early in August 1804, the tedium of continual studies was relieved when the Earl of Harrington visited the college, reviewed the cadets and praised them lavishly, informing the King that the cadets were a great credit to the institution. But Alexander certainly did not reciprocate the Earl's praise:

I had the honour of being bugle-man to the whole. I never in my life saw such an ill dressed man a Lord. We were all drawn up in line to receive him. I could not conceive what the Captain meant when he gave the word present arms on an odd looking man with a thread-bare brown coat coming on parade. This shows that appearances should not be much attended to.

The following month there was considerable more drama at the college when, following Alexander's description:

Their [sic] has been a great mutiny here & ten of the Cadets who stood up for independence have been expelled by order of His Majesty. We expected the Duke of York here there being so much ceremony urged upon the occasion. Our two Captains fell in on the right & left, the Major in the centre, & our Colonel in front. When the Governor came in front of the parade, the Drum beat the general salute. After the ceremony of saluting was over we were formed into a square when the prisoners were brought in to the midst. The Governor read His Majesty's sentence which was that their swords should be broke over their heads & dismissed from the college with every mark of ignominy. I am sure if a few more are not expelled soon the College will never go on—it has got a very bad name indeed in short. I am almost ashamed to appear in its uniform there being such a number of theives & cut throats about it. I quite detest the place. I feel more uncomfortable than ever. I wish I was to leave it tomorrow.

In subsequent letters, Alexander gave the following amusing details of the events that had led to the mutiny:

You wished to know the greivances of the insurgents were that we were to much confined & grievously muck'd about by a new Captain who is as stupid as he is severe & the Col favouring so much as he does for any one who can spare him a brace of hares or pheasants is sure not to be forgotten as soon as the first indulgence is ask'd for him. A son of the Earl of Harrington's was sent to the Hospital for a disease you may guess at and letting of a few prisoners was made a non-com officer about a month after & I believe if the Lieut Governor had not opposed it he would have had a badge of merit. These partialities created a great noise in College for some time; some even had the impudence to pass the Col saying I am going to get the—tonight that I may be made Non-Com tomorrow.

Clearly Alexander was referring to the Earl's son getting a venereal disease, and the word he has omitted out of a sense of decorum is either 'pox' or 'clap'!

Alexander also related to Andrew Virtue what the plotters had attempted and the effect of their expulsion:

> The poor fellows who are gone I believe are for the most part received by their relations—they must feel very much shock'd at such a disgrace never to be deemed worthy to wear a sword in His Majesty's service. I am sorry to say out of the nine who were expelled 4 were Scotchmen—one the Nephew of Boyd Alexander's of South Barr & the other a son of a Mr Napier's of Militman (?) somewhere near Paisley; the other two come from somewhere near Edinburgh, one of their names is Brown & the other Grant; the latter was an East India Cadet belonging to the Engineers—a very fine young man and a particular friend of mine, he never acquainted me with the rebellion which I am very glad of because if he had I should have been esteemed as bad as any if I had not discovered it which I certainly would not have done but might have advised him against it. The plan was rather dangerous—to blow up a hay rick, break the Parson's & one of the Captn's heads, demolish nigh 200 stand (?) of arms & to entirely deface the College unless their grievances had been redressed. However I was not quite such a fool as to join them.

Until Alexander had finally revealed all the details of the plot, his father was particularly anxious that he might in some way have become involved and thereby 'ruined for ever'—as he had heard separately of the disgrace of Boyd Alexander's nephew and Mr Napier's son. However, he was finally reassured that Alexander had more sense than that.

Meanwhile the steady pressure exerted by Alexander through his many requests to be permitted to leave the college and depart for India was finally achieving results. His father eventually realised that he had been studying hard and that if he was given permission by the college to leave, this was actually recognition that he had achieved the necessary level of competence. Alexander had, in fact, already advised that Mr Scott, a professor of Persian and Arabic at Marlow, had recommended at East

India House that he should be permitted to leave for India at the vacation. So when, at the end of October, Alexander wrote:

> I spoke to Colonel Butler today & he told me that (that) I could get a certificate from the Collegiate Board of the exact description that Mr Elphinstone told me I should proceed to India with. Now if it be Mr Speirs wish that I should proceed to India there must be a letter written to Mr E requesting him to write to Col B to know if I can receive the certificate. Without this be done I cannot receive my certificate. I wish you would let Mr Speirs know this & that it would require as much dispatch as possible. If this certificate be had before the vacation it will save the expense of staying here which I am sure will not be small.

His father, on reading the above, finally wrote to Mr Elphinstone as follows:

Eldersly 1st Nov 1804

My dear Sir,

I have this day a letter from my Boy; you had the goodness to send to Great Marlow. He is most anxious to get to India as he says what is true: this is the time to go for speedy promotion. He assures me that Colonel Butler informed him he should procure for him such a Certificate from the Collegiate Board as you would wish to have.

I have the honour to be my dear Sir,
Yours most Sincerely
Archd Spiers

However, Alexander's expectation that he could actually leave for India before the holiday was not to be realised. By the middle of November, his impatience was again showing:

> Since I answered yours of the 2d Novr I have heard no tidings relating to my departure for India which makes me think Mr Elphinstone has not written to Col. Butler about my certificate

or the Col. would have spoken to me about it. I took the opportunity yesterday of writing Mr E by a cadet going to the India House. I do not know whether it was wrong in me doing so or not, but Mr E is so very slow in his movements I thought a letter might stir him on a little. I would be much obliged to you to speak to Mr Speirs for a little more money as I was obliged to subscribe for some fire works &c on the 5th Novr as the other cadets & Non. Com. Officers did the like & I believe I owe some little to our Drumer for letters & this is about the time he makes up his accounts £1: 10 I believe will pay him & the other things I have to pay for. There were 3 of our officers left us the beginning of this week and I have heard from good authority I shall be Ensign before or after the Vacation if I come back.

This was only one of innumerable requests for extra cash—he had in fact only the previous week received £2 to cover some earlier debts. But he was quite right in his prediction that he would be promoted, and only three days later he was able to report: 'What I prognosticated in my last is come to pass this afternoon. I was advanced to the rank of Ensign here at College which may convince Mr Speirs I have behaved well at least. I have superseded 6 Ser(gean)ts. I shall require a feather and sword knot whether I shall want a sash or not I am not certain but I shall not be in a hurry as perhaps Mr Speirs has got a different Ansr. to his letter than I have to mine. From what Mr Elphinstone says I do (not) think I shall be able to proceed to India this season which I am very sorry for but I trust Mr Speirs has had better luck in his application and all will be well. I suppose Mr Speirs will have no objections these things here & Mr Ticking to pay for them another £ will be necessary as the servants will expect more from an Ensn. than a Serjt.' It is amusing to note how Alexander invariably finds some excuse to ask for more cash, and of course he was well aware that his promotion would create a favorable atmosphere in this case.

By now, though, the college term was drawing to a close, and once again the thorny problem of where Alexander was to stay during the holidays had not been finalised. In September, Alexander had again been invited by Sir William Clayton to spend the holidays with him, but Alexander had declined to accept, saying that he was returning home. He certainly did not want to stay at Professor Ticken's house again, saying:

> There is one of the Professors here acquainted with Mr
> Elphinstone. If Mr Speirs has no objections I shall request him
> when he writes to Mr E to acquaint him what kind of
> accommodation we have here in the vacation—twenty Cadets in
> a house with only 4 rooms chok'd full of beds & our sitting room
> not larger than your office & these Cadets are of the very worse
> kind—indeed one of our punishments & one of the worst is
> keeping some of the worst Cadets here during the vacation.

Fortunately for Alexander, though, he did not need to stay at Mr
Ticken's over-crowded house for long. On 19 November he heard from
one of William Elphinstone's sons (who was staying at the college with
one of the professors) that he would go to India that season. And, shortly
afterwards, Mr Elphinstone invited Alexander to stay at his house for
the vacation.

Alexander must have had slightly mixed feelings about accepting this
invitation, as he had earlier written to Walter Logan saying: 'If you would
be so good as to entreat Mr Speirs to allow me to visit some of my friends
in Scotland before I go to India perhaps never to see them again. Excuse
this trouble.'[6] But this request seems to have been ignored, and in fact
Alexander was quite right in assuming that he would never again see his
friends in Scotland, as he didn't have any time for such a visit, his time
being taken up in preparing for his travel to India, from where he never
returned.

The holidays commenced on 29 November, and Alexander spent a
week or so at Mr Ticken's house before going to stay at the Elphinstone's
house at No 2 Harley Street in London. Whilst there, Mr Ticken wrote
the following letter to Walter Logan—displaying the general high opinion
in which Alexander was held at the College:

> In compliance with your request transmitted to me in August last,
> I have provided Cadet Ensign Speirs with such necessaries and
> such sums of money as to the best of my judgment, I have
> thought necessary for him considering his age, rank at College
> &c. He is now at the Honble Mr Elphinstones in order to try
> if he can go out to India with the next Fleet. I am, myself, very

sorry that he should wish to leave the College before the expiration of another year, as no young man stands higher (I believe) than he does, in the estimation of both Officers and Professors, and as his rank in the Company's service is still going on, his stay at College another year holds very great advantages particularly this, that as the greatest part of the time he already has spent at the College, has necessarily been directed to the first rudiments of Science, and as he is happily over the most difficult and most disgusting part of his education, it would be a pity, that after having laid so good a foundation, he should by his not giving himself sufficient time destroy, or at best, render abortive, those seeds which with care and labour, for the last 18 months, have been implanted in him. I expect him down now, every day from Mr Elphinstones, and shall, for his sake, be happy to hear that he can't go out for at least some months to come… Mr Speirs is a very good young man and as he is both from his age and Military Rank entitled to the treatment of a man, I shall be thankful for a line as early as possible, giving me some sort of hint for the regulation of his finances, for the remainder of the vacation; for if Mr Elphinstone introduce him to much company, this few days he is spending with him, I imagine he will find his 5 Guineas very short when he returns to me.

In fact Alexander did not return to Mr Ticken's house, but stayed on with Mr Elphinstone until he had been fully kitted out for the journey to India. This was a long process, as cadets needed a vast amount of clothes and other kit, both to last them for the long sea voyage and for their stay in India. Mr Ticken had been asked to oversee and authorise payments as necessary, but without being given guidance on spending limits. He wrote, somewhat apprehensively, to Walter Logan on 11 February 1805:

I have anxiously expected to hear from you for several days past, my young friend Speirs having been ordered by Mr Elphinstone to complete himself in his necessaries as soon as possible, stating to him, then, that he would perhaps sail in 8 days at longest. Speirs of course applied to me, I did not know which way to act, for the best—but at any rate conceived that the most eligible way would

be to order certain portions of his articles, leaving it open for you
or his father to make what additions you might think proper; for
Cadets are sent out, at almost any price from 150, to 400 or 500£.
Therefore I have merely ordered what he cannot possibly do
without and wait to hear from you how far it is to be extended.
The list I sent you, contains very many articles more (in number)
than they are obliged to take, at the same time it contains nothing
more than any young man, as a Gentleman, takes with him. He
has now ready (instead of those as the list states) 48 superior Calico
shirts—which is too little, I conceive he ought at least to have 36
more, as the voyage is long, and none can be washed on board—
and towards the latter end of the voyage he must have 1 each day.
It would be more satisfaction for me to hear from you or Mr Speirs
who I find is in Devon, giving me some direction as to number
or expense—which would guide me, as at present I am working
with him entirely in the dark. I therefore hope you will answer
this immediately, in order that his final equipment may not take
place, without my having a guide to regulate his expenses.[6]

Alexander evidently spent January and most of February 1805 visiting
large stores both in Marlow and London to buy all the kit. Then, on
23 February, he was finally ready and he set out by stage coach with his
trunks to Portsmouth, having been provided with £15 by Mrs Elizabeth
Elphinstone for the journey and to get his trunks on board. Alexander
had spent a total of £178-7-2 on equipping himself, which seems quite
moderate when compared with the range of £150 to £400 or £500 quoted
by Mr Ticken. Indeed, in a letter to Alexander's aunt Martha (wife of
Peter Speirs of Culcreuch), who was staying in London at the time, Mrs
Elphinstone said:

I hope the expense of our young friend's outfit will not appear
extravagant—it is really rather under the generality of cadets. At
the same time I am sensible the charges Tradesmen are now
obliged to make (from the increase of taxes on every article of
subsistence) must appear enormous. I take the liberty of
mentioning this circumstance—as Mr Alexr Speirs (very
properly) seemed to think it would in a sum total appear a great
deal. I beg to offer my Comps to Miss Graham & Mr Spiers.

But Archibald Speirs clearly thought his son's final bill was excessive and he evidently sent a strongly worded letter of reproof to Mr Ticken, who replied:

I was considerably hurt at that letter, fearing that after all the pains I had taken, to be right, some mistake had arisen as to the outfit of Mr Speirs; during the vacation, when it was first likely he was to go out soon, I received a letter from him saying, that Mr Elphinstone had told him he was likely to go in a fortnight, and expressing his fears that he should be obliged to be fitted out in a hurry from the Slop Shops in London with things ready made—to this I could make no reply, in a few days came Mr Logan's letter, requesting me to send him a list of necessaries &c. Alexander got one from Mr Elphinstone Junior, a copy of which I enclosed to Mr Logan, and stated at the same time that I thought it an extravagant one, I also sent Mr Logan a real list of necessaries and had certainly no thought of ordering a single article, without a prior order. Alexr was continually wishing me to let his shirts at least be made up under the eye of Mrs Ticken, this I resisted, till he got his discharge from College, he was then at my house and as I knew that Mr Elphinstone had told him, he would sail in 10 days, and as he stated to me, that he had not heard either from you or Mr Logan how he was to be fitted out, I then ordered 6 shirts to be put in hand, and requested him to write the same evening to Mr Logan and also to you, informing you of these circumstances and begging you to write immediately, to say how and where he was to be completed, on the blank side of his letter to Mr Logan I wrote a few lines myself, stating this to him; he understood you were at Farringdon, and as there are four places of that name in different Counties, he directed a separate letter to each, for fear he might not direct to the light, not knowing which you were at—we waited till 6 shirts were ready, we heard nothing from you or Mr Logan, and 6 more were ordered, and so on, as I took particular care to order but a few things at a time, in case an answer should arrive from you, none however came; and he constantly stated to me, that he had not heard from you anything to the contrary of his being fitted out here. You mention

Capt Gray in your letter, I assure you Sir, I never heard the Gent's name mentioned & as I never either saw or heard from him or of him, its impossible, that I should act under his directions. You will find that the amount by the vouchers sent Mr Logan to be 178.7.2—the lowest estimate given by Welch & Stalkers house, was 169 odd, this small deviation arose from his ordering 10£ worth of things from his Ship at Portsmouth, and some things he had, which were not included in the list of 169£... I now come to the most painful part of what I have to say—in your letter (which did not arrive till after Alexr had sailed) you seem to intimate that you were doubtful that some articles might be charged, which he never received. Surely, Sir, the respectability of my public situation, without any personal knowledge of me, might have been sufficient to keep even the shadow of such a suspicion from the mind of any Gentleman, that I had any concern with. However, permit me to state on my *Honor* or if you request it, on my *Oath*, that I did most consciously examine every article supplied to him, as if it had been for myself, and also that every article charged, he has received, and perhaps 'tis necessary also to declare on *Honor*, that my situation here is that of a Gentleman, and that of all the young men I ever had, or have now under my own immediate care, I never did either directly or indirectly receive any emolument, from any money or monies, laid out for their use.

On arrival at Portsmouth, Alexander was directed to his ship—the *Surrey*—a sailing ship of 819 tons built by Dudman in 1804, with a length of 143ft 11ins and having three decks, with 6ft 2ins headroom between decks. He boarded the ship along with numerous other army officers including nine other cadets, of whom six were bound for Bengal and the rest (including himself) were bound for Madras. From there he wrote this last letter—this time directly to his father:

Surrey Mother Bank
March 6th 1805

Honoured Sir,

I am now on board the Surrey bound for Bengal & will sail with the first fair wind. I gave Mr P Speirs an outline of the expenses

I had incurred in fitting myself out which I believe he transmitted to you but since that I have had occasion for some other necessary items and some cash: I took the liberty of writing to Mr Elphinstone and stated what I wanted which I dare say he will send to me, but I have received nothing from him. Indeed I have not had time. I thought I should let you know in case he should think proper to send me anything and I not have an opportunity of acquainting you with it before I sailed. Mr Elphinstone told me to inform you that letters to Lord Cornwallis & Gen Lake would be of infinite use to me in India and if you sent them to his house in London he would forward them to me by the first opportunity. I am very uncomfortably situated here having no cabin of my own but obliged to borrow one from one of my companions for a moment to write this. If I should survive the voyage I shall if you have no objections let you know how I am situated. Impressed with the highest sense of gratitude for the many and great favours you have conferred upon me.

I remain

Your most obedt &c
Alexr Speirs

P.S. I signed the person's account who fitted me out in linen &c & altered some articles that were charged which I did not receive. I had from Mr Ticking during the vacation £12 for pocket money &c.

A.S.

In fact the first fair wind came early the following day, 7 March, when the Captain, John Cumberledge, gave orders for all passengers to return on board and at 11am the anchors were weighed. The journey to India took just over four months—a relatively uneventful voyage, except for the death of a soldier one evening just before their arrival at Madras, his body being committed to the deep the following morning. Alexander's first sight of India came a few days later, on 14 July, when the coast of Madras was finally sighted. And this is where a minor discrepancy arises: according to the ship's log, Alexander departed from the ship on 17 July, when the ship docked at Madras. But Alexander had been nominated for the Bengal service, so he almost certainly remained on board for a further three weeks, until the *Surrey* landed at Calcutta on 9 August.

All of Alexander's dreams were now merging into reality—his first impressions of that fascinating country, India, being of the incredible heat and humidity, the vast seething population, the squalor of the cities and the desperate poverty of the natives. How could fortunes be made in this country, he must have wondered. But he was committed now, and still excited by the knowledge of how different his life was going to be.

Alexander was soon enrolled as a Lieutenant in the first battalion of the 23rd Bengal Native Infantry, initially under basic training and then on active service with his Regiment. I must however, generally draw a veil over most of the next eighteen years, when Alexander was on Regimental duty, simply because there is so little information available to distinguish his own part in operations by his Regiment.

The only glimpse into his life over that period comes from a letter written to his father in September 1808. Evidently his father had by now relaxed his previous rule of only dealing with Alexander through intermediaries, and must have expressed disappointment that Alexander had not yet achieved promotion—triggering the following response:

You may depend upon it that no want of attention either to my duty or studies prevented me from having an Adjutancy or Qr. Mastership, there are only one of the former to each Battn & one of the latter to a Regt. No officer can hold either of those appointments in any Corps but in the one to which he belongs & the penalty of changing Corps is the same as in the King's Regts i.e. entering Junior of the Regt. The above appointments are only to be held by Subalterns & are in the gift of the Comdr in Chief with whom I have not the smallest interest, neither of the above have been vacant since I joined the Corps. I can have a good recommendation from the Comdg Officer of the Regt whenever I wish, if it would be of any service to me; had Major Munro whom I mentioned to you in a former letter gone home last year you would I think have had an opportunity of forming a better opinion of me than you seem to have at present.

Alexander was writing from Dewaree, fifty miles south of Delhi, his Regiment being on Garrison duty for the imperial city. So, he was able to offer to send his father anything he wished from India. Evidently his father assumed that a Lieutenant like Alexander was well-paid, but conditions for Officers of the Company had recently been made much less favourable, as Alexander hastened to point out, complaining that since they no longer received 'double *Batta*', Lieutenants were on just over half their previous pay, and that 'every thing likewise is excessively dear now, more especially in the Upper Provinces. We pay three guineas for a hat, eight ditto for leather pantaloons & so on in proportion. I wrote to a friend of mine in Calcutta to let me know the price of a good common hunting watch such as I could get for ten or fifteen Guineas in England, as mine was reported irreparable. He said he had inquired and found that I could not get a good one for less than four hundred & fifty rupees which is upwards of fifty £ Sterling. This made me think I might be able to do without one. From this small specimen you may guess how far our allowances go, however bad they are I hope soon to be able to inform you that I am above the world & live as well too (as I have always done) as any person on Subaltern's allowances in the Battn.'

Despite his father's expectations, Alexander had to wait until May 1813 before being made Acting Adjutant of his Regiment, and another two years before advancing to the post of Interpreter and Quarter Master. Then, in 1816 he reached the rank of Captain-Lieutenant. In June 1818, shortly after his promotion to the rank of Captain, he was appointed as Brigade Major to the advanced Rajpootana Force (the role of a Brigade Major being to assist in the command of the Brigade).

Meanwhile, he had evidently met the Indian woman who became his partner and lived with him for the rest of his life (and whom he eventually married in February 1847, when he was on his death-bed). Her name was Helen Beg, a native Christian and the daughter of a Moslem, Hossen Alli Beg. Alexander knew her affectionately by the name of Bibi Bunnoo. Over an eighteen-year period she bore him eight children. Their first borne, Archibald and Grace, were twins, born at Meerut on 23 February 1817 and baptised later that year at the Chaplain's station there. After Archibald and Grace, three more daughters were born, followed by three more sons—the last son (my great-grandfather) being born in 1835. Although only his first two children were baptised in India, it was easy to identify all of these children, because they were all mentioned in his will. However, there were perhaps more children who died before he wrote his will. There is, in fact, strong evidence that he had at least one more daughter. This assumption is supported by an ancient record of a grave of 'Miss Spiers' at Kalundri, which was where Alex had lived during the monsoon season when he was Agent at Sirohi. I have myself seen this grave, which is clearly that of an infant, but it is now without any markings. However, the local people confirmed to me that it was the grave of an English girl, the daughter of the 'Burrah Sahib' of Sirohi.

We can now resume Alexander's story in 1823, when he commenced the political duties that were to comprise the remainder of his long career. In the second decade of the nineteenth century and particularly after the decisive victory of Lord Hastings in his operations against the Mahratta empire early in 1818, following which Hastings had proclaimed the universal sovereignty of the Company throughout India, the majority of the Rajput states had (with some gentle encouragement from local British Political Agents) been keen to sign treaties which gave them the protection and assistance of the British Government in the governance of their states, in return for some loss of revenue. The Rajput States welcomed the prospect of peace in their lands and the assistance of the British Forces in preventing border skirmishes or invasions since the Mahrattas and Pindarees had invaded and laid waste to their lands in the past. And, by 1823, Sirohi was the only state that had not yet signed such a treaty.

Since 1818, Sirohi State had made several representations to the British Government, seeking such a treaty, but a major obstacle was the fact that the neighbouring State of Jodhpur claimed sovereignty over Sirohi. Before any negotiations could commence, this claim needed to be investigated. This investigation had now been completed, showing conclusive evidence that Sirohi had always been an independent State, and that Jodhpur, its more powerful neighbour, had no justification for the claim of overall sovereignty. Accordingly, in a letter to Major General Sir David Ochterlony (the Resident in Malwa and Rajputana), the Governor General authorised him to send an officer to Sirohi to assess the current situation, investigate the claims made by Jodhpur on the spot, assist the Rao in restoring his state's affairs and to propose forming such a treaty—the officer picked for these duties being Captain Alexander Speirs (or Alex as he was commonly known).

Shortly before this, Alex had already been taken off his Military duties at Nimach and sent to Udaipur, where he had been acting from mid-March 1823 as assistant to the Political Agent there, covering for the sick Captain Waugh. But only after a month at Udaipur, he was relieved from this temporary post as a result of being selected for the mission to Sirohi.

Hence, after being furnished with copies of all previous correspondence relating to Sirohi, Alex was duly sent on this mission. On his arrival at Sirohi, Alex immediately found a potential obstacle to the proposed treaty, namely, that Uday Bhan, the Rao, had been deposed from the Gaddi (throne) in 1818 and that Sheo Singh, his younger brother, was then governing the state, having assumed the title of Rao. It soon became clear that Sheo Singh had taken this action with the blessings of the four principal chiefs, or Thakurs, after they had suffered tyranny and oppression for several years under Uday Bhan's rule. A further impediment to the proposed treaty was the existing lawlessness. It necessitated keeping a military corps in order to protect commerce on the old-established route from Gujarat to the Northern Provinces, which passed through the state of Sirohi, as well as to ensure security of property within Sirohi. Normally, such a force was only maintained if paid for directly by the ruler, or if the Company's share of the revenue would adequately support it. However, Alex did not think that the revenue from the State would rise to such a level for several years, as only a small proportion of the country was currently under agriculture, great tracts of previously farmed land having been laid to waste due to the ravages of marauding gangs of Bhils and Meenas. In fact, Rao Sheo Singh's own share of the revenue was so low that it barely enabled him to support his family, let alone a military corps.

Further enquiries by Alex revealed that Uday Bhan had only ruled for a short period after the death of his father, during which time he had had raised the demands for tribute from the people 'to such a pitch of aggression, added to the most wanton and glaring outrages upon the domestic feelings and habits of his subjects that indignation at the...effects of his unbridled excesses compelled them to break at once the claim of hereditary obedience and to provide for their own security by disarming their oppressor'. The chiefs had then placed Uday Bhan's younger brother, Sheo Singh, who was then only a boy and clearly merely a tool in their hands, on the Gaddi and had reduced his hereditary right to claim a fixed proportion of the land revenue as tribute to a mere voluntary contribution from themselves.

As a result, Rao Sheo Singh had never received sufficient revenue to enable him to properly govern the country, to maintain an adequate army, or even to maintain his own family in a manner befitting a ruler. In fact, Alex shortly observed 'one abortive effort made by him to maintain a small body of men in order to restore tranquillity to his state, and of its almost immediate failure, leaving him to combat with debt and the loss of his family ornaments and insignia'. The greed of the Thakurs, who had deposed Uday Bhan and recognised Sheo Singh as their Rao without providing him with adequate revenue, had led to the current situation where marauding gangs were able to plunder freely throughout the land. This provided the Thakurs with a further excuse to avoid adequate payments towards the state treasury. Moreover, this lawless condition had, over the eight year period of Sheo Singh's reign, also deprived the state of any passing commercial trade, taxes on which had been the principal source of revenue for the late Rao, Sheo Singh's father, Rao Vairisal II.

When Sir David Ochterlony suggested that a treaty could only be made with the established ruler under the normal rules of primogeniture (i.e. with Uday Bhan), the Thakurs became so alarmed, that they attempted to legitimise the rule of Rao Sheo Singh by investing him with the Tukha. They proceeded to do so, despite Alex's remonstrance that such an action should await the sanction of the British Government in the wake of the pending treaty. On hearing this, Sir David Ochterlony confirmed that the only basis on which a treaty could be made with Rao Sheo Singh was in the event of his assuming the title of Regent, and renouncing the investiture. Alex duly advised Rao Sheo Singh of this condition, and, since the latter was clearly unable to gain proper control of the affairs of his state without the assistance of the British, he readily accepted the renunciation of the investiture and that he should henceforth 'be styled Mookhtar (ie. Regent) on the part of his brother and acknowledge the right of succession of his brother's children to the Guddy'. However, in checking the conditions of a draft treaty which Alex presented to him, Sheo Singh did make the point that he would not expect to be deprived of the Regency during his own life in the event that Uday Bhan subsequently had any male children. As he was most insistent on this point, Alex amended the treaty to allow Sheo Singh to retain the Regency during his natural life, and that only on his demise would the succession revert to any lawful heirs of Uday Bhan. The Governor General accepted this modification in the treaty, which was duly signed, commenting that Alex's actions were 'considered to be highly judicious and satisfactory'.

Naturally, as the East India Company had always been primarily a trading company, some eventual profit in the form of revenue was expected in return for their aid in the governance of Sirohi. Hence, one of Alex's main tasks was to establish the total value of the state's annual harvest in grain, sugarcane, indigo, cotton etc., from which estimates and agreements for the amount of tax to be levied could be drawn up. He did this extremely conscientiously, touring from village to village, and providing the government with a general description and location of each village, checking their previous assessments and comparing them with his own observations on the quality of the soil, the number of ploughs in the village, the number of wells in use (which is a good indicator of the likely produce of the soil in such a dry climate), and actual yields in the current year. He continued this work for a full year in the state of Sirohi, by the end of which he had provided the government with a vast amount of data, leading to the unfortunate overall conclusion that his first impression of the desolate condition of the state was well founded. There was indeed little likelihood that the gross revenue would cover the costs of providing such troops as were necessary for maintaining law and order for many years to come.

At this stage, Alex's mission (which was to conduct initial negotiations, form a treaty with Sirohi and provide an administrative framework for a local agent to take over) was clearly drawing to a close, and he would have been recalled to his military duties, but for the following recommendation by Sir David Ochterlony:

> The zeal, attention and activity of Captain Speirs have been conspicuous from his first mission to this petty and unfortunate Principality to the present moment, and I cannot report the termination of operations without calling the attention of Government to his merits and services and assuring His Lordship

in Council that he has been and still is suffering a possible loss by his meritorious exertions—his appointment in the military line being filled up by an officiating substitute, and his civil allowances unsettled, he has been precluded from drawing any salary from either branch of the service, and instead of remitting his monthly savings to his Agent, has been compelled to run in debt to Native bankers for subsistence. ... I hope I may be permitted to recommend that Captain Speirs should receive the salary and allowances of a local Agent from the date of his departure from Neemutch to take charge of the Oodeepore Agency, and that he be nominated permanent Agent in Surhooee (sic) with the usual allowances of a Local Agent.

Faced with such lavish praise by the distinguished veteran campaigner, the Governor General was happy to follow this recommendation, and so began Alex's official career as a Political Agent, starting on a salary of 1200 rupees per month.

Throughout Alex's time as Agent at Sirohi, he was very conscious of the unfriendly and aggressive attitude of the State of Marwar (or Jodhpur) towards Sirohi. Marwar's ruler, Man Singh, openly encouraged acts of aggression on its borders, which had become Sirohi's chief problem. Initially, Alex managed to effect a partial control of these border aggressions by the employment of a detachment of two hundred Horse from the 4th Regiment of Local Horse. But Government was unhappy to provide its own forces on a regular basis for such patrols, deeming normal border control to be a duty of the State. However, as Alex pointed out in many letters on the subject, this was a case where the neighbouring and far more powerful State, Marwar, was taking no steps to control their own subjects, even though they had the means to do so, and was evidently encouraging the attacks. Clearly Marwar was acting contrary to its own treaty, which required that it should control its own borders and punish any of its subjects committing aggressions in neighbouring territories. So when, in December 1826, Sir Charles Metcalfe (the Resident at Dehli) suggested that the Detachment of Local Horse should be withdrawn, Alex put forward a well-argued case for the formation of a separate corps of about six hundred men together with two hundred Irregular Horse, to patrol the borders and to be placed under his supervision, the corps being funded by both of the States. Sir Charles Metcalfe was impressed with Alex's proposals, and forwarded them to the Governor General for approval. However, after some further correspondence, no firm decision was made, and then, when Sir Edward Colebrook replaced Sir Charles Metcalfe as Resident at Delhi, the momentum was further lost, resulting in no action.

At an early stage in his Political Superintendence at Sirohi, Alex had selected two places for his residence and office during the year. His main staff office and main residence were at Sirohi, in temporary buildings he had arranged to be erected at his own expense, but as Sirohi is in a valley at the base of a range of high hills and in those days the town was completely surrounded by jungle, it was not a very healthy place to live in during the rainy season. Consequently, at that time of the year, he and his office staff would decamp to other temporary buildings he had erected near the village of Kalundri, about thirteen miles outside Sirohi. But by June 1826, all of these temporary buildings were in a poor state of repair, and Alex was concerned for the welfare of his staff if they were to stay in them during the rainy season. In an effort to rationalise his office requirements, he selected a comparatively open spot, about a mile outside Sirohi, where he hoped the atmosphere would be healthy enough to remain throughout the year. Unfortunately, though, when he arranged for excavations for a well in the spot, no water was found even after a considerable depth had been reached, and the effort had to be abandoned when hard rock was eventually struck. All this had been carried out at Alex's own expense, and he had till then also had to bear the additional costs of keeping a mobile establishment of servants, followers and cattle to enable him to move about the territory of Sirohi, which was still in a comparatively lawless state.

Now Alex rightly sought the assistance of the government to provide for his office accommodation, leaving them the choice of erecting it at Sirohi, Kalundree or at both places. In its usual way, though, the government was in no rush to commit itself to such expense until it was satisfied that the Agent's position at Sirohi was likely to be a permanent one, and until Alex had submitted for approval plans of the proposed building and detailed estimates of the cost involved, which he did in December of that year. Without any formal training in building construction, agents like Alex were still expected to produce reliable estimates for such building work and in his case Alex had to estimate for the transport of all necessary woodwork from the timber depot via Ajmer, none of suitable quality being locally available. Eventually, by the time the government had actually sanctioned the work ten months later, Alex had been forced to commence construction of a permanent bungalow at Sirohi, again at his own expense, as otherwise he and his staff would have had inadequate shelter during the monsoon season. However, the sanction of a total sum of 8,281 rupees for construction left Alex free to finish the building he had already commenced and to erect another at Kalundree, providing this total amount was not exceeded. As Alex had been unable to wait for the formal permission before commencing the work, naturally he had to supervise the foundation work himself, even though untrained in building construction. But, in giving permission for the work and approval of the expenditure, the government also agreed to provide an overseer from the Office of the Superintendent of Public Buildings at Nasirabad to supervise the remaining work.

In fact, Alex's estimate proved to be too low, as he could not hire workmen locally and had to send for a labour-force from Nimach and Nasirabad, which involved paying much higher rates. Consequently, he could only afford to alter the bungalow at Sirohi to make it suitable as an Agency building, the cost of this work leaving insufficient funds to commence another building at Kalundree. The fact that Alex was still owed Rs 1950 for construction of the building four years later shows how much risk and expense Political Agents were expected to bear on their own account during those times.

After continuing for four years in his post at Sirohi, Alex was given the first extension of his duties in November 1827, when he was asked by the Resident at Delhi, Sir Edward Colebrooke (who had recently replaced Sir Charles Theophilus Metcalfe as Resident), to take charge of actions in the Udaipur state against the ravages of gangs of Bhils and Grasseahs in the hilly areas, who would not accept the authority of the Rana of Udaipur, and who were aided and abetted in their insurrection by the outlawed Thakur Daulat Singh. This came about due to the death of Captain Black, who had been serving at Udaipur solely in this capacity and had suffered a considerable setback with his initial force of 152 horse and 1475 infantry in a disastrous engagement near the town of Khairwara, but was now to be equipped with a force from Nimach under Colonel Burgh of 20 Companies of Infantry, 200 Irregular Cavalry and 100 Pioneers. Unfortunately, Captain Black had died whilst on his way to meet this strengthened force, whereupon Alex was asked to take charge of the operations (in addition to his normal duties). In his letter to the Governor General on the subject, Sir Edward Colebrooke commented: 'From Captain Speirs' local experience in regard to their tribes I am led to hope that the loss of Captain Black's services at the present moment though much lamented may be in a great measure compensated', with which the Governor General fully agreed, adding that he 'anticipates great advantage from the employment of the services of the above officer on that delicate and important duty'.

The government was indeed not disappointed in this respect. Although he was aware that Dowlut Singh had refused all previous peaceful gestures, Alex halted the advance of the force initially as a last ditch attempt to resolve the issues which had kept Dowlut Singh in a state of rebellion for the past four years. Dowlut Singh had previously been the Minister to the former Rao of Jowass (who had since been deposed), with responsibility for collecting revenues—a very lucrative appointment as he was only bound to pass on a percentage of such revenues to the Rao. His appointment was clearly not hereditary but subject to the discretion of the former ruler of Jowass. Dowlut Singh's rebellion, thus, had been an expression of his desire to be reinstated to his previous position, which in turn depended on the reinstatement of the former chief. At first, he tried to negotiate only on this condition and it took Alex some time, through a series of exchanged messages, to convince him that this stance could never be accepted but that, if he was prepared to surrender and submit himself to the decision of the British Government, his case would be heard fairly.

Even at this stage, Dowlut Singh showed considerable apprehension at the thought of actually meeting Alex, who received a message that 'the Taccoor had been hovering about camp all the previous day, but was too much alarmed to come in, that if I would then go out a short distance he would accompany me to my tent.' The following day Dowlut Singh again changed his mind and sent Alex a message saying that he would meet him in any village but would not come to his camp. The import of this was clear; that despite Alex's assurances, 'at present he was too much alarmed to do so being well aware of the numerous atrocities which had been ascribed to him and which he apprehended could not be entirely forgiven, that he would send in Govindah Khawass and some of his people to remain with me...that I might place some confidence in his sincerity and entirely forgive him all his former delinquencies, or rather those attributed to him and when he had satisfied himself that this was the case he would come to me when and where I might direct.'

Such an anxiety felt by wrong-doers at actually submitting themselves to British justice, even after receiving the most generous assurances, was something encountered only too frequently by Alex in his long political career. But nearly always, by gentle persuasion and by 'bending over backwards' to accommodate their concerns, Alex would manage to dispel their fears and reinforce the trust thus established by treating them as humanely as possible. In this case, however, it shortly became clear that Dowlut Singh was buying time by playing a double-game: whilst he was sending these apparently conciliatory messages, he kept changing the terms on which he would meet Alex, rendering such a meeting extremely improbable. All this time, he was assembling forces against the Company. Eventually, in early January 1828, Alex recognised that diplomatic measures were simply having no effect. He, therefore, called on Colonel Burgh to continue his advance and to attack and pursue Dowlut Singh and his followers, acquainting him with the situation:

> I am informed that Dowlut Singh is at the village of Dheukwass about three and a half cos to the South West of our present camp and has with him about three hundred men armed with matchlocks and between three and four hundred armed with bows and arrows. It is also extremely probable that the Bheels of the neighbouring villages may join him. He has himself intimated to me the hostile intentions of his followers and those at present with him.

In fact, Dowlut Singh tried to conceal his intentions by sending one of his men to Alex 'with a message that Dowlut Sing had desired him to say that he himself had no hostile intentions and would never meet the British Troops, but that a number of Grasseas from Panurwah and elsewhere had collected in the neighborhood and meant to oppose the Force on its march unless the estate of Jowass was restored to the Rao and...that our troops should not be advanced into their territory. No reply was sent to these propositions.'

The ensuing action started very much in favour of the Bhils, whose guerrilla attacks in fairly wild countryside were hard to counteract using conventional military tactics. Alex had received intelligence that Dowlut Singh's deputy, Govinda Khuwass, was occupying the village of Kankur Sangwara, so, before commencing an attack on the village, two Thanas (or Police posts), each with about 200 matchlock-men, were sent to occupy both of the passes leading out from that village in order to cut off any attempted escape of the rebels when the village was attacked. But word of the troop movements had already reached Govinda Khuwass, who promptly sent his own matchlock-men to positions above the passes, from where they attacked the Thanas before the attack on the village could take place. As a result, four of the troops were killed, another four wounded and three horses also injured.[27] As the element of surprise was missing now, the troops were withdrawn on this occasion. However, they continued to pursue Dowlut Singh's followers over the next few weeks.

Eventually, the tactic of continual harassment paid off and on 11 February 1828, Alex received a delegation consisting of the Rana of Panurwa and several prominent local chiefs who were 'very anxious to know what was to be done in regard to Dowlut Sing. I replied that he had left me nothing else to do than to attack and pursue him and his adherents, that I had offered him a full pardon and the restoration of all lands held by him or his forefathers; what else he could desire I knew not; as to giving over Jowass to him which he appeared to wish for, it could never be listened to. I added that if Govt should determine to restore Jowass it would be to the Rao of that territory who was alive and perfectly competent in such an event occurring to appoint his own Minister... They said that Dowlut Sing was not so foolish as to persist in making any such request and begged to know if in the event of his now throwing himself on my mercy what he had to expect. I replied that though he little deserved any consideration from me in consequence of his people having fired on our foraging parties, yet I was still willing to act as favorably towards him as I could.'

Once again, Dowlut Singh showed considerable apprehension and wanted to make sure that the terms agreed on suited him before surrendering himself. Alex describes it in his report:

I was given to understand that several messages had passed between Taccoor Dowlut Singh and the Chief of Panurwa, after which I was asked if it was my intention to visit once more the places of residence of the three Chieftains of Panurwa, Joora and Ohgna. My reply was that I did. When I was asked if I would meet Dowlut Singh at the Rana's house on my arrival at Panurwa, to which I consented... In the morning and on a visit Dowlut Singh made me in the evening he said he was ready to attend to whatever I required of him, he was willing either to become an active servant of the State or if that was not expected of him, to sit at home and till his lands, in which latter case he only wished sufficient to subsist himself. I told him that I by no means wished him to remain inactive but was anxious to benefit from the advice and assistance of a man of his reputed abilities and experience... I offered him his hereditary lands and rents as I had done formerly. He begged that I would not be offended if he declined these offers for the present under any circumstances because if he accepted them he would be thought by the world to have become a traitor to and have deserted the cause of his master the Rao of Jowass; that he was willing to accept whatever stipend I offered him or which his services might merit, but should his master's lands be restored, he would of course look for and expect what he and his forefathers held under that Chief... I told him that the restoration of the lands of the Rao of Jowass did not rest with me but with Govt and that I could not condemn his motives for refusing the lands which his ancestors had held, and requested he would give me a memorandum in regard to his wishes for support... I added that his exertions for the restoration of good order and peaceable habits amongst these wild tribes were more likely to obtain the favorable consideration of Govt for his master's lands than the conduct he had hitherto pursued, and recommended a trial of this line of conduct in preference to that which he admitted he was so heavily tired of and had led him such a life of difficulty and danger for over two years.

Alex further goes on to say:

I know not yet what his propositions for provision are likely to be, but I would recommend a liberal stipend for him as giving him an interest in upholding our rule and in the preservation of good order and as the best security in my opinion for binding him to our own interests and those which we would wish to uphold.[28]

In fact, Dowlut Singh asked for a stipend of a hundred rupees a month, which was approved on Alex's recommendation. Before receiving this, however, the Thakur had to provide written engagements for his future good behaviour. In this way, Alex obtained the allegiance of this previously rebellious chief, who was now prepared to act constructively in assisting with the pacification of the hill tribes. Thereafter, Dowlut Singh frequently accompanied Alex on difficult missions even assisting him in tricky negotiations, which was much appreciated as he undoubtedly held a lot of influence with all classes of people.

Alex's leading role in the transformation of this rebel was well received by the government, and I believe it probably influenced the decision to upgrade him to the rank of Major from April of that year. However, this was not the only outcome. Such skills in diplomacy were in short supply at the time, hence, the Governor General also decided to increase Alex's responsibility to cover the superintendence of the hilly areas of the neighbouring States of Udaipur, Dungarpur and Jawass.[29] This was a quite an extra responsibility, as it was here that the lawless Bheel and Grassia tribes lived—these being the tribes who refused to acknowledge the supremacy of the actual heads of State, and who caused continuous trouble with their plundering raids on peaceful valley villages. Fortunately for Alex, the government recognised that extra responsibility merited extra pay and Alex received an additional 300 rupees a month as his reward.

Alex continued with his political duties at Sirohi for another four years, before showing signs of restlessness. He had by then served at Sirohi for nine years in total, with ever-increasing responsibilities, and his work had always received fulsome praise from his superiors. Clearly, he was hoping for a promotion and was probably aware that the government was proposing to form a new agency at Ajmer, with responsibility for all the Rajputana States. So, learning that the Governor General, Lord William Bentinck, was visiting Ajmer on his tour of the country, Alex wrote seeking permission to wait upon him there. At the time, Alex had been showing Lord Clare, the Governor of Bombay, (who was himself travelling to Ajmer to meet the Governor General) the sights around Sirohi. Alex received a reply, giving him permission and asking him 'to accompany His Lordship (Lord Clare) to Ajmer rendering him such attentions as your political station and influence may furnish the means and opportunity of doing.' Alex seemed to have achieved some success because three months later he was informed of his appointment as Superintendent of Ajmer in the following resolution:

> The Honorable the Vice President in Council is please to pass the following appointments on the nomination of the Right Hon'ble the Govr. Genl. Lt. Colonel Abraham Lockett Governor General's Agent for Rajpootana States and Commissioner for Ajmer with a consolidated salary of sixty thousand rupees per annum. Major A. Spiers, Superintendant of Ajmer and First Assistant to the Governor General's Agent in Rajpootana. Major A. Spiers will continue to draw his present allowances as Political Agent at Sirohi.

When my father discovered the letter from Alexander Speirs describing his first days at Marlow, we naturally assumed that Alexander, being illegitimate, was being sent off to India as a way of ridding his father of any embarrassment. My later discovery of the forty other letters written by Alexander from Marlow seemed to reinforce this impression, as it was clear that Alexander was not permitted to write directly to his father. So I was quite surprised when I found a further four letters written by Alex from India, directly to his father. Three of these letters were written in 1832, the year of his father's death, and they clearly indicate both a continuous correspondence and a warm relationship (in one of the letters Alex asks his father whether he has received the Sirohi-made matchlock gun and sword he had sent him, and thanks his father for sending the 'Cabinet Cyclopaedia').

These letters also refer specifically to Alex's visit to meet the Governor General at Ajmer and state his subsequent reactions. In the first letter, dated 23 March 1832, Alex says:

> I have been moving about with very little intermission since the middle of Dec last, I joined Lord Clare the Governor of Bombay

at the frontier station of that army & about eighteen miles distant from my own boundary on the 24th of that month & attended him through my district, shewing him over the mountain of Aboo, its temples & remarkable places, shortly after His Lordship had left my charge I was directed to attend him to Ajmer where he was proceeding to meet our Governor General Lord Wm Bentinck, where we arrived on the 18th of January. I remained there with him till the 11th February, when I was directed to proceed with His Lordship to the boundary of the Bengal territories to the Eastward of the Arabulla Hills to the Westward of which I had gone up with him & by which he had an opportunity of seeing Oodeypore, the Capital of the Hindoos & the residence of their King, the Rana, he there visited the palaces, lakes & islands of that potentate, all of which he greatly admired; he said he had seen nothing in Europe to surpass them & that the embankments forming the lakes, from the great labour and expense bestowed on them, as well as their strength & beauty were worthy of the best days of Greece or Rome. I am quite of the same opinion; after conveying Lord Clare to the point directed, I left him on the 14th of this month & am now on my return homewards, during the time I was with His Lordship I experienced the greatest kindness & attention from him & he would have gladly taken me still further with him. He has given me the kindest invitations to visit him at Bombay, in Ireland or England or wherever he may be. I admired him much as far as I saw of him as a Statesman (I mean as an Indian Governor) & a gentleman...

Alex talks about his experiences with the then Governor General, Lord William Bentinck, in his letters.

During the time I was at Ajmer Lord & Lady William Bentinck were very kind to me. I had several long and private conversations with his Lordship & he was pleased to tell Lord Clare that he had got much good & interesting information from me, for which by the bye he thanked me when I departed from him; he said too that he made no promise but that when he told me that no officer stood higher in his estimation than myself, that I might suppose I should not be forgotten by him & if he can, in the new arrangements he is about to make for this quarter, he will serve me. Sweet words cost him nothing & they butters no parsnips as the proverb has it, I am however inclined to trust him as he is not often lavish of his commendations. He also told Lord Clare I should be provided for.

In his second letter, written a month later, Alex was already wondering whether he was right to have trusted Lord Bentinck's sweet words, but he only reveals his true feelings in the third letter, written just after receiving the news of his posting to Ajmer. He says:

You never wrote a truer word than 'that there was no dependence to be placed in the words or professions of great me', not withstanding what I wrote to you of our Governor General's sweet words to me, he has just removed me from this place where I was independant, to the superintendanceship of the Province of Ajmere & as first assistant to his Agent for Rajpootana, this will entail upon me the whole of the judicial & fiscal duties of that Province, besides a great deal of drudgery as an afsistant & this too without giving me a single farthing of additional salary to sweeten the annoyance, I had almost said degradation, of being made an assistant & that too after being nine years a Political Agent & receiving on all occasions the applause of Government where there was an opening for so doing, even from Lord W. B. himself. He has made my immediate superior Colonel Lockett (though a senior officer to me in the army, yet a junior in the Political Department by two years or nearly so) Agent to the Governor General for Rajpootana & Commissioner for Ajmere with a salary of 60,000 Rs a year, my allowances are not one third of this. Colonel L's is entirely a new appointment & every claim and consideration appears to have been sacrificed to aggrandize his charge & increase its dignity and his personal allowances. I know and feel confident that he has not done half the works in the department which I have done & has been in a pleasant part of the country & in society whereas I have been laboring for the last nine years in almost a state of banishment, amongst a set of savages & cut off from all society. They may talk of our Governor General's high feelings of justice & impartiality but I have never discovered or experienced them as yet... This business has so disgusted me with the service & the country that I would renounce both & tell the Governor General he might bestow his assistantships on whom he pleased had I even a tolerable competency in regard to fortune, but as I unfortunately have not, I must just grin & bear till better times come round upon us and which I hope will be soon.

It is abundantly clear that Alex was hoping, and had reasonable grounds to expect, to be offered the post of Agent to the Governor General for Rajpootana and felt betrayed at having been offered the post of an assistant. In fact, Sir Charles Metcalfe, a gifted administrator who had become Resident at Delhi at the age of twenty-seven and who was now a member of the Supreme Council of India and deputy to the Governor General, seems to have thought that Alex deserved a higher post. In a private letter to Lord William Bentinck, dated 29 February 1832, he wrote '...Major Speirs, whom you think of as Lockett's second at Ajmere, is I believe an excellent man; very steady and conciliatory, and in every respect worthy of notice and promotion.'[2] I consider that the phrases I have underlined indicate his polite disagreement with the Governor General's view.

However, much though he would have liked to resign, Alex indicated that he could not afford to do so, and he had to endure another seven years before finally achieving the status of British Resident. His statement that he did not even have 'a tolerable competency as regards to fortune' leads me to a further speculation. A story that has been handed down to me through generations in our family is that Alex had been about to retire in about 1830, but lost all of his savings in the crash of one of the Calcutta banking houses, either Palmer and Co, or Colvin & Co. I think this statement implies that his loss occurred due to the collapse of Palmer & Co in 1830. (Colvin & Co only collapsed in 1833).

Alex received the letter directing him to take up his appointment at Ajmer on 19 May 1832, but he could not procure transport for the removal of his property until 3 June, when he commenced on his journey to Ajmer. Before setting out, he had instructed the majority of his Infantry and Horse Escort to disband and rejoin their respective Corps, as, despite Alex's advice that the Political Agent should be based at Sirohi, Government had decided to economise by directing that his replacement, Captain Pasley, should manage the Sirohi and Doongerpoor Agency from Nimach. Alex took along with him a small party of his Infantry escort as his personal guard for the journey and, with the sedate pace of travel by bullock carts, the 200 mile journey from Sirohi took two weeks to complete. After taking one day to settle in, he formally took over the duties of Superintendent from the Honorable RJ Moore on 18 June.

My use of the term 'to settle in' was in fact quite a euphemism. Alex discovered to his dismay that the Superintendent's residence was in a very bad order—with most of the terraces broken up, much of the window glass being broken and many doors and chawkhuts needing repair or replacement. The building previously used as a Court and as offices for the staff of writers had been virtually dismantled. This building was originally a tomb, and had now been returned to that state and handed back to the family who owned it. Alex quite naturally asked the government to sanction repairs to his residence and recommended that a new building be erected for use as offices. But new regulations were now in force, whereby Political Agents were now supposed to fund their accommodation from their salary. Consequently, the government refused to repair the accommodation or to fund new offices, leaving Alex considerably worse off than he had been in his appointment at Sirohi.[5]

To make matters worse, the government was also cutting back on staff, and Alex found that, although he had the usual staff of English, Persian and Hindi writers, the two assistants to the previous Superintendent, the Honorable Richard Cavendish, had been assigned to other posts—so that he was left without a single assistant. This would have made it impracticable for Alex to start his impending tour through the province to make the new settlement of Land Revenue. This was urgently required as the next five-yearly settlement was overdue. But the government was clearly on a massive economy drive and would not countenance any replacement appointments, except suggesting that Alex should 'borrow' an assistant from Lt Colonel Lockett, Alex's immediate superior officer at Ajmer.

Time went by and almost eighteen months after taking up his post, an event occurred which should have led to the realisation of Alex's ambitions for advancement. In November 1833, Lt Col Lockett was suddenly taken seriously ill, departing urgently for the Cape of Good Hope on two years' sick leave, leaving Alex to take over the duties of Agent to the Governor General. But any hopes that Alex might have had regarding the confirmation of his appointment were dashed a few months later when the Governor General appointed Major Alves to the post and transferred Alex to replace Captain Pasley as the Political Agent at Nimach. Lord William Bentinck justified this decision thus:

> I am induced to propose this arrangement from the necessity that is so apparent of providing a more efficient officer for the charge than Captain Pasley and from the recollection of the successful management of his former charge at Serowhee.

But I can hardly imagine how Alex must have felt at once again being passed over for promotion by someone who claimed that he rated Alex as one of the best Political Agents. And Alex must have been particularly incensed when it was made plain to him that the Agency at Nimach came under the Rajpootana charge, which meant that he would be subservient to Major Alves although being promoted to the rank of Lieutenant Colonel the previous year.

As fate would have it, Alex duly handed over the Rajputana Agency to Major Alves and travelled to Nimach, arriving there three weeks later. At Nimach, there was a former Residency building from the time when Major General Sir David Ochterlony had ruled the former Malwa and Rajputana Agency from there. Alex was given permission to use the Northern wing of the Residency as an office for the Nimach Agency. But he soon realised that this area of the building was uninhabitable, all doors having been removed and the walls and ceilings needing plastering. And there were other serious defects too—'The stairs leading to the upper rooms are without banister on which account, as they are very narrow, they are in their present state somewhat dangerous, more especially in coming out of the room towards the top of the stairs...A covering too of the aperture leading to the top of the house is urgently required to prevent the whole of that immediate (interior) quarter of the house being injured by the weather. This opening is at present uncovered.' So, once again Alex found himself obliged to provide out of his own pocket the accommodation for his office staff until the government finally saw it fit to pay for this essential work almost eighteen months later and to grant him an office allowance in the interim. Alex's duties at Nimach involved extensive travelling as he was expected to simultaneously control other States too including his former charge, Sirohi, for which he received little extra remuneration, finally causing him to give vent to his feelings in this letter:

> That I shall be a sufferer and to a considerable extent in a pecuniary point of view by my removal to this Agency there can be no doubt, unless Govt. will take into consideration the travelling expenses which are entailed upon me in moving about to the different States under my charge, involving a circuit of 442 measured miles over certainly the worst roads in India and thro' jungles which speedily destroy every description of camp equipage and where supplies are difficult to be had and high priced. The very trifling addition to my allowances on removal to this Agency can be considered a mere nominal augmentation to what I should have received had I remained at Sirowi with the pay of my increased Mily rank which I was there entitled to. I beg leave to state that I have been employed as a Poll Agent since March 1823 and that no officer in the Dept in that situation has enjoyed fewer advantages in terms of allowances than myself either during that time or at present. As to my services I shall say nothing; they are before Govt.

But this plea seems to have fallen on deaf ears as the reply from the government states that giving Alex a special deputation allowance would be against established rules and that funds were not available to increase his salary.

Meanwhile, Alex's prospects did improve somewhat, and I suspect this was because Lord William Bentinck resigned as Governor General in March 1835 and was succeeded temporarily by Sir Charles Metcalfe who, as the reader will recall, seems to have had a high regard for Alex's capabilities as well as a recognition that he deserved to be rewarded for taking on extra responsibilities. I am sure that it was Sir Charles Metcalfe who agreed to Alex being given the additional responsibility of the State of Udaipur, even though by the time the announcement was made in March 1836, he had just been succeeded by Lord Auckland as Governor General. However, it was certainly Sir Charles Metcalfe, in his new role as Lieutenant Governor of the North Western Provinces, who made a strong recommendation to Lord Auckland that Alex should receive an increase in pay of Rs 500 per month, making his new salary Rs 2500 per month, adding 'that Lt. Coll. Speirs is a very meritorious officer, and his services in this department entitle him in the opinion of the Lt. Govr. to every possible consideration from the Govt.' And now, to give the reader a better idea of how Alex had been imposed upon previously in terms of pay, I will quote from his application for this additional allowance:

> The charge which I now hold was formerly held by three distinct Pol Agents, Vizt: Major Cobbe, Meywar; Captain Macdonald, Bauger and Kauntal: and Major Speirs, Sirowi. The officer who had that situation here alone received a higher salary, besides other advantages, than I do at present.

However, Alex's new superior officer, Major Alves, does seem to have been conscious of the fact that Alex had far more experience than himself, and fully supported Alex being given the extra responsibilities, leaving him free to stay at Nimach, Sirohi or Udaipur at different times to suit the demands of the post.

Sir Charles Metcalfe shortly gave Alex a further important duty that of being present at a high-profile trial in Jaipur to ensure that the sentencing was fair. In the following extract from a letter to his cousin in Scotland, dated 14 June 1836, Alex himself describes his new responsibilities:

> Since I wrote to you last, Government has added greatly to my charges by transferring to it the State of Meywar, the head of which is the Rana of Oodypoor, the King of the Hindoos! This adds greatly to the respectability of my situation & to my work, it may also to my allowances eventually, but it has not as yet. I believe I have principally to thank my friend Sir C. Metcalfe for this. He has also recently selected me for an important duty & which I am now on my way to take charge of—Viz: to be present at a Court which is to be assembled by the Jyepoor Govt for the trial of the parties implicated in the outrages committed at Jyepoor on the 4th June 1833 in which Mr Blake of the C.S. was

killed & Colonel Alves was wounded. I am merely to interfere
so far as to prevent any vindictive proceedings against them, but
not to take any active part in the proceedings or sentences.
Government directed an officer of Character & Experience to be
selected for this duty by the Lt Governor of the Western
Provinces & he has made choice of me, at which I feel much
gratified. I know not whether it is likely to be of any pecuniary
benefit to me, though it is likely to give me great additional
trouble & a very hot and annoying march at the very worst season
of the year.

The cousin to whom Alex was writing was Alexander Graham Speirs,
who was by now MP for Paisley and who had already succeeded his father,
Peter Speirs, as proprietor of Culcreuch. In the letter, Alex was also
replying to news of the death of 'poor Matilda' and gave instructions on
disposal of his legacy from her. Almost certainly, he was referring to his
half-sister, Matilda, who had died late in 1832. Again, I find it quite
surprising that Alex (being an illegitimate son born before his father's
marriage) had a close enough relationship with his half-sisters that he
should receive a legacy from one of them. But he had clearly kept a
regular correspondence with each of his cousins, as he asked in the same
letter whether his cousin Archibald (who was by now a magistrate and
Collector at Allahabad) had arrived home safely on his furlough. And he
also felt himself sufficiently a member of the main family to ask
Alexander (of Culcreuch) to make up a seal for him, bearing the Speirs
arms and crest.

Evidently, Alex received this seal (in the form of a ring) and it seems
to have been passed down through the family. My grand-mother appears
to have inherited it—saying in a letter to my uncle in 1964:

>...the grounds of the house of Lady Anne Speirs had large
>elaborate iron gates and empanelled in those gates was the
>[Speirs] crest and motto, the same as on a ring meant for sealing
>letters which I used to wear.

After four and a half years of controlling three States from Nimach,
Alex's dream of gaining one of the top political posts came true. A vacancy
had occurred at Ajmer when Lt Col Alves resigned his position as Agent

to the Governor General for Rajpootana. In the subsequent re-shuffle of posts to fill this vacancy, Lt Col Sutherland, who had been British Resident at Gwalior, was instructed to take over the vacancy at Ajmer, while Alex was instructed to officiate as Resident at Gwalior. So, on 1 January 1839, Alex duly handed over the Nimach post (which had since been renamed 'Meywar Political Agency' to emphasise the importance of the Udaipur state) to his successor and set out a few days later for Gwalior, reaching there on 29 January. However, having formally taken over the duties from Sutherland and after being presented to Maharaja Junkojee Rao Scindia of Gwalior, Alex was asked to attend an urgent inquiry at Jhansi, where the succession to that Raj was being challenged by several contenders. So, for about a month whilst the inquiry was in progress, Alex had to leave his first assistant, Lieutenant Richard Ellis, in charge at Gwalior.

No sooner had Alex returned to resume his duties at Gwalior, than he received the first of many khureetas from the Baiza Baee, the Maharaja's 'adoptive' mother and widow of the former ruler, Maharaja Dowlut Rao Scindia. However, Alex was aware of the fact that Baiza Baee, a spirited Mahratta lady, had ambitions to interfere in the running of the State since she had ruled for a number of years as Regent after her husband's death in 1827 and during Junkojee Rao Scindia's minority. Baiza Baee had actually ruled firmly and fairly but had treated the young Prince harshly, keeping him under restraint and excluding his name from the State seal, intriguing to remain Regent for life. (Dowlut Rao Scindia had left no sons, and Junkojee was simply a close relative whom the Court had chosen to succeed to the throne). But Junkojee had eventually managed to flee to the Residency for protection, which had led to a stirring against Baiza Baee and finally to her expulsion from the State when Junkojee finally commenced his reign as Maharaja in 1833. Alex knew that the Maharaja would not tolerate any interference by Baiza Baee, so he always replied politely but firmly resisting her attempts to regain some influence in the State affairs.

Alex was not exactly ecstatic when his salary as Resident at Gwalior was fixed at rupees 3,012 per month, only rupees 512 above his previous salary since the increment was not even two-thirds of the salary of rupees 5,000 per month that he had quoted to Lt Col Lockett at Ajmer in 1832. As the appointment was (initially) temporary, the Company had rules allowing the appointee to draw half of the salary for his previous post and half of the salary of the person whom he replaced. In this case he had replaced Lt Col Sutherland on a salary of rupees 4166 per month but he was instructed that military pay had to be deducted before making the calculation, so once again he lost out in terms of pay compared to other Residents.

The only description of Alex that I have ever come across is the following rather unflattering excerpt from Emily Eden's book, *Up the Country*, written as a series of diary entries while she was accompanying her brother, the Governor General, Lord Auckland, on his long, slow tour of the Upper Provinces (the tour had started in Calcutta in October 1837 and only returned there on 1 March 1840!):

> Dec 10th 1839—There is a Colonel E. come into camp today: he is the Resident at Gwalior, and is come to fetch us. He is about the largest man I ever saw, and always brings his own chair with him, because he cannot fit into any other. He has lived so entirely with natives that I fancy he very seldom sits in a chair at all, and I suppose he is, as he says, very shy of white females, for it was impossible to get an answer from him... To finish off Colonel E., I must mention that the officer who commands his escort is called Snook, and that his godfathers, to make it worse, called him Violet. He is a little man, about five feet high, and is supposed to have called out three people for calling him Snooks instead of Snook.

Emily Eden was obviously highly amused by some of the officers' names because referring to another meeting with Alex on 4 January 1840, she says:

> E. is the Gwalior Resident, and is on the same fat scale with everything else, except little Violet Snook, who is trotting about the street very busily. It is rather curious that the camp should contain three officers rejoicing in the names of Violet Snook, Gandy Gaitskell and Orlando Stubbs. Are they common names in England? Gandy Gaitskell we are uncommonly intimate with; he is always on guard, and always dining here. Orlando Stubbs is a novelty.

Emily had arranged to meet Alex and his contingent of officers after church the next day (being a Sunday) and she continues with her lively entry, mainly about Violet Snook:

> They live five miles off, so Colonel E. gave them a breakfast before church, and when I went out this morning early, they were all arriving, and Violet Snook was rushing in and out in a violent state of excitement, receiving his brother officers, shaking hands and bowing and ordering, and in short it was quite pleasant to see a Violet with such spirits, and a Snook with such manners. They all came after church, and seemed a gentleman-like set.

Interestingly, whilst Emily Eden's book is peppered with the use of initials, often altered as in the case of the reference to Alex as 'Colonel E,' she is far less discreet with other officers. 'Violet Snook' was almost certainly Lt John V. Snook of the 23rd Native Infantry; Gandy Gaiskell was another Lieutenant, in the 26th Native Infantry, which was on escort duty for the Governor General's tour; and Orlando Stubbs was a Lieutenant Colonel in the 53rd Native Infantry, doing duty at Gwalior as Commandant of Scindia's Reformed Contingent.

I would have liked to have added to Emily Eden's pen-picture by enclosing a photograph of Alex's portrait, which was painted whilst he was Resident at Gwalior and which was seen by my family hanging in the Residency in about 1930, together with those of many other Residents at Gwalior. Unfortunately, though, I have been unable to trace this portrait, which seems to have disappeared since independence, along with the portraits of the other Gwalior Residents.

The description given by Emily Eden does give some weight to my view that Alex's duties as Resident at Gwalior generally involved a great deal of ceremony and were probably less demanding than his previous duties when he needed to tour several States and personally arbitrate in hundreds of legal matters and disputes. Now, as Resident, his duties were more static and he had a larger staff to whom he could delegate some of these duties.

In particular, Alex had many dealings and much correspondence with Major William Sleeman, who was by then the General Superintendent in charge of the Thuggee Department based in Moradabad, and who liaised with many Political Agents and Residents in order to help eradicate the practice of thuggee in the states under their control. Initially, it was agreed that Sleeman could send his assistant Captain Graham into the Gwalior state with an armed force to round up thugs and dacoits and send them for trial by the Maharaja's Government with Alex presiding at the trials. In one such trial in the autumn of 1840, twenty dacoits were tried of whom thirteen were found guilty of robbery in Gwalior territory, five were found guilty in the Company's territory and two were acquitted. But such outside interference did not suit the Maharaja and moreover the detailed investigations of such cases were highly time-consuming for Alex. So, it was agreed with the Maharaja that Alex's assistant, Richard Ellis, should be put in charge of capturing the thugs and dacoits, effectively forming a separate Thuggee Office at Gwalior.

I will now turn to a series of events that unfolded at Gwalior over the next two years: In February 1841, Alex learned that Junkojee Rao Scindia was confined to his bed with a debilitating sickness that left him very weak. Whilst Alex was eventually able to visit the Maharaja, who claimed that he felt much better, Alex felt the need to warn the government of several potentially serious problems if the Maharaja succumbed to his illness. The first problem that Alex reported to Lord Auckland was the fact that the Maharaja was childless and that his wife was very young—too young to be left to decide on a successor by herself (it was usual for such a choice to be left to the widow if not already decided by the ruler). And, stemming from this was the fact that Scindia's five ministers did not see eye to eye on any matter despite the fact that they were expected not only to continue governing the country, but also appoint a Regent from amongst them to rule during the minority of the successor. In Alex's opinion, only one of the ministers, the Mama Sahib, had sufficient authority and was capable of acting as Regent. Now clearly a subject such as the succession to the throne had to be broached in a very tactful manner, and a time of illness was not appropriate. But unfortunately no such opportunity presented itself since the Maharaja was again taken seriously ill in August 1842. This bout of sickness was more prolonged, leaving him unable to attend to State business for several months and the government in a state of turmoil as none of the Scindia's ministers was prepared to take decisions on their own busy as they were in constant in-fighting. The situation was made worse by the fact that the Maharaja would not admit Alex or any of his Ministers to his bedside, so that even urgent matters could not be resolved.

With the Maharaja's health in a perilous state and no possibility of him choosing a successor, Alex made discreet inquiries to help in the eventual choice. He produced for the Governor General a genealogical chart of the Scindia family, which showed that two boys aged about three and eight were nearest in line to the succession, the elder boy probably having the best claim. During the succeeding months, Alex barely managed to visit the Maharaja two or three times, and in each instance his health was too poor to permit more than a desultory chat about the affairs of State. He also refused to be seen by the Residency surgeon, Dr Irvine. Maharaja Junkojee Rao Scindia finally expired, after another debilitating attack of his illness, in the evening of the 7 February 1843.

At first all seemed to go on smoothly—Alex was shortly invited to attend at the palace, where he was met by the five ministers and other Court officials, and after expressions of condolence, the ministers confirmed that they accepted Tara Bai (the Maharaja's young widow) as their sovereign mistress and that those present had selected Bageerut Rao, the elder of the two boys that Alex had already decided upon, as the successor to the throne. On being led to the purdah curtain, Alex gathered that Tara Bai was in full agreement, telling him that the Maharaja had instructed her several months before to adopt Bageerut Rao as her son and successor in the event of his death. So, with general agreement on the succession, it only remained for a Regent to be chosen. Since both Tara Bai and Bageerut Rao were too young to manage state affairs. Alex now confirmed to Lord Ellenborough (who had succeeded Lord Auckland as Governor General the previous year) the advice given to Lord Auckland that 'the Mama Sahib (the maternal uncle of the late Maharaja) appears to me to possess the greatest influence of any person about this Court and seems to be attached to our interests. He would perhaps be the person best calculated to place at the head of the Regency.' Lord Ellenborough agreed with Alex and authorised him to nominate the Mama Sahib as Regent.

Now this was the most delicate phase of the operation (bearing in mind that the ministers could never agree, and they were thus unlikely to readily accept one of their number as Regent) and the first signs of trouble duly emerged as soon as Alex broached the subject through his envoy, the Durbar Vakeel. The Vakeel informed Alex that the young widow was being strongly influenced by a female servant named Naurungee (who was notorious for her intrigues) to delay the appointment of a Regent so that the former ministers could carry on the government as before. Three ministers were also involved in this, including one known as the Dada Khasgee Walla, whom they proposed for the office of Regent, although he was probably the most inefficient of all the ministers.

Alex decided to try and settle the matter on 22 February, the day when the young Maharaja was to be installed on the Gaddi (throne). So he went to the palace early that morning, where he was met by the Durbar Vakeel, who informed him that he had met the three ministers and with great difficulty persuaded them to agree to the nomination of the Mama Sahib as Regent, obtain the consent of the Maharani and to his nomination being publicly declared immediately after the new Maharaja had been placed on the throne.

The ministers were then brought before Alex and they confirmed their agreement on the appointment of Mama Sahib as Regent. Alex did note, though, that the other ministers still wished to allow the young Tara Bai to have a strong voice in the running of the government. So he told them that that the Regent's power should be uncontrolled and that both they and the Maharani should delegate to him the fullest powers and that if they or others were to interfere with him by bringing orders to him from the Rani, all his efforts for the good of the Country would be paralysed and affairs would remain in the same state of confusion. This they agreed to abide by. So the Mama Sahib was duly called in, and he made a solemn undertaking to forget any previous enmity and to treat them fairly. Now, as Alex reported:

> The hour for placing the Maharaja on the throne having arrived, the Ministers left me, when after a short period, the Durbar Vakeel, the officers who accompanied me and myself entered the hall of audience, which I found crowded with the principal officers of the State, and influential people of all classes. I was conducted to the neighbourhood of the Purdah behind which the Maharani was sitting, where I met the young Maharaja standing to receive me, from whence I led him to the Guddee on which I placed him,

about ½ an hour after sunrise, when a heavy discharge of Guns and small arms in honour of the event immediately took place, and which continued for some time... The usual Khillat was then presented on the part of the Governor General on occasions of this description, consisting of 7 trays of jewels; 24 trays of clothes; 5 trays of articles of European manufacture, with an elephant and two horses, all richly caparisoned. On the termination of this ceremony, one of the turbans which formed part of this present, and which was richly ornamented with jewels was taken up by one of the Chiefs and that which the Maharaja wore and much of the same description, was removed and the former put on by the Minister, behind a temporary screen of cloth drawn in front of the Maharaja, on the removal of which cloth a Royal Salute was directed to be fired. The Ministers, the officers who accompanied me and myself then went and sat down on each side of the purdah above alluded to, when the Maharanee expressed her gratitude to the Governor General for his friendship...After some consultation between the Ministers and the Ranee, she said that she approved of the Mama Sahib being nominated Regent (Mookhtar) and ordered him to be invested with a dress on that account, which having been effected we returned to our seats near to the Guddee, when the Ministers proclaimed that he had been nominated to that distinguished post, which appeared to give great and general satisfaction... The Ministers and all the influential people of the Court then came forward with their respective presents to the young Maharaja, which he continued to receive till he appeared quite worn out from fatigue, when I took my leave, after receiving the usual ceremonies of Utr and Pawn.

But the appearance of agreement was unfortunately illusory and transient. Alex soon realised that intrigues were occurring behind the scenes, over which he had no possible control. The woman Narungee was in league with the minister Dada Khasgee Walla and both were scheming to overthrow the Mama Sahib so that the Dada Khasgee Walla could become Regent. Moreover, both Narungee and the Dada Khasgee Walla exerted a great deal of influence over Tara Bai, who was only twelve years old, and a virtual puppet in their hands. They reinforced her belief that she should have ultimate control over the Regent's actions—all the time persuading her to adopt their agenda. On occasions, Narungee simply issued orders in Tara Bai's name. In this situation it became impossible for the Mama Sahib to govern, as his orders were continually being challenged or disobeyed. Alex then agreed with the Governor General that the diplomatic removal of Narungee from Gwalior was essential to the survival of the Regency, as she seemed to be at the centre of all the trouble. Eventually, after a month of such chaos, Alex managed to persuade the young Maharani to part with her favourite without causing a scene—Narungee being bribed with the offer of a village worth Rs 3000 per annum to depart.

Lord Ellenborough seemed quite satisfied with this result, Alex being informed of 'the Governor General's entire approval of your conduct during the proceedings with respect to the woman Narungee and (of) His Lordship's congratulations on the success which has so far apparently attended your exertions'. However, although Narungee's removal from the palace improved matters for a while, the Dada Khasgee Walla had by now gained considerable influence over Tara Bai in his own right, and he still aimed to overthrow the Mama Sahib. He started spreading dissatisfaction amongst the troops in the large Gwalior army to achieve his objective. This was not difficult as, due to inaction during the late Maharaja's long illness, the troops had not been paid for a considerable time—eighteen months in the case of the Cavalry and twelve months in the case of the Artillery and Infantry. When the Mama Sahib attempted to remedy this situation by withdrawing thirty-three lakh rupees from the treasury to reduce the arrears in pay, he received an angry message from the young Tara Bai denying him permission to do so. It was clear that she was being manipulated by the Khasgee Walla, with the intention of destabilising the army. The Khasgee Walla, however, covered his tracks well. Matters eventually came to a head on 21 May, when Alex was informed by a messenger that Tara Bai had assembled the officers and Chiefs in Camp, with the exception of the Regent and the Durbar Vakeel, and advised them that, although she had appointed the Mama Sahib as Regent, she had several causes of complaint against him and now wished to remove him from office. The following morning, Alex attended a Durbar with the same assembly, where he was able to speak to Tara Bai from behind the purdah. It turned out that two of her principal complaints against the Mama Sahib were the earlier removal of Narungee and his current intention to remove the Khasgee Walla from Court. Alex informed her that Narungee had quit the court voluntarily and that the Khasgee Walla had actually applied to him for permission to leave Gwalior. He could not therefore consider the removal of the Regent on such slight grounds. However, the young Rani was adamant that she would not continue with the Mama Sahib as Regent whereupon Alex told her that he did not accept that this was her real view, but that he believed she was being manipulated by evil advisers. After briefly remonstrating with the Khasgee Walla about his actions, Alex withdrew from the Durbar.

It turned out that the reason for the Mama Sahib's absence at the Durbar was that the Khasgee Walla had given orders for the troops to seize him and place guards over his house. The officers concerned however were not prepared to do so at which point the Khasgee Walla's followers demanded that the Mama Sahib should leave Gwalior. The Mama Sahib had politely declined, saying he would do so only if he were assured that the order came directly from the Rani. Following this, guards were left in the area, preventing anyone from visiting the Mama Sahib.

The Dada Khasgee Walla's intentions were now becoming clear. By preventing the Mama Sahib from paying the troops their dues and doing so himself, he hoped to buy the army's loyalty and use the troops to support his power struggle. Hearing that the Khasgee Walla had just paid the troops, Alex reported:

They still in general feel well disposed to support the Mama's cause and have been heard to say that the Khasgee Walla and his party had them formerly upwards of a year in arrears, that the Mama has paid them up six months at once and was about to pay them two months more, that the Dada had given them four months and wished them in consequence to seize the Mama to serve his own purposes and then get them a year in arrears again, but that they would not seize the Mama.

But within a week, the situation had changed and more troops were openly supporting the Khasgee Walla with only Colonel Baptiste's force remaining loyal to the Mama Sahib. The problem was that loyal subjects felt it their duty to support the Maharani and did not know that she was being manipulated by the Khasgee Walla. A few days later the issue was forced when all of the army Commandants were asked to attend a Durbar at the palace. On arrival, each was asked to sign a declaration stating their wish that the Mama Sahib should be removed from office as Regent. Those who declined to sign, were told that they would be forbidden to enter the palace or attend Durbars in future. Eventually under this duress, all of the officers complied. Clearly now the Mama Sahib's position had become hopeless.

One event which had occurred just prior to this, and which now assumed greater significance, was that the Mama Sahib had arranged for the young Maharaja to marry his niece—the marriage having taken place the day before Tara Bai first notified her desire to remove the Mama Sahib from office. Lord Ellenborough correctly deduced from this:

> The Mama Sahib had probably owed his downfall to the very measure upon which he most confidently relied for the securing of his Power, namely to the marriage of his niece to the Maha Rajah, which he very improperly managed without communication with you. It is most probable that the Dada Khasgee Walla represented this measure to the Maha Ranee as intended to lead to the setting aside of Her Highness and to the conducting of the Government by the Mama Sahib in the MahaRaja's name without allowing to H.H. any participation therein. The very sudden change in the position of affairs at Gwalior is so identical in point of time with the marriage, and the Dada Khasgee Walla, at first reduced to despair by that event and thinking only of his safety by retiring from Gwalior was so soon the prime mover of everything within the Palace that it is no more than a fair conclusion that having obtained accefs to the Mahuranee he so alarmed her by his representation of the effect of the marriage upon her future position as to induce H.H. blindly to aid all his designs.

Now that the Khasgee Walla had forced the army Commandants to seek the removal of the Mama Sahib, events moved fast. Two days later, the Mama Sahib received a deputation from the officers, asking him to leave Gwalior. On his initial refusal to do so, he swiftly found his house surrounded by four Companies and two field guns. Much alarmed, he appealed to the Resident for advice and Alex very sensibly suggested that he make a virtue of necessity and that he should leave the territory provided he was assured of safe passage. This was granted to him, and he made his retreat from Gwalior the following evening, on the 5 June 1843.

Shortly afterwards, Alex was instructed by the Governor General firstly to break off all official discourse with the Gwalior Government and then to make what would appear to be a routine visit to Dholpur, a town about forty miles north of Gwalior, where there was a bungalow occasionally occupied by the Resident during the rainy season. On his arrival at Dholpur, Lord Ellenborough's secretary sent Alex the following secret message:

> The Govr. Genl. directs me to inform you that his impression is that it would be inexpedient for you to return to Gwalior until some Govt. shall be created there having the appearance of good intention & giving the promise of stability, or until the Maharanee & the Chiefs may earnestly call upon you for your assistance in enabling them to form such a Govt.

He went on to instruct that Alex should not return to Gwalior without his express sanction. The object of this was clear—to send an unambiguous message to the Maharani and her followers that their recent actions were so strongly disapproved of by the British Government that their Resident had been withdrawn, but without formally stating this in writing.

These measures were also intended to spread alarm, to test the allegiance of Tara Bai and of the army to Dada Khasgee Walla—and for a while they were reasonably effectual. The total interruption of communication only lasted for a few days, but this break was sufficient to cause Tara Bai to send a Khureeta confirming that although she could not agree to the reinstatement of the Mama Sahib as Regent, she would take no steps to appoint another minister without the approval of the British Government. She also implored Alex to return to Gwalior—but he was able to blithely assure her that his stay at Dholpur was simply a routine visit. More vital, however, was the effect of the news on the army, since the Khasgee Walla's increasing power depended on the allegiance of the army. It soon emerged that Colonels Baptiste and Jacobs, who controlled large regiments of the 40,000 strong Gwalior army, had never accepted the Khasgee Walla's cause. However, realising this, the Khasgee Walla tried to curry favour with their troops through his control of their pay, inciting them to mutiny against their Colonels. Within two weeks he had achieved this aim in the case of Colonel Baptiste's Regiments—the troops deserted to join the Khasgee Walla, beating and mistreating their officers before deserting. Alex received a petition from eighty-eight officers of his regiments, stating that they had 'been seized upon yesterday night, tied up to the guns, cruelly beaten and turned out all in a flock like sheep with our single suit of clothes on our body & locked out of our houses and lines, this has been done to us by the tyranny of the usurper Dada Khasgee Walla and the Baee Sahib & were, by his orders, kicked, thumped & ill used cruelly and we are now suffering starvation for the last two days, not being allowed to go into our lines to take our property, children, wives and families. The usurpers and the ruling powers of Gwalior greatly dread our joining the British therefore we have thus been treated…' But Alex was powerless to help them, as the Company's troops were not yet assembled in the vicinity.

Settling at Dholpur, Alex quickly established a network of messengers and spies to keep him informed of all that went on at Gwalior. It was clear that the Dada Khasgee Walla had effectively taken control of the state and was by now able to coerce Tara Bai into agreeing to all of his actions. His control of the state was, however, only to the extent of issuing orders that would assist his power struggle and there was no semblance of governance—the country being in a state of anarchy and the army in disarray. Within a few weeks, he had sacked the few court officers who could have formed an administration and had replaced them with known trouble-makers, who were given large bribes to assist his cause. Although few people really supported him, it was very difficult to oust him, as Alex reported:

> The whole of the influential Chiefs & officers of the Durbar, hold aloof from the Khasgee Walla & his measures. It is said that they have entered into a combination amongst themselves, at all costs to remove the Khasgee Walla, as an enemy to the peace and well being of the State, but he shelters himself very closely in the Palace, where he has doubled the guards & seldom moves out & then only when strongly guarded; besides, there is not in my opinion a man of resolution amongst the Chiefs to undertake such an enterprise, though I am told they have a large proportion of the troops in their favor.

Eventually, in early October 1843, the Dada Khasgee Walla over-reached himself when he detained several Khureetas that both Alex and the Governor General had addressed to Tara Bai thereby proving that he had usurped her authority (until then he had shielded himself behind the fact that the Maharani would always issue orders confirming his instructions). Realising that the Khureetas had not been received by Tara Bai, Alex wrote to her stating that it was now clear that the Dada Khasgee Walla's actions had caused a rupture between the two Governments, that he had assumed the power of Maharaja and that whilst he remained in her territories 'it is obvious that there can be no hope of friendship between the two Govts. I have therefore ordered the Meer Munshee and all other British Subjects to quit the Residency and immediately to join me at Dholepore. The only means of bringing about a renewal of friendship is to send the Dada Khasgee Walla to me.' Thus Alex informed her that he was now officially quitting the Residency. The action was also sufficient for Lord Ellenborough to issue a proclamation stating that the British Government fully supported the succession of the young Maharaja 'but the Dada Khasgee Walla usurps the Guddee, for he conceals from the Maharanee and from the Durbar the Khureetas addressed to her Highness by the Govr Genl and represents matters not as they are but as for his own purposes he wishes them to appear. The British Govt which recognises the succession of the Maharaja cannot recognise the supercession of the Dada Khasgee Walla...' It seems that this proclamation was sufficient to push the Chiefs into an attempt at seizing the Khasgee Walla, which they eventually managed with the support of the troops of the Maharaj Campoo, who stormed the palace and eventually took him by force. On learning of his seizure, the Governor General wrote to Tara Bai, requesting that the Khasgee Walla should be handed over to the British for punishment, as it was deemed that if he was detained within the Gwalior territory, there was still a strong potential for him to incite his followers to cause further disruption. But she refused, and her refusal was evidence that it was not only the Khasgee Walla who had been advising her—Alex now realised that her father, Jeswunt Rao Goorpurra, had all along been promoting the Khasgee Walla's cause.

Tara Bai's refusal to hand over the Khasgee Walla had severe consequences for the Gwalior state. Until this point, Lord Ellenborough was prepared to wait for some semblance of order to be established in the state and had accepted the notion that the Maharani was under the Khasgee Walla's malign control. But Alex advised the Governor General that 'the three Chiefs who are anxious of restoring friendly relations with our Govt. and who now hold the Dada Khasgee Walla in their hands are, together with the Maharaj camp on whose support they appear to be solely able to rely, placed in peril by the artillery and the more numerous troops in the interest of the Dada Khasgee Walla, by whom they are represented to be surrounded'. So it was clear that armed intervention was now becoming necessary. When she persisted in her refusal, the Governor General finally decided that British forces must enter the Gwalior state and take control until order was re-established. A large armed force had already been assembled and when Lord Ellenborough arrived at Agra on 10 December, he gave orders for its advance into the Gwalior territory.

Before concluding the story of these events, I must here mention that on 6 December, Alex was finally released from his post as Resident at Gwalior and departed for his new post at Nagpur. The circumstances were as follows: Two months previously, the Governor General had issued orders that Alex was to take over from Major Wilkinson as Resident at Nagpur and that the Gwalior State would now come under Lt Col W.H. Sleeman, the Governor General's Agent in Saugor and Bundelkhand. It was made clear to Alex, though, that this measure was not in any way a reflection on his performance, but was intended as a mark of strong disapproval of events at Gwalior—which would henceforth have reduced status. Sleeman was instructed to manage affairs at Gwalior from his office at Jhansi, leaving only his assistant, Captain Sir R. Shakespear, to occupy the Residency. When Alex asked if he should proceed to Nagpur after Captain Shakespear's arrival at Gwalior, however, he was firmly told 'your abrupt departure in the midst of a transaction might evidently prejudice its issue, and reference should be had only to the public service at Gwalior in determining the period at which you should set out for Nagpore'. The Governor General clearly wanted Alex alone to liaise with the Gwalior Durbar whilst there was still some hope of achieving a diplomatic solution to the crisis. He was only permitted to leave when all hope was lost. And, when Sleeman took over from Alex and made an initial contact with the Durbar, he was forcibly told that:

The Governor General considers it to be very prejudicial to the success of the negotiations which may be carried on from hence under his own immediate direction that you, having no specific instructions and being necessarily unacquainted with the views which may be entertained from time to time by his Lordship with respect to events daily occurring at Gwalior and the course to be pursued thereupon should hold any communications whatever with the Durbar or any person on its behalf and you will accordingly refrain therefrom.

After the British forces commenced their march, it only took a further six days before Tara Bai yielded to the pressure to hand over the Khasgee Walla. Captain Shakespear was sent to receive him and detain him at Dholpur. But by now Lord Ellenborough was not content to accept this delayed gesture and wanted to ensure that all disturbances at Gwalior were over. So he did not halt the advance, but instructed Sir Hugh Gough, the Commander in Chief to continue towards Gwalior. On learning that the British army was in the Chambal, the boundary between Agra and Gwalior States, a deputation of the most influential chiefs was sent to request that the Maharani and young prince could wait on the Governor General at his current location. But Lord Ellenborough would not wait, so a compromise was reached whereby the meeting should take place at Hingona, within the Gwalior state and twenty-three miles from the capital. The troops, however, would not permit the Royal party to leave Gwalior, marching themselves from there and proclaiming that they would drive the British back across the Chambal—and they nearly did that too.

Having waited in vain for two days at Hingona, Lord Ellenborough directed Sir Hugh Gough to advance to Gwalior, heading for Chounda, where Scindia's army was known to have been present. But he did not know that during the night seven battalions with twenty guns of heavy calibre had moved unobserved to Maharajpore and entrenched themselves there. Meanwhile, the British troops advanced towards Maharajpore, where they intended to have breakfast, without even having taken the normal precaution of reconnaissance, so scornful were they of the enemy's capabilities. (Their march was described as a military promenade, the Governor General and the wives of the chief officers accompanying the procession on elephants.) Suddenly, though, pandemonium broke out when the first volley was fired by the enemy from their hidden batteries. As Lord Ellenborough pointedly stated, when the battle commenced, everybody and everything was out of place. The siege train had been left behind on the surrender of the Khasgee Walla and the light field pieces of the army were no match for the heavy ordnance of the enemy. The day was saved, though, by the tactics of Sir Hugh Gough, who sent wave upon wave of troops to attack the enemy batteries. Eventually, the batteries fell silent and the battle was won, but at a cost of a thousand killed and wounded out of a total force of 12,000 (the Mahratta force was said to number about 14,000).

This victory left Lord Ellenborough with the future of the state of Gwalior at his disposal, but rather than annexing the kingdom, he simply curtailed its independence. Tara Bai was deposed from the office of regent and forced to retire from public life on an allowance of three lakhs a year; a council of regency was set up, with instructions that they were to act implicitly on the advice of the Resident; and the army was reduced to only 9,000 men, with a separate British contingent of 10,000 men. As previously stated, these severe impositions were all the direct consequence of Tara Bai's refusal to hand over the Dada Khasgee Walla until too late. In her banishment, she may well have pondered over some advice that Alex had given her in a Khureeta, just before leaving for his new post:

> The Right Honourable the Govr. Genl. is shortly expected to arrive at Agra. If, before his arrival, the Khasgee Walla has not been sent to Agra, it is impossible to say what his Lordship may order or how affairs may end. Therefore, if your Highness is desirous to preserve the prosperity of your Govt. and the friendship between the States, you will not delay in sending the Khasgee Walla immediately to Agra.

In the meantime, Alex was on his long march to his new post at Nagpur, reaching there at the end of January and officially taking over from Major Wilkinson on 1 February 1844. On the following day, the Rajah of Nagpur, Rughagee Bhonsla, held a durbar at the palace, when Alex was formally introduced—the Rajah sending Lord Ellenborough the following obsequiously flattering account of his meeting with Alex:

> I have long heard his praises, but when we became acquainted I fully perceived his genius, his good qualities and disposition.

In a repetition of his past experiences on taking over at the Sirohi, Ajmer and Nimach Political Agencies, Alex found the Residency building in a very dilapidated state, mainly due to decayed roof thatch allowing leaks to occur throughout the building. On the upper storey, only one room was usable, the other two rooms being merely spaces covered by the thatched roof, but without walls or ceiling. There was a separate office building, but this was in an even worse state, large plants and shrubs having taken root in the walls and split the masonry in many places. But only a small portion of this building was needed for offices, so Alex recommended that the remainder should be demolished and the materials used for repairs to the rest of the building. One particular proposal that Alex made was to raise the roof of the banqueting hall by 3½ ft as the room was too ill-lit by day and too stuffy at night for its purpose. (I can certainly vouch for the effectiveness of this modification, the room now being quite magnificent). In this case, the government was remarkably quick in approving most of his proposals, scarcely more than three weeks after his submissions.

Lord Ellenborough kept his word that his position as Resident at Nagpur was not to be considered as a demotion, and he did so in the most effective way possible—by increasing Alex's salary from Rs 4,155 to Rs 4,503 per month. However, in reality the Bhonsla state was much less prestigious than Scindia's dominions had been before the disturbances at Gwalior. I will not enter into a detailed account of his duties at Nagpur until his death three years later. It should suffice to say that they were mainly routine matters, made pleasant by the fact that Rajah Rughagee Bhonsla was very accommodating to the British. Alex still had many dealings with Lt Col Sleeman, particularly when the latter needed 400 cavalrymen to help in keeping the valley of the Nurbudda in order. The Rajah was happy to oblige with the loan of a detachment from the Nagpur Horse for this purpose. One particular event was that Alex's third daughter, Helen, was married in the Residency in October 1844 to Joseph Fisher Stevens, a Lieutenant in the 18th Madras Native Infantry, which at that time was attached to the Nagpur Subsidiary Force.

We now turn to 12 February 1847, when, without prior warning, Alex wrote to the government enclosing a letter from the Residency Surgeon, John Macintire, stating that he was in a bad state of health and urgently needed a change of climate, recommending that he should be allowed to proceed to Bombay and potentially be granted leave to travel to Europe on a sick certificate. Ten days later, Alex was granted six months' leave on medical certificate, with permission to visit the Bombay Presidency—where the Company's doctors would examine him and make a final decision on whether he should be granted leave to travel to Europe. He was also given permission to be accompanied on his journey by Dr Macintire until he met up with his son-in-law, Surgeon Benjamin White, who was travelling out from Bombay to meet up with Alex. Over the next few days, Alex made final preparations for his sick leave, giving his bankers Power of Attorney over his affairs, so that his salary could be drawn and paid in to his account. In doing so, he disclosed that his illness was 'a violent attack of dyspepsia, which does not appear to be inclined to leave me.'

Alex, however, did not even reach Bombay. He set out on his journey on 26 February accompanied by Dr Macintire, having handed over the responsibility of the Residency to his assistant, Captain Ramsay. After they had travelled for about hundred miles, they met up with Benjamin White, who took over the responsibility of Alex's care from Dr Macintire, and they continued for a further hundred miles until they reached the military cantonment at Jalna. And the last record of him is a brief letter from the Commandant at Jalna dated 19 March 1847, informing the government that Alex had died there at about 10 o'clock that morning.

Hence, Alex never realised his ambition of retiring to his native Scotland with his hard-earned fortune. There is a large obelisk, some twenty feet tall, dedicated to his memory in the cemetery at Jalna. The inscription reads as follows:

Here lie the mortal remains of Alexander Speirs Esqre., Colonel in the Bengal Infantry and son of Archibald Speirs Esqre. of Elderslie. Arrived in India in 1805 and serving his Honorable Masters with unwearied industry, acknowledged ability and eminent success, rose through successive distinguished posts in the Political Department to the high station of Representative of the Court of Nagpore. Died at Jalna on 19th March 1847 in the 60th year of his age and the 43rd year of an unbroken residence in India.

My own view is simply that he is an ancestor of whom I am proud. Whilst many in the Company's service achieved far greater distinction, Alex was a very conscientious worker, renowned for his good judgment, and there are few who could match his forty-three years in such a hot country without ever taking a furlough—until it was too late. Sadly, though, the ruse in which his father had connived of lying about his age when he joined the Company's service meant that even his gravestone inscription is incorrect—he was actually in his 62nd year.

1

THE ELUSIVE DR SHORT

THE READER, NOTING THE ENIGMATIC TITLE OF THIS CHAPTER, MAY BE excused for asking the obvious questions: Who exactly was this Doctor Short? What made him so elusive and what connection did he have with the subject of this book, *The Wasikadars of Awadh*?

In response to these questions, let me begin by briefly recounting a story that my father, Lawrence, told me as a child—a story which has been passed down verbally through four generations of our family.

Joseph Short was one of my great-great-grandfathers, through the marriage in 1866 of his daughter, Rachael to my great-grandfather, John Speirs. He was the youngest son of a Doctor Short and his Armenian wife (both of whose Christian names were unknown by our family), and had three other siblings–Mary, the eldest, followed by John and Eliza. Both John and Eliza were said to be deranged, although Eliza's mental instability was apparently less pronounced than John's and she was reputed merely to suffer from palpitations.

We understood that the Short family had been living in Kanpur and in the year 1817, decided to move to Lucknow. Mary had been sent on ahead of her parents in a palanquin and she was near the city of Lucknow when further progress was suddenly interrupted by the approach of the Nawab of Oudh, Ghazi-ud-din Hyder, who was returning to Lucknow from his hunting lodge with his large entourage. Now clearly it would have been gross *lese Majeste* to have continued their journey in front of

SHORT FAMILY TREE

NOTE: Characters shown in bold type also appear in other trees.

Doctor James Short
b. 1788
d. 1807
m. Mary (Armenian widow of Mr Carrapiet)

Mary Angela
(later known as Sultan
Murrium Begum)
b. c 1806
d. 1849 Lucknow
m. Ghazi-ud-din Haidar 1st King
of Oudh

John (insane)
d. 1857 in mutiny

Eliza (suffered
palpitations)
m. Major Thomas Besant

Thomas Richard
b. 1841 Lucknow
d. 1904 Norwich

Joseph
b. 1813
d. 1870 Lucknow
had 8 illegal
children by 5
slave girls
m(1) Jane
Huggins 1830
who d. 1849
m(2) Amelia
1860
who d. 1891
Lucknow

James
Macdonald
b. c 1841
d. 1919
m. 1861 Nancy

14 Children

Martin
b. c 1846
m. 1892 Jane

George
b. c 1850
d. 1890

William
George by
Piari Begum
b. 1879

Emma
b. c 1852

Isaac
b. c
1856

Georgiana
b. c 1857
d. 1904

Isabella
b. c 1858
d. 1931

Edwin
b. 1859
Calcutta
d. 1927
m. 1874
Alice Francis

Mary
b. 1875

RaChael
b. 1846
d. 1882
buried Lucknow
m. 1866
John Speirs

7 children
(see Speirs tree)

Benjamin Joseph
b. 1856
d. 1896
m. 1880 Susan
Gardner

Louisa Florence
b. 1881
d. 1881

Margaret
b. 1857
m. 1880 Henry
Snell

6 children
(see Snell tree)

Elisa
b. 1878
d. 1910
(illeg)
Mary
alias
Akhtar

Alice
b. 1881
d. 1940
m. 1909
Augustus
Sangster
(who d.
1925)

Louisa
b. 1883
d. 1908

Frederick
b. 1885
d. 1939
m(1) Grace Roullett
m(2) Bandetta
Theresa
m(3) Mary Lopez
nee Short

Stanley Seabright

Edward Duhan
(who d. 1858 at
Calcutta)
(see Duhan
tree)

Mary
b. 1831
d. 1904
Lucknow
m. 1845

Helen
b. 1837
m. Joseph
Johannes

(see Johannes
tree)

Nelly
b. 1842
d. 1906
buried Lucknow
m. 1860
Arthur Edward
Quieros

(see Quieros
tree)

Marcelina
b. 1847
m. 1866
John James
Bourbon

2 Sons, 1 daughter
(see Bourbon tree)

the Court procession, so her bearers set down the palanquin at a respectful distance by the side of the road, to allow the Nawab's party unimpeded progress. Mary had stepped out of the palanquin to watch the procession of court followers, camels and ornately caparisoned elephants, one of which carried the magnificent royal Howdah. She was in turn noticed and admired by the Nawab, who, on learning that she was unaccompanied by her parents or any guardian, gave orders that she should accompany him to Lucknow.

And our story simply relates that by the time her parents arrived in Lucknow, Ghazi-ud-din Hyder had married Mary after persuading her to adopt the Muslim faith, under which she was given the name Sultan Murium Begum. Mary, who was then still only about ten or eleven years old, had always been close to her youngest brother (himself then only an infant), and it was agreed that he should live in the palace with her. So, Joseph spent his childhood in the Farhad Buksh palace at Lucknow, where he was brought up by Mary (or Murium Begum as I shall hereafter call her) as though he was her child and where he fairly naturally adopted the Muslim style of dress, although both he and Murium Begum had actually retained their family's Roman Catholic beliefs. Murium Begum was, we understood, one of Ghazi-ud-din Hyder's favourite wives and, in recognition of the fact, he had bestowed a wasika of 2,500 rupees per month on her (the wasika being a pension to be paid to her during her lifetime, one-third of which she could will to whosoever she wished, the remaining two-thirds to be reserved for the maintenance of the holy Shia Muslim shrines at Kerbala and Nushruf. The monthly payments were to be made in perpetuity to the descendants of the legatee named in her will by the British Government as part of the agreed terms under which Ghazi-ud-din-Hyder had loaned a crore rupees to the British Government).

We knew little else about their lives beyond the fact that Murium Begum had died of tuberculosis a few years before the mutiny, having previously bequeathed the full one-third of her wasika to her brother Joseph; that John had died during the siege of Lucknow when, in a moment of frenzy, he had rushed out from his safe hideout into the mob of insurgents and had been killed; that Eliza had married a Captain Besant and had a son called Dick, but her eventual fate was unknown; and lastly that Joseph had escaped at night during the mutiny from his hideout, which was close to the river Gomti, descending the steps cut into the river-bank walls to a waiting boat which took him to a cave where other refugees had gathered. From there, the party of refugees had travelled to Kanpur towards safety, but not before Joseph had been robbed of the jewels which he had taken with him to ensure his immediate security in those troubled times. We also understood that Joseph had married twice, our family being descended from his daughter, Rachael, by his second wife (who was supposed to have been Murium Begum's maid-servant). And finally we knew that Joseph had arranged for his sister's burial in a domed tomb in the Kaisar Pasand Cemetery and that his remains were interred in St Joseph's Cathedral in Hazratganj.

So, there, in four brief paragraphs, is the family tradition that I would like to present to the reader as 'Exhibit A' in the story of the lives of Joseph Short and Murium Begum related in subsequent chapters. Now clearly family traditions can often rightly be held in suspicion by biographers, as there are many instances where subsequent research has found such traditions to have no factual foundation whatsoever. However, I believe, that particularly where the later research does support the tradition, it can reasonably be presented verbatim, leaving the reader free to judge for himself whether he (or she) accepts those facts that are not actually confirmed by the research.

It would be a normal expectation in reading any biography to be given a reasonable introduction to the subject in the form of an outline of the lives of the subject's parents. This of course brings me to Doctor Short, Joseph and Mary's father and the subject of this chapter. Naturally, one of my aims in the research for this biography was to positively identify who he was, where he came from and other facts about him. But I was also aware that my father, Lawrence, had made repeated efforts over a number of years to track him down and had merely ended up with two possible candidates, viz; Doctor James Short, who had joined the HEIC's Bombay service in 1788 as an Assistant Surgeon and had been posted as a Surgeon to the Baghdad Residency in 1800; and Doctor Michael Short, who had travelled to Madras in 1821 and applied to the HEIC for a post of an Assistant Surgeon there. His application was initially rejected on the grounds that he had no diploma certificate to prove his medical qualifications, and after a long delay the Medical Board at Madras rejected him in May 1823 after examining him in surgery and finding him not qualified.

Of these two possible candidates, James Short was and still remains the most likely one by far, particularly when the following sources are taken into account:

1. In his book *A History of Armenians in India*[1], Mesrovb Seth gave ,quite an accurate account of the Murium Begum story, and included the following statements: '...In 1813, an English doctor, James Short, of the Honorable East India Company's service, married at Patna an Armenian lady, Mary by name, the widow of an Armenian merchant named Minas. One of their daughters, named Mariam, became one of the queens of Ghaziuddin Hyder (the first King of Oude)' and '...the marriage was celebrated by an Armenian bishop, named Arathoon, and the witness to the marriage was a Mr Carrapiet, an Armenian resident of Patna'.

2. A translation of the Urdu book *Begammat-i-Awadh*[2] by Sheikh Tassaduque Hussain which deals with the story of Murium Begum includes the following statement: 'Sultan Maryam Begum, daughter of Doctor Short of the Baghdad Political Agency, was by nationality Armenian and Christian by religion. In the third year after the accession of Ghazi-al-din Haidar, in 1817, her mother came with her from Cawnpore to Lucknow...'

The reader will note that Seth not only named Dr James Short, but also gave very specific details about his marriage, suggesting that they had been taken from a marriage register entry. Also, although Seth does not mention whether Dr Short had worked at the consulate in Baghdad and Sheikh Tassaduque Hussain does not mention his first name, both references could refer to the same person, namely the Dr James Short of the HEIC who, as previously mentioned, can be shown from the Company records to have worked at Baghdad.

But let me now mention the obstacles that need to be overcome before either of these candidates could be shown to have been Joseph and Mary's father. In James Short's case, the records clearly show that following several years' service with his military regiment on the Malabar coast[3], during which time he had received his promotion from Assistant to full Surgeon, he was appointed 'to the Medical duties of the Durbar of the Bacha of Baghdad, acting at the same time under the instructions of the Resident...' at the beginning of August 1800.[4] Although it is not exactly clear as to when he reached Baghdad, it can be assumed that he probably arrived there around December 1800. However, he himself confirmed in a letter that he was relieved from this post on 8 November 1802 in order to return to the Presidency of Bombay[5]. Whilst on his travels, he fell seriously ill at Bussorah[5], as he vividly described in a letter to the Resident at Baghdad.

> I have had a most severe attack of a liver complaint, from which, after the application of three Blisters & enormous quantities of Mercury, I am only so far recovered as to be enabled to sit up for a short time and to walk a little about my room. The complaint has reduced so much, that I am only able to write you a few lines.[5A]

After recuperating for three months, he decided to travel by a country ship to Bombay, arriving there at the end of April 1803. At Bombay, he was examined by the Company's doctors, who pronounced him to be in need of a change of climate. Accordingly, he was granted a furlough to Europe on sick certificate on 10 June 1803[6]. He sailed from Bombay on the Company's ship *Lonjee Family*, which left for England on 8 July 1803, accompanied only by his native servant John de Cruz (there is no mention of him being accompanied by a wife or children). He reached England in the middle of December 1803 and eventually died at Exmouth in March 1807[7] having made a will in which his estate was divided between his father and sisters. Again, there was no mention of his wife and four children.[8]

So, clearly, either Seth has got his marriage date of 1813 wrong, or he is referring to another Dr James Short. But the records of the Company servants are very precise, particularly in the case of Surgeons, and there simply was no other Dr James Short in the HEIC at that time. Moreover, the Dr James Short whose history I have traced, does not appear to have gone anywhere near Patna before his brief service in Baghdad, and there was insufficient time afterwards, before his arrival at Bombay to commence his sick furlough in June 1803. Turning to the reference from *Begammat-i-Awadh*, I believe this to be somewhat more encouraging because it simply says that Mary Short was his daughter, without mentioning his marriage at Patna or a date after his death. So it could be argued that Seth simply got his facts wrong about the marriage at Patna, but that Dr James Short had children (either within or outside of marriage) by an Armenian woman whilst he was working at Baghdad. But even this theory presents difficulties—(1) his stated age at both of his marriages and (2) a comment on a petition he made in 1858 that he 'was a man aged about 45 years'.[9] These statements each indicate that Joseph Short was born in about 1813—i.e. ten years after Dr James Short left India 'unaccompanied by a wife', and six years after his death. Joseph Short's death certificate in fact gives his age as fifty-three, which would imply that he was born in about 1816. This evidence clearly shows that Dr James Short could not have been his father.

Turning now to the only other candidate (within the service of the HEIC), Dr Michael Short, I believe that he can be dismissed as 'extremely unlikely' simply because his probable arrival date in India was July 1820 at the earliest[10], which would mean that Mary and Joseph must have been children from a marriage in England, and this in turn would suggest that their mother was very unlikely to have been an Armenian. Moreover, if he was their father, both references quoted above would be completely wrong, either regarding a marriage at Patna or service at Baghdad.

Having informed the reader about our family's problems in identifying exactly who Doctor Short was, I can now add with some confidence that we are not alone in this. The following is taken from the judicial summary in response to a petition by Joseph Short's widow, Amelia in 1871 for a one-third share of his wasika, following his death in 1870:

This Mary Short is shewn to have been an Armenian by birth and by religion, who Doctor Short was cannot be ascertained. The tradition that he was English is probably correct but whether he was English proper, Scotch or Irish, Protestant or Roman Catholic—no one can say positively and in a case turning on marriage this is important especially if as is afserted he was a Protestant which is probable from Joseph Short having been married by the Protestant Chaplain at Cawnpore... If therefore we believe the witness Gabriel whose mother was God-daughter to this Mary Short she was not married to Doctor Short... If we believe Mrs Moses then he was married at Patna according to the Armenian creed or ceremony by an Armenian Bishop and such a marriage was by the then law of England void. I think it clear that Mary Short had been previously married to a Mr Carrapiet an Armenian for not only does Gabriel assert this but the witness Bibi Catherine herself baptised by an Armenian priest at the instance of Mary Short says that Mary Short told her that her husband had died in his own city Bagdad some years ago... Doctor Short's origin is therefore unknown a valid marriage is not shewn and if the evidence as to marriage be true then the marriage is void and the children are illegitimate... As to Sooltan Murium Begum herself we first find her as a child with her mother at Agra, Doctor Short having then died or deserted his family.[11]

Hopefully, the reader can now see the problem that I face—if legal proceedings within a year of Joseph Short's death were unable to establish his parentage (on which the whole case rested, as Amelia Short's inheritance of Joseph's wasika depended on which country's laws were deemed to apply), then what chance do I stand, one hundred and thirty years later, when there are no witnesses available to cross-examine, and when the amount of accessible data on such relatively unknown people is obviously meagre?

However, combining all of these pieces of often contradictory evidence, I believe that a reasonable interpretation can be provided by the following scenario: Doctor James Short of the HEIC service had met Mary, the widow of Mr Carrapiet, whilst he was working at the Baghdad consulate between late 1800 and November 1802. They became lovers (probably without getting married) leading to the birth of Mary and possibly John and Eliza, but **not Joseph**. Whether or not she had married James Short, Mary evidently treated the partnership as marriage and assumed the surname Short. She probably accompanied James Short, with their children, when he went on his leave from Baghdad. However, on the way he fell seriously ill. Subsequently, the family split up at Bombay and he returned to England on sick furlough, where he died in 1807. Effectively widowed twice, Mary Short continued travelling across India and settled in Kanpur with her family. Whilst living there, she had an affair with another man (unknown name) and Joseph was the product of this liaison, being born in 1813. However, as far as the children were concerned, they were simply brothers and sisters, and their mother obviously did not disillusion them about their mixed parentage.

In producing the above summary, I have leant heavily on the statements in the evidence given in 1871, since these were made in a court of law by witnesses who had obviously known Mary Short because the court statements pre-date Sheikh Tassaduque Hussain's book by twenty-five years and Mesrovb Seth's book by sixty-six years. These statements clearly indicate that Joseph and Mary's mother was an Armenian named Mary, the widow of a Mr Carrapiet. However, the marriage in Patna seems highly debatable, as there was insufficient time and it is only claimed by one witness while contradicted by another. It seems probable that Seth was told the same story as was related by the witness Mrs Moses but when writing his book he confused her version of the events and mentioned Carrapiet as the witness to James Short's marriage rather than her deceased husband. I trust that the reader will agree that my hypothesis is a reasonable one, being supported not only by the HEIC records, but by most of the statements made in early books as well as the original court statements. But I do not feel justified in giving whatever additional data I have on Dr James Short's life, since I cannot be sure that he was actually the father and also since such data as I have does not add significantly to our knowledge of him as a person.

And finally, as a reaffirmation of his elusive nature, my last ditch attempts to establish whether Dr James Short of the HEIC was indeed the father of Murium Begum have ended inconclusively. In a letter that he wrote from Bombay whilst awaiting a medical report, Dr Short confirmed that he had travelled from Bussorah to Bombay by 'Country ship'. So I decided that a check on the logs of any likely Country ships must be worthwhile, as would a check on the logs of any likely ships for his eventual return to England—since hopefully these might reveal whether he was accompanied by his family. Unfortunately though, in the case of the Country ships, no logs for that period appear to have survived. And in the case of his journey to England, I can only report that he travelled, accompanied only by his native servant, John de Cruz, on the ship *Lonjee Family* which departed from Bombay on 7 July and reached England on 13 December 1803.[12] But in the case of this journey, the fact that he was not accompanied by his family still fits my theory. Only if his family happened to have accompanied him to England (and subsequently returned to India) could the relationship be demonstrated. So, the verdict must remain as 'not proven'.

2

Sultan Murium Begum

IN THE LAST CHAPTER, I TOLD THE STORY OF HOW MARY SHORT WAS effectively 'kidnapped' by Ghazi-ud-din Haidar and how, by the time her parent(s) arrived at Lucknow, they found that she was already married to him. Now I hasten to add that I have no means of substantiating that story, beyond simply verifying that it has been as faithfully presented as passed down to me by my father, who had in turn been told the story by his father and so on for a further two generations.[1] And I must add here that there is a quite different story given in two Urdu books— *Quaisar-ut-Tawareech* (or The King of Histories) by Kamal-ud-din Haidar, which was printed in 1890, and *Begammat-i-Awadh* (or The Begums of Awadh) by Sheikh Tassaduque Hussain, printed in 1896. So, in order to give the reader a balanced picture, I now give a translation of the relevant section from the latter book (both books relate substantially the same story):

> Sultan Murium Begum, daughter of Doctor Short of the Bagdad Political Agency, was by nationality Armenian and Christian by religion. In the third year after the accession of Ghazi-ud-din

[1] This same 'kidnap' story was also related to my second cousins. But amazingly Mrs Nandini Shepherd of Kanpur recalls that the same story was read to her from a Persian book during a history lesson at Loreto Convent in 1968. Unfortunately, though, I have been unable to trace the Persian book!

Haidar, in 1817, her mother came with her from Kanpur to Lucknow and stayed in a rented house on the far side of the Goomti river in the Haidarabad locality. Ghazi-ud-din Haidar used to take the air on that side, and for a year Murium Begum would do herself up in European clothes and greet his Majesty. Her mother desired to make the Nawab as a moth to the candle of her daughter's face and thus to acquire the property and riches with which to spend one's life in pleasure and comfort. But for a period the Nawab wasn't affected. In the end, however, the arrow of the plan hit its mark.

One night the attachment sown by that delicate rose took root in the Nawab's mind, and, when midnight had passed, he sent his favourite, Mir Kallu, with Ministers and torch-bearer to summon them. The mother began to say to Mir Kallu that they had lost hope and now wished to return to Cawnpore, and that they were only waiting for the expenses of the journey. In a brief space of time, though, Miss Short, finely attired and prepared, was in the rooms of the Furrah Buksh Palace. His Majesty, seeing her, full of a thousand longings, told her to take a box of three lakh Rupees' worth of studded jewels from a table and, when she had put them on, to come to him. After she had accordingly waited on His Majesty, he gave her five thousand Rupees and suffered her to depart.

As reported by Mirza Kamal-ud-Din, the compiler of the *Quaisar-ut-Tawareekh*, the condition of her mother at that time passed all bounds and she was overcome by an excess of joy. They performed their thanksgiving in the courtyard.

A few days later, once again at night-time, he summoned her and bestowed a box of gems and jewels, two thousand rupees, one thousand Ashrafis and three folds of embroidered cloth. Then a few days later still he called her and gave her a devotional meal with his own hand and initiated her into the Islamic faith. Outwardly and of her own free will, she then swore the Muslim profession of faith. He then said, 'I have made you my Begum'. She made a vow and after her acceptance of Islam, was called 'Sultan Begum'.... One day after this he presented her with studded bangles worth a lakh of rupees in which white and pink diamonds were set, and with a nose-ring of the same value; and, having given five thousand Dirhams, he presented about twelve Dirhams for the preservation of the harem. He gave her a palanquin to mount on and appointed Zafar-ud-Daula Captain Fateh Ali Khan to see after the preparation of her necessaries.[1]

Clearly, there is a major difference between the two versions. Also, the above tale includes a considerable amount of detail whereas by the time the story reached my ears our family version was much sparser in details surrounding the actual wedding. However, during the Nawabi period, there were numerous writers employed to record every single event that took place within the palace or affecting the Nawab, and it can reasonably be assumed that the version given in the above books was based on such palace news reports. To explain the discrepancy I would simply put the following queries to the reader: If our family version (effectively involving a kidnap by the Nawab) was true, is it likely that the Court writers would have dared to report it? And if Mary Short's mother had complained publicly about the kidnapping of her daughter, would they not be tempted to produce an alternative and more acceptable version, which laid the blame on the 'scheming mother', rather than the Nawab? On the other hand, the 1871 judicial summary mentioned in Chapter 3 of this book includes the following statement, which not only supports the version of *Quaisar-ut-Tawareekh* but also casts doubt on whether there had been a formal marriage ceremony.

...She was brought to Lucknow and at a very tender age was by her mother given as a concubine to a Mahomedan King of Oudh...for marriage undoubtedly there was none[2].

Again, though one might as well ask where this specific information came from, since it is highly unlikely that such personal events at the Muslim Court would have been revealed to the British Resident at the time. And having said that, I shall desist from further speculation as I certainly have no personal axe to grind on the subject and am content to simply state that either version is possible. I leave the reader to make up his or her own mind. So, let us now continue the story of Sultan Murium Begum.

Ghazi-ud-din Haidar undoubtedly had strong feelings for his Vilayuti Mahul (being fair-skinned and of English/Armenian descent, Murium Begum was generally known as the Vilayuti or foreign Begum). He arranged to have a magnificent garden constructed for her on the banks of the Gomti River, appropriately known as the Vilayuti Bagh, where many flowers, shrubs and plants of European origin were cultivated, some of these having been sent from the Botanical Gardens in Calcutta. The garden was about two hundred metres square, having decorative walls on three sides and with a flight of steps descending to the river on the fourth side. The garden was set out in fairly formal style, with a central tank feeding numerous fountains and having straight paved walks alongside flower beds and several barahdaries and summer-houses—as described by a European visitor in 1846.[3] The Nawab and Murium Begum used to stroll here in the evenings or they would come for a picnic and boating in the river. Unfortunately, little can now be seen of this garden, which is totally neglected and whose brick and stucco structures are now in ruins.[4]

There is an amusing story connected to Murium Begum. Once, she casually mentioned to Ghazi-ud-din Haidar that the King of Delhi had given his favourite wife a dress worth one and a half lakh rupees (a fabulous sum for a dress for the time, being equivalent to £15,000). Not to be outdone by the King of Delhi, Ghazi-ud-din Haidar promptly said that he would give her a similar dress. When the dress was finally made, encrusted with diamonds, pearls and using the finest silks, it had actually cost the Nawab four and a half lakh rupees. Ghazi-ud-din Haidar wished to show Murium Begum to the Court in this dress, so he asked that she should be dressed up and presented to the Durbar. When she had been carefully dressed and made-up for the occasion, Murium Begum asked her maid-servant how she looked in the dress. The maid-servant replied: 'Your Highness, you look absolutely beautiful. If only the day will come that your servant will also receive a gift like that'. At this Murium Begum replied: 'Take the dress, it is now yours! Put it on and go to His Majesty at the Durbar.' The maid did as she was instructed. Not surprisingly, Ghazi-ud-din Haidar was furious when the maid appeared at the Durbar and he stormed back to Murium Begum asking why she had sent her maid-servant in her place. In reply Murium Begum said: 'My Lord, I am your servant and so is she. What difference is there between one servant and another?' It is apparent that Murium Begum was quite a feisty lady, prepared to defy her husband occasionally—and no doubt her strong character enhanced her attraction to him.

Ghazi-ud-din Haidar had several other wives, and I will here provide the reader with a brief portrait of them, in order to put his marriage with Murium Begum into context. His first (and principal) wife, Badshah Begum, came from a respectable but modest family and was the daughter of Mubashir Khan Munajjam-ul-Mulk, a noble who was also an astrologer, had studied at the Delhi Observatory and produced almanacs for noble families. The marriage, which took place in 1794–5, had been arranged by Ghazi-ud-din's father, Saadat Ali Khan. Badshah Begum was a well-educated girl of striking features, with a strong and dominant character, which soon led to a rift with her husband after she learned of his affair with her maid-servant, Subh Dowlat. When Nasir-ud-din Haidar, Ghazi-ud-din Haidar's son and heir, was born to the maid in 1803, Badshah Begum did not stand by idly, but arranged for the maid to be killed. The same fate would have befallen Nasir-ud-din Haidar if a stewardess had not prevented his murder.

Naturally, such behaviour though partly understandable, did not endear Ghazi-ud-din Haidar to his chief consort, and they thereafter lived separate lives to the extent that he demanded that she should remove herself from the palace and live in the town (although he relented when she refused to do so). It is said that even when she visited him on his death-bed, he refused to relent and covered his eyes rather than see her. However, after his death she remained as a powerful force in the palace, and it was she who, on Nasir-ud-din Haidar's death in 1837, attempted to place her grandson, Munna Jan, (whose paternity was disputed) on the throne. This led the Resident to finally gain control and place the Company's 'puppet' Muhammed Ali on the throne, causing her eventual downfall. Thereafter, she was imprisoned alongwith Munna Jan in Chunnar Fort.

Ghazi-ud-din Haidar's second wife known as Mubaruck Mahal, formerly Mariam, was the daughter of Colonel Aish and his Hindu wife. Mariam was a charming and cultured woman, who had met and attracted Ghazi-ud-din Haidar on his visit to Kanpur in October 1814 to meet the Governor General, Lord Hastings. He had subsequently brought her back to Lucknow and, after converting her to Islam, had married her in 1815. She was undoubtedly his favourite wife, as evidenced by the fact that he bestowed on her the largest pension of all his wives, rupees ten thousand per month. She was a gentle and sweet woman who quickly became a favourite at Court and was allowed to take over many of the functions of the Chief Consort, much to the chagrin of Badshah Begum. She died on 30 January 1840, and was buried at the Shah Najaf Imambara, alongside the tomb of her late husband.[5]

Besides Mary Short (or Murium Begum) whom the Nawab had met and married in 1817-18, Ghazi-ud-din Haidar had two more formal marriages. Surfaraz Mahal, an extremely attractive and dusky girl, belonged to Malihabad and was originally a Sunni Moslem. Her marriage to Ghazi-ud-din Haidar took place after she converted to the Shia faith. She was left a wasika of one thousand rupees a month, although her servants and dependents received a separate allowance of rupees 929. After Ghazi-ud-din Haidar's death, she lived at the Machi Bhawan, but later shifted to a house in Mahmood Nagar when the Machi Bhawan was raised to the ground by the British during the mutiny.

Ghazi-ud-din's last wife was known as Mumtaz Mahal. A Hindu by birth, she was converted to Islam by her father, Urai Lal. After her husband's death, she dressed only in white and lived behind the Shah Najaf Imambara. When she died in 1896, she was buried there, alongside her late husband, Mubaruck Mahal and Surfaruz Mahal.[5A]

The above mentioned were Ghazi-ud-din Haidar's 'official' wives whom it is assumed that he married by the formal Nikah ceremony, and who are mentioned in numerous histories of the Nawabs of Awadh. Besides these, Ghazi-ud-din Haidar evidently had a vast number of inferior wives, whose existence has not generally been acknowledged. However, in a rather poignant letter written in November 1858, after the annexation of Awadh (and thirty-one years after Ghazi-ud-din Haidar's death), the Chief Commissioner gave the Governor General a list of forty-six 'females of the Mahul of Ghazeeoodeen Hyder' and asked what should be done to support them, adding that 'most of the females were the inferior wives of the King, they are all very aged, and several are in very destitute circumstances'. The list certainly corroborates his description—the ages given are all between forty-eight and sixty-six years, and the pensions vary between three and fifty rupees a month, with descriptions such as 'earns a living by serving' or 'earns a livelihood by grinding corn' or 'living in great destititution' being applied against some of those earning the lesser pensions[6]. Presumably, the King actually had more inferior wives than the forty-six listed, as one can reasonably assume that some would have died before 1858.

Ghazi-ud-din Haidar himself was described in 1824 as 'rather a tall man, and being long-backed and sitting on a somewhat higher cushion than his neighbours, looks particularly so at his own table. He has evidently been very handsome, and has still good features and a pleasing countenance, though he looks considerably older than he chooses his painter to represent him. His curling hair and whiskers are quite grey, and his complexion has grown, I understand, much darker within these last few years, being now indeed perhaps the darkest in his court... The King of Oude, however, is evidently fond of dress, and is said to be a critic in that of others as well as his own... His manners are very gentlemanly and elegant, though the European ladies who visit his Court complain that he seldom pays them any attention... He is said to be naturally just and kind-hearted, and with all who have access to him he is extremely popular. No single act of violence or oppression has ever been ascribed to him or supposed to have been perpetrated with his knowledge, and his errors have been a want of method and economy in his expenses, a want of accessibility to his subjects, a blind confidence in favourites.' The above description was provided by Bishop Reginald Heber, when he visited Lucknow during a protracted tour of Northern India in the years 1824-25, which he had started at Calcutta, the centre of his vast diocese.[7]

Reginald Heber gave a vivid description of a breakfast at the palace with Ghazi-ud-din Haidar. He travelled there with the Resident in open palanquins, accompanied by a large procession of men armed with silver sticks. On arrival, 'the King received us, first embracing the Resident, then me. He next offered an arm to each of us, and led us into a long and handsome, but rather narrow, gallery, with good portraits of his father and Lord Hastings over the two chimney-pieces, and some very splendid glass lustres hanging from the ceiling. The furniture was altogether English, and there was a long table in the middle of the room, set out with breakfast, and some fine French and English china. He sate down in a gilt arm-chair in the centre of one side, motioning us to be seated on either hand. The Prime Minister sate down opposite, and the rest...was filled from the Residency, and about an equal number of natives, among whom were one of the King's grandsons... The King began by putting a large hot roll on the Resident's plate, and another on mine, then sent similar rolls to the young Nawab his grandson... Coffee, tea, butter, eggs and fish were then carried round by servants, and things proceeded much as at a public breakfast in England. The King had some mess of his own in a beautiful covered French cup, but the other Mussulmans eat as the Europeans did. There was a pillaw, which the King recommended to me, and which I was bound to taste, though with some reluctance. I was surprised, however, to find that this really was an excellent thing, with neither ghee nor garlic, and with no fault except perhaps, that it was too dry, and too exclusively fowl, rice and spices... During the meal, which was not very long, for nobody ate much, the conversation was made up chiefly of questions from the King as to the countries I had visited, the length of time in India and objects of my present journey... I took care to thank him for his kindness in sending the guard and the Aumeen to meet me, as also for the loan of the elephant and chariot. I understood pretty well all which he said, though he does not speak very distinctly, but I seldom...answered without interpretation.'[7]

The Bishop ascribed Ghazi-ud-din Haidar's inability to govern effectively, and the consequent desolate state of the Country to the fact that he was 'disliked by his father, Saadat Ali, who had kept him back from all public affairs, and thrown him entirely into the hands of servants. To the first of these circumstances may be ascribed his fondness for literary and philosophical pursuits, to the second the ascendancy which his khansaman Minister has gained over him. Saadat Ali, himself a man of talents, fond of business and well qualified for it, left him a country with six millions of people, a fertile soil, a clear revenue of two millions sterling... and no army to maintain except for police and parade... Different circumstances however soon blighted these golden promises. The principal of these was perhaps the young Nawab's aversion to public business. His education had been merely Asiatic, for Saadat Ali had kept his son from all European intercourse and instruction. He was fond, however, of study and in all points of Oriental Philology and Philosophy, is really reckoned a learned man, besides having a strong taste for mechanics and chemistry. But these are not the proper or most necessary pursuits of a King, and have rather tended to divert his mind from the duties of his situation...'[7]

Bishop Heber then went on to explain how Ghazi-ud-din Haidar had been timid in his attempts to remove the haughty and imperious Resident John Baillie, and that he had ended up by sacking his own able Minister Hakeem Mehdee rather than admit his real purpose. 'The then Resident of Lucknow [John Baillie] was said to interfere too much in the private affairs of the King. The Minister [Hakeem Mehdee] would not allow it and the King was so much irritated by this real, or supposed interference that he sent private intelligence to Lord Hastings... The King's servants, worked upon the King's timidity by representing the danger of coming to an open quarrel with the Resident... The King retracted his complaint and ascribed it to the incorrect information and bad advice of the Hukeem Mehdee, who was in consequence deprived of many of his principal employments...'[7]

This had occurred within a few months of Ghazi-ud-din Haidar's ascension to the throne in July 1814. In fact, John Baillie's disrespectful and imperious manner had been previously complained of by Ghazi-ud-din Haidar's father, Sadat Ali Khan, but Ghazi-ud-din Haidar did not have the courage to persist with his own claim, and not only blamed Hakeem Mehdee but also the Residency Surgeon, Dr Low and two other Residency staff. This left the Governor General, Lord Hastings, in a quandary as it was quite evident to him that the King was not telling the truth[8]. So he ended up by leaving Baillie as Resident for a further year, before finally removing him from the post. Meanwhile, Ghazi-ud-din Haidar had replaced the efficient Minister Hakeem Mehdee by an unscrupulous scoundrel, Aga Meer, who had previously been his khansaman, but elevated himself to this position through his influence over the King. During Aga Meer's term as Chief Minister, the people of Awadh suffered many years of misrule and oppression, as he assumed most of the executive power, whilst the King took no active interest in governance of the country. The explanation (given above) by Bishop Heber that Ghazi-ud-din-Haidar's lack of interest in governing the country was due to the inadequate preparation accorded to him by his father is almost certainly correct. Sadat Ali Khan was a confident ruler who had maintained full executive control of Awadh, having placed men dependent on himself in positions of authority. However, he had not trusted his eldest son and had therefore appointed his second son, Shams ud-Daula as his deputy, intending him to become his successor. So, when Ghazi-ud-din-Haidar had succeeded to the throne with the support of the East India Company, he was highly ill-prepared for governance.[8A]

Although he was a weak ruler, Ghazi-ud-din Haidar was a personable man, and life for his favourite begums must have been pleasant in his lifetime. Indeed, it is clear from the terms of endearment towards her late husband in her will 'may Holy God perfume the tomb of blessed memory' that Murium Begum reciprocated his affection for her, but when he died in 1827, her status within the palace inevitably suffered. The begums of former monarchs had little of the freedom that they were allowed whilst their spouses were there to indulge their every whim, but were looked upon with suspicion by the new rulers as being likely to seek solace or romance elsewhere.

Although at her marriage, she had apparently freely accepted Islam, Murium Begum undoubtedly held strong Roman Catholic beliefs, even to the extent that, when the Armenian bishop from Julfa paid a visit to Lucknow in 1833, he was warmly received by her and held a divine service in a room at the palace, which had been improvised to serve as a chapel. This service was attended by Murium Begum and all her Armenian servants, who took Holy Communion at the hands of the Armenian Bishop. And, before the Bishop left Lucknow, the devout Armenian Queen presented him with a complete set of very expensive robes and sacred vestments for his use during his Indian tour. This description was related by George Aviet Zachariah, who had accompanied the bishop as a deacon.[9]

The affection and high esteem with which Murium Begum had been regarded by Ghazi-ud-din Haidar during his lifetime which led to her having an exalted status within the Farhad Buksh palace, is clearly highlighted by the fact that after his death she would dare to hold Holy Communion whilst living in a Muslim palace. (It appears that this was a regular event, as it was later testified that she 'frequently received the Blessed sacrament at the hands of the then Roman Catholic Priest of Lucknow').[9A] A further demonstration of his esteem was his bestowal on her of a wasika of rupees two thousand and five hundred per month during her lifetime, one third of which she was free to pass on to whomsoever she chose, their heirs to receive the wasika in perpetuity. This, of course, is the wasika that she later willed to Joseph Short which the writer is entitled to claim being his direct descendant.

Only a few years after Ghazi-ud-din Haidar's death, Murium Begum's health started deteriorating and she was eventually diagnosed as suffering from consumption (or tuberculosis), which she suffered continuously over a twenty year period. During that time, she made numerous requests to be permitted to leave the Awadh territories for a healthier climate due to her illness, but the successive Kings of Awadh felt unable to grant such permission, fearing that disrepute or scandal could be brought onto their Court if a begum of a deceased King were free to associate with commoners. So, like Ghazi-ud-din's most favoured wife, Mubarak Mahal (who had also made similar petitions, although not for health reasons) Murium Begum was not given permission, and spent most of her later years confined to the palace. She did in fact try to obtain the assistance of the British Resident, with several letters and petitions between 1836 and 1848 which made out the case that the terms of payment of her wasika by the British Government were that it should be payable 'in whatsoever City or Country she may reside' and that they therefore had an implied duty to assist her to change her place of residence. However, she did not receive much support from the various Residents.

Colonel John Low was the first Resident to receive applications from her but, although he considered that she had a valid case (i.e. he believed that the clause had been inserted in the Treaty in order to allow for this actual event of the widows wishing to leave the Kingdom of Awadh), he took no action whatsoever for a period of two years. During this period, he received five letters from her on the subject but he neither replied nor forwarded these letters to the government for a decision. He referred the matter to the government only when he was departing on sick leave for the Cape of Good Hope in November 1838. But even the then Governor General (Lord Auckland) declined to intervene in what was considered to be a delicate matter affecting the Royal household, merely stating his hope that the King might be persuaded to grant permission.

The following reply came when the acting Resident, John Caulfield, asked King Muhammed Ali Shah for his response to the Governor General's request:

His Majesty the King of Oude although he would cheerfully

comply with His Lordship's wishes, is nevertheless averse to sanction the unusual measure of Ladies connected with his Court and family retiring from under the legitimate guardianship of those who are by custom and duty responsible for their honour, which, cannot be sullied without the Royal *damum* (a figurative term for reputation) becoming tarnished. His Majesty has in consequence of a communication with Captain Paton previous to my arrival, signed a written document sanctioning the departure of the Moobaruck Muhul Princess to Mecca, but has expressed much displeasure at Sooltan Murium Begum's desiring to leave. The Minister in placing the permission for Moobaruck Muhul's leaving Lucknow in my hands made known without disguise or preface that His Majesty granted it with seeming reluctance, as he considered such a proceeding at variance with established usage and inconsistent with the sanctity of the Haram. His Majesty, added the Minister, is confident that the retirement of the Moobaruck Muhul lady will be the prelude to many applications from other Ladies of the family who may have intrigues political, or amatory in which they desire to indulge.[10]

Noting the strong views expressed by the King of Awadh, Lord Auckland decided not to pursue the matter further, and instructed the Resident to do likewise. Thereafter, Murium Begum's fate was sealed and all her petitions to leave the Kingdom received the stock response that she must first obtain the King's permission. But the King clearly did not believe that her health was the primary reason for Murium Begum to leave Awadh, preferring to assume that she was seeking male company. Whether or not the latter was true, there is little doubt that she suffered from ill-health for many years. In 1843, Amjad Ali Shah, who succeeded to the throne of Awadh after his father Muhammed Ali Shah's death the previous year, evidently finally accepted that Murium Begum 'was laid up with consumption, that the attendance of the Doctors had proved unavailing and that they had therefore recommended her to leave this Country and proceed to some other climate for the benefit of her health, accompanied with the certificates of her Physicians and her request to be permitted to depart agreeably therewith'. However, he still refused to permit her to leave Awadh, stating that there were several places within the Kingdom with a more salubrious climate, where she could go for treatment if absolutely necessary. (I personally doubt whether there are such places, but that she would have perhaps needed the cooler climate of a hill-station).

After her request was again turned down by the new monarch, Murium Begum decided that a British Doctor's opinion might hold more sway with the Resident, so she arranged to be seen by the Residency Surgeon, Doctor Login, who certified:

> I do hereby certify that I have professionally enquired into the case of Sultaun Muriam Begum, and after careful examination I am of opinion that change of air to Bengal for a few months will be highly conducive to her recovery.

Lucknow   Signed/ J Spencer Login MD
May 5th 1843   Residency Surgeon[11]

But even this had little effect, as the Resident managed to conveniently 'lose' the certificate for several years and failed to notify the government of the evident seriousness of her illness. In the meantime, Murium Begum herself was pre-occupied with her deteriorating health, and soon had to accept the fact that if the British Government were not going to assist her, she had no realistic chance of getting the necessary change of climate which in turn implied that her chances of eventual recovery were slim. So, recognising that her end was near, she shortly executed her will (in Persian), a translation of which is given in the appendix.

In her will, Murium Begum made reference to the wasika of Rs 2,500 per month bestowed on her by her late husband, Ghazi-ud-din Haidar, over which she had the power to will one third (or Rs 833-5-4) to whomsoever she wished. From this wasika, she allocated Rs 33-5-4 to be shared by Hakim Mahomed Ali, her Physician, and by Moosamut Cheotee Khannum for 'her fidelity and good services', the remaining Rs 800 of this one-third portion being given to her brother Joseph 'whom from his infancy I brought up under my care and protection like my own son'. However, she did make further stipulations regarding Joseph's inheritance, as follows:

This allowance for my brother's expenses and to give

maintenance and clothing to my other brother John Short (who is insane) and my youngest sister Eliza (who is attacked with severe palpitation also) in case of her husband and son will not support her under such circumstance my said brother will also give her food and clothing rupees 750 and also to be disbursed by my brother's own hands and direction and after my brother's demise to be acted in the same manner by his heirs. In repairs, illuminations and charity of the Roman Catholic Churches rupees fifty vizt Lucknow rupees twenty and Cawnpore rupees thirty.

She also directed that Joseph should make all her funeral arrangements and have discretion over the erection of a tomb. And finally, regarding all of her property, she pronounced:

After my demise my said brother will be sole proprietor of all my household property including jewels, cash, Booneead Munzil premises as well as all and every property of mine and after my demise the male and female slaves and Abyssinian females who are left my brother has full power over them either to keep them or let them free and no other person has liberty to interfere respecting them.[12]

So that, besides the small bequests to two servants and to the churches at Lucknow and Cawnpore, Joseph inherited all of her wealth.

Still suffering from recurring bouts of tuberculosis, Murium Begum's last years were further saddened by two more impositions. Early in 1847 she discovered that her Mootsuddee (accounts clerk), who had been managing her affairs for many years, had been embezzling not only her money, but also many items of her property. Her accounts were in total disarray and the clerk, named Sookhundum, had removed the correct papers, so that she had no means of ascertaining how much had been misappropriated by him. At first, she wrote to the King, Amjad Ali Shah, who gave orders for the Mootsuddee to repay all that had been taken, but there was no follow up of these orders. The Mootsuddee simply ignored the royal command. Not wishing to repeat her request to the King, she then wrote to the Resident, Colonel Richmond: '...I hope from your kindness that such measures will be taken that the man will give my accounts and money or that the subject may be brought to

His Majesty's notice in an official note, in order that His officers may properly threaten him to pay the embezzled money and the accounts connected with it. And as I have been for some years troubled with consumption, and now in consequence of Sookhundum's dishonesty and ingratitude entertain different notions and am in grief, I have certain necessary words to say worthy of being told. If you will kindly authorize Dr Login and also 2 or 3 Doctors from the Cantonments to come to my house, and consult about my sickness and report to you what I may say respecting my funeral and burial you will much oblige me... Formerly Dr Login examined my sickness and gave me a certificate for a change of air, and I made a request to go away from this place for my recovery, and not to derive pleasure, which was not allowed, although it is written in the Deed of Engagement that wherever they (the Pensioners) may reside they will be paid in the coin of the Country. I trust you will favour me with a satisfactory answer.'[13]

However Lt Col Richmond, the Resident, merely replied with condolences on her ill-health, rather than providing the assistance she had requested. By now, the Residents were clearly following a course of non-interference with the Begums of Awadh, even though the Treaty under which they received their wasikas stipulated that 'the British Government will always protect the honour of the stipendiaries who will be paid out of this fund, and it will be the protector of their possessions such as houses and gardens (whether bestowed by the King of Oude or purchased or built by themselves from the hands of the Sovereigns and their enemies and in whatever city or country they may, be their allowance may be paid to them there.'[14]

The second imposition on Murium Begum occurred a year later, when Lt Col Richmond issued orders that Muhuldars should be appointed to stay in the muhuls (or palaces) of each of the widowed begums. They were entrusted to report to the British Government twice a month on everything that took place there, and to report immediately in the case of any improper conduct. Now the reason for this imposition of 'female spies' on the begums was the known misconduct of one of the widows of King Nasir-ud-din Haidar, named Taj Mahal, who had taken to heavy drinking and moreover had given birth to a child long after the death of Nasir-ud-din Haidar. This behaviour had caused considerable distress to the King (Wajid Ali Shah) who had suggested that eunuchs should be placed in each of the muhuls to guard over the activities of the begums, but Colonel Richmond feared that 'His Majesty was surrounded by those who would doubtless take advantage of this occasion to press hardly on the Begums for purposes of private emolument, and my fear that should such authority be conceded to the King, a difficulty would arise in discovering and preventing harsh treatment, led me to meet His Majesty's views as far as I could, in keeping order in the Muhuls by the appointment on my part to each of a Muhuldar, or female house servant, whose residence in the Muhul would act as a check.'[15]

Although Colonel Richmond's alternative was clearly less draconian than the King's original suggestion, it took no account of the fact that the other begums might be innocent of such misdeeds and would resent the slur on their characters by this imposition as can be clearly discerned from Murium Begum's response to the Resident's orders.

From Sultaun Murriam Begum to Colonel Richmond Resident of Lucknow dated 7th February 1848
After compliments

I have received a notice bearing the seal of the Resident's Court, in substance as follows namely: That Muhuldars on salaries of ten rupees per mensem each will be appointed by the Government to note the proceedings that take place in the Muhuls of the Stipendiary whether good or evil, should the Muhuldars conceal any circumstance they shall be considered guilty. The perusal of the notice has thrown me into considerable distress, for if the servants of the British Government without proof of guilt, assume so much severity, and adopt new rules contrary to ancient practice, what are we to expect from others. Not that I entertain any apprehension from the appointment of a Muhuldar (it is a well known saying "He fears not to render an account whose accounts are correct") but it is astonishing and painful to reflect that notwithstanding you are aware of the condition of my health and of the propriety of my behaviour how I have for the last 20 years, since the death of His late Majesty conducted myself, that I have up to the date of this letter had respect to my honor and Character, that no misconduct on the part of my servants has ever taken place, that I have for years been a prey to disease and that my days and nights are spent in contemplating the state of my health with reference to which the Residency Surgeon gave me a certificate recommending change of climate, you should without proof of misconduct on my part include my name among those of the rest... Severity and durance are certainly due to those who misconduct themselves but it is improper to include with the guilty, and to cast imputations upon, and disgrace, such as are innocent, for the public will necessarily question—if they did nothing amiss, why did the Government appoint Muhuldars over them? I beg that if any misbehaviour (which God forbid) imputed to me should reach your ears, you will acquaint me with it, and after investigation visit me with whatever penalty the Laws provide. But in the absence of crime, I cannot help observing my sanction to the appointment of a Muhuldar over myself would be a tacit acknowledgement of guilt. I beg you will let me know your opinion on the subject that I may escape this disgrace... The Muhuldars moreover deeming themselves the servants of the Government will wish us to conciliate, and submit to them, and demand an increase of salary, and should we fail to pay them the respect they may think due to them, they will take every opportunity to defame us. How then under these circumstances are we to exist, and how long to reply to their fabrications. It is mentioned in the 4th Article of the accompanying copy of the Treaty, that the Government will protect the honour of the Stipendiary, but when a mere Muhuldar is at liberty to menace and oppose us, what becomes of our honour and character.[16]

Now I should in all fairness mention here that the Urdu book *Begammat-i-Awadh* refers to the fact that after the death of Ghazi-ud-din Haidar, Murium Begum became intimate with a Hakeem. His name is not mentioned, but I would presume that this is the same Hakeem Muhammed Ali to whom she granted a wasika of rupees fifteen a month 'in recompense due by me to his duties as Physician'. It is not possible to say whether they had intimate relations, but such stories and intrigues were rife in Muslim palaces and I feel it is unjustified to pronounce them as lovers simply on the grounds that he was granted a wasika (which was the least bequeathed by her to anyone) by Murium

Begum. Also, although she could obviously have been bluffing, Murium Begum in her letter has effectively challenged the Resident to show that she had ever misbehaved. Clearly, such a tactic could have backfired in a very embarrassing way if there was indeed some truth to the allegations.

Subsequently, she received a very curt and insulting reply from the Resident stating: 'Muhuldars will be appointed without doubt, and the objections of no-one attended to. It is therefore requested that no further trouble be given on the subject by lengthy and useless communications'[15], In spite of that, she did not leave the matter at rest, but sent a petition to the Governor General, stating once again the grounds on which she sought positive assistance from the British Government, both to be allowed to leave Awadh and for the removal of the Muhuldar from her palace. The full text of this petition is given below:

To,
The Right Hon'ble James Andrew
Earl of Dalhousie K I
Governor General of India in Council
&ca &ca &ca &ca &ca &ca

The memorial of Sultan Mariam Begum one of the widows of the late Abdool Muzzuffer Moizod Deen, Gazeeood Deen Hyder King of Oudh,
    Sheweth,

That the said King of Oude on advancing the British Government the loan of one crore of rupees in perpetuity entered into a treaty with it dated 17th August 1825, containing among others the following conditions:

Article 3rd

The British Government guarantees that it will pay for ever the monthly sums hereafter mentioned out of the interest of the above loan to the persons set forth in this instrument in the current coin of the place where they may reside without any reduction whatever.

Article 4th

The Hon'ble Company will always protect the honour of the stipendiaries who will be paid out of this fund, and it will be the protector of their possessions (whether bestowed by the King of Oude or purchased or built by themselves) from the hands of the Sovereigns and their enemies and in whatever City or Country they may be their allowances will be paid to them there.

That your Memorialist is one of the widows of the King for whose maintenance and protection from insult and dishonour provision has been made in that Treaty, and that the stipend of 2,500 Rupees secured to her by Article 3rd of the said Treaty has been regularly paid to her by the British Government.

That the concluding portions of paragraphs 3rd and 4th of the Treaty, to which your Memorialist would draw your Lordship's attention, stipulate that the stipends shall be paid to the stipendiaries wherever or in whatever City or Country they may reside, in effect acknowledging their right to freedom of action and liberty to reside in whatever City or Country their inclinations, health, or other circumstance may lead them. Of this liberty contemplated by the treaty your Memorialist has been debarred as will appear from the following statements.

That your Memorialist has been labouring under consumption for about 21 years; that in the year 1843 finding the disease to have progressed to an alarming extent she sent for the Residency Surgeon Dr J.S. Login who after a careful examination of her case gave her a certificate (No 9 of the documents appended hereto) recommending change of climate and a sojourn in Bengal as most calculated to benefit her health, your Memorialist therefore considering herself under the Articles of the Treaty of the British Government entitled to claim the interference and protection of the British Representative addressed a letter to him stating her desire to leave the Country and to retire to some climate more congenial to her health, begging he would use his influence with the King in the matters, but the reply of that Officer (your Memorialist regrets to state) was to the effect that removal from Oude was opposed to the wishes of the King and that she could not be permitted to depart beyond the frontiers of his Dominions; finding however her case daily assuming a more serious aspect, she was compelled repeatedly to address letters to the several Residents at this Court on the subject but without success, until in a manner at once indecorous and disrespectful she was peremptorily informed by the present Resident that she should make no further communication on the matter.

That your Memorialist is not aware of any reasons why His Majesty should desire to restrain her to reside within the confines of his dominions, where her health has suffered so much and so long, and prevent her from seeking an improvement in her health by that change of climate which a medical officer of experience considers the only means of relief to a person in her situation.

That your Memorialist is not singular in her application to be allowed to remove to another Country as other ladies of the Royal Family have solicited and obtained permission to do so; that Shumsoonissa Begum the widow of the late King of Oude, Asufood Dowlah, who though refused permission by the late King Sadut Ally Khan to leave the kingdom obtained the sanction of the Resident of the time to do so, and was furnished with an escort to secure her from molestation during her progress. That the interference of the Resident on behalf of this lady, although she was not placed by her deceased Royal Consort under the protection of the British Government, gives your Memorialist a stronger claim than she could have preferred to the interference of the British Government, seeing that an express provision has been made in the treaty to insure to her protection of the Government and liberty to reside wherever she may find it most suitable.

That another widow of His late Majesty Gazee oo Deen Hyder, named Fatima Begum was permitted by the reigning King to leave his territories from which it will appear to your Lordship that even His Majesty does not consider it improper for members of the Royal Family to reside beyond his dominions, and your Memorialist cannot suppose that she is alone to be deprived of this advantage because her late Royal Consort has secured to her the shield of British protection and a guarantee that her allowance shall be paid to her through the British Government wherever she may reside. That your Lordship must be satisfied from the medical certificate produced by her that the object of your Memorialist in wishing to leave the Kingdom is no other than the benefit of her declining health, but if any doubts be entertained as to whether any present necessity exists for such a step she is anxious that your Lordship should be satisfied on the point by the appointment of a committee of British medical officers for the establishment of the fact.

That your Memorialist has to complain not only of a restraint put upon her movements contrary to the stipulations made by her late Royal Consort, with the British Government, but of a gross outrage upon her honour, the protection of which was one of the principal objects of His late Majesty in making the Treaty. That although the 4th Article of the Treaty provides that 'the Hon'ble Company will always protect the honour of the stipendiaries', it will rest with your Lordship on a consideration of the following circumstances to determine how far the British Representative at Lucknow has carried out the stipulations entered into by the British Government.

That in consequence of the misconduct of Newaub Tauj Muhul widow of the late Nusseerood Deen Hyder King of Oude, His Majesty placed her in durance and not satisfied with doing so, he has appointed muhuldars or female overseers as spies over all the Begums included in the Treaty, disgracing them thus, in the estimation of all the Royal family and of the public at large, by subjecting them to imputations which the conduct of the said Begum must necessarily give rise to notwithstanding that the age and infirm condition of your Memorialist are such as should render her, above all suspicion and that her character has ever challenged the strictest scrutiny. That in disregard of the spirit of Article 4th of the Treaty which guarantees protection to her property, her person and her honour, the Resident in the most disrespectful style intimated to your Memorialist in reply to her representations that 'Mahuldars will be appointed and the objections of no one attended to' and that 'it is proper that with reference to this matter he be no more troubled with lengthy and useless communications'.

Under these circumstances, while on the one hand, the life of your Memorialist is endangered by disease against which she is not allowed to use the most appropriate remedy, and her honour insulted on the other, not only by the King of Oude but also by the delegate of the British Government she has no resource than to throw herself upon the protection of the Supreme Government begging it will take its serious consideration the tenor of the Treaty—which entitles her to its safeguard, and justice and to order the Resident of Lucknow not only to rescind the obnoxious measure he has adopted, or permitted to be adopted, but to allow her to leave the Dominions of the Kingdom to reside in the territories of the East India Company.

That your Memorialist submits, that in seeking the interference of your Lordship with His Majesty the King of Oude for the removal of the stain cast upon her honor and for permission to reside within the British territories, she is not praying for aught than can be considered objectionable on political grounds, since the treaty entered into by her late Royal Consort with the British Government was contemplated by him as calculated to meet the very circumstances in which your Memorialist is now unhappily placed and your Memorialist is confident that your Lordship will not withhold from her that protection which the Treaty expressly guarantees to her.

That your Memorialist is fully sensible of the resentment her appeal to your Lordship is calculated to provoke against her in the event of her failing to obtain redress but she leaves her case in your Lordship's hands in full reliance upon your Lordship's sympathy for her unfortunate condition and readiness to fulfil the obligations undertaken by the British Government, and your Memorialist as in duty bound will ever pray

Signed / J. A. Fenwick
Vakeel of Sooltan Murium Begum[17]

However, there is no record of any positive response being sent to Murium Begum before the event which she had been predicting for so long—her death from tuberculosis. Murium Begum died at around 9 pm on 6 April 1849, at the age of about forty-three. So, sadly, her untimely death proved that she had indeed needed to leave Lucknow for the sake of her health, but from the British Government's standpoint, it seems that it merely relieved them of further troublesome correspondence!

Finally, though, her death seems to have caused the Resident to properly examine the obligations and responsibilities of the British Government under the Treaty. Shortly after her demise, the King of Awadh received a copy of her will. He objected to its validity and claimed that the one-third of her wasika which she had bequeathed to her brother should be bestowed on the royal family on the grounds that her reversion to the Christian faith had invalidated the will. He further suggested that the remaining two-thirds could be disposed of by agreement between the two governments. However, the Resident replied speedily 'that it was guaranteed in the Deed of Agreement of AD 1825 that the late Sultan Murium Begum should be allowed to bequeath a third part of her allowance to whomsoever and for whatsoever purpose she pleased, and this proves that the power was given to her free from any conditions, and therefore he could never have any hesitation in accepting the will as valid: Also that the British Government would have had no objection to the cooperation of the Oude Govt, in the expenditure of the remaining two thirds of the late Begum's allowance in charitable purposes, but His late Majesty Ghazeeooddeen Hyder had expressly requested that the Rulers of Oude should not be permitted to interfere in any way and the Governor General had agreed thereto, therefore it was impracticable.'[18]

We have now come to the end of Murium Begum's remarkable story. It simply remains to be said that she was buried in the small Roman Catholic cemetery at Kaisar Pasand in Lucknow, her grave being enclosed within a marble tomb under a large dome supported by eight brick columns, all stuccoed and painted white. The ceremony was conducted by her younger brother Joseph, who also arranged for her tomb to be erected. The beautiful marble tomb was destroyed during the mutiny, but the dome and columns looked very imposing even when my grandfather took a photograph of the tomb in the 1920s. Sadly, this is no longer the case, and the tomb is likely to crumble to the ground unless repairs are carried out before long.

3

JOSEPH SHORT

MURIUM BEGUM'S LIFE, I AM SURE THE READER WILL AGREE, WAS RATHER a sad one. Whatever happiness she had derived from her marriage to Ghazi-ud-din Haidar must have seemed a distant memory during her last twenty-two years of continual illness, confined to a palace while her health gradually worsened, with much reduced status and with no children to give her a sense of fulfilment. But her brother, Joseph, by contrast, certainly seems to have enjoyed his life!

Whilst Murium Begum evidently was a devout Roman Catholic, her brother didn't take his religion quite so seriously. Although he professed the Roman Catholic faith, in practice he lived a life more akin to that of a Mohammedan gentleman which was hardly surprising as, during his formative years, he had been brought up in a Shia Muslim palace. Before the mutiny, he owned two large and luxurious houses in Golaganj. In one he lived with his Christian wife, and in the other with the slave girls left to him by Murium Begum in her will! In fact, in a court case heard shortly after his death in order to determine how his wasika should be distributed, it was stated that Murium Begum herself had arranged his first marriage to an English girl and had also given him one of her slave girls as a concubine, at about the time that she wrote her will in 1844.[1]

According to the transcript of the above case, Murium Begum had 'brought up her brother as a nominal Christian and caused him and a girl professing Christianity to be sent to Cawnpore to be married by the

Protestant Chaplain and that they were so married appears from the certified extract from the Registers. But at the same time up to the date of making her will she lived according to customs of Mahomedans. Joseph Short did the same up to a much later date. At the time her will was made Joseph Short had issue by this Christian wife as well as by the present Amelia Short then a Mussulman and unmarried and Sooltan Murium Begum herself presented him with a slave girl as concubine.'[1]

Each of these court statements is borne out by other evidence. In the case of his first marriage, the records of the Kanpur Chaplaincy station show that Joseph Short was married there to Jane Huggens, the daughter of James Huggens (a soldier in HM's 9th Lancers), on 7 June 1830 by the Assistant Chaplain, James Whiting. Jane was only fourteen at the time and evidently illiterate since in place of a signature she made 'her mark'. Joseph, on the other hand, was shown as being seventeen (which is one of the pieces of evidence that he was born in about 1813 and therefore could not have been the son of the Dr James Short who had died in 1807 as mentioned in Chapter 1).

Little is known about Joseph's first wife, Jane, except that she bore him four daughters (Mary, Helen, Nelly and Marcelina) over the next sixteen years before dying (according to her children's testimony) in December 1849. The links of Joseph Short's family with Kanpur are surely borne out by the fact that he went there to get married, and also that his mother later died in about 1842 'whilst on her way to Cawnpore'. The probability of his parents being Roman Catholics is highlighted by the testimony that his mother 'was buried in the Roman Catholic cemetery'.[1A]

Joseph Short's second wife, Amelia, gave evidence of her origins. She came from a Shia Muslim family and was originally known as Wuzeer Begum before her conversion to Christianity in 1860. Initially, she lived in the Muhul of Sultan Murium Begum (which supports our family legend that she had indeed previously been Murium Begum's maid-servant). One day, King Nasir-ud-din Hyder approached her insisting that she and Joseph should be married by the full Nikah ceremony.[1A] So, although Joseph already had a Christian wife, he complied and married her by Muslim rites. Later though, after the death of Joseph's first wife, and following Amelia's conversion to Christianity, the couple went through a Christian marriage ceremony at St Joseph's Church in 1860.

Joseph Short himself provided evidence to the effect that he had treated the slave girls left to him by Murium Begum as his concubines– he named five of his slave girls and the children they had borne to him in his Persian 'warisnama' given to the Lucknow Wasika Office in 1863 (A warisnama was a sworn legal statement of true heirs, required from and provided by each Wasikadar in order to ensure that his wasika should be distributed correctly on his death). The translation of Joseph Short's warisnama (which throws light on his colourful life) is given in the appendix within clause five of Amelia Short's petition. It confirms that besides having four children by his first wife, Jane, and three by his second wife, Amelia, he had a further eight children by the five slave girls! (Joseph Short's children are shown in the family tree on page 2). It is interesting to speculate how many children he may have actually sired in addition to the fifteen children named in the warisnama as infant mortality in those days was high.

Evidently Mufsummat Illaheejan was the slave girl given by Murium Begum to Joseph as a concubine, since the stated age of Macdonald Short indicates that this liaison had started in 1841 or earlier, during Joseph's marriage to Jane Huggens. We know little about Jane (although our family knew about each of her four children except Mary Duhan). However, as Mary Duhan features quite prominently in this story, I will introduce her first. Mary was Joseph's eldest daughter, born in 1831. When aged twenty-seven, she was described as being 'a half-caste and of native manners, but her children are of a lighter complexion'.[2] At the tender age of fifteen, she was married in Lucknow to Edward Montegue Crawford Duhan, the youngest son of James Duhan, an Irish merchant who had arrived in India in 1791 illegally (i.e. without the consent of the H.E.I.C.) and had settled in Kanpur. James had been supplying European goods to the Court of Awadh since 1798 but he was frequently in trouble with the Magistrates at Kanpur for selling illegal liquor to the English troops 'many of whose lives had been paid as a forfeit to the improvident use of it'.[3] In December 1816, he wrote to the Resident asking for permission to set up a shop in Lucknow on the pretext that there was currently no European shop in Lucknow and 'that it would be of great convenience to Gentlemen residing in that city'.[4] This shop was later set up, and also a 'Duhan Hotel' near the Residency. In this way, the family had gradually developed their business interests in Lucknow. Edward was seventeen years older than Mary and was the tutor to Nawab Moobarizood Dowlah at the time of their marriage. However, after the annexation of Awadh, he had taken a position as a copyist in the Judicial Commissioner's Office at Lucknow, starting his career there in 1856 on a salary of hundred rupees a month.[5] Interestingly, in a character reference, two of his colleagues, James Orning and W. Hutton, had stated that Edward was very regular in his attendance and bore a good character.[5]

Let us now turn to the event that devastated and transformed so many lives in Lucknow—the siege of the Residency during the mutiny of 1857 (or the first war of Indian Independence). At the time, Joseph Short had two large prestigious houses in Golaganj, a district of Lucknow just south of the Residency compound, and in the same locality as the Johannes House (which was mined and blown up by the British Sappers during the siege as it became a favourite stronghold for rebels due to its prominent position overlooking the Residency).

On the outbreak of hostilities, Joseph Short chose to remain at home rather than taking refuge in the Residency, presuming that his Moslem dress and manners would protect him from attack by the rebels. But as we might guess he was wrong in this assumption and his houses were quickly looted by the rebel army. Consequently, fearing for his life, he went into hiding in the city with his family. They found refuge in the house of a policeman, Hasan Ali Khan, in the Daulatganj district. Remaining long in any place of hiding was of course precarious for both parties, so the family moved to the house of Mirza Mohammed Taqi, the grandson of Nawab Amir al-Daula Haidar Beg, in the Mansurnagar district. Another Christian, Ratan Sahib*, had also taken shelter in that house along with his family. One day, Ratan Sahib's* eldest child, Muhammad Askari, demanded that Joseph Short should give him some jewellery that Joseph had brought with him, or face exposure. Knowing that Ratan Sahib* was also in hiding there, Joseph assumed that the young man was merely bluffing and refused to hand over his jewels. But this

---

*The story as related above is taken from a translation of *Begammat-i-Awadh* by Sheikh Tussaduque Husain. I am indebted to Dr Rosie Llewellyn Jones for pointing out that quite probably 'Ratan Sahib' was none other than Felix Rotton, who was known to have converted to Islam and to have fought against the British along with his Anglo-Indian sons.

was no bluff, and Muhammad Askari thereupon went to the Collector, Husam al-Daula Yusuf Khan, and reported to him that there were English people concealed in the district.[6]

On receiving this intelligence, the Collector sent a note to his brother, the army general Nasir al-Daula Muhammad Hilli Khan, more commonly known as Mammu Khan. Now Mammu Khan used to work closely with Begum Hazrat Mahal, the mother of the proclaimed ruler Birjis Qadr and leader of the rebellion Regent during Birjis Qadr's minority. He immediately sent out a platoon of soldiers with Muhammad Askari to Mirza Mohammad Taqi's house. Shortly, all the Europeans were captured and, with their hands bound, were taken to the Dar-i-Daulat by way of the main meeting square. Once there, all the prisoners were drawn up in a line before Begum Hazrat Mahal, whose soldiers seemed eager to shoot them all. However, Muftahud-Daula interceded on their behalf, informing the Begum that amongst the group was Joseph Short, the brother of Sultan Murium Begum. With a little embroidery of the truth, he informed her that everyone knew that Joseph Short was a Muslim. The fabrication was of course considerably helped by the fact that his dress and manners had always been those of a Muslim. Joseph Short was then brought before the Begum, who inspected his attire and, after further questioning, accepted that he was a Muslim noble and stated that her Government would protect his honour and dignity. She ordered that his hands (and those of his family) should be unbound and ordered them to be taken care of and given into the charge of Darogha (police inspector) Mir Wajid Ali.

Darogha Mir Wajid Ali then installed them in a rented house and, to ensure their safety, floated a story that Joseph Johannes, Joseph Short's son-in-law, who had been captured along with Joseph Short, was a maker of percussion caps for guns, which would be of great use to the rebel army.[6]

The reader may well have heard previously of Darogha Mir Wajid Ali, who achieved fame for his role in the rescue of 'the English Captives of Oudh'[7]. Mir Wajid Ali had assisted Sir Mountstuart Jackson and his sister Madeline, Captain Philip Orr and his wife and child, three year-old orphan Sophy Christian and several other people who were all held at Kaisarbagh, at great risk to himself—firstly by ensuring that the leg-irons of the captives were removed and thereafter that all the prisoners were well cared for and fed during their confinement. Not only that, he then arranged for the ladies' surreptitious removal to a house occupied by the Sultan Muhul and his own wife and children, from where they were rescued along with Mir Wajid Ali's family by the British troops. (The men in the party had been murdered by the troops of the Moulvi of Faizabad several months ago and young Sophy Christian had died of starvation). The Moulvi evidently suspected that Mir Wajid Ali was assisting the captives and was already heading for the house with a considerable force when Wajid Ali's brother-in-law begged the assistance of a party of Gurkhas headed by Captains MacNeill and Bogle who managed to reach the spot in time and rescued the captives just before the arrival of the Moulvi's troops.[7]

Joseph Short, being of mixed parentage, was probably viewed with some suspicion by the British Authorities which is why the story of his escape was never publicised in the same manner as that of Mrs Orr and Miss Jackson. However, when he subsequently applied in April 1858 to Major General Outram (the Chief Commissioner of Awadh) to have his wasika reinstated, an investigation of his conduct during the mutiny had to be carried out, as wasikas were only reinstated to those who had remained loyal to the British during the mutiny. The report on his conduct states:

> During the occupation of Lucknow by the insurgents, Mr Short was imprisoned with his son-in-law Mr Joseph Johannes. Captn Orr of the Intelligence Department gives a certificate to this effect. On the capture of the city by our troops, Mr Short got away with the ladies who were saved to Maharajah Jung Bahadoor's camp.

Joseph Johannes has been mentioned above as being imprisoned with Joseph Short, and as his family is closely inter-related with ours, I think its time we acquaint ourselves with him. Joseph was one of the two sons of Jacob Johannes, an Armenian who had served for forty-two years as a Lieutenant in the King of Awadh's service. He had eventually been discharged following the annexation of Awadh on a pension of hundred rupees a month.[9] At this time, he was Adjutant of an infantry Regiment as well as a courtier at the Awadh Durbar. However, such service did not preclude other simultaneous occupations (with the permission of the King of Awadh) and Jacob had converted a house in Golaganj, close to the Residency and opposite the Brigade

Mess, into a shop from which he supplied European articles to the community for twenty years. (The property known as Johannes House was actually inherited from Jacob's father-in-law Mr D.G. Braganca, Head Assistant in the Residency[10]). This business had been highly profitable, such that by the time of the mutiny, the shop premises, together with the associated dwelling-house and godowns were valued at 32,000 rupees, and the contents of the shop at 20,000 rupees[11] making Jacob Johannes the richest merchant in Lucknow. All the property was lost during the outbreak. With the rapid advance of the rebels after the battle of Chinhut, it had not been possible to include Johannes house within the Residency defences which was subsequently taken over as a stronghold by the rebels. Later, it was mined and blown up by the order of Major General Sir John Inglis.

Joseph Johannes himself had also been a Lieutenant in the King of Awadh's service, having served for eighteen years in the King's Body Guard, a Cavalry Corps, before being discharged on a pension of rupees fifty a month at annexation.[12] He was reputedly an accomplished scholar and had written some beautiful poems in Urdu[12A], besides being an artist. He later employed his aesthetic talents to become an early photographer[12B]. Joseph Johannes had married Joseph Short's daughter Helen some time before the mutiny, but the records of the marriage or any children prior to 1857 were lost when the Church Registers were carelessly left behind on the evacuation of the Residency in November 1857. Before the mutiny they had lived in a house in Golaganj, close to Gubbins battery as well as his father's house (Johannes House).[13] However, needless to say, after his release from captivity, when Joseph returned to his house in the spring of 1858, he found that it had been ransacked by the insurgents. On his return, Joseph applied to Sir James Outram, the Chief Commissioner of Awadh, for the arrears in his Government pension. Interestingly, in this letter he referred to 'the active part I have taken with regard to the release of Miss Jackson and Mrs Captain P. Orr' the circumstances of which 'you must have been made acquainted with by Captain Orr'. Unfortunately, though, Joseph did not elaborate on exactly how he had assisted in their release.[13A]

Joseph and Helen had two sons and three daughters after the mutiny. One of his daughters, Eva Florence, married my great uncle William Speirs in 1889. John Joseph, one of his sons (known as Joey Johannes and a photographer by profession), was a great friend of William Speirs. He will appear in a later chapter.

Let us now turn to the fate of Joseph's eldest daughter, Mary, and her husband, Edward Duhan during the mutiny. By now, Edward and Mary were proud parents of three children—Edward (aged ten), Joseph (aged six) and Roseline (aged three). As a Government employee, Edward Duhan had been urged to take shelter in the Residency after the compound had been fortified in June 1857 at the instigation of Sir Henry Lawrence, the Chief Commissioner of Awadh. Accordingly, he and his family had entered the Residency towards the end of June. At the time, it appeared (deceptively) quiet in the area and Mary had decided to take the opportunity of visiting some relations in another part of the town, taking the children with her. She set out in the morning on 30 June and expected to return that very afternoon. However, that was the fateful day of the defeat of Sir Henry Lawrence's troops in the battle of Chinhut, from where the British troops retreated to the Residency, harassed all the way by the much larger rebel army.[14] Mary was of course unable to return to the Bailie-guard that day, or in fact thereafter—as the defeat at Chinhut was the precursor to the siege of the Residency. She and her children were shortly held as captives by the rebels and placed under the charge of Nawab Mahmud Tuhka Khan, who in fact treated her very kindly. Later she, like Joseph Short and Joseph Johannes, was placed under the control of Darogha Mir Wajid Ali—although in a different part of the city. She evidently had quite a high degree of freedom, as when she was subsequently released by Raja Man Singh into the hands of Charles Wingfield, the Commissioner at Gorakhpur, she was able to provide him with valuable intelligence about the state of affairs in Lucknow. The following is taken from Wingfield's letter to G. Edmonstone, Secretary to the Governor of Bengal:

> She swears confidently to Mrs Orr and Miss Jackson & another lady name unknown being still alive & under the care of the same Darogah Wahid Ally. She had not seen them however for they were in a different part of the city. About 5 months ago she says, during the rains 32 women children & men were brought into Lucknow from the districts & there murdered. She does not know their names but heard that one of the victims was brought

to jail only ten days before. About two months back Capt Orr & some five or 6 other gentlemen were murdered. The three ladies before alluded to as still alive were of this party... Besides these she mentions many East Indians & their families still living in Lucknow—Govr Hare & family—Mrs Wroughton & family—Mrs Francis & family—Mrs Baily & family. Many of these she says are so dark that they pass for natives and are in no danger of their lives. They are not even confined or watched. Nawaub Numwur oodowla & Mooroom ooddowla were plundered of everything and the former was imprisoned & cruelly maltreated. She represents the mother of the boy whom they have set up for King as very bloodthirsty & having herself given the order for the execution of the prisoners. The Chief officers or Generals as they are termed of the rebels are Munner Khan, Shurf O Dowla (the Cashmiree) Nurga Hyder (who got a pension from Govt) & Mozuffur Khan. When she left Lucknow it was full of sepoys, at 60,000 she heard their number stated but there were not all old sepoys, more than half were recruits for whenever a sepoy is killed in action another man is enlisted in his place.[14]

Mary Duhan and her children had apparently been released from Lucknow through the agency of Raja Man Singh, who appears to have fought against the British and then regretted it. 'Man Singh, she says, told her he did not mean to fight against us and he saw how useless it was & he wished to save his life. He told her he would try to get the other ladies away from Lucknow & she knows he is spending money with that object.'[14] In order to facilitate her release, Raja Man Singh had sent his Vakil, Anant Ram, to Mary's place of captivity who then managed to escort her family safely to Man Singh's fort at Shahganj. From there, the family had later been taken to Gorakhpur and left in the safe hands of the Commissioner, Charles Wingfield, arriving at Gorakhpur early in February 1858. (This same Vakil later rescued Mrs Orr's daughter, carrying her through the city at great risk and passing through the enemy's camp, before reaching the safety of the British army camp at Alam Bagh on 7 March 1858). Raja Man Singh was later rewarded for his protection of Mary and other captives with a remission of 20,000 rupees otherwise payable from his Jagir.[15]

Meanwhile, Mary's husband Edward had been helping with the defence of the Residency, being posted at Sago's Garrison. This was a small single-storeyed building to the South-East of the Residency compound, which had formerly belonged to a school-mistress, Mrs Sago. It was particularly vulnerable, being exposed on three sides to the enemy.[15A] He served there, undertaking long and arduous sentry duties alongside William Sangster, F.J. Quieros, Mr Hutton, Mr Ewart and many others. He was noted by his colleagues (James Orning and M Hutton) as being one of the most willing of the Garrison, always ready at his post and doing everything that was required of him. However, quite naturally, as time went by he became more and more anxious about the fate of his wife and children, not having seen or heard from them since they had left the Residency just before the siege. His worries about his family and the exposure consequent on the long sentry duties eventually affected his health, and he often succumbed to illness. Mr Ewart, who was an apothecary, generally attended to Edward during his frequent illnesses.[16]

Finally, when Sir Colin Campbell's troops forced their way into the compound on 17 November, Edward's ordeals at the Residency were brought to an end. Over the next few days, the women and children were carefully withdrawn, without a single casualty. Then, at midnight on 22 November, Edward left his post in Sago's Garrison and withdrew along with all the remaining defenders of the Residency to Alam Bagh. From there, together with most of the refugees from the conflict at Lucknow, he travelled via Kanpur to Allahabad, where they remained for about a month, waiting until the roads were safer, before leaving for the comparative safety of Calcutta.

A relief fund had been set up at Calcutta, and the Honorary Secretary, Mr M. Wylie, granted Edward subsistence from the fund, in the absence of any possible employment. But he still underwent nearly three months of further uncertainty regarding the fate of his wife and children, until at last he heard of their release from captivity in February 1858. Finally, the family were reunited when Mary and the children joined him at Calcutta a short time later. However, Mary's joy at being reunited with her husband was shortlived. After the re-capture of Lucknow (completed on 21 March 1858) and the restoration of a semblance of order in the city, Government servants were instructed to return to take up their posts again. But Edward, still weak from his privations and illnesses during the siege of Lucknow, was unable to comply with the orders. He fell critically ill and died there a few months later. And, to add to Mary's woes besides being widowed at the age of twenty-seven, she shortly realised to her consternation that she was pregnant with her fourth child. This baby girl, named Jane Alice Angeline, was born in January 1859 but sadly did not survive long and was subsequently buried in the dissenter's burial ground in March 1860, at the age of fourteen months.

The relief fund, under Mr Wylie, continued to support the widowed Mary and her children, granting her sixty rupees per month as a temporary measure on the assumption that she should shortly be able to claim a widow's pension of that amount on account of her husband's Government service and the fact that his death resulted from the hardship he had suffered during the siege. Mary's moving letter of application for the grant of such a pension is given below:[16]

> To T.D. Forsyth Esq
> Secy to the Commr of Oude
> Lucknow

Sir,

My husband, the late Mr Duhan, was a public servant and up to the day when the civil functions ceased to operate he was employed as an assistant in the office of the Judicial Commr of Lucknow. During the most harassing and hazardous siege of that place he, in common with other uncovenanted Servants of Govt endured privation and met his assailant with Christian fortitude and becoming loyalty. On the 30th June [1]/57 he entered the Residency Garrison a hail and hearty man and left it on the 22nd [1]/57 Nov a mere shadow of himself; shattered in his constitution and broken in spirit chiefly from the risk and fatigue he had endured and partly from the dismal prospect he had before him for he never regained his former appointment with Govt. Shortly after evacuating the Garrison he came down to Calcutta where his wants were supplied by the generosity of Mr Wylie from the relief fund. After my husband's arrival in Calcutta he had but a few months and at last sunk under the debility of the whole physical system.

Being thus left a destitute widow the only resort now left to me is to lay my helpless case before you in hope that you will by your generous interposition in my behalf secure for me from Govt a similar pension to those settled upon other widows.
It may be necessary here to mention that Mr Wylie still allows me 60Rs a month by way of temporary maintenance.

30 April 1/59   Your Obdtt humble St
Cal: No 6   Mary Duhan
Wellesley Square
1st Lane

At first Mary's application for a widow's pension seemed to proceed well, particularly when the government decided to refer back to her for the names and ages of her children, as they would also be entitled to pension of sixteen rupees a month. But the stumbling-block came when she had to prove that Edward's death was caused by exposure and fatigue during the siege. She was asked to produce a certificate to this effect from the doctor (Sub Assistant Surgeon Ameen ood Deen Khan) who had attended her husband during his final illness. To her dismay she found that this was not possible as the doctor himself had died! So Mary wrote to other volunteers who had served with her husband at Sago's Garrison, asking them to confirm the details of his illness whilst at the Residency. Several of them, including Dr Ewart, William Sangster, William Morgan, Felix Quieros and M Hutton did so, but the Government was not satisfied with these statements—nor even with the statement of the Calcutta Relief Fund Committee, who likewise thought that Edward Duhan's final illness and death had been caused by his suffering at Lucknow. Hence, despite Mary's evident distressed circumstances and the fact that her husband had died following loyal service at the Residency, she was never granted a widow's pension.[16]

We shall now continue with the story of Joseph Short, the protagonist of this chapter. We left him having been freed from captivity into Maharajah Jung Bahadur's camp in mid March 1858 and subsequently applying to the Chief Commissioner of Awadh to have his wasika reinstated. The report on his conduct during the mutiny was verified by Captain Adolphus P. Orr, in charge of the Intelligence Department, (he was the brother of the murdered Captain Phillip Orr of 'the English Captives of Oudh') and the reinstatement of his wasika was thereafter recommended by the new Chief Commissioner of Awadh, R. Montgomery and sanctioned by the Governor General in July 1858.[17] Joseph had already returned to his home in Golaganj, but shortly had to leave Lucknow, as all city inhabitants apart from Government servants were obliged to do in the aftermath of the siege until permitted to return by the British authorities. He therefore went to live in Calcutta until mid 1859, staying in a house at 32 South Colinja Lane. (He evidently took his slave-girls along with him to Calcutta, as his youngest son, Edwin, was born there to the slave-girl Peearee on 6 May 1859).

The situation with which Joseph was confronted on his return to Lucknow is most vividly described by him in his letter dated 10 February 1862 and his subsequent petition to the Viceroy, the Earl of Elgin (both reproduced in full in the Appendix). In Joseph's letter, addressed to the Chief Commissioner of Oudh, he describes how he found on his arrival at Lucknow that both of his large houses in Golaganj, which he valued at Rs 25,000, were in the process of being demolished by British military engineers. Such demolitions occurred on a massive scale in Lucknow following the recapture of the city after the siege of the Residency. Colonel Robert Napier of the Bengal Engineers, who arrived with the relieving force, had produced a plan on 26 March 1858 to render the city safe from future attack. The plan, which he oversaw and which led to the destruction of two-fifths of the city over the next few years, involved creating military 'strong-posts' with wide roads radiating through the previously dense city, in order to facilitate rapid troop movements to any trouble-spots[18]. Joseph went on to explain that his subsequent application to the Commissioner for compensation was referred to the 'Nazool officer', Mr Elliott, who made enquiries and reported 'on the 4th August/59 that the said houses were actually demolished by the Engineer Department and estimated at Rupees 7,500, on which Mr Elliott ordered Moonshee Ramdyal to select a house for me, several small houses were shewn me in which a Christian could not think of living in fact they were more to be classed with huts than houses which might be made habitable for any respectable person and as those houses did not suit me nor would they have been of any use to me especially as I had no place where to lay my head in with my large family who were likewise suffering the same inconveniences as myself from want of accommodation, I was compelled to rent a house in the suburbs of the city.'[19]

Joseph described many subsequent applications to various officers, which eventually resulted in his being given Oomrao Begum's house situated near the Kaisar Pasand, valued at Rs 7,000, in February 1861. But he had only taken over that house for three days and had just commenced clearing it of rubbish when he was informed that this house too was due for immediate demolition! His appeal to halt the demolition was too late, though, and the house was duly demolished. Homeless again, Joseph next appealed to the Commissioner, Colonel Abbott, in September 1861, to grant him a 'Nazool house', known as Sufder Bagh, which had then come up for sale at a price of Rs 6000. But the officers refused to suspend the sale, despite Joseph's protestation that in similar circumstances Joseph Johannes was given a Nazool house that had been put up for sale. The situation subsequently deteriorated since the officers denied that he had a valid claim at all, even though Joseph informed the Chief Commissioner that his 'claim has been established by the City Magistrate Mr Wood from his demolition register and also by Mr Wylie the then Nazool officer, as also by...' In his subsequent appeal to the Viceroy, Joseph made the following intriguing reference to a report by the Deputy Commissioner on his circumstances:

...that Your Petitioner was a Wuseekadar of the Oudh Government drawing so much per Memsem that he pursued no trade, and that he was given to keeping pigeons (fancy ones) and moreover was in the habit of taking doses of opium, hence Your Memorialist was not a fit object of consideration. Your Memorialist humbly begs to state that in regard to his being a Wuseekadar (Pensioner) of the Oudh Government there is no doubt, that Your Memorialist has on his farm yard a few Pigeons as many Noblemen and Gentlemen of respectability in India, yea even in England have for their use and amusement—and as regards Opium eating Your Memorialist begs humbly to ignore the use of that drug. This Your Memorialist can establish by reference to most of the respectable Christian and Native Community who have been acquainted with Your Memorialist prior to British Rule in Oudh and up to the present period.[19]

It is not possible to conclusively prove now that Joseph Short's statement is correct, as the relevant files of the Chief Commissioner's Office no longer exist. However, his story certainly 'rings true', particularly as he names the officials with whom he was corresponding and the precise date of each event. But the actual policy of the British Government is neatly summed up in the following official notes attached to the file:

> The Petitioner prays for compensation for his houses destroyed. The City of Lucknow was prize of war, and when the Engineer Dept set to work raising forts for its protection when re-occupied, houses were demolished over a very wide area, and compensation given in no case. The claim is groundless, and any precedent admitting such a claim would bring on a host of others. 31st May 62.[20]

Nevertheless, the Nazool officers were evidently empowered to compensate European householders for loss of property by assigning 'Nazool' houses to them. (I should here explain that the word 'Nazool' simply means Government property—and this of course applied to all property in the City, which was treated as prize of war). Joseph's son-in-law, Joseph Johannes was more successful in a similar claim of compensation for his destroyed property, being awarded a Nazool house and later being permitted to buy five shops adjoining the house.[21] It seems to me that Joseph simply encountered a mixture of double-dealing and jealousy from the officials he was dealing with—who probably resented giving a valuable property to a man who was only part English, dressed like a Muslim and had no need to work due to his wealth. Such resentment appears as an undertone in the memo by the Deputy Commissioner when forwarding the petition in which he states that 'Mr Short follows no trade or profession, but appears to be chiefly occupied with fancy pigeons and opium, he has a small garden and a Waseeka of 800/- monthly and is reported to be wealthy as his sister was the Walayutee Begum married to Ghazeeooddeen Hyder King of Oude. The house in Golaganj is said to have been worth some 8000/- and was previous to the mutiny occupied by the family of his eldest daughter (Mrs Duhan).'[22]

Needless to say, Joseph did not succeed in claiming compensation, particularly when condemned for opium-eating. On the basis that there is no smoke without fire, I presume, that despite his denials he was declared an opium user. But it is difficult to understand why this should condemn him as unworthy of compensation, since the consumption of opium was regarded as a fashionable pursuit by the wealthy in those times, unlike the modern connotations of a dangerous addiction.

Admitting defeat in his battle for compensation, Joseph shortly left Fakir Mohammad Khan's hatta, where he had been staying whilst awaiting the results of his claim. (Fakir Mohammad Khan's hatta was in the Deorhi Aghamir area of the city, to the East of the Residency compound. There still exists a building labelled Faqir Mohammad Manzil in the area, on Subhash Marg.). He then bought a house in Kaisar Bagh, close to Neil's gate—one of the original gateways to the now-demolished Kaisar Bagh palace, originally known as Sher Darwaza but re-named in honour of Colonel James Neill, who had fallen there on 25 September 1857 in the first assault on the Residency under General Havelock. This gateway is close to the Begum Hazrat Mahal Park, less than a half-kilometre from the Chattar Manzil palace where Joseph had been brought up by Murium Begum. Hence, he never strayed far from familiar territory.

It was from this house that a joint family marriage was arranged in April 1866. Joseph's daughter Marcelina (by his first wife) was to marry John James Bourbon, a twenty-nine year-old clerk from Agra. John Bourbon was reputedly descended from the French royal family, his ancestor being Jean Philippe de Bourbon, Duke de Bourbon and Comte de Montpesier, who had left France and arrived via Venice, Egypt and Ethiopia at the Court of Akbar Khan in 1560.[23] Simultaneously, Joseph's daughter Rachael was to marry my great-grandfather, John Speirs (whose life is covered in a later chapter). The ceremony was held at 10 am on Monday, 23 April at St Paul's Roman Catholic Church. After the ceremony, the guests were invited back to Joseph and Amelia Short's house for cakes and wine, and they returned at 7.30 pm that evening for a dinner party. Rather amazingly, two of the original invitations to this joint wedding have survived.[24]

I will now return to amplify a comment I made at the beginning of this chapter: that Joseph Short didn't take his religion quite so seriously as his sister, Murium Begum. The reader will recall that under her will, Joseph Short was to be granted 800 rupees a month, of which 750 rupees were for himself and 50 rupees were 'to be disbursed by my brother's own hands and discretion and after my brother's demise to be acted in the same manner by his heirs in repairs, illuminations and charity of the Roman Catholic Churches at Cawnpore and Lucknow'. Shortly after her death, the Resident, Sir William Sleeman, took a Persian document from Joseph Short, confirming that he would pay the legacies of both the Roman Catholic churches regularly every month and a copy of this document was also sent to the Reverend Adeodatus, the Priest at Lucknow who was to receive the legacies.

For a few months, Joseph paid the legacies regularly as agreed, but thereafter the payments were made very irregularly. However, it was not until 1854 or 1855 that Sir William Sleeman wrote to the Revd Adeodatus to check that the payments were being made—when he was told about the irregularity of payments. Sleeman then fell ill and went on sick leave, so it was left to his successor, Sir James Outram, to deal with the problem. Sir James Outram, on examining the will and the original treaty of 1825, decided that the payments should be made direct from the treasury in view of Joseph Short's default. So direct payments were made to the Revd Adeodatus from then onwards, until all wasika payments were halted by the siege of the Residency in June 1857.[25] The Revd Adeodatus then took refuge in the Bailie Guard, alongside Jacob Johannes, but he eventually died whilst on his way to Allahabad as a result of the exposure and harsh conditions suffered during the siege. (The refugees from the siege travelled the last forty miles of the journey to Allahabad by train and, according to one source Revd Adeodatus expired peacefully in his compartment just as the train pulled in to Allahabad station.[25A])

When peace had been restored, Joseph was granted the full wasika of eight hundred rupees, and evidently took no steps towards paying the fifty rupees to the Roman Catholic Church—as the Revd Lewis shortly wrote to Government on behalf of the RC Church asking to be paid arrears of 1500 rupees.[26] However, as pointed out in his letter reproduced below, Joseph did have two facts in his favour: it appears that the Revd Adeodatus had treated the legacy as a personal pension (clearly not the intention) and moreover by this time, there were no chapels at Lucknow or Cawnpore. (The previous chapel at Lucknow had been erected in 1824 by Father Adeodatus on four bighas of land in Golaganj but this chapel had been destroyed during the mutiny and the land was subsequently sold to finance the erection of the new churches in Hazratganj and Dilkusha[27]).

To Lieutt JF MacAndrew,
Offg Secy to the Chief Commr of Oudh, Lucknow

Sir,

I beg to acknowledge the receipt on the 3rd Instt of your letter No 1491 D/ 29th Ulto calling on me for an explanation of the reasons which induced me to withhold the monthly payment of 50 Rs bequeathed by the Will of Sooltan Murium Begum towards the support of the Roman Catholic Chapels at Lucknow and Cawnpore.

In reply I take the liberty to state for the information of the Chief Commissioner as follows.

The claim of Revd Lewis will be found to be entirely ungrounded, as it is distinctly stated therein, that of the Rs 833/5/4 bequeathed by the Begum, I am entitled to 800 Rs pm from which 50 Rs is to be spent 'at my discretion for the illumination, repairs & ca of the Chapels' and not for the personal support of the Priest; or to be given to him direct, if it were so, why would it not have been stipulated in the will accordingly, as has been done in the case of the other two stipendiaries under the same will who secure their respective allowances directly.

In the time of the Resident Colonel Sleeman when the will was enforced, I was paid the 800 Rs in full and spent the amount of 50 Rs at my own discretion for the purpose to which it was attributed. If the Priest was entitled to receive the 50 Rs direct, it would have been paid to him.

During the time Genl Outram was Resident here, Revd Adeodatus made some representations to him and prevailed on him to order the payment to him (Revd A) of the 50 Rs. To this measure I objected, and even did not draw my Waseeka for some time, but of course I could not resist the order of the authorities. I was obliged to yield and having come to an understanding with the Revd Adeodatus I continued to pay him the amount of course on the condition that it would be spent in the same manner.

On the reoccupation of Lucknow my case was investigated & my claim to the full amount of 800 Rs was admitted by Mr Williams and the Chief Commr and on the receipt of the Govt sanction when the Waseeka was issued to me Mr Williams who was in charge of the Treasury and was perfectly acquainted with all the particulars of this Waseeka never made any alteration with regard to the 50 Rs besides this amount is only to be spent for the illumination, repairs &ca of the Chapels; and there is no Chapel now either here or at Cawnpore, but in the event of the Chapels being replaced I shall of course continue to disburse the amount as usual.

With this explanation I leave it to the kind consideration of the Chief Commr and trusting he will extend his protection to me.

> I beg to remain
> Sir,
> Your most obdt Servt
> J Short

P.S. As Revd Lewis claims the 50 Rs I beg he be called upon to produce any document he may possess of Sooltan Murium Begum substantiating the claim.
Lucknow
The 12th of Augt 1859[28]

The Chief Commissioner, however, did not accept this explanation, and shortly arranged again for the fifty rupees to be deducted and paid directly to the new priest at Lucknow, Father William Gleeson. Eventually though, Joseph refused to draw his pension at all unless he received the full amount, and at this stage he petitioned the government. He took such a strong action because as he had stated in his petition he had 'ascertained that from the first June one thousand eight hundred and fifty nine up to November one thousand eight hundred and sixty no portion of the rupees thirty a month has ever been received by the Chaplain of Cawnpore for the purposes directed by the said will although the full rupees fifty were paid monthly direct to the Reverend Father Gleeson the Chaplain of Lucknow.'[29]

Now I am by no means an apologist for Joseph Short's behaviour— as it is clear that he must have only paid the fifty rupees very occasionally when it was left to him. But the following certificate which he had received from the Chaplain at Kanpur, and enclosed within his petition, does strongly reinforce his argument that the money being paid to the Lucknow priest on behalf of the Kanpur Church was being misappropriated:

Cawnpore 4.9.1861

I the undersigned do declare upon my honour that since I have been at Cawnpore from the 1ˢᵗ June 1859 I never either heard or received any money from Miss Short's bequest of 50 Rs a month for this chapel nor I have authorized any person at Lucknow to draw the amount nor I had heard anything about it except this day from Mr F Menzies.

F Alphonsus
C Chaplain

P.S. I prefer to draw the money from Mr Short direct than through any other person.[29]

In this case, Joseph Short's petition was more successful as the government recognised that it would lose any legal challenge to the unorthodox withholding of fifty rupees a month by the Chief Commissioner. The Wasika Office was bound to pay Joseph the full amount stipulated in Murium Begum's will and, if Joseph did not pay the Lucknow and Kanpur churches the fifty rupees, the church representatives would need to sue him in a Civil Court. Thus, Joseph achieved his aim of increasing his wasika by unscrupulous means to eight hundred rupees a month, as the church did not take any legal action against him.

The fact that Joseph Short thereafter considered his pension to be the full eight hundred rupees is surely demonstrated by the entry register to La Martiniere School, which school his sons Martin, George and Benjamin attended in the mid 1860s. In each case, the register records Joseph's income as eight hundred rupees a month.

It's time we draw the story of Joseph's life to a close, there being nothing further to relate beyond the fact that he died due to apoplexy at his house in Kaisar Bagh at about 2pm in the afternoon on 26 February 1870.[29A] Interestingly, the burial register for St Paul's church records his profession as 'Native Christian and proprietor'—which seems to reinforce the impression that he was always considered to have native, or Muslim manners. On the other hand, though, the Right Revd P. Losi, Bishop of Patna, said that he had known Joseph personally since 1862 and could certify that he was a practising Roman Catholic.

However, one mystery still persists. The record clearly shows that he was buried in the chapel at the new church of St Joseph's which had been built in Hazratganj in 1868, by permission of the Bishop. His widow, Amelia, in fact stated that his grave was in the main aisle of the chapel, immediately facing the altar. This church certainly had a chapel with several graves but it was demolished in 1969 to make way for the new Cathedral of St Joseph's. Unfortunately, despite the expressed wish of Bishop Conrad de Vito of Lucknow that these grave-stones should be carefully removed and replaced after the bodies had been re-interred, I have been unable to find any trace of them. Hence, Joseph Short's final resting place remains to be a mystery.

To conclude this chapter, I will now relate what little I have found out about Joseph Short's sister Eliza, who our family believed had married a Major Besant and had a son named Dick. Armed only with those legends, my first discovery was a record of the baptism at Lucknow of Richard Thomas Besant on 31 May 1841 to 'Captn Besant and Eliza his wife'. Now clearly this was a promising start, but with no marriage record being found, no Christian name for Captain Besant and no maiden name for Captain Besant's wife, I could not prove that this Eliza is indeed the sister of Joseph Short.

The only Captain Besant who seemed to be a possible contender as the father in this record is Captain Thomas Henry Gatehouse Besant, who, though never served at Lucknow, yet took leave on 'personal affairs' to visit Lucknow and Kanpur from July to September 1837. However, he subsequently had the charge of stores on the abortive Afghanistan campaign from December 1838 to about March 1840 and does not appear to have a chance of visiting Lucknow thereafter until he returned to England on a final sick certificate in 1845, by which time he had been promoted to Major. Hardly a promising candidate—I am sure the reader will agree.

However, I decided to try to locate Major Besant in England, and shortly discovered him in the 1851 census living at Dorchester with his wife, Sarah E. Besant and his son Thomas R. Besant who was shown as aged ten and born in the East Indies. So the trail was getting warmer again! But, even though Thomas R. Besant was almost certainly the same person who had been baptised ten years before as Richard Thomas Besant, how could I prove that his mother was indeed Eliza Short?

The answer, when it came, was certainly not proof—but I would rate it as strong circumstantial evidence. It is also a very sad tale. The following is an extract from the will of Thomas Henry Gatehouse Besant (who died at Dorchester in February 1874 leaving all his property to his wife and daughter and the residue to a trust for their benefit):

>...and after the decease of both my said wife and daughter for the benefit of my illegitimate son Thomas Richard Besant who is now in a Private Lunatic Asylum kept by Mrs Rackham at Catton near Norwich and I desire that in the event of means being available my said son shall be placed in the Dorset County Asylum as a non pauper but should the means not be forthcoming he must be placed in that establishment as a pauper patient my said son having no nearer relation in India or elsewhere than first cousins who are in needy circumstances...[30]

Richard Besant (as I shall call him) never had any reprieve from his confinement in asylums. He was admitted to the Catton Private Asylum in July 1854, when he was only thirteen. In March 1879 he was transferred to the Norwich County Asylum 'his friends having failed to pay for his maintenance for a long time past, he has been made a pauper and admitted here'.[31] And he remained incarcerated at that asylum until relief finally came to him on 4 June 1904. Taking a stroll in the grounds on a fine summer's afternoon, he was noticed to collapse suddenly, and was pronounced dead by the resident doctor.[32] He died aged sixty-three, having spent almost fifty years confined to a lunatic asylum.

His case-notes on admission to the Norwich Asylum indicate a harmless, good-tempered person enjoying good health, but with slightly dirty habits and a tendency to wet himself occasionally. The main signs of dementia were in his conversation, which was 'very incoherent and disconnected, & he appears to be the subject of delusions for fancying himself a great person & possessed of much money &ca'.[33] I cannot help wondering whether these delusions included telling the asylum staff that his aunt had been a Queen of Awadh, who had passed her large inheritance on to his uncle so that his relations in India had never had to work!

My opinion is that the fact that Richard Besant suffered from some sort of dementia, like Eliza and John Short, indicates some kind of congenital dementia running in the family, and he was indeed the son of Eliza Short. But whether Thomas Henry Gatehouse Besant had actually married Eliza Short is open to question. If there had been a marriage, the records are probably amongst those destroyed after being left in the Residency at the end of the siege. Murium Begum, in her will, clearly refers to Eliza's husband and child, but she also implies that the relationship was not a sound one, or she would not have made provision for Eliza's support 'in the event that her husband and son do not support her'. And this precaution seems to have been born out by Thomas Besant's subsequent actions.

4

Wasikas, Court Cases and Scandals

It is doubtful whether the representatives of the Honourable East India Company who negotiated the three 'Oudh loans' really appreciated the administrative and legal difficulties that would later ensue from the granting of wasikas. Urgently needing to refill the Company's empty coffers in order to support the war in Nepal, Lord Hastings (and subsequently Lord Amherst) cast a greedy eye on the massive wealth accumulated by the Vizier of Awadh, who was persuaded to grant a loan of a crore of rupees. On Saadat Ali Khan's untimely death during these negotiations, his successor, the more pliant and suggestible Ghazi-ud-din Haidar eagerly renewed the offer and, with some arm-twisting by the Resident Mordaunt Ricketts, subsequently 'volunteered' further two large loans. The terms of these loans, which were granted 'in perpetuity', specified that in lieu of paying interest at five percent, wasikas should be paid to the chosen ministers and begums, and to their descendants, also in perpetuity. The word 'Wasika' seems to have been derived from the Persian 'Vasiqueh', which means a bond or pledge and a 'Wasikadar' was therefore a holder of this bond.

At first, of course, the administration was relatively simple. The newly created Wasika Office merely had the duty of paying the stipulated amounts on a monthly basis to the chosen recipients. It was only on their (and their descendants') deaths that the complications started to emerge.

Firstly, it was necessary to be certain who were the actual direct descendants, for which purpose 'warisnamas' were sworn by the wasikadars, in which they named their descendants. Thereafter, questions arose which could not be simply resolved: Were legitimate and illegitimate heirs to be treated equally? Were the wives (or husbands) of wasikadars entitled to a share? Did the religious beliefs of the families affect their entitlement (i.e. should Christian or Muslim or other law be applied in the case of disputes)? Which court (if any) had jurisdiction in the case of disputes? Could wasikadars disinherit any heirs for misbehaviour? Did the British Government have the power of disinheriting recipients? If the Wasika Office mistakenly paid sums to people not entitled to receive them, who was liable to make recompense?

All of these questions, and more, arose in the fractious disputes that occurred following Joseph Short's death some of which were not resolved even sixteen years later. The fact that the family members would willingly fight each other in order to maximise their own wasika payments surely adds weight to the saying that 'money is the root of all evil'.

Joseph's remains had hardly been laid to rest in the chapel at St Joseph's Church in Hazratganj before the disputes began. Initially, Joseph's children by his first wife, Jane, led by Mary Duhan, claimed that his wasika should be distributed amongst the four of them only, as they were the legitimate children of a Christian marriage, whilst all his other children were either the products of his liaisons with Muslim slave girls (and therefore illegitimate) or the children born to his second wife, Amelia, prior to marriage (and also therefore illegitimate). However, in his warisnama, Joseph Short himself had not distinguished between his legitimate or illegitimate children, but had named all of them and had also included his wife, Amelia as an heir. Moreover, he had specifically repudiated the right of Macdonald Short, his son by the slave girl Mussumat Illaheejan, to claim his share on the grounds that 'his conduct is very bad'. Likewise, he had repudiated his daughters Isabella, Emma and Georgiana because their slave girl mothers had deserted with them to Calcutta.[1]

Immediately, the children by the slave girls countered their exclusion using the argument that Joseph and their mothers were Muslims and that rights of succession should be determined by Muslim, not Christian, law.

The Wasika Office could not resolve disputes of this complexity, so the case was referred to the Judicial Commissioner's Office for an opinion. On examining the Persian text of Murium Begum's will, the Judicial Commissioner decided that neither Muslim nor Christian law was intended to apply. Instead the natural law of succession (i.e. that all of the heirs of his body were to be treated equally, without regard to whether they were legitimate or illegitimate, Christian or Muslim) should be adopted. This meant that, despite Joseph Short's exclusion of four of his children, the decision was made that they should inherit equally with the other children. (Although in practice as no-one knew the whereabouts of Isabella, Emma or Georgiana, their shares of wasika were held, pending their re-appearance). He further stated that Joseph's widow, Amelia, had no legal right to a share. However, in applying this recommendation in an order made on 7 September 1870, Colonel Barrow, the Officiating Chief Commissioner decided to grant her fifty rupees a month for life only, to be deducted from the shares of the children.[1]

Now Amelia Short had declined to get involved in the wrangling up to this time, being confident that she was entitled to receive a one-third share of her husband's wasika under the provisions of the Indian Succession Act of 1865. But she was not prepared to accept an arbitrary and conditional pension as advocated by Colonel Barrow. So, my great-grandfather, John Speirs, (who was Amelia's son-in-law) sent a highly well-phrased petition to the Chief Commissioner on his return from leave, asking him to correct the injustice that Amelia had suffered at the hands of Colonel Barrow. Although John Speirs had no legal training, he produced a very coherent argument which, in my view, was not improved upon when Amelia subsequently had to engage solicitors to take matters further. Predictably though, the Chief Commissioner refused to amend Colonel Barrow's order.[1A]

So Amelia then arranged for her solicitor, Mr Justinian Watkins of Calcutta to petition the government on her behalf. He did so, sending the petition to the Viceroy, Earl Mayo, which made out the case that wives or husbands of wasikadars were entitled to a one-third share of their spouse's wasikas under the Indian Succession Act, and quoting numerous examples where this rule had been applied. But the government was extremely unwilling to get involved in such appeals as, if such a precedent was set, its officers might easily be swamped with endless litigation. Hence, Amelia was informed that the government could not take a decision on a case of this kind on the grounds that, 'Its duty is simply to pay the money to the proper parties. Who those parties are must in case of dispute be settled by the Civil Courts.'[1]

From a perusal of the government's comments on her petition, it is clear that referring Amelia to the Civil Courts was certainly not its only option and that the Viceroy could have easily amended the Chief Commissioner's orders. Moreover, the Civil Courts had been expressly prohibited from involving themselves in wasika disputes and particularly from taking decisions that would affect the actual payments of wasikas. As a result, Amelia's subsequent suit in the Civil Court was dismissed in July 1873 and she was unable to get the case re-heard until she had applied to the government for a certificate granting the court jurisdiction to act in her case. Having already effectively directed Amelia to the Civil Courts, the government could not with propriety refuse her this certificate, but the Chief Commissioner's thoughts on the matter are interesting, particularly his disparaging comments about wasikadars:

If the present petition be granted, it will form a precedent, and the Chief Commissioner therefore considers it his duty to point out the very serious evils which will be the result of permitting Waseekadars to appeal in this way, from the decision of the Chief Commissioner, in the Civil Court... The Waseekadars generally are idle and thriftless; with few exceptions they are heavily in debt, they belong to a litigious class, and how to deal with these people whose circumstances have already attracted the special attention of His Excellency the Viceroy is becoming a great political difficulty; their families increase as fast as their pensions by continual redistribution decrease. To allow the Waseekadars to dispute in the Civil Court the decision of the Chief Commissioner whenever they happen to be dissatisfied with it, will be to add greatly to the difficulties which have already to be faced in dealing with them by affording them an additional means of beggaring themselves, for the loser will almost as a matter of course be ruined by the expense of litigation and the winner will come out of the contest severely crippled if not in an equally bad plight.[2]

Clearly, the Chief Commissioner was prejudiced in advocating that the wasikadars should not be permitted to challenge his decisions in the Courts, but he hit the nail on the head with his comment about ruining themselves by the expense of litigation. Amelia had in fact refused to accept the fifty rupees per month awarded to her by the Chief Commissioner (as this could be deemed to be an acceptance of his award) and had been forced to borrow many thousands of rupees from native bankers, at very high rates of interest, in order to pursue her case. But, by the time of her suit in 1873, being unable to borrow further money to continue her case, she had been obliged to dispense with her solicitor and file her suit *in forma pauperis*.[3]

Eventually, though, the government did supply the required certificate and, in a subsequent civil case in May 1876, it was decreed that Amelia was entitled to the full one-third of Joseph's wasika as originally claimed. However, this was not the end of the matter, as meanwhile the Wasika Department, even though they were aware of Amelia's claim, had been paying out the full wasika to Joseph's children. So by the time she was finally paid arrears of wasika in March 1877, instead of being paid the awarded sum of 21,056 rupees, she was only given the accrued sum of 6,173 rupees at the rate of fifty rupees a month as originally awarded by the Chief Commissioner, and she was owed 14,853 rupees which had already been disbursed to Joseph Short's children.

Amelia did not initially pursue the government for the amount owed, as some of Joseph Short's children had filed appeals and she was advised to wait until the time when all such appeals had expired, which occurred in 1883. She was by then an old woman and was looking after my great-grandfather John Speirs's children because his wife (her daughter Rachel) had died the previous year. John decided to take up her case himself without employing solicitors, as Amelia had already incurred debts of 9,500 rupees in legal costs—more than she had received in 1877. So she granted him Power of Attorney in her affairs and John proceeded to petition the government for the money owed. Although at first the government prevaricated and stated that Amelia should claim the money from Joseph Short's children, his petitions eventually met with some success when, without of course admitting liability, the government offered half the sum claimed. In 1887 John was eventually forced to accept this sum on Amelia's behalf, as the government refused to reconsider the case and threatened to withdraw their offer.

But Amelia did not have long to enjoy her money. In November 1891, at the age of sixty-seven, she died at John's home in Lucknow of breast cancer. At the family's request, and as she was the sister-in-law of a former Queen of Awadh, the city magistrate and Bishop Tesli gave permission for her remains to be buried in the chapel at St Joseph's Church in Hazratganj, alongside her late husband. However, such special status has not helped to preserve either tomb, both of which seem to have been destroyed when the church was demolished in 1968 to make way for the new cathedral.

Once again, as in Joseph Short's case, Amelia's death was the inevitable trigger for further family disputes. The Wasika Officer had, quite reasonably, distributed her hard-won share of Joseph Short's wasika to her descendents (i.e. her surviving children Benjamin Joseph Short and Margaret Snell and her grandchildren by her deceased daughter, Alexander, William Sleeman and Winifred Speirs). But Joseph Short's other nine children, led by Mary Duhan petitioned the Viceroy stating that Amelia Short's one-third share was a life-interest only and that' on her death this wasika should revert to be shared equally amongst all twelve surviving children.[4]

Now by this time, probably following the embarrassment felt by the government in their dealings with Amelia Short, the precedent had been set that wasikadars could petition the government in the case of disputes, rather than being obliged to institute proceedings in the Civil Courts. Also, it had been established that the Indian Succession Act did apply to cases where a spouse had been named as an heir. Hence, in this case, a decision was quickly forthcoming from the government, dismissing the claim of the half-siblings and awarding Amelia's wasika to her own children and grand-children only.

Besides being the cause of many family feuds, wasika claims also often inadvertently led to the revelation of 'skeletons in the cupboard'. When Amelia's younger brother, Benjamin Joseph Short, died five years later, there were three sets of claimants to his wasika, which exposed Benjamin's turbulent married life.

In 1880, Benjamin had married Susan Gardner, the daughter of Alan Hyde Gardner, a zamindar from Manowta village, Etah district (I will return later to mention this interesting family connection). The marriage, however, was neither fruitful nor successful. According to my grandfather's testimony in the subsequent court case to determine who should inherit the wasika, the couple could never agree and she had left him permanently in 1893. Thereafter she did not even claim maintenance from him till the time of his death. Indeed, Benjamin Short had stated his belief that Susan had been unfaithful to him and he had consequently omitted her name from his will.[5]

Susan's father, Alan Hyde Gardner, represented her in Court and submitted a long letter from her stating:

Shortly before my husband's death, his ill-treatment in drunken fits had compelled me to seek the protection of the magistrate, but as he made a promise before that officer not to give me any cause for complaint in future, I readily agreed to go back to his house and went. But he soon reverted to his old habits, and I had no other alternative but to take shelter under the roof of my father in the district of Etah. I remained till my husband's death. He had inserted my name in the former warisnama, but subsequently in 1893 he omitted my name without, however, assigning any reason, or even expressing that he wanted to disinherit me. I take the liberty to submit that the above-mentioned MacDonald Short had been excluded from inheritance by his father in express terms, and yet the authorities allowed him a share in common with others. But in my case my husband does not exclude me in express terms, nor does he assign any reason.

In further support of his daughter, Alan Hyde Gardner confirmed that 'Mr Benjamin Short was a drunkard. He used to spend every pice and did not give expenses for his wife. In the Court the husband and wife compromised. I know nothing about the will referred to in Mr Speirs' statement. My daughter was on good terms with her husband. She was living with him. She now and then used to go to collect the revenue of her own village. Susan knew of her husband's sickness. She did not attend his deathbed, because she had gone out to collect the revenue from her village'.[5]

Whether or not Susan had been unfaithful to him, it was clear that Benjamin had been unfaithful to her, as one of the claimants to the wasika was a Muslim woman, Piari Khanum, who claimed that Benjamin had married her (by the Nikah ceremony) and that she had two children by him. Although Benjamin, in a statement made to the Civil Judge in 1893, had said:

> I know Piari Khanum since she began living with my brother George. I have had no sexual intercourse with her. She has had three children. One is my brother George Short's, I can't say who is the father of the other two. She has given birth to 2 children since the death of George—the first was born about a year after his death.

However, a barrister Mr J.B. Boyle, appearing on behalf of Piari Khanum, flatly contradicted Benjamin's sworn statement and advised the Court that Benjamin himself had told him that two of Piari Khanum's children were his own. Mr Boyle did not know the children's names, but was able to confirm from his own knowledge that Piari had been Benjamin's mistress for many years. Mr Boyle did not, though, attempt to support Piari's claim that she was married to Benjamin.[5]

My grandfather, Sleeman Speirs, who was at the time only twenty-one years old and studying law (and who eventually became a very successful advocate), cross-examined the Barrister. From his cross-examination it was established that such children, being illegitimate and not mentioned in the warisnama, had no automatic rights of inheritance. The Court also accepted that Benjamin's omission of Susan from his warisnama was a deliberate act, due to the breakdown of their marriage, and that this precluded her from succeeding to the wasika. So the case was decided against both Susan Short and Piari Khanum and in favour of Benjamin's surviving sister, niece and nephews, represented by Sleeman Speirs. However, Sleeman and his brothers did not want their aunt to suffer, so they willingly agreed to allow her a life-time pension of forty rupees a month from their wasikas—equivalent to the one third that she would have been able to inherit if mentioned in the warisnama (but reverting to them on her death).

Once again, Benjamin Short's half-siblings Mary Duhan, Ellen Johannes, Nelly Quieros and Marcelina Bourbon tried to get a share of his wasika as in the case of Amelia Short's wasika. Again though, on being cross-examined by my grandfather, it was established that Benjamin's wasika was not just a life-interest and should be distributed only to his true sisters in accordance with his warisnama. Hence, this claim too was dismissed.[5]

I had mentioned above that Susan Gardner was the daughter of Alan Hyde Gardner, and I will now return to dwell a bit further on this family connection. Alan Hyde Gardner was the son of Stewart William Gardner who had come out to India in 1828 as an Ensign in the 28th Regiment of Native Infantry. In India, Stewart Gardner met his close relative Col William Linnaeus Gardner (the adventurer who, arriving in India in 1790, had fought as a mercenary for the Mahrattas and who eventually joined the Company's army and became the founder of Gardner's Horse). Subsequently, Stewart had wooed and married the Colonel's granddaughter, Hirmoonee—this story being told in Fanny Parks' fascinating book *Wanderings of a Pilgrim in Search of the Picturesque*. The marriage took place at Agra in August 1834, witnessed by William Linnaeus Gardner (strangely, the marriage certificate refers to her as Jane, rather than Hirmoonee Gardner). The old Colonel was by then a rich man, living in retirement at Khasgunge on the income from several villages that he owned. He had promised Stewart who was still an ensign with little income, £100 a year besides his military pay. However, this allowance had not materialised since the Colonel was then in his dotage and died peacefully within the year leaving Stewart some villages said to generate this income, but which generated a mere fraction of it. Meanwhile, Stewart in expectation of the allowance and in frustration at still being an Ensign after eight years of service had resigned his commission. From then onwards his family's fortune depreciated from bad to worse. The family survived on the income from the aforesaid villages, which were at Manowta, in Etah district near Khasgunge, but living in penury.[6]

Now Stewart was the cousin of Sir Alan Legge Gardner, the third Baron of Uttoxeter, who died in November 1883 leaving no legitimate heirs to the Barony. (Sir Alan Legge Gardner, in typical Gardner defiance of the conventional, had five illegitimate children by his mistress, the beautiful young actress Julia Fortescue, only marrying her many years later).[6]

Stewart Gardner's father, Rear Admiral Francis Faringdon Gardner, was the next eldest brother to the second Baron Gardner. Therefore, on the death of the third Baron without any legitimate heir and with no younger brother, Stewart's descendents had a valid first claim to the Barony (Stewart himself had died the previous year). So Alan Hyde Gardner, Stewart's eldest son, was persuaded to present his case and claim the Barony. This was however a very difficult thing to achieve with limited funds from an obscure village in Awadh, particularly as he could not afford to travel to England to present his case properly. It seems that he did carry out the initial moves towards doing so and through his lawyer Dr Mayor (?), entered his claim to the Barony in Debrett's Peerage in about 1884. At this point, Stewart alienated his lawyer by taking him to Court for not returning some family papers, and the claim never went any further.[7]

The title to the Barony certainly remained dormant until at least 1956, when my grandfather took the following cutting from the *Times* dated 9 May titled 'Claim to Dormant Barony' which stated:

Lieutenant-Commander David William Hyde Gardner, R.N., stated last night that he intends to apply for a dormant peerage already claimed by a 75 year old man living in a village in India. Since the death of the third baron in 1883, the barony of Gardner has been dormant, although Burke's Peerage comments that 'an heir obviously exists'. Burke's says that the right to the title has not been established. Both Burke's and Debrett's name as the claimant Alan Legge Gardner, of Village Bhnowta, Dadri, Dist Bulandshahr, United Provinces, India. He claims to be a direct descendant of the first Baron Gardner of Uttoxeter, in the County of Stafford, Admiral of the Blue, who died in 1809... Lieutenant-Commander Gardner, aged 43, married with two sons, aged 17 and 10, and a daughter aged 15, is on the staff of the Commodore, R.N. Barracks, Lee-on-Solent. He told a reporter 'I have never met Alan Legge, who is a descendant of my great-great-grandfather's brother, Stewart William Gardner. Stewart William was in India as an Ensign in the 28th Regiment Native Indian Regiment and married an Indian princess and had many sons'.[8].

Susan Short died just five years after the death of her husband in January 1901. As it had already been established that her pension was a life-interest only, her wasika automatically reverted to my grandfather, his brothers, sister and their aunt.

The next death in the family was that of my great-grandfather who died in 1907 at the age of seventy-two. Again, the files in the Wasika Office dealing with the subsequent distribution of his wasika reveal a minor 'skeleton in the cupboard'. My father and his siblings had only ever been told that they had two uncles, Alexander and William and no mention had ever been made of an aunt, Winifred. I recall how astounded my father was when, in 1979 on a trip to India, I found his grandmother's grave and told him that the inscription mentioned her seven children. In fact, subsequent research revealed that twin boys, Henry and Frederick Speirs, had died as infants and a sister, Veronica, had died of small-pox aged five. Now it is quite understandable that no mention would be made of uncles and aunts who had died in infancy. But why should they not be told about an aunt, living in Lucknow, close to their uncle?

Winifred had married Jacob Edgar Quieros, a member of an old Lucknow family of Spanish origins. I do not believe that this alone would have caused the evident shame that prevented my grandfather from telling his children about his sister. The following notes from the Wasika Office offer the clue:

> Distribution of John Speirs, deceased. ...Winifred Speirs has put in an appearance today. She states that she has become Mahomedan now... The record keeper's report is correct. I understand however that Mrs Winifred Speirs has become a pervert [sic], & has consequently changed her original name of Quieros to Speirs her maiden name since 1904. I believe she is now in the keeping of a Mahommedan, but the fact of her having changed her religion does not seem to affect her right to inheritance, except in so far that her case should, I think, now be regulated.[8]

It seems that the fact that Winifred had evidently deserted her husband and was now living with a native Indian, having converted to the Muslim faith was so shocking to the family that they denied her existence. I cannot wholly blame my grandfather for never mentioning his sister, even though this cutting off of contact must have seemed very harsh to her. Instead, I blame the prejudices of the time. My grandfather and his brothers knew perfectly well that they were of mixed race—but from their skin-colouring they appeared to be English, and that was sufficient to enable them to have successful careers as lawyers, instead of being constrained to follow the only careers that were deemed suitable for Anglo-Indians. They had seen how their own father had suffered, spending his whole working life as an Engineer constructing railways on a pittance of a salary, because his skin-colouring revealed his 'Anglo-Indian' descent. They did not want their children to suffer a similar prejudice and hence any evidence of inter-marriage or relationships with Indians was simply obliterated from the 'family memory'. It was far safer never to mention such facts, so that one's appearance of being a Pukka Sahib would never be questioned.

5

JOSEPH SHORT'S CHILDREN BY SLAVE~GIRLS

MOST FAMILY-HISTORY RESEARCHERS FEEL A BUZZ OF EXCITEMENT EACH time they find another family member's baptism, marriage or death recorded in a church register—particularly when the entry provides new information about the existence of a wife or child. So fellow researchers will surely appreciate how grateful and excited I was when I was given permission to freely search through all the old registers at St Joseph's Cathedral in Lucknow, where our family ancestors had been baptised and married over a period of eighty years. The three-day long search proved to be very productive, yielding a vast amount of data sufficient to produce several family trees.

Most researchers also probably take the register entries at face value, possibly making some allowance for adjustment of stated ages at marriage etc. I hope that they will take the following example as a message of warning—never take anything at face value!

One of the entries that I had taken down on my research trip in 2001 concerned the baptism of William George, a son to George and Catherine Short on the third of June. Now I was fairly certain that the father named here was one of Joseph Short's sons by his slave girls, particularly as the God-parents were named as Winifred Speirs and Benjamin Short—his half-siblings. And this has proved correct. However, subsequent examination of the record file held in the Wasika Office at Lucknow concerning George Short's demise unravels a very different story.

From witness statements made to the Wasika Officer following George's death, it is clear that he never had a wife named Catherine. However, for some time he had an affair with a married Muslim woman, known as Piari Khanum.[1] Now Piari Khanum lived in Husainabad, but in a separate house from her husband, Sheik Mohammad Abbas—and it seems that George was one of the several lovers who used to visit her there.[1] The boy, originally named Bakur, and subsequently baptised as William George Short, was born to Piari Khanum in November 1879 while her husband was alive.

It appears that Sheik Mohammad Abbas was aware of his wife's infidelity and had refused to maintain her son. He, however, had died in about 1885, and shortly thereafter George had moved in to live with Piari Khanum at her house in Husainabad. Then, early in 1887, the couple came with the boy William to live in the Short family house in Kaisar Bagh (Joseph Short's former home, where his widow Amelia now lived with her son Benjamin and her grandsons Alexander, William and Sleeman Speirs). And it was while they lived there that the boy was baptised at St Joseph's Church as 'William George, son of George and Catherine Short.' However, Piari Khanum was already tiring of her relationship with George Short in favour of his half-brother, Benjamin, as described by my great-uncle, Alexander Speirs:

The open flirtations progressing in the immorality that she carried on with Benjamin Short made me believe that she was not a modest woman. Then I went to Mussoorie. On my return in December 1887 I found that the woman Chhoti had deserted George Short & lived in open concubinage with my uncle Benjamin and this is being carried on up to this date.

---

[1]Piari Khanum was also known as Mussumat Chhote. At the hearing, twelve witnesses confirmed in a written statement that 'George Short during his life-time married one Mussummat Chhote Hurmozee the sister of Mussummat Chhote according to Mohammedan law [and] that the said marriage though presumably invalid according to English law would under Mohammedan law be valid & make any legal intercourse between George Short & Mussummat Chote impossible.' The witnesses confirmed, though, that George 'for a short time kept the said Mussummat Chote as his mistress, who subsequently left him for the protection of his brother and under her influence got the said Bakur the son of Sheik Mohamed Abbas baptised as William Short his son by Catherine his wife. The said George Short had no wife of that name [and] in fact the said George Short was never married.' (Presumably the last statement refers to marriage by Christian rites.)

Although Benjamin Short later swore that Piari Khanum had not been his mistress, too many other witnesses confirmed this as a fact for there to be any doubt. In fact, Martin Short produced a letter in his brother George's handwriting, confirming that when he was drunk one night Benjamin had sworn that he loved Piari Khanum. Shortly after this, George had moved out of the house, taking his son William with him.[1]

Now whether William was actually George's son is certainly open to question, as several witnesses confirmed that Piari Khanum had relationships with a number of men. In fact, my great-grandfather John Speirs had met George Short accompanied by the boy on one occasion and, being shocked by William's behaviour, had asked George whether he was his son—to which George had replied, 'No, he is the son of the woman I am keeping, but he is not my son.' Moreover, after George's death, ten of his siblings challenged whether William was really his son— only Benjamin (who was clearly not an unbiased witness) stated that he definitely was George's son. However, in assessing whether William should inherit his father's wasika, the Wasika Officer took the view that George evidently treated him as though he were his son, noting that William called George 'Abba' (or father). Also, since George had signed a warisnama naming William as his son and heir, he believed it should be accepted in the absence of proof to the contrary.

When George Short died in April 1890 of bronchitis (being barely forty), quite a long protracted battle ensued over the upbringing of William. George had clearly intended his son to be brought up as a Roman Catholic, having enrolled him as a day-scholar at the newly formed St Francis College only two days after his baptism in June 1887. But William's mother was a Muslim and clearly a woman of very loose morals, whom the Wasika Officer did not consider fit to be entrusted with his welfare. This distrust proved to be justified when it became apparent that Piari Khanum was neither looking after her son nor sending him to school. So the Wasika Officer, Mr W.H. Cobb, with the sanction of the District Commissioner, took matters in his own hands by acting as William's guardian (and thus being able to ensure that his large wasika allowance was properly spent on his upbringing).

In order to arrange for William's education, Mr Cobb then wrote in September 1890 to Revd Father Bartholomew, the Principal of St Francis College (and also the Parish Priest of the adjacent St Joseph's

Church in Hazratganj), asking if William could become a boarder at the College. But Father Bartholomew had to point out that as the school had only taken their first pupils in 1886, they had not yet completed the accommodation for boarders. He suggested that in the meantime William should be sent to St Michael's Catholic Boarding School at Bankipur (near Patna). First, though, Father Bartholomew was asked to buy four suits for William, as his mother had left him only with very shabby clothes. Arrangements were then made to send him there, but at the last moment William became 'affected with Itch' (a contagious disease caused by the itch mite, which burrows in the skin, causing irritation). As a result, Father Bartholomew suggested that he should remain at Lucknow until he had been cured.[2]

Meanwhile Piari Khanum wrote to Mr Cobb, apparently suddenly concerned about her son's welfare and suggesting that she would send him to any school he wished. However, her real motive of getting hold of her son's wasika allowance was evident from her request that he should 'kindly allow the full amount of pension to her son William Short, from which the expenses for his schooling, maintenance, &ca &ca will be defrayed, and a monthly account of the minor's expenses, will be submitted to the Wasika Office...' Needless to say, the Wasika Officer ignored this request.

It seems that William did not actually attend the school in Bankipur but instead remained at St Francis College, Lucknow where he was finally enrolled as a boarder in December 1890. Only a few months later his grandmother, Amelia Short, entered the fray, with the following petition to the Commissioner of Lucknow:

Honoured Sir,

I most humbly beg to state that by order Mr Cobb C.S. late officer in chg Wasequa, Lucknow my grandson William Short (son of George Short deceased) was placed in charge of the Roman Catholic Chaplain and made to live as a boarder in the Chapel Compound. I was at first quite pleased at this, but the other day on Sunday I went to Chapel and after Mass I wished to speak with my child but the native woman servant or clerk in charge of the boy, would not allow him to come near me even, and when I called the lad to me the woman began to speak to the poor boy in a most harsh and unbecoming manner for a common servant—it was shameful to see the way she behaved and altho' my heart yearning to embrace my boy yet in spite of my begging of her to let the boy come to me she spoke in a most rude manner & would not let the lad stir even, besides this the boy is fretting very much being suddenly separated from me & all his relatives—besides his food being also suddenly changed quite disagrees with him, he is getting thinner and thinner daily and is quite changed; under the circumstances and as the life of my grand-son is too dear to me, I hasten to lay the facts before you and to earnestly crave that my grandson may be made over to me to take care of and bring up, and as I am a Roman Catholic myself, I will send him daily to the Roman Catholic School he now attends and also send him to Chapel as he now goes. I only wish to save my poor child from a premature grave for the boy will surely suffer if he is treated in the manner he is now—if you are a parent I appeal to your feeling as one to take my case into your kind consideration and order that my poor boy William Short may be made over to me, and for this act of benevolence & charitable kindness I shall ever bless you and pray for your prosperity.

I have the honour to be,

Honored Sir,

D/ Lucknow   Your most obedt Servt
The 6th May/91   Amelia M. Short [2]

However, the Wasika Officer would not relinquish his guardianship, even though Amelia confirmed that she had also brought up William's father, George Short and all of his brothers. He simply informed Amelia that according to the rules of St Francis' school, parents of boarders could only visit their sons once a month and that she should apply to Father Bartholomew to see if he would relax this regulation. In fact, as Amelia herself died merely six months later, it would only have caused further disruption if she had been granted guardianship.

Meanwhile, William's mother Piari Khanum, still pursuing the prize of control over William's wasika allowance, made her bid for guardianship jointly with Benjamin Short in an application to the District Judge. It seems likely that neither the Wasika Officer nor the Lucknow Commissioner were consulted in this application, because the District Judge simply granted the couple guardianship. Armed with the Judge's order, Mr Boyle, Benjamin Short's barrister, came to St Francis School early in December 1891 and demanded that William should be handed over to him. Although Father Bartholomew had several misgivings about William's mother, confiding to the Wasika Officer that 'she brings with her persons whom I object to' he added that 'Master William Short at present is doing well and has reached that age at which boys understand everything and I do not think that such intercourse with his mother will do him any good, may well do a great deal of harm'. However, he had no choice in the matter, as otherwise he would have been held to be in contempt of court.[2]

As a result, William was withdrawn from St Francis' school and handed over to the care of Benjamin Short and his mistress, who did however state in a message that they would be willing to send William back to St Francis School as a day-boy. But the Wasika Officer was not satisfied with this situation, so he immediately made a fresh application to the District Judge, who, on hearing about Piari Khanum's character, appointed the Wasika Officer as William's guardian once again. It appears though that he did not rescind his earlier order, so that effectively Piari Khanum, Benjamin Short and the Wasika Officer were joint guardians.

Faced with this unhappy compromise, Mr Cobb, the Wasika Officer, evidently decided that it would be better for William to be sent to a school far from Lucknow, where his mother would have no opportunity of visiting him and disrupting his studies. Therefore, arrangements were made to send William to St Joseph's College, the boarding-school for European boys run by the Irish Christian Brothers at Nainital. Once again, Father Bartholomew was asked to ensure that William was properly 'kitted out' for the school, so he visited Whiteaway, Laidlaw & Co in Hazratganj and bought all the required clothes, towels, sheets, blankets etc for William, before arranging his journey to Nainital in mid-February 1892.[2]

However, after William had only been at St Joseph's College for a few months, the Judicial Commissioner decided to set aside the District Judge's second ruling and ordered that 'the Wasika Officer should apply for removal of the mother of minor from guardianship & for his sole appointment to the District Judge'. The Judicial Commissioner clearly intended that there should be a speedy transfer of guardianship to the Wasika Officer alone, and that William should remain at St Joseph's College until this had been effected. But in practice this process took a whole year, during which time Piari Khanum continued to be William's guardian. During this period, Piari Khanum swiftly removed William from St Joseph's College and eventually enrolled him as a day-boy at the Centennial School[1] which at that time was in Husainabad, close to the Gomti River, behind Sheesh Mahal.[2]

Finally, in July 1893, Mr Cobb's application for sole guardianship of William was heard before the District Judge of Lucknow. Several witnesses testified that Benjamin Short was in a very poor state of health, mainly due to excessive drinking. He in fact admitted that for some time he had been ill with fistula and that he could barely walk a quarter of a mile. Stating that he still wanted to remain as William's guardian, he confirmed that William now lived with him and that he would allow Piari Khanum to visit her son occasionally and not to live with him. Benjamin maintained that he had never had sexual intercourse with Piari Khanum and was not the father of her other two children, although each of the other witnesses confirmed that Piari had lived with Benjamin as his mistress for some time, and that, although they no longer lived together, she still used to visit and spend the night with Benjamin. Others also confirmed that, contrary to Benjamin's statement, William did often live at his mother's house. Accordingly, the judge ruled that neither Benjamin nor Piari Khanum were fit to act as guardians and that the Wasika Officer should become the sole guardian.[1]

Thus, after three years of legal battle the issue was finally settled, and William was once again sent to St Francis School under the care of the Wasika Officer. He stayed there for the rest of his school-days and,

---

[2] A Mission school had been established at Husainabad in February 1864 by the Revd L.H. Messmore. It was renamed as the Centennial School in 1877, in honour of the centenary of the American Methodist Mission. The school did not transfer to its current site in Golaganj until 1921. The pupils at all times have generally been Indian children, either Hindu or Muslim, the school having no authority to teach Christianity. Piari probably chose this school because she did not want her son to be given a Christian upbringing.

according to Father Bartholomew, was always polite and made good progress in his studies. But the situation suddenly changed on 3 June 1899, when William had been granted leave by Father Bartholomew to visit his uncle, Martin Short, who was staying at the Prince of Wales Hotel. This however, was simply an excuse for William to leave the school premises, as Father Bartholomew discovered later that day when he received the following letter from Mr Boyle, Benjamin Short's former Barrister:

Lucknow June 3-99
Revd Fr Bartholomew, Lucknow

Sir,

Mr Boyle having gone for the day on a case to Barabanki he has asked me on behalf of Mr William Short, and himself as legal adviser, to write and inform you that Mr Short has from today accepted service under Mr Boyle, and is now in his house. As you are aware, the guardianship which you have hitherto exercised over Mr Short ceased yesterday by virtue of his majority today, and by the order of the District Judge (Mr Bateman) made on the 27 May last (a certified copy of which has been shown to you) Mr Short is now at perfect liberty to deal with himself and his property as he likes. As Mr Short will probably stay here for a few days, before arranging for his future residence, Mr Boyle will be glad if you will send over per bearer the box of clothing and any other little things which Mr. Short may have left with you. Mr Boyle also requests that you will be good enough not to interfere in any way with Mr Short's wasika account as he intends to deal with it himself and without any reference to you. Any interference on his property would be illegal and Mr Boyle hopes that you will not force unpleasant issues in the matter. From the nature of this communication you will gather that Mr Short has not run away from school and any statement to that effect from you will be contrary to the truth and unfair to Mr Short

Yrs faithfully,
Dn Banain
For J.B. Boyle Esq[2]

In this way, William Short's school-days ended quite dramatically. Unfortunately though, all the good intentions of the Wasika Officer and Father Bartholomew to ensure, that William received a 'good Roman Catholic upbringing' in accordance with his late father's wishes came to naught. At some stage in his life, William converted to the Shia Muslim faith and was renamed as Baqur Husain. He married at least twice, taking a 'mutah' wife, Mehdi Begam, and later a Nikah wife, Masjidi Begam, by whom he had one surviving son, James Joseph Short (alias Haidar Abbas), born in 1947. Not only that, the intentions of the authorities to keep him separated from his mother also seem to have had little effect. William obviously kept a sufficiently close relationship with Piari Begam to mention her, aged sixty-two, as his heir in his first warisnama made in 1928 (she had probably died by the time he made out his next list of heirs in 1948). He eventually died in January 1961 in Mohalla Ramganj, Lucknow leaving his widow Masjidi Begam and his son, Haidar Abbas, to inherit his wasika.[3]

Let us now turn to the life of Joseph Short's eldest son, James Macdonald Short, who was born in about 1841 to the slave-girl Ellaheejaun.[3]

The reader may recall that Macdonald Short had evidently displeased his father (who did not approve of his conduct), as a result of which he had struck him off the list of heirs in his warisnama. Unfortunately, Joseph never divulged the reasons for his dislike for Macdonald in detail to enable us to judge whether his son deserved such harsh treatment. But this meant that Macdonald had to employ crafty tactics in order to ensure that he did actually inherit a share of his father's wasika when Joseph died in 1870. His stratagem involved stating that both Joseph Short and Murium Begum had been practising Muslims for most of their lives, whilst all other witnesses confirmed the established fact that they had really been Roman Catholics, although they had naturally adopted

---

[3] Interestingly, according to the testimony of Macdonald and Martin Short, their mother Elajeejaun and two other slave-girls, Sewtee and Nowrozee, were originally given to Sultan Murium Begum by her Khawas, Hussain Ufza. Murium Begum later gave them to her brother as his 'Slave-wives' or Hurrums—even though Joseph had by then married his first Christian wife, Jane Huggins. Hence, Murium Begum certainly appears to have been complicit in her brother's extra-marital affairs.

a Muslim lifestyle. He went so far as to say that his father observed all Muslim rites until finally renouncing Islam in 1860, despite knowing that Joseph had gone to great lengths to ensure his sister had a Roman Catholic burial in 1849. Macdonald's reason for distorting the truth was quite transparent—he stood a far greater chance of inheriting the wasika if he could establish that Islamic law should prevail rather than Christian law, under which he would not inherit due to his illegitimacy. In fact he need not have worried, as the Commissioner's final decision was that neither Christian nor Muslim law should apply, but the 'law of the body' under which all of Joseph's progeny, whether legitimate or illegitimate, Christian or Muslim, should inherit equally. And the Commissioner also decided to ignore the fact that Joseph had specifically disinherited Macdonald (and his half-sisters Emma, Georgiana and Isabella) and to grant them an equal inheritance.

Whether or not he was consciously trying to follow his father's example, Macdonald Short's life certainly mirrored that of Joseph Short in two aspects—namely in the large number of children he had and the variety of mothers by whom they were born! In June 1861 he had married Nancy Orr, daughter of Alexander Orr—whose family had lived in Lucknow since 1779 and had prospered as merchants and traders.[4] The marriage however was not a successful one, and Nancy had apparently left Macdonald some time in 1882, as he later described in a letter dated March 1917:

> my wife Mrs Nancy Short, having left me, since last 35 years, lives with a man by name Delaver Husain and remained with that man for about 8 years, when, after leaving her, gone away Mrs. Nancy Short put forward her claims for maintenance allowance as a lawful married wife before Major Horsford, City Magistrate of Lucknow. This officer was in charge of the Husainabad Endowment where I was serving as a Head Clerk and he was Wasika Officer of Lucknow. I regret to mention here that I could not put forward my grievances before him through shame because she (my wife) took my honour by living with the said man having gone through an adultery...[5]

Nancy appears to have borne only two children to Macdonald, both of whom died in infancy: a daughter, named Mary Magdelene (who died aged twenty-six months and whose grave can still be seen in the 'Chiria Jhil' cemetery in the gardens of the Mother Theresa home in Sapru Marg[4]) and a son named Alexander (born in 1865, and who died of a cough and fever aged only nine months). Macdonald's version of Nancy's departure may not be entirely accurate, as the baptism records of St Patrick's Church in Kanpur show that his next child, Elizabeth, was born to 'Rosabella Short' in September 1877. Clearly, if Nancy did leave him in 1882, her departure may well have been caused by his liaison with Bella, who went on to bear him at least six children.

On the other hand, though, there is a record of a maintenance order having been granted to Nancy Short by the City Magistrate in December 1882, whereby Macdonald agreed to pay her ten rupees a month. This would imply that Nancy had actually left him eight years before this, as Macdonald stated that the claim was made after her affair with Delaver Husain. And Nancy's subsequent behaviour does raise a major question about her moral standards. At a hearing in 1914 the Lucknow City Magistrate refused to increase the allowance Macdonald paid her on the grounds that 'she earned a certain income from the disgraceful trade of pimp'.[5]

The identity of Macdonald's first mistress, Bella, is not altogether clear. In 1907 he confirmed that five of his surviving children were born to a Christian woman 'Bella', but their baptismal certificates either show a blank for the mother's name or simply 'Rosabella' without mention of any surname. In the case of her son Julian, though, there is no record of baptism. However, in a later warisnama, James mentions a son 'Simon Joseph Ernest' of the same age as Julian, and his certificate of baptism shows 'Isabella Simon' as the mother. Now this would suggest that Julian is probably the same person as Simon Joseph Ernest—in which case Bella's full name was Isabella Simon.

Macdonald's second mistress was a Muslim woman, Zainab Begam who bore him a further six children between 1890 and 1905 while he was still living with Bella. He took them all to St Joseph's Church, Hazratganj in October 1907 and, after Zainab Begam had first been converted to

---

[4] The grave inscription, which says, 'Sacred to the memory of Mary Magdaline the only beloved child of James McDonald & Nancy Short d 3/ 6/1864 age2y2m3d' is the only record of her existence. Neither baptism nor burial register entries seem to have survived.

Christianity and baptised under the name of Jane, all six children were then baptised in a joint ceremony. In the case of his youngest son, Jacob, aged only two, it was fortunate that he was baptised then, because he succumbed to small-pox just two months later and his existence would have been unknown to us all.

In this way, like his father, Macdonald sired fourteen children[5] over a period of forty-three years to several women, only one of whom was his wife. And, like his father, he maintained both his mistresses for many years—both Bella and Zainab Begam still being in his keeping when he died in 1919 at Mohalla Khayaliganj Thana in Hazratganj. But, unlike Joseph Short, Macdonald needed to work for his living. He took various clerical jobs, working in the Customs Department at Lucknow prior to 1865, and then for the Police Department in the 1870s. He was working at Allahabad as a clerk in 1880, later returning to Lucknow as Head Clerk at the Wasika Office in Husainabad. But he was dismissed from this post for misconduct in 1892. He probably retired at this stage, and appears to have been living at Barabanki in 1907, at the time of the mass

---

[5] In 1906, McDonald listed five children born to Bella as: Elizabeth, Angelina, William, Charles and Julian. However, a twenty-one year old son named James had died the previous year from consumption, so it is reasonable to suppose that he was also Bella's child. In the case of his second mistress, Zainab Begum, he listed her children as Mary, John, Ada, Ellen, Rosy and Jacob.

Each of Macdonald's daughters seems to have married (with the possible exception of Elizabeth, who still retained the surname Short although she had six children by Mirza Ahmad Jan—perhaps through a Mutah marriage). Ada married Timothy Smith, an assistant station master at Khagola, and Rosy married Ronald Bruce-Hamilton, an assistant manager for a transport company—the Smith family eventually settling at Wellesley College, Nainital and the Bruce-Hamiltons at New Delhi, before both families eventually left for England some time after 1940. Ellen married Mr Collett and settled in Meerut, living at 62A, the Mall. Mary married George Lopez, who worked in the Government Telegraph Office, and went to live in village Kashipur, Unrao. Angelina married Cyril Medley, remaining in Lucknow, where she had three children: Gladys, Noel Charles and Horace Macdonald. (Gladys married Mr Alney, and had five children, including Patrick and Juliet, who also remained in Lucknow. Their families still live in Lucknow, although they have both died).

Macdonald's eldest surviving son, William, died childless at Kanpur in 1963. His second son, Charles, married Elizabeth Joseph in 1912 and they had one son, Francis Anthony. As mentioned later in the chapter, he fell on hard times in 1921. The fate of Julian and John is not known by the author.

Christenings of Zainab Begam and their children. But by 1914 he had returned to live at Maqbara Amjad Ali Shah (close to Hazratganj).

Although he was seventy-eight when he died, Macdonald's youngest daughters Ellen and Rosy were at the time still at school in Kanpur, where they were placed under the guardianship of the Collector until they reached the age of majority.[5]

Macdonald's second surviving son, Charles, seems to have fallen on hard times. He went on military service in Mesopotamia [now Iraq], serving there until 1921. When he returned to Lucknow he was in a poor state of health, suffering from a hacking cough and rheumatism, bad enough to prevent him from working. With steadily mounting bills, he was eventually forced to apply to have his wasika commuted (i.e. discontinued in exchange for a lump-sum). But even though the Wasika Officer accepted that his was a deserving case, the commutation process dragged out for over two years despite numerous appeals from Charles, which met with typical bureaucratic indifference.[6]

Martin Short was Macdonald Short's younger brother, born in about 1846 to the slave-girl Ellaheejaun. Far less is known about him than his elder brother, although the records of La Martiniere College show that he attended it as a day scholar from March 1863 to November 1867 (his half-brothers George and Benjamin Joseph Short also attended the same institution as day scholars during this same period). Martin seems to have followed the precedent set by his father and by Macdonald, in having children by a Muslim woman and later arranging for her to be baptised as a Christian prior to their marriage. His consort's (Christian) name was Agnes Jane, and she bore him four children between 1878 and 1885. The first two, Mary Eliza and Alice Jane Short were baptised at the RC Church in Benares in 1882, where he was working at the time for the O&R Railway. His other children, Louisa Florence and Frederick Martin Short were baptised at St Joseph's Church in Lucknow in July 1892, on the same day that his consort was converted from Islam to Christianity before they got married. By this time he listed his occupation simply as 'Wasikadar' implying one assumes that he was no longer working, but just living on his wasika of Rs41 10As 8P.

Let us now turn to Martin's daughter Alice who lived quite a turbulent life. She had married Augustus William Sangster at St Joseph's Church, Lucknow in July 1909. He worked at the time in the Printing

Press Office of the O&R Railway at Lucknow, and came from a family long resident at Lucknow and having a history of loyal service to the British Government—as described below.

Augustus's grandfather, William Sangster, born around 1800, seems to have been the first of the family to live in Lucknow. At the tender age of fourteen, the British Government awarded him a pension since his father, George Sangster, an old Mahratta Officer, had been killed for refusing to fight against the British during the Mahratta wars.[7] William had lived at Lucknow and had served as a writer at the Residency from 1827 to 1859, when he finally retired. He had, however, been suspended from his post for almost four years between 1852 and 1856 for some suspected misdemeanour but had been completely exonerated and granted a full pension on retirement. When he was re-employed in 1856, his duties were listed as 'Persian Interpreter to the King of Oude'. And during the following year he had endured the siege of the Residency, fighting alongside Edward Duhan (Joseph Short's son-in-law), Felix John Quieros, James Orning and Mr Hutton in Sago's Garrison. He lived on as a pensioner to the grand age of eighty-one, dying of old age in September 1881.

The Sangster family had remained in Lucknow, and Augustus's father (also named William) had served as a writer and subsequently as record-keeper at the Judicial Commissioner's Office in Lucknow (working alongside my grandfather's elder brother William Speirs, and also John Ernest Johannes). Augustus's mother, Charlotte, also came from a noted Lucknow family, being the daughter of Augustus Manuel, a pleader at the law-courts.

Although Augustus and Alice Sangster did not have any children, Alice's unmarried elder sister Eliza had given birth to a daughter about a year before their wedding, following an affair with a Hindu. However, Eliza had died suddenly from fever when her daughter Mary was barely two years old. So, in order to avoid a family scandal over the illegitimate birth, Augustus and Alice adopted Mary, getting her baptised at St Joseph's Church in March 1911, but without revealing the name of her true mother or of the Hindu father. And only a few years later, Alice similarly adopted her brother Frederick's infant son when his first wife Grace suddenly died after a severe attack of diarrhoea in May 1917. Frederick went on to marry twice more, but never reclaimed his son, Stanley Seabright, stating bitterly in his warisnama:

I disclaim my son Stanley who was taken from me in his infancy (when his mother died) by my sister Alice Sangster and her husband the late A.W. Sangster as their own child son and heir and he bears the name Sangster and not mine[8] .

For a number of years, Augustus and Alice Sangster appear to have lived happily with their adopted children. They lived at Chaulakhi in Banks Road, and sent Mary to St Agnes School near Charbagh and Stanley to St Francis School in Hazratganj, while Augustus worked as Deputy Superintendent at the O&R Railway Printing Press.

But then in 1921 Augustus started behaving erratically at work, explaining to his new manager that he was unable to apply himself due to family troubles (although others in the office thought that he was just upset at being superseded for the post of Superintendent by his new manager). He returned from six weeks' leave of absence apparently better and continued to work normally—interrupted though by another period of stress-related leave in 1924, when he admitted to problems in his marital relationship. A colleague described him at this time as being 'a bit mad. He never used to sleep or eat and he used to roam about the house. He was alright in other ways except that he used to lose his temper often. He used to walk about and...used to chase people, and we used to be afraid to go to his bungalow. I went to see him once as he was my officer, and he said "get out". He threatened me with his fist.'

Matters came to a head in May 1925 when he again became highly agitated and eventually told his manager, Mr Willmer, that he wanted to alter the declaration for his Provident Fund saying, 'I cannot get on with my wife so I want to make another declaration'. Initially, he made out this declaration (in the form of a will) leaving half of the pension to Alice and a quarter each to their adopted son and daughter. But he swiftly ripped this form up and confessed to his clerk that he needed advice saying, 'I do not know what to do, my brains are worried. You had better advise me.' He went on to tell the clerk that he was very concerned because his adopted daughter 'went out on a bicycle and some Muhammadan made love to her' and he had quarrelled with his wife because she did not keep watch over her. He was also worried because he had lost money at the races and become a pauper. But when the poor clerk pointed out that only Augustus could decide how to bequeath his money, he eventually made out other forms, which were again duly witnessed. However, he was evidently under great stress and was soon taken from work and placed under his doctor's supervision. He did return to work briefly in June but, as Mr Willmer described, 'his brain seemed to become benumbed. He was not fit for work. I sent for him and he was brought to office and his arms were rigid and his mouth open and could not recognize anyone. He did not appear to be in his senses'.[9] The following week he was dead.

It was only after Augustus' death that the accusations began to fly between his widow Alice and his adopted daughter Mary. Apparently, Mary had fallen in love with a Muslim man, Akhtar Mirza, who had converted her to Islam under the new name Kaniz Fatima Begam, following which the couple had been married in the house of a Maulvi in Golaganj about two months before Augustus' death. According to Mary, her father had simply not approved of the marriage taking place in his home, but had told her that she could come back after the marriage. Now this would seem very surprising, because such a radical change of religious faith generally led to great bitterness and estrangement within the family. This explains Augustus' disturbed behaviour since he was traumatised by Mary's act. But Mary went on to lay the blame for her father's behaviour on Alice, making the following statement:

> My father did not rebuke my mother for letting me go out alone on a bicycle. My father became angry with my mother about 4 years before he died. He used to be angry every day. He used to beat her also. She also used to beat him. This beating used to take place in my presence and mother used to set a bull-dog at my father. On one occasion I rescued my father from the bull-dog. He only got struck from the paws. My mother only once set a bull-dog on my father. My father turned out my mother from the house. The bull-dog stayed with my father. My father turned out my mother 5 or 6 months before he died. When my father was sick she came again to attend to him but he tried to beat her again but she ran away. My father gave my mother Rs 50 a month for clothes. She went and lived in an empty room in the same compound where we were. The affair of the bulldog was 3 years before his death. My father used to rebuke her for wandering about and then she used to get angry and beat him. My mother began the marpit (hitting) and then my father also

beat her. My father did not go to make any complaint to any officer to avoid disgrace and there was no case instituted. The office people used to tell my father that my mother used to wander and that her conduct was bad. Then he became angry. I also used to complain of my mother's conduct. When I made complaints about her then my father turned her out. This was about 6 months before he died. I told my father that my mother used to go out at night when he was asleep. Once he noticed himself and beat her. I have seen my mother with the man and she is still with the man. His name is Nazar Khan. He is a Kabuli. The Kabuli lives at her house. He is a poor man. He does no work. My mother maintains him. She keeps this man in the house not as a Chaukidar, not as a servant, but as a husband. Sometimes he cooks the food. He also does other odd jobs. When my father turned out my mother 6 months before his death this Kabuli was living with my mother even then. He used to come secretly at night. My father knew about it. I also told my father about it. So far as I know my father never spoke to this Kabuli. My father got angry with the servant Baqar because he did not tell him about my mother. Sometimes my father used to be angry with the clerks in the office when the work was bad. My father was ill about 5 years before he died. He had fever and cough. He had no other illness. My father did not divorce my mother to avoid publicity and disgrace. I have not seen my mother with any man except this Kabuli. I was married 2 months before my father died.[9]

However, when Alice Sangster gave evidence, she stated that she and her husband had loved each other very much and never quarrelled for a single day. She explained that her husband's behaviour changed because of his mental illness. She stated:

...about 18 months before my husband died he became mad, i.e. his brain became deranged. He used to throw chairs down and beat the children. He said that he would kill everyone. He was attended by many doctors. Doctor Hunter wanted to send him to lunatic asylum but I begged him not to send him there, because he was very weak and he would die there. It was a year before he died when Colonel Hunter wanted to send him to lunatic asylum. He took leave of six months.

Alice also said that she had been told by Mr Wilmer that Augustus had made out a will in her favour and that, after Augustus' death, she had sent her servant to his office to collect the will and any other personal papers. The servant told her that there was a quarrel. 'He told me that the will was found in a drawer and Akhtar Mirza was tearing it up. The servant seized it from Mr Akhtar Mirza and gave it to Mr Wilmer and so I got it torn.'

Following this incident, Alice had instituted a court case against Mary and her husband. It seems that Mary was claiming to be her daughter in order to claim inheritance through Augustus' will. To prove her wrong, Alice obtained Mary's baptism certificate and arranged for the priest, Father Angelo, to confirm in court that Mary was adopted by the couple. Alice now confirmed that Mary 'was about 2 years old when we started to maintain her. Her mother had died. Her natural father allowed us to take away the child and bring her up. The girl was educated in St Agnes' School near Charbagh in Lucknow. She remained in school up to about the age of 15. She used to ride a bicycle and my husband was annoyed. She used to wander about and he heard that she was carrying on with some Mohammedans. The girl ran away with Akhtar Mirza. Neither I nor my husband knew anything about it before. My husband was ready to send them to jail. My husband used to be very angry as I did not stop the girl going out on a bicycle. I have a bull-dog still. My husband was very fond of it. Muhammad Ali, Taluqdar, gave it to me as a present when it was small. This dog has never bitten anyone. The dog used to run at dark people. I never set the dog on my husband. I never beat my husband. He never beat me. I do not know about any Kabuli but once I had a Nepalese, Hindu servant. He went away 2 months before my husband died. He used to work for my husband as a bearer etc. My husband never turned me out of the house. Mary Akhtar used not to tell tales about me but we used to quarrel a great deal. She wanted to marry some Muhammadan but I did not give my consent. She became jealous. She was angry with me. My husband did not turn me out 6 months before his death. He never turned me out for a single day. He did not give me allowance of Rs 50, and a separate Kothi in the same compound. He used to give me his full pay. I never heard from my husband that he had made a declaration giving half of his fund to Mary Akhtar and half to Stanley Short, and not a penny to me. I do not know why he should have done so.'

With such contradictory versions of the same events, it can only be a matter of conjecture where the actual truth lies. In my view, there is probably some truth in both the accounts. Bearing in mind that Augustus had shown signs of emotional disturbance for four years, and had complained of 'family troubles' it seems likely that the original cause was a deteriorating relationship with his wife rather than just 'becoming mad' as Alice claimed. And quite probably, in such a situation, she may have sought solace elsewhere. His wife's infidelity might have led to an escalation in his demented behaviour. Clearly, though, he was also extremely distressed by the fact that Mary had run off and married a Muslim. This would explain why he felt the need for help from colleagues in deciding how to change his will as he simply could not decide whether to leave any money to either of them. It also seems clear that Mary and her husband were being highly deceitful over Augustus' will, and were probably trying to destroy it when caught by Alice's servant. In the end, the court accepted Alice's version, and she was granted the assets in Augustus' Provident Fund, which amounted to Rs 16,677—quite a respectable sum in those days.

So far, we have covered the lives of Joseph Short's first three sons by slave-girls; Macdonald, Martin & George Short. His next son by a slave-girl was Isaac, born in about 1856 to Naurojee Khanum, another of the slave-girls given to him by Sultan Murium Begum. Although Isaac was given a Christian name, he was not baptised before Joseph's death and appears to have opted for his mother's religion i.e. Islam. His mother, Naurojee, looked after him after Joseph's death, asking the Wasika Officer to arrange for her to receive his wasika, as otherwise she could not afford to continue his education. Little is known about his later life, except some amusing details which show how people try to distort previously stated facts to suit the situation.

Isaac had converted to Islam and changed his name to Amir Mirza in 1890, shortly before marrying a Muslim woman, Hamza Begum, in January 1891 by the full Nikah ceremony. They had a son, Faiyaz Mirza, who was born, according to Hamza Begam, about fifteen months later. Isaac had entered both of their names in his warisnama in 1893. But the marriage evidently did not last, and the couple must have separated shortly thereafter, before divorcing in March 1895. During their separation, Hamza Begam had applied for maintenance for herself and her son, and the court accepted her evidence. Consequently, she was granted rupees twenty per month until June 1895. This included three and a half months for Idaat (a period fixed after divorce by Muslim law in case the husband wishes to reunite with his divorced wife). She had also been granted rupees five per month after the divorce for maintenance of their son.

Isaac (or Amir Mirza) soon married another Muslim woman, Mussumat Imaman, and had two further daughters by her, Amir Begum and Ahmadi Begum, whose names were entered in a warisnama in 1897. But he did not enter the name of his son Faiyaz Mirza, which was challenged by Hamza Begum and he was called to the Wasika Office to offer an explanation. Amir Mirza now stated that Hamza Begum had been his mistress only and that they had sexual relations for a year before he had contracted the Nikah. He claimed that Faiyaz Mirza was not his son at all, but had an unknown father. He further added that 'when I married her she was pregnant. She used to have intercourse with others also. I was deceived into taking her by marriage. In the Warisnama of 1893 I entered Faiyaz Mirza's name as I was not in my senses then.' But the Wasika Officer realised that this was a typical story when a former lover had fallen out of favour and, noting that Amir Mirza was paying maintenance for him, accepted that it was proved that Faiyaz Mirza was his son. Later still, Amir Mirza wrote another wasika in 1916, again omitting Faiyaz Mirza's name as an heir. However, by then he had forgotten what he had said in 1897, and merely said that Faiyaz had been conceived illicitly before marriage, not remembering his previous claim that Faiyaz was 'not from my seed'. [I am unsure how this matter was finally resolved, because most of the relevant file is in Urdu.][10]

Joseph Short's last son by his 'hurrums' was Edwin, born to Mussumat Peearee, Joseph Short's own slave, in May 1859. Like Isaac, Edwin had not been christened before Joseph's death in 1870, but this omission was rectified the following year, when he was baptised by Father Lewis at St Joseph's Church. At about this time he was living in Kaisarbagh with his half-sister Margaret Snell. Margaret also owned the house next door, which she rented to a Muslim girl named Malka Begum and it wasn't long before Edwin formed an attachment with Malka. According to Margaret, the couple were married 'in my house at

Kaisarbagh (Shair Darwaza) in my presence' but at the same time Margaret mentioned that Malka Begum was first baptised under the name Alice before being married to Edwin in church (this is confirmed by the records of St Joseph's Church, which show that they were married in October 1874, when Edward was just fifteen). In fact, Alice herself confirmed the somewhat unusual circumstances of her marriage saying:

I was lawfully married to Edwin Short ascending to Christian religion in the R.C. Church... Father Lewis consecrated the marriage. In those days I was living with my brothers & mother in Luchha Shuba. Mrs Snell also took part in my marriage. The ceremony took place in the latter's house.[11]

Edwin and Alice (or Malka Begum) continued to live at Margaret Snell's house for about six months until, following some unpleasantness between the two families, Edwin rented a prostitute's house in Wazirganj and they moved there. Alice had become pregnant whilst living with the Snells, and their daughter was born shortly after their move to Wazirganj, being christened as Mary Josephine Short. According to Alice's testimony, Edwin and Alice had other children who later died (presumably they died young, as no baptism records have been found). But, not long after his marriage, Edwin had begun an affair with a woman from the Bazaar known as Amina Begum. Eventually, he began to openly live with her as his mistress, which naturally led to a breakdown of his marriage. As a result, Alice and Edwin separated although they never actually divorced, and Edwin continued living with Amina Begum for the rest of his life. Meanwhile, Alice reverted to Islam (and to her former name of Malka Begum) and their daughter Mary Josephine, having been abandoned by Edwin, also converted to Islam, and was given the name Mariam Begum.

Now Amina Begum already had a daughter, named Shahzadi, who was aged about six at the time she commenced her affair with Edwin, and who naturally lived with Edwin and Amina Begum. And it was Shahzadi who, many years later, became the mistress of my great-uncle, Alexander Speirs and bore him three children. But we will dwell upon their lives later.

It is here that the tale takes a Machiavellian turn because at some stage Edwin evidently deliberately renamed Shahzadi as Mary Josephine Short, even though she had no blood connection to him, and despite the fact that this was exactly the same name as his real daughter by Malka Begum. While she lived as his mistress, Shahzadi had borne Alexander Speirs two daughters who survived and an elder daughter who died. But when their affair was over, Shahzadi decided to convert to Islam and married a Muslim, moving from Lucknow to Malihabad. Her eldest surviving daughter, Alice Mary Speirs, was thereafter brought up by Edwin and Amina Begum. Edwin evidently treated her as though she was his own granddaughter.

Doubtless, Edwin's original reason for re-naming Shahzadi as Mary Josephine was to ensure that she would be accepted as his daughter and could eventually inherit his wasika. He had previously made out a warisnama listing Malka Begum as his wife and Mary Josephine as his daughter. He hoped that Shahzadi could take over the role of his daughter without being challenged. However, when Shahzadi married a Muslim and converted to Islam, Edwin decided to disinherit her, but still kept up the pretence that she was his daughter, so that he could pass the wasika to his 'granddaughter' Alice Mary Speirs. When challenged by the Wasika Officer, Edwin made the following statement on oath:

As I am a Catholic I can't marry a second wife. I kept another woman Amina Begam a Mohamedan & she bore me a daughter Mary Josephine here who is at Malihabad... The latter girl is my illegitimate offspring. The wirasatnama filed by me in 1893 before Mr Radice contained the name of my daughter Mary Josephine who was living with me at that time. I wrote this letter...revoking & cancelling the wirasatnama filed by me in 1893. The reason of this was that my daughter Mary Josephine left my protection and turned a Mahomedan and married a Mohamedan at Malihabad where she went to live. I discarded and disowned her and hence cut her off from being my heir. Before her turning Mohamedan she lived with Alexander Spiers, pleader at Fyzabad as his mistress and Alice Mary was the offspring of this connection. She was not married to Mr A. Spiers but lived with him as his mistress. Mr. Spiers has been paying Rs 8/- p.m. to his daughter through the Alliance Bank Lucknow as pocket money to her. I have no other heir but my grand-daughter Alice Mary.

Edwin then turned to his real daughter, who was in court, and said of her:

Miss Mary Josephine Short is the daughter of Malka Begum & from whose seed I cannot say. I married her about 35 or 40 years ago, but she deserted me & there was a judicial separation between us under the orders of the then Judge Mr R. Scatt... Malika Begum had become a convert to Christianity; her Christian name of her daughter is not Mary Josephine but she has assumed a wrong name to pass herself off as my daughter.

Edwin used a similar ploy to that used by Isaac Short, in claiming that Mary Josephine was not from his seed, but he went on to state that she had assumed a wrong name to claim inheritance. In doing so, and by saying that Shahzadi was his daughter by Amina Begum, he was simply trying to invert the truth. His evidence was quickly dismissed though, as Margaret Snell was able to testify that Mary Josephine had been conceived in her house, and she and other witnesses confirmed that Shahzadi was six years old when Amina Begum became Edwin's mistress. Finally, he did admit that Mary Josephine was his daughter, but said he wished to disinherit her because she had turned to Islam and never cared for him. In fact, he achieved this intention in the end, by the simple expedient of making a will, leaving his wasika to Alice Mary Speirs. But in this case, he took care not to perjure himself, merely confirming that she was the daughter of his nephew Alec Speirs, and not trying to claim that she was his granddaughter.

Edwin lived in the Maqbara Amjad Ali Shah area of Lal Bagh until his death in March 1927 of heart failure, at the age of sixty-seven. He evidently bore great affection for his great-niece, as he not only left her his full wasika allowance of rupees forty-one per month, but he also asked her to arrange for masses to be said by the Roman Catholic Chaplain of St Joseph's Church for the benefit of his soul.[11]

6
WAHIDUNNISSA BEGUM'S STORY

THE ASTUTE READER MAY HAVE NOTICED THAT IN THE LAST CHAPTER I only covered the lives of Joseph Short's five sons by slave girls, completely omitting any reference to his three daughters, Emma, Georgiana and Isabella. The reason is quite simple—as their mothers had absconded with them to Calcutta when they were young, the three girls 'disappeared' without a trace and never returned to claim their share of wasika when Joseph Short died.

Joseph had actually disinherited these daughters because they had been taken away from his protection but the final decision of the Wasika Officer had been that they, along with Macdonald Short (who had also been disinherited) should receive equal shares in his wasika with his other eleven children. But as their whereabouts were not known, for over four years their wasika allowances were accrued, until the Wasika Officer agreed to share their allowances between the other twelve children, on receiving their assurance that such payments would be reimbursed if Emma, Georgiana or Isabella ever re-appeared.[1] Evidently none of the three girls ever returned to press their claims.

Quite by chance, though, I looked closely at a file relating to a claim for wasika made in July 1905 by a Muslim woman, Wahidunnissa Begum. The file revealed that she claimed to be the daughter of Emma Short, although she referred to her mother by the Muslim name Amir Begum. She said that Amir Begum had married Maulvi Syed Zain-ul-Abidin, a sub-Judge, at Benares in 1869 or 1870. She was one of the five daughters and four sons of Amir Begum and now lived in Aligarh, with her retired father. Her mother had died at Moradabad on 20 May 1886 and was buried there in Kasisahib Bagh. Wahidunnissa was now claiming her share of Emma's wasika, back-dated for the thirty-five years since Joseph Short had died.

However, her evidence, although strong, was not conclusive. She claimed (through her husband, Sayed Wali Hasan, a Mukhtar of the Aligarh Court) that Macdonald Short had visited them a few times in Agra and Moradabad. Macdonald Short, on his part, denied such visits, although he confirmed that he had 'met and talked to Maulvi Zain-ul-Abidin at Lucknow on two or three occasions and found that although the latter knew everything about the Short family he did not care to apply for the small wasika his wife Emma was entitled to'. Macdonald admitted though that he had been told that Maulvi Zain-ul-Abidin 'was married to one of my sisters. Her name was Emma Short. I do not know whether she was also called Amir Begam. I was not present at the marriage but I was told by my brother the late Martin Short that Emma Short was married to Maulvi Zain-ul-Abdin. When the mutiny took place we were very young & we all separated from each other. Emma never visited Lucknow after the mutiny. We never saw her after that'. Whilst Joseph Short's other children denied any knowledge of Emma Short's marriage or whereabouts, Edward Duhan (the son of Mary Duhan) admitted:

> It is not true that the whereabouts of Emma Short & her mother were not known at the time of Joseph Short's death. I heard that Emma was married to a Mahomedan in Govt Service.

And another witness, a resident of Aligarh, stated that he had been shown a portrait of Joseph Short, hanging in the drawing-room of Maulvi Zain-ul-Abidin.

On balance I felt it was quite likely that Wahidunnissa's claim was true, and it certainly seems to have worried the twenty-two heirs of Joseph Short who would have their wasikas reduced if the claim was accepted. Not surprisingly, they sent the Wasika Officer a torrent of petitions. Besides simply stating that they had never heard of Wahidunnissa, a common theme of these petitions related to the thirty-five years it had taken for the claim to be presented. The petitioners quoted Brown's Legal Maxims: 'The laws assist those who are vigilant, not those who sleep over their rights'. But they were also concerned that the Wasika Officer would make an arbitrary decision which would be costly to have reversed, so they correctly pointed out that such a challenge should be referred to the Civil Courts, as the 'duty of Government is simply to pay the money to the proper parties. Who those parties are, must, in case of dispute, be settled by the Civil Courts'. Their fears seemed unfounded as the Wasika Officer eventually ruled that the claim should be dismissed as 'not proven'.

However, I was not content to leave the case as it stood. My strong hunch was that Wahidunnissa had been telling the truth about her parentage, but had simply been unable to substantiate her story. So, on my next trip to India I decided that I must try to locate some descendents of Maulvi Zain-ul-Abidin to confirm my theory.

Naturally, my expectations of success in this quest were pretty low, as more than a hundred years had elapsed and the difficulty of tracing descendents in a country as large as India was great. All that I had when I started my search was a list of the names and occupations of Wahidunnissa's eight siblings and the fact that in 1905 she lived at 'Tarwala Bungalow, Aligarh'. Fortunately, some brilliant detective work by a friend gave me the name of a descendent still living in Aligarh, so the following day I caught the early morning train to Aligarh from Delhi. But I only had a name, without address or contact details, so it was still a tall order to find one person in a city of half a million!

However, I began to realise that I might even succeed when I took a rickshaw to Aligarh University and found myself travelling along 'Zain-ul-Abidin Road'. Clearly, the implication of this title was that the Maulvi had been a person of significance. The principal of the University soon confirmed that Syed Zain-ul-Abidin had been a very close friend of Sir Syed Ahmad Khan, the founder of the MAO College (Muslim Anglo-Oriental College), which later became Aligarh Muslim University. The two had met at Ghazipur, where Zain-ul-Abidin presided as sub-judge and where Sir Syed founded a Muslim school in 1863. Zain-ul-Abidin had moved to Aligarh on his retirement to aid his friend with the founding of the college. And it turned out that Wahidunnissa Begum's address, 'Tarwala Bungalow', was Zain-ul-Abidin's home in Aligarh. Unfortunately, the house was demolished many years ago, but soon any disappointment evaporated when a staff-member said that he could take me to meet a great-grandson of Zain-ul-Abidin.

So, within only three hours of arriving in Aligarh, I found myself knocking at the door of Nurul Abidin, the first of several descendants of Syed Zain-ul-Abidin whom I met on this research trip. Nurul and his cousin Ehtisham were both fascinated when I showed them Wahidunnissa's petition, and quickly confirmed that the statements she had made about her parentage and the names and occupations of her siblings were correct. However, they knew few details about their great-grandmother and could not say whether she was originally known as Emma Short, or was one of Joseph Short's daughters. Nurul, though, showed me two old photographs, one of a European man in Muslim garb, the other of a light-skinned Anglo-Indian woman in a sari. I am now glad that I took copies of these two old photos, even though he did not know who they were, merely that they were ancestors, thought to be brother and sister. It was only later in my tour, when I managed to contact another cousin and her mother, living in Bhopal that the final pieces of the jigsaw puzzle clicked into place—revealing that they are all my third-cousins.

At Bhopal I met Asma Mannan and her mother, a surviving granddaughter of Syed Zain-ul-Abidin. She recalled that her grandmother was called both Amir Begum and Emma Short. She also knew that Joseph Short was her grandmother's father. Now this memory alone is surely good enough to persuade any who may doubt that the connection is proved. But Asma's mother also had some very strong corroborating evidence, in the form of a small brass casket, with an inscription in Urdu carved around the sides. The casket contains just two photographs—one is a picture of her grandmother's grave, quite an elaborate one, with a lamp-post and cast-iron fencing around it—and the other is a picture of her grandmother, exactly the same photo shown to me by Nurul Abidin. And the main piece of corroborating evidence is the Urdu inscription around the casket, which states 'died and buried at Moradabad in 1886'— exactly as stated by Wahidunnissa in her petition.

Clearly, the photograph of the woman is Emma Short, but then who is the man? Now Nurul Abidin thought that they were brother and sister, but Emma definitely had no brothers. I am convinced that this photograph is of Joseph Short, partly because he is dressed exactly as he was always described—i.e. a European man who was in the habit of wearing Muslim clothing. Also, there is a clear family likeness between him and Emma Short. And finally, on studying this photograph, it is clear that it is not a direct photograph of a person, but a photograph of a portrait. And, as previously mentioned, a witness had confirmed seeing a portrait of Joseph Short in Zain-ul-Abidin's drawing-room. It seems that the original has disappeared, but fortunately someone took a photograph of the portrait, which has remained within the family.

Whilst I was delighted to have proved the connection between our families, the descendents of Syed Zain-ul-Abidin had more to offer. Apparently, Emma Short's mother, the slave-girl Muhboob Jan, was known in her old age as Bi Nanna. And shortly before her death in the 1920s, she had told her own vivid story about her escape from Lucknow during the mutiny to her great-grandson, Syed Badruddin, the son of one of Wahidunnissa's younger brothers, who later produced an article for the MAO College magazine. The following is a translation of the original Urdu text of 'Bi Nanna's tale', kindly carried out for me by Nurul Abidin's sister, Tayyaba Qidwai:

> Before I tell you the story of the trials and tribulations of Mutiny, as told by Bi Nanna (Madame Grandma), let me tell you something about Bi Nanna, as she is no more with us.
>
> Bi Nanna belonged to the prestigious family of the Nawabs of Awadh and lived in the grandiose Palaces of Lucknow. In this atmosphere of comfort and luxury, sorrow and suffering were alien to her. Her husband was the Waseeqahdaar (Pensioner) of a noble family of Lucknow. The upheavals of Mutiny, led to Bi Nanna leaving her home in Lucknow and landing at Mutya Burj (Earthen Turret) in Calcutta. Till the end of her life she sung praises of her beloved husband's love and faithfulness and also remembered Lucknow fondly.
>
> She loved her little grandchildren and would take an interest in the tiniest details of their lives. At night she would lie down under a huge thatched roof, hugging her little ones to her bosom and lovingly putting them to sleep. There were no lullabies or fairy tales, but she would narrate to them with moistened eyes, the decline of the Royal Family of Awadh, the calamity of the Mutiny and the tale of her own tragic travails.

I also had the chance to meet her. She welcomed me with open arms with her usual warmth and charm. She talked nineteen to the dozen and also told me about the tragedy of her life. This is what I am going to narrate to you now. I never did know her name. But the young and old all called her – Bi Nanna. She was of medium height, had a glowing fair complexion and a full set of teeth, belying a ripe old age of around 80 years. What exquisite manners and deportment! To me she was the personification of perfect Eastern Culture. Well versed in the etiquette and finery of Awadh Tehzeeb, her flawless chaste language was often interlaced with verses of exquisite Urdu poetry.

She was proficient in stitchery and craft. But her speciality was in the Art of Cooking. The delicacies and treats which she prepared in her kitchen were the most perfect that I have ever tasted. She was the most perfect woman of the East whom I have ever met. Now listen to Granny's tale in her own words:

Oh My son! What do you ask about the Mutiny! May God protect even the seventh enemy from the scourge of Mutiny. What can I say now—was it a storm? The death knoll for the Last Judgement? Or a striking infliction on us from the skies, which struck instantaneously and refused to go away?

Listen—one afternoon we were sitting after lunch in the room of Chattar Manzil, which faces the River Gomti, chatting with each other, when there was a loud cry of—'They are coming! They are coming!' These words were like arrows, which pierced the thin armour of sensibility, which was left in the ensuing confusion. With God's grace, an inspiration clicked in my mind and I started throwing all my expensive possessions in the artificial spring in the Palace. The rest I put on the steps and covered it with a rag, just like a cat trying to hide its excreta. Then I picked up my 9 month-old daughter and ran. One of my step sons-in-law, who was extremely emaciated and had swellings in his groin, lamented and pleaded with me to take him along. I readily agreed, saying that wherever I go you will come too. I held on to his finger and hid my little girl in the enormous folds of my long and flowing skirt and ran out. I had just stepped out when those damned mutineers reached us. I was terrified out of my wits. Holding on to my two handicapped wards, I got inside a small ante-room nearby and shut the wooden door. But our bad luck was moving much ahead of us. The ante-room had a window with glass louvers and those accursed mutineers, put their glittering sword blades through these teasing us, scaring us. Every time the tip of those blades passed close by, I would shudder and move right and then left, dodging it. The throat was so parched due to constant invocation of prayers, that I could hardly utter any words from the mouth. It was as if our very souls were hung on the hangman's noose! Finally, the attackers got tired of the exercise of threatening and frightening us and mercifully left. I waited for a few minutes for the air to clear and then emerged quietly muttering, 'Oh God, help us!'

Look at the turn of fate—the ladies who would always be covered and shrouded and who dared not even look at the sun directly; who had not even put their bare feet on the ground, were that day running hither and thither like the partridges whose nests had been destroyed. Their delicate feet were swollen and bleeding on the pebbled ground, their lips were cracked and peeling, their hearts trembled in fear—it was a terrible sight to see them in this plight. This blood-curdling scene was enough to stop the heart of many.

So I kept watching these scenes, tears trickling down my eyes and holding on to the two poor, weak souls in my care, walked the streets till I reached the Imambada of Hussainabad.

There seeing the rubies and emeralds studded in the canopies, I shuddered to think that within no time, these would be all looted. Then thinking that since these did belong to my family, I took a handful of the precious gems and put them carefully in the upper fold of my skirt and ran from there. Due to my anxiety and terror, my limbs were as heavy as lead.

Then there was another concern. My baby daughter was very fair complexioned and rosy cheeked and the mutineers had no hesitation in shooting their arrows at anyone with a fair complexion and blue eyes. So I was more concerned for her than me. Then I thought of a way out. I took the black soot from the back of an iron griddle, and blackened her face, wrapped her in the flowing folds of my skirt and hugged her to my chest. Two miles from Lucknow, there was an iron bridge on the River Gomti and I crossed that to enter a small village called Hyderabad. My baby's Nanny used to live in that village and I made my way to her house. But, upon seeing me the Nanny got extremely panicky, as my presence was a threat to her own safety. She begged me to leave, saying that since I was from the Royal Family, the mutineers would surely kill her if they found out that she had given shelter to me. But I begged her for her help at this terrible turn of events and even offered the jewels which I had 'stolen' as a bribe. Finally, she relented and showed some compassion by giving me and my baby some tattered clothes to cover our identities and gave us some dry bread to eat. I also thankfully got rid of my expensive clothes, which could have spelt the death of both me and my child. From here, fate took a strange turn.

I became the servant in the house of one who herself had served me. I would work in her house and stitched clothes to earn some money. The hand which would always lift to give, now spread out to receive. This is what befell me.

Now listen to what happened to my husband and other male members of my family. Since my husband was very fair and handsome, the mutineers thought that he was an Englishman. There were other 12 members of the family, who were also mistaken to be the Gora Sahibs (white men) and so all of them were tied with ropes and locked up. So I not only worked to feed myself and my baby, but I also took supplies to my family members in jail. Finally they were freed with the help of Kotwal (Mayor) Hassan Raza Khan, who told them that these people were from the family of Sultan Maryam Begum's brother, Mirza Yusuf Ali and that they should not be tortured. He said The Royal Family members followed an Islamic way of life and to punish them would not serve any objective. So after this plea, mercifully they were released. After this horrifying experience, they all changed their appearances. They grew long beards, wore flowing robes, with a long cap, had olive beads round their necks and would forever be reciting 'Ya Ali' as their fingers rapidly worked on the beads of the rosary in their hands. So in this way, they passed their time till Lucknow was freed. What else could the poor men do!

Mirza Burgis Qadr, who was on the throne, and his mother went to Nepal after the victory. There was a lot of rejoicing in Lucknow after the victory. The English flag was hoisted where the officers of the British Raj and the commoners gathered and the mutineers were pardoned. I also left Lucknow and via Banaras went to Mutya Burj to meet my relatives.

Oh what has become of the world! It has changed completely. Not only the earth but even the skies seem to have changed.'[3]

Besides being a very vivid recollection of events at the time of the mutiny, Bi Nanna's tale includes several details which support and some which seem to contradict the fact that she was Muhboob Jan, Joseph Short's slave-wife. Clearly she has named 'Sultan Maryam Begum's brother, Mirza Yusuf Ali' as her husband. Now in Wahidunnissa Begum's petition, she also refers to Joseph Short as having the Muslim alias of 'Sahib Mirza'—so there seems to be no doubt that Bi Nanna is referring to Joseph Short, particularly as the story she relates of his detention along with other members of his family matches Joseph Short's own story. The story also includes the fact that her husband was fair, like an Englishman—and of course Joseph was half English, half Armenian, so this can be taken as a supporting fact. In relating the story, Syed Zainuddeen has mentioned that Bi Nanna's husband was a Wasikadar of a noble family of Awadh—which is of course true of Joseph Short.

At the same time, there are elements of Bi Nanna's tale that cast some doubt on her origins as a slave-girl. From what she says, she appears to have been living a pampered life in the Chattar Manzil Palace at the time of the rebellion rather than a life of drudgery as a slave-girl. I think that this can simply be explained by the assumption that when Joseph Short took Muhboob Jan as his hurrum (slave-wife), he no longer treated her as a slave but gave her the respect and lifestyle that a wife deserves. Presumably, she had remained in the Chattar Manzil Palace rather than joining her husband in his luxurious houses in Golaganj because their relationship was waning by this time. And, although she doesn't mention deserting Joseph Short, she confirms having left Lucknow and moving to Calcutta. (Joseph Short stated that she took her two daughters and left his protection for Calcutta). Another mystery is that Bi Nanna mentions taking her nine month old daughter (Georgiana) with her but fails to mention her other daughter, Emma, who was aged about five at the time. However, one must recall that the story has been told second-hand, and was related by Bi Nanna about sixty years after the event. In my opinion, these elements of doubt are slight and outweighed by the other evidence supporting the fact that Bi Nanna must have been Joseph Short's slave-wife, Muhboob Jan.

And now, to conclude this chapter, I must reiterate my firm belief that Syed Zain-ul-Abidin had married Emma, the daughter of Joseph Short by his slave-wife, Muhboob Jan. And this means that Nurul Abidin, Ehtisham and Asma Mannan are my third cousins and are, of course, entitled to receive a share of Joseph Short's wasika. So, unlike my grandfather and his brothers, who fought Wahidunnissa's claim, I would encourage these third cousins to press their own claims. I offer my assistance to help them win their rightful share of this royal legacy.

7

The Duhan Family

James Duhan was the first member of the Duhan family to settle in Bengal. A trader from Ireland, he had come to India in 1792 and had settled in Kanpur in August 1806. At that time, Kanpur was rapidly developing from the insignificant village that it was four decades earlier. In 1765, the Company's army had caused the Mahratta army to take flight and then set up camp at Jajmau, a few miles from the village of Kanpur. This encampment became permanent in succeeding years because the treaty of Allahabad, which was signed by Lord Clive in the same year, required the Company's army to defend the Nawab of Awadh against the Mahrattas. For this purpose, Kanpur was strategically well-located.

The military camp at Kanpur gradually developed into a vast sprawling cantonment, stretching for seven miles along the banks of Ganges, with 6,600 troops stationed there by 1778. A large bazaar sprang up to cater to the needs of the sepoys. European traders from Calcutta also started setting up 'Europe shops' which sold European goods, brought up-river from Calcutta. All such traders had to obtain permits from the Company to settle up-country, and by 1804, nine European traders were listed at Kanpur.[1] James Duhan joined them two years later, probably having previously traded from Calcutta.

Now the military authorities had long been aware that drunkenness was a serious problem amongst European soldiers stationed in Cantonments. Indeed, almost eighty percent of deaths amongst soldiers

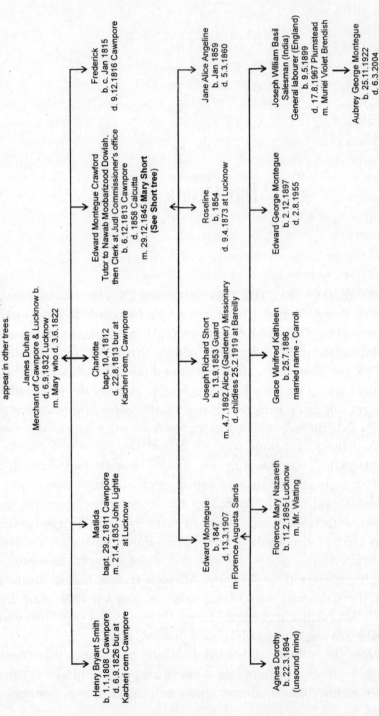

DUHAN FAMILY TREE

NOTE: Characters shown in bold type also appear in other trees.

James Duhan
Merchant of Cawnpore & Lucknow b.
d. 6.9.1832 Lucknow
m. Mary who d. 3.6.1822

Matilda
bapt. 29.2.1811 Cawnpore
m. 21.4.1835 John Lightle
at Lucknow

Henry Bryant Smith
b. 1.1.1808 Cawnpore
d. 6.9.1826 bur at
Kacheri cem Cawnpore

Charlotte
bapt. 10.4.1812
d. 22.8.1813 bur at
Kacheri cem, Cawnpore

Frederick
b. c. Jan 1815
d. 9.12.1816 Cawnpore

Edward Montegue Crawford
Tutor to Nawab Moobarizood Dowlah,
then Clerk at Judl Commissioner's office
b. 6.12.1813 Cawnpore
d. 1858 Calcutta
m. 29.12.1845 **Mary Short**
(See Short tree)

Edward Montegue
b. 1847
d. 13.3.1907
m Florence Augusta Sands

Joseph Richard Short
b. 13.9.1853 Guard
m. 4.7.1892 Alice (Gardener) Missionary
d. childless 25.2.1919 at Bareilly

Roseline
b. 1854
d. 9.4.1873 at Lucknow

Jane Alice Angeline
b. Jan 1859
d. 5.3.1860

Agnes Dorothy
b. 22.3.1894
(unsound mind)

Florence Mary Nazareth
b. 11.2.1895 Lucknow
m. Mr. Watting

Grace Winifred Kathleen
b. 25.7.1896
married name - Carroll

Edward George Montegue
b. 2.12.1897
d. 2.8.1955

Joseph William Basil
Salesman (India)
General labourer (England)
b. 9.5.1899
d. 17.8.1967 Plumstead
m. Muriel Violet Brendish

Aubrey George Montegue
b. 25.11.1922
d. 6.3.2004
m. 7.10.1942 Lyra Teresa Sullivan

were attributed to alchoholism. Accordingly, a law was passed in 1803 banning the sale of locally produced spirits, which, being cheap and highly intoxicating, were considered to be the chief cause of the menace. Under this law, only one merchant, granted licence as a sutler, could sell liquor in each cantonment area. In Kanpur, James Duhan soon became notorious for selling large quantities of 'Bengal Rum' to the soldiers in defiance of the ban on such sales by unauthorised merchants. Eventually, a suit was brought against him by Mr Hill, the sutler to the Cantonments, who paid a tax to Government of nine rupees a day for the privilege and was not going to take competition from unauthorised merchants lying down. Consequently, James was charged and summoned to appear before the Magistrate of Kanpur. In court, James acknowledged that he had been selling rum, but brazenly stated that it was pure Jamaica Rum and was therefore not subject to the ban, which only applied to local produce. However, the evidence against him was substantial. Firstly, he had been selling rum at four rupees a gallon, for which price he could not have purchased rum from Jamaica. Also, a number of witnesses came forward to testify that the rum was much harsher than Jamaica Rum; one witness (who evidently had considerable knowledge about rum) stated that:

> Jamaica Rum drinks mild and pleasant. It is not fiery and pungent like this, and according to the age is mild in proportion. I have bought it seven years of age and 2 days old, it is not high color'd and tastes of the cane. There is a fine oil in good Jamaican Rum. It sticks to the glass, running down the side of it, after pouring out a part of it.[2]

The magistrate, John Ryley, accordingly found James guilty as charged and levied a fine of 810 rupees. But when the Court Chupprassee came with the court order to collect the fine, James twice told him that he was too busy, asking him to return the following day. On the third day, when the Chupprassee again demanded the payment, he reported that 'Mr Duhan told me that he would neither pay the money nor accompany me to the Court, gave me abusive language, and assailed me with Brick Bats one of which struck me on the arm the mark of which is still apparent.'

James was evidently a volatile person, who was not easily intimidated by legal processes. But he realised that he had overstepped the mark on this occasion, sending the magistrate the following rather unconvincing excuse for his actions:

Sir,

I have to apologise for an error I committed yesterday and I hope when I candidly inform you that it was really a mistake that you will not be displeased but pardon it altogether.

On my return from Major Voyles sale I was much fatigued by exertion and I was scarcely seated when several Hircarrahs annoyed me with verbal messages for their Masters' purchases, I referred them all to the moonshy and desired them to go to Major Voyles Bungalow, and that he would deliver the Property— some were very troublesome and plagued me much. After they were gone the Pean of the Court came to me for an answer— as he termed it to his Master's Chit, and not recollecting the man and supposing that he wanted some purchases from the Auction Room I accordingly referred him to the moonshy who would do his business. The man would not go away altho' I repeatedly desired him to go to the moonshy and that he would deliver his master's purchase. I entirely mistook the man and did not know him, and as I was engaged with a Gentleman in conversation he annoyed me very much which caused me to lose temper desired the man to go about his business and to go to Hell. I did not discover the mistake until the Peon quit the Premises and as it was a mistake altogether I hope you will have the goodness to look over it.

Cawnpore—29th Augt 1812　　　　　　　I am, &ca (Signed)
　　　　　　　　　　　　　　　　　　J. Duhan.[3]

Predictably, the response from John Ryley confirmed that James' behaviour constituted resistance to the due process of the court, and he was told to consider himself 'under the Custody of this Court and upon no account to quit Cawnpore without permission previously obtained for that purpose from this Court'. But James had already sought legal advice (which informed him that the magistrate had exceeded his authority by levying such a fine on a European) and he wrote back questioning the jurisdiction of the Zila Court in the case, saying that although he would pay the money, it was to be held until the case had been tried by a higher court. In the same letter, he also cast doubt on the court process saying that two of the witnesses who had signed affidavits to the effect that the liquor he had sold was Bengal Rum now denied this and said that the evidence had been wrongly transcribed in Court.[3]

Needless to say, James' response did not endear himself to the magistrate, who promptly submitted all papers in the case to the government at Fort William, for consideration by the Governor General. However, John Ryley must have felt quite abashed when he received a reply stating that although the government had no doubt of the justness of his conclusions, 'Mr Duhan being a British Subject the Governor General in Council would have supposed that you must have been perfectly sensible that he was only amenable to the jurisdiction of the Supreme Court & that the powers & authority vested by the Regulations in the Zillah and City Judges did not in any manner extend to persons of that description'.

As a result, John Ryley was forced to repay the fine incorrectly imposed on James Duhan, although the government did ask him to inform James 'that should he again commit the offence of selling Spirituous Liquors in opposition to the rules established with respect to that point, his License for residing in the Interior of the Country will be withdrawn'. The Magistrate was also advised to 'report every occurrence of that nature which may hereafter take place on the part of Mr Duhan or any other British Subjects for the information and orders of Government' and naturally he took great care to do so, having effectively lost his initial legal dual with James.

The Magistrate, in turn, had also pointed out that many European shopkeepers of Kanpur had become extremely self-willed and tended to take no notice of the military or civil authorities. Clearly, James belonged to this independent group, and he must have felt that the local Magistrate was fairly powerless to act which is why he ignored the Magistrate's warning and continued supplying locally produced liquor to the troops. Then the Commanding Officer of HM's 67th Regiment wrote to James asking him not to 'sell any Wines or Liquors of any description to the Soldiers of the Regiment under his Command, their wives, or the Native women kept by them, without a written order countersigned by him'. To which James brazenly replied that he was 'not in the habit of disposing of Spirituous Liquors to Soldiers, to their wives, or Native Women kept by them, without a chit from an Officer requesting of me to do so. I declare to you that even on producing such a Document, I comply with much reluctance, because it would not be to my Interest, being so extensive in business as I am, to encourage such people to my House, and another reason, such sales are very trifling with me indeed. I always understood that a Captain or a Subaltern Officer had the priviledges of granting a deserving Man, occasionally, a Liquor Chit. However, as it is contrary to the Colonel's wish that a compliance be made, even in these cases, you will be pleased to inform him that unless a Chit be produced bearing his signature, I will not furnish the article required and to prevent my giving umbrage to any Gentleman I shall state that it is the Colonel's request'.[4] But of course James had no intention of actually complying with the Colonel's order!

It was not long, therefore, before he was again 'caught in the act' when the Bazaar Sergeant seized a half a gallon of spirits that had just been sold by James to a Captain in the 67th Regiment. In this case, James simply denied having supplied the liquor but he was trapped later when he sent the Officer a further half-gallon in compensation for the quantity seized and the officer reported this to the Bazaar Sergeant. On being charged, James managed to infuriate the Magistrate with his colourful counter-accusations, referring to the 'malicious intent on the part of the Bazar Serjeant, to injure me, from the cause of my having refused him Credit for the purchase of Goods, as a person universally known to be in the habit of Continual intoxication, as well as wanting in the principles of Honesty...'

But in submitting the case to the government for further orders, John Ryley somewhat defeated his own cause by pointing out that 'James Duhan is one of the principal European Shop Keepers at Cawnpoor that his concerns are I believe extensive, and that consequently his utter ruin (or at all events, a very considerable loss) would be the result of his License to reside in the interior being cancelled.'[5] Naturally, the government took due note of this warning and decided to let James off with a strong warning that if he transgressed again, his licence to remain at Kanpur would be withdrawn.

From James' point of view, though, it seemed that the government was only bluffing and that he could continue behaving in the same manner with impunity. But the final straw came only a few months later when he was accused of 'insolent and wantonly offensive behaviour' towards the Commanding Officer of the 53rd Regiment of Foot. When this incident was reported to the government, his licence to reside in Kanpur was revoked in January 1814 and he was instructed to report to Calcutta. But, in the same letter, James was given the breathing space he needed by being told that he could have three months to wind up his affairs at Kanpur. He replied as follows:

Sir,

I have the honour to acknowledge the receipt of your letter, dated the 14th of January, which reached me on the 3rd of the present month communicating the orders of His Excellency the Right Honourable the Governor General in Council. I beg leave Sir, most respectfully to assure you, that I will return to Calcutta at the expiration of the time to which my residence at this station has been limited, should I not be indulged with longer time.

I had the honour of addressing the Earl of Moira on the 15th and 28th of last month, and I trust the respectable testimonials which I enclosed of my character will induce his Lordship to extend my Residence at this station to the period of twenty months, to enable me to collect my outstanding Debts, which exceeds One Lack and a half of Rupees, Bills, Bonds, and Promissory Notes, exceeding 60,000 Rupees have been sent in to the General in Command of this Station, for collection, and altho' it is now nearly one month, yet not a single Rupee have I realized.

Lord Minto was graciously pleased to direct Circular letters to be written from the Adjutant General's Office to Commanding Officers, ordering them to afford me assistance in realizing my Debts; Seven months have nearly passed over and I have not received one Rupee.

Cawnpore　　　　　　　　　　　　I have &ca
February 10th 1814　　　　　　　　Signed/ J. Duhan[6]

In response to his petition, James was granted a further three months to collect his debts and close his shop. Evidently though, this time period too was insufficient to collect his dues, but nevertheless he returned to Calcutta as instructed. It appears that he was now in deep financial distress because on arrival at Calcutta he again urgently petitioned the Governor General, requesting a further year to collect the debts owed by Officers of the Company's army. Although he had been told that the previous three-month extension was the last that would be granted, the government relented on learning that James' wife Mary was heavily pregnant with their last child. So, in mid-December 1814 James was permitted to return to Kanpur for another year to wind up his business there. He was told that he would not be permitted to re-open a 'Europe Shop' in Kanpur under any circumstance, but on giving a pledge of future good behaviour, he could open a shop at Dinapore after the one-year period.

James reached Kanpur on 1 February 1815 and reported his arrival to the government who confirmed that his one-year period would start from that date. His wife, Mary, evidently gave birth to their fifth child, Frederick, only a few days after their arrival so one can only imagine that the long journey from Calcutta must have been quite hazardous for her at such a late stage of pregnancy. Their child, though, only survived for twenty months and was buried at Kanpur in December 1816.

It seems that James probably gained permission to extend his stay at Kanpur because he was evidently there when his son died, and a few days later he was writing to the government with the following request:

Cawnpore
17th Decr 1816

Sir,

I most respectfully beg leave to inform you that in consequence of there being no Europe shops at Lucknow, I have been written to by several English Gentlemen requesting that I would open a shop under the superintendence of an intelligent moonshy, and that it would be of great convenience to Gentlemen residing in that city. I further beg to state that, I have been supplying the Court of Lucknow with Europe Goods these eighteen years, during which time my conduct gave general satisfaction. I will feel much obliged by your obtaining me permission to establish a shop at Lucknow and to go over for a few days two or three times every year.

It is attended with great inconvenience and expense of breakage
sending articles over on hackerries to Lucknow to prevent which
I wish to transport my property on boats up the Goomty.
I hope you will excuse the trouble.
I have the honour to be

Sir

Your most obedt. Servt.
(signed) J. Duhan[7]

At this stage, though, the 'trail' left by James Duhan in official
correspondence runs cold presumably because he had learnt his lesson
that it is unwise to defy Government orders after he was forced to close
down his shop at Kanpur. It is not clear in fact whether he did actually
leave Kanpur, as successive Bengal Directories still show a listing for
'James Duhan, merchant & trader, Cawnpore' until 1824, when the entry
changes to 'James Duhan, Europe Shop keeper & Auctioneer, Cawnpore'.
From these entries (the fact that his wife Mary died at Kanpur in 1822
and that his eldest son died there in 1826), it is reasonable to suppose
that somehow he persuaded the authorities at Kanpur to allow him and
his family to remain there, and was eventually permitted to re-open a
'Europe Shop' there in about 1824. It also seems likely that he opened
the 'Europe Shop' at Lucknow, as it was there that he died in 1832 and
it was also at Lucknow that his son, Edward Duhan, married Mary Short
in 1830.

What is clear, though, is that James' fortune suffered a severe reversal
in the years up to his death—almost certainly due to losses sustained
from the forced closure of his shop, as predicted by the Collector of
Kanpur. In his will, written only two months before his death, he left
his 'houses and grounds at Cawnpore' together with his stock-in-trade
and outstanding debts to be divided equally between his 'lawful and well
beloved wife Elizabeth Duhan' and his only surviving son and daughter,
Edward Crawford and Matilda Duhan—with his furniture and plate being
divided just between Elizabeth and Matilda(evidently he had re-married
after the death of his first wife, Mary, in 1822.) However, his will was
clearly an over-optimistic document, as James had neglected to mention
two substantial loans. His widow shortly wrote to the Registrar of Deaths
at Calcutta:

Sir,

I beg leave to enclose the Will of my late Husband, which was once forwarded to you by Mr Middleton who was appointed an Executor to the Estate of the assets. I cannot give you any information whatever as the Accounts are in a very confused state his effects here were Seized by 'Sha Beharry Loll's' Ghomastas for a debt of upwards of 14,000 Rs. I have a list of the whole and am ready to forward it if desired.

Being fully aware of the Insolvency of his affairs I declined administering. Since his death I have not received a fraction of the outstanding Balances due him indeed we experienced great difficulty in preventing money sufficient to defray his funeral Expenses &ca &ca. Immediately after his death I took the necessary precaution to pack up the Books, Letters, Chits &ca &ca for the future disposal of which I must be guided by your advice. I would have sent the Will before but have been confined to my Room the last three months from severe indisposition. Mr Duhan being so much in debt we were left in a most distressed state so much so that Drs Campbell and Stevenson kindly undertook to raise a subscription for our benefit.

I am Sir,

Lucknow
January 29th 1833

Yours obediently,
Elizabeth Duhan.[8]

Robert Middleton, the other named Executor, also refused to administer James Duhan's estate and it was at this stage that a relative, William Duhan, successfully petitioned to administer the estate. William's petition refers to 'certain differences [that] existed between [James Duhan] and your Petitioner regarding some money transactions', which had been resolved in July 1822 by a bond requiring James to pay William Rs 17,769—11As within twelve months. James had apparently failed to repay the money and, including interest, slightly more was now owed to William who declared on oath that he was unlikely to receive more than Rs 5000 of this debt from the administration. Clearly, this indicated that James Duhan was insolvent at his death.

Unfortunately, the precise family relationship between James Duhan and William Duhan is unclear. The most likely explanation is that two branches of the family (which has an unusual surname) had settled at Kanpur, as other unidentified members appear in directories. James was undoubtedly the first member of the Duhan family to have settled in India, having arrived in 1792 from Ireland. The earliest directories show only James Duhan, as a 'merchant and trader at Cawnpore' but by 1824 the Bengal Directory also lists: 'Duhan, James jun, Assistant to Tulloh & Co' and 'Duhan, William, Assistant to Hamilton & Co.' Confusingly, James Duhan junior had also evidently opened a shop within the military cantonment at Kanpur, as he came to the attention of the government when he was sued in court for not paying bills submitted by two natives in August 1820. William Duhan (who obtained probate of James Duhan's estate) died at Kanpur in 1850, aged fifty-eight. He was probably a nephew of James, and possibly the son of a George Duhan who died at Lucknow in 1840.

Escaping now from the confusion over these Duhan family members, let us return to James Duhan's family—in particular to his surviving son, Edward Crawford Duhan. The reader will recall from Chapter 3 that Edward had moved to Lucknow where he was working as tutor to Nawab Moobarizood Dowlah at the time of his marriage to Mary Short. The harrowing tale of how Edward had remained at the Residency, fighting at Sago's Garrison, while his wife and children were trapped outside the Residency has already been told.

Widowed at the age of twenty-seven and with three young children to care for[9] after Edward's death, Mary had been supported by the relief fund at Calcutta until her return to Lucknow some time after June 1859. At Lucknow, she continued her fight to receive a widow's pension, but this was eventually refused in July 1860 because she was unable to prove that her husband's death was solely due to his exposure during the siege of the Residency.[10]

Before the mutiny, Mary Duhan had lived with her family in one of Joseph Short's two large houses in Golaganj. But these houses had been demolished by the British as part of the massive clearance operations once peace had been established, in order to render the city less vulnerable to further uprisings. It is reasonable to assume that when she returned to Lucknow in 1859 as a widow with three children and no means of support, that she must have turned again to her father for shelter. So I would presume that she lived with Joseph Short at Mohammed Khan's hatta until 1862, and remained with him in one of the houses that he subsequently bought in Kaisar Bagh.

However, Mary must have found it difficult to cope with her children as a widow (she never re-married—which was unusual in those days). When her younger son, Joseph, was sent to La Martiniere School in 1862, William Sangster is named as his guardian—implying that near-relatives were asked to assist her. Joseph was expelled from the school four years later, although the reason for his expulsion is not mentioned. Her elder son, Edward, had left the family home by 1872, when he was employed as an Accountant for the Awadh and Rohilkhand Railway at Bareilly. The following year, however, another tragedy occurred in the home, when Mary's only surviving daughter, Roseline, caught a fever which grew steadily worse until she died from it.

By now, Mary's father Joseph Short had been dead for three years, and Mary had become one of the most active campaigners to maximise the wasikas given to herself and her married sisters, Nelly Quieros, Ellen Johannes and Marcelina Bourbon—on the grounds that they were Joseph's only legitimate children. When this claim failed, and the Chief Commissioner ruled that all of Joseph's children should inherit equally, Mary next led the challenge to Amelia Short's claim to a widow's one-third share of the wasika. (Her leadership is shown by the fact that her name invariably precedes those of the other claimants, and also that she wrote confirming that correspondence should be addressed to her).[11]

Even after Amelia Short eventually (at massive personal cost) won her battle to receive a widow's one-third share of the wasika, Mary accepted this judgment only partially. Although she did not further contest the decision, she waited until Amelia herself died, and then immediately petitioned on behalf of herself, her sisters and half-siblings for a share in Amelia's one-third share. My great-grandfather led the defence against Mary's claim, pointing out quite correctly that the award to Amelia had been made in a Court of Law and was unconditional, not just a life-interest. Mary again lost this case, the decision being taken that only Amelia's children could inherit her wasika, in accordance with her warisnama.

Mary continued fighting for wasika rights well into her old age. At the age of sixty-five she again petitioned the Wasika Office on the death

Alex Speirs, the tobacco merchant

Mary Buchanan, wife of Alex Speirs

The Nagpur Residency

(possibly) Sultan Murium Begum

Nawab Ghazi-ud-din Haidar

Sadat Khan, the founder of the Awadh dynasty

A woman from the harem

Map of Lucknow (1857)

Murium Begum's tomb at Kaisar Pasand in Lucknow

Mrs. & Mr. **SHORT** present their compliments to

The Miss ....

and solicit the favor of _____ attendance at the ROMAN
CATHOLIC CHAPEL, Banks Road, Lucknow, on _Monday_
the _28th_ April at _10_ A. M., to witness the Nuptials of
THEIR DAUGHTERS

MISS RACHEL SHORT, ⎱ & ⎰ MISS MARSELINA SHORT,
TO ⎰   ⎱ TO
JOHN A. SPEIRS,   J. J. BOURBON.

and thence to their Residence, near Neil's Gate, to partake of
Cake and Wine.

N. B. _____ Company is also solicited to a Dinner Party
at 7-30 P. M. of the said day.

The Short Wedding Invitation

Begum Hazrat Mahal

A scene of the siege in Lucknow (1857)

The Residency in Lucknow after the siege

Joseph Short   Amir Begum or Emma Short

The brass casket belonging to Emma Short with inscription in Urdu: 'died and buried at Moradabad in 1886'

Syed Zain-ul-Abidin

Wredenhall Pogson

(left to right) Lawrence, Mac, Jean, John with Sleeman (1924)

Alexander Speirs

Sleeman & Alexander

Allahabad High School

The Moradabad Lawyers

Sleeman & Christie at their first home in Moradabad (1905)

An old photograph of Houston House

(left to right) Bill, John, Alec at Margate (1914)

Sleeman in England (1914)

Saharanpur Trial Lawyers

Silverwood, Musoorie

Sleeman at Fairlawns

Sleeman in old age with the author's
sister Valerie (1958)

Bill & Sleeman at
Alexander's Grave

William (sitting far left) at a garden party with daughters Mary and
Margaret sitting on the ground, right (1911)

(left to right) Bill, John, Alec (1913)

Jean & Lawrence

John & Lawrence

St Joseph's College and St Mary's Convent as viewed from Philander

Lawrence & his girlfriend

Alec (extreme left) and Bill (extreme right) with clergyman & son (centre)

Lawrence, John, Mac & Jean   Jean & Mac   Marjory

Motorbike outing c. 1907. On bike at left: Sleeman and Chris Speirs. On central bike: John and Catherine Gordon (dog on lap) with her sister Joan behind. On bike at right: Ernest and Florence Gordon, with daughter Joan. By kind permission of Gay Geugan & Shirley Fox

of Benjamin Joseph Short, her half-brother. Again, though, she lost the claim as half-siblings only had rights to succession in the absence of direct heirs or siblings of the deceased—which was not the case. Regrettably, all her actions must be taken to imply a continual feud between the Duhan and Speirs family, as otherwise she would surely have accepted her half-siblings' rights and not have continually taken legal proceedings against them. A pointer to such a feud is the fact that my father knew the names of all his father's cousins (Bourbon, Johannes, Mellor, Short, Sinclair) except the Duhan family. Presumably, this was because my grandfather did not wish to associate with those cousins. A sad state of affairs indeed!

Mary died at Lucknow in April 1904 at the stated age of eighty (her actual age was around seventy-three), of 'complicated diseases'—whatever that may mean! She was given a funeral with Roman Catholic rights by Father Lewis, the Rector of St Francis School. Sadly, considering the number of wasika battles that she had lost in her lifetime, even the bequest made in her will could not be complied with. She had brought up her niece, Annie Johannes, from childhood, and accordingly had willed that Annie should receive a third-share of her wasika along with her two sons. But, as previously explained, wasikas can only be passed to close relatives (such as a niece) in the absence of any direct heirs. The Wasika Officer therefore rejected the claim made by Annie La Frenais (her married name) and awarded the wasika just to Mary's sons, Edward and Joseph Duhan.

The Duhan family stayed on in India for a considerable period and I will here briefly mention their later history:

Mary's elder son, Edward Montegue continued working for the railways for the rest of his life, switching in about 1880 from accountancy to becoming a Supervisor in the Railway Postal Mail Service. In November 1890, he married Augusta Florence Sands at St Thomas Cathedral, Bombay. Over the next nine years, Augusta bore him three daughters (Agnes, Florence and Grace) and two sons (Edward George and Joseph William), before she herself succumbed to typhoid, dying at Bankipore in 1900 aged only thirty. Only seven years later, Edward Montegue followed his wife to the grave, dying of Bright's disease at Lucknow in March 1907. He evidently knew that he was dying, as his will was dated only nine days before his death. In his will, he appointed his brother Joseph Richard as the guardian of his two sons, and the Lady Superior of the Bankipore Convent (where they were studying) as the guardian of his three daughters. His wasika was provided exclusively for his eldest daughter Agnes, as she was stated to be of unsound mind.

Mary's younger son, Joseph Richard, was working as a guard when he married Alice

Gardener, a teacher of Lucknow, at Sitapur in 1892. But he later switched career, and is shown as 'Superintendent of the Maharajah's stables' at Bharatpur between 1900 and 1909, when he worked in a similar appointment for the Nawab of Rampur State. He seems, though, to have kept a house in Lucknow, as he wrote from 11 Mission Road, Lucknow in 1907. He died, childless at Bareilly on 25 February 1919 of chronic kidney failure. His wife, Alice inherited his wasika on his death, when she was living at 'Pandey Lodge, Bhim Tal'. She died at Lucknow on 25 March 1923, and her grave is still there in the Nishat Ganj cemetery.

Turning to Edward Montegue Duhan's children, I have already mentioned that his eldest daughter, Agnes, was said to be of unsound mind. She died some time in late 1935 or early 1936 and the wasika she had received was then distributed to her brothers and sisters. Florence Mary Nazareth, the second sister, was born at Lucknow in February 1895, and baptised at St Paul's church a month later. The only clue I have to her later life is that she had married a Mr Watling and was living at 116, Ripon Street, Calcutta in August 1940. Grace Winifred Kathleen, the next sister, was born at Bankipore in July 1896 and baptised at St Joseph's Convent there in November 1896. When Agnes died, Grace had married a Mr Carroll and was living at 7 Elliott Lane, Calcutta. She was obviously quite a feisty lady, and was certainly not prepared to put up with the endless bureaucratic delays and obstacles that the Wasika Office caused her before she finally received her entitlement, complaining to the Accountant General that 'It is to be regretted that a Government Department like the Wasika Office is permitted to depart from its traditions and give people who have dealings with them the amount of trouble which the Wasika Office has done. I have complied with every request of the Wasika Officer, but he has deliberately and obviously gone to the extremity of creating awkward situations, thereby delaying payment. This fact has even been remarked by the Bank...'

The first of Edward Montegue Duhan's sons, Edward George, was born on 2 December 1897. I know little about him, beyond the fact that he was living at Khagul Road, Dinapore in 1929 and at 'back of Railway Station, Vizagapatam' in 1934, which suggests that he worked for the railways. However, like his uncle, Joseph Richard Duhan, Edward George seems to have retained his connections with Lucknow, as he died there of dysentery in 1955, receiving a Roman Catholic burial by Father Clement. Confusingly, under 'Occupation' in his death certificate, is written: c/o Basil Duhan, Spectrum, Lall Bagh, Lucknow—again, though, reinforcing the likelihood that the Duhan family still lived and worked in Lucknow in 1955.

Edward Montegue Duhan's last child, Joseph William Basil Duhan was born in May 1899. He married Muriel Violet Brendish and was working as a salesman at Agra when their only son, Aubrey George Duhan was born in 1922. In 1933, however, he was working for the East Indian Railway at Gaya, living at 42 Hindley Road. Clearly, though, he retained some connection with Lucknow in 1955 (see address given in the last paragraph). He died at Plumstead, England in 1967.[12]

Finally, to confirm the Duhan family's long residence in Lucknow, I must point to an entry in the St Francis School registers, showing that Aubrey George Duhan had sent his eldest son, Keith, to Kindergarten class there in 1948/49. Starting with Edward Crawford's marriage at Lucknow in 1830, the records suggest that the Duhan family lived in this historic city for at least one hundred and twenty eight years.

8

THE QUEIROS FAMILY

THE SPANISH FAMILY OF QUEIROS (ALSO SPELLED AS QUIEROS OR QUIROS) occupies a prominent place amongst the mixed-race families that settled in Lucknow during the Nawabi period. Having arrived at Lucknow in 1787, the family remained there both throughout the insurrection of 1857 (when three members received awards for their assistance in the defence of the Residency) and well beyond independence—two members were still living there in 1988.

Joseph Queiros was the first member of the Queiros family to set foot in India. Born in 1760, he was a descendent of a Spanish noble family who trace their ancestry to Spain in the ninth century. He was the son of a Commodore of the Spanish Royal Navy, his full title being 'Don Joseph Chamois de Queiros'. He had travelled to India as a young man and subsequently settled in Calcutta, where in 1784 he set up a business as an auctioneer, dealing mainly in property and paintings. Several advertisements of the period show that his business started thriving within a year or two. Even in 1784, when his business was still in its infancy, Joseph Quieros 'proposed a raffle of old masters—first prize being 19 pictures worth £500'.[1]

He not only auctioned houses for others, but also bought several properties in Calcutta. In 1784, he bought an upper-roomed house in Calcutta for Rs 50,000 along with two partners, and they subsequently mortgaged that property to 'The Bengal Insurance Company'. He also formed a co-partnership with a capital of Rs 70,000 with Joseph Bernard Smith and Anthony Lambert. But when Smith wanted to return to England in February 1786, the partnership was dissolved by mortgaging a house to Lambert for Rs 5 only, in lieu of a bond to pay the latter Rs 35,000 with interest at twelve percent.[1A]

It was around this time, in October 1786, that Claude Martin came to stay in Calcutta for a period of about six months. Claude Martin was an enterprising Frenchman from Lyons who had joined the French East India Company as a common soldier, fighting under the unpopular Lally against the British who were laying siege to Pondicherry in 1760. Martin had, along with many other disenchanted French soldiers, deserted to join the Honorable Company's army when the tide turned against the French. Initially, he had enrolled as an Ensign and helped to set up a 'Free French Company' whose main purpose was to round up deserters from the French army. Martin progressed rapidly, later becoming a surveyor, and assisting in the survey of Awadh. This led him to establish his residence in Lucknow. He started exerting considerable influence there when he befriended the Nawab Vizier, Asaf-ud-Dowlah and the British Resident, John Bristow. Shortly after, when Asaf-ud-Dowlah ascended the masnud (throne) in 1775, Martin was appointed Superintendent of the Vizier's arsenal, whilst retaining his army rank as Captain. In the intervening years, he amassed a large fortune mainly on account of his connections with the Nawab.[2]

The chief motive of his extended trip to Calcutta was to gain an introduction to the new Governor General, Lord Cornwallis (Claude Martin was renowned for getting considerable benefit from his connections with people in power). During his stay, Martin met Joseph Queiros and persuaded him to join him in Lucknow as his 'man of affairs'. In fact, it seems highly probable that Claude Martin had met Joseph Quieros previously too. One of the ways in which Martin had impressed Nawab Asaf-ud-Dowlah was by conducting several experiments with hot-air balloons. An article in the *Calcutta Gazette* dated 15 August 1785 refers to a 'plan and drawing of the improved balloon which is hung up for inspection at the house of Mr Joseph Quieros'.[3] The ownership of this plan surely implies that Joseph Queiros knew the man who was conducting the experiments.

Soon, Joseph Queiros wound up his auction business at Calcutta and moved to Lucknow to work for Claude Martin some time in 1787.

Initially, though, Joseph stayed at Benares for a few months. Joseph's primary responsibility was to act as a steward for the estate at Najafgarh (near Kanpur) that Martin had bought the previous year, and which was being developed into an indigo farm. It seems that Martin wished to exploit the business acumen that Joseph had demonstrated by building up a thriving auction business in a relatively short time. So, only two years after employing him at Najafgarh, Martin suggested that Joseph should join him as a partner (along with another friend, Benoit de Boigne) in a Company trading in 'piece goods'—lengths of cloth made in factories in Northern Awadh. Each of the partners was to contribute a lakh of rupees to the partnership, Claude Martin loaning Joseph Queiros his share.[4]

Predictably, whilst Martin and his friend de Boigne assumed a passive role in this business venture, it was Joseph Queiros who was sent out to the aurangs at Tanda, near the Himalayan foothills, to distribute advance funds for cloth manufacture as well as to check the quality of the finished goods. Aurangs were the Indian factories where weavers would contract through a middle-man (or gomasta) to supply a certain amount and quality of cloth on payment of an advance to cover their sustenance. Claude Martin does not seem to have wholly trusted his steward in this venture, sending him further instructions only a week after he had left, spelling out the problems of advancing money through the gomastas early on. This could lead to an excessive price being paid, as competitive bidding later in the harvesting season brought prices down. The other problem that Martin went to great lengths to outline was the possibility of receiving inferior goods, which could be avoided by ensuring that the cloths were marked and that agreements were made specifying the exact quality required.

Martin was probably apprehensive because Joseph Queiros did not have any prior experience in the textiles business. But he seems to have made little allowance for the fact that Joseph Queiros stood to lose his own stake in the business as well. It is not clear how profitable this business was, as seasonal prices fluctuated considerably. However, Martin and Queiros seem to have persevered (probably having bought out de Boigne's share in the business when he returned to Europe) right until Martin's death in 1800.[4]

The two men evidently became quite friendly, to the extent that Claude Martin became the godparent to one of Joseph's children, Claude

QUIEROS FAMILY TREE

NOTE: Characters shown in bold type also appear in other trees.

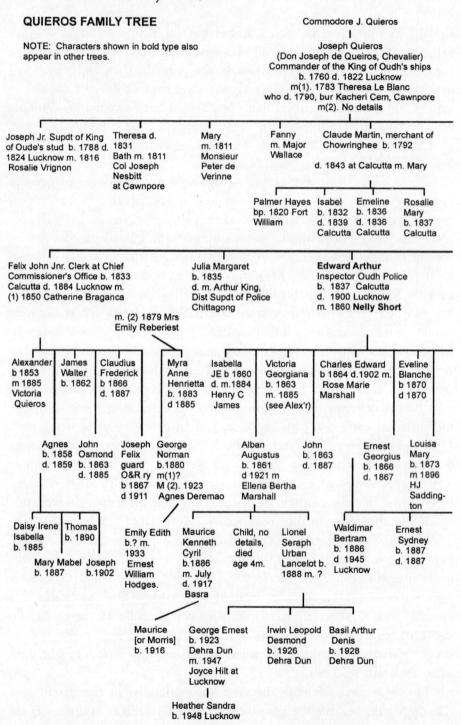

Commodore J. Quieros

Joseph Quieros
(Don Joseph de Queiros, Chevalier)
Commander of the King of Oudh's ships
b. 1760 d. 1822 Lucknow
m(1). 1783 Theresa Le Blanc
who d. 1790, bur Kacheri Cem, Cawnpore
m(2). No details

Joseph Jr. Supdt of King of Oude's stud b. 1788 d. 1824 Lucknow m. 1816 Rosalie Vrignon

Theresa d. 1831 Bath m. 1811 Col Joseph Nesbitt at Cawnpore

Mary m. 1811 Monsieur Peter de Verinne

Fanny m. Major Wallace

Claude Martin, merchant of Chowringhee b. 1792

d. 1843 at Calcutta m. Mary

Palmer Hayes bp. 1820 Fort William

Isabel b. 1832 d. 1839 Calcutta

Emeline b. 1836 d. 1836 Calcutta

Rosalie Mary b. 1837 Calcutta

Felix John Jnr. Clerk at Chief Commissioner's Office b. 1833 Calcutta d. 1884 Lucknow m. (1) 1850 Catherine Braganca

Julia Margaret b. 1835 d. m. Arthur King, Dist Supdt of Police Chittagong

Edward Arthur Inspector Oudh Police b. 1837 Calcutta d. 1900 Lucknow m. 1860 **Nelly Short**

m. (2) 1879 Mrs Emily Reberiest

Alexander b 1853 m 1885 Victoria Quieros

James Walter b. 1862

Claudius Frederick b 1866 d. 1887

Myra Anne Henrietta b. 1883 d 1885

Isabella JE b 1860 d. m.1884 Henry C James

Victoria Georgiana b. 1863 m. 1885 (see Alex'r)

Charles Edward b 1864 d.1902 m. Rose Marie Marshall

Eveline Blanche b 1870 d 1870

Agnes b. 1858 d. 1859

John Osmond b. 1863 d. 1885

Joseph Felix guard O&R ry b 1867 d 1911

George Norman b.1880 m(1)? M (2). 1923 Agnes Deremao

Alban Augustus b. 1861 d 1921 m Ellena Bertha Marshall

John b. 1863 d. 1887

Ernest Georgius b. 1866 d. 1867

Louisa Mary b. 1873 m 1896 HJ Saddington

Daisy Irene Isabella b. 1885

Thomas b. 1890

Emily Edith b.? m. 1933 Ernest William Hodges.

Maurice Kenneth Cyril b.1886 m. July d. 1917 Basra

Child, no details, died age 4m.

Lionel Seraph Urban Lancelot b. 1888 m. ?

Waldimar Bertram b. 1886 d 1945 Lucknow

Ernest Sydney b. 1887 d. 1887

Mary Mabel b. 1887

Joseph b.1902

Maurice [or Morris] b. 1916

George Ernest b. 1923 Dehra Dun m. 1947 Joyce Hilt at Lucknow

Irwin Leopold Desmond b. 1926 Dehra Dun

Basil Arthur Denis b. 1928 Dehra Dun

Heather Sandra b. 1948 Lucknow

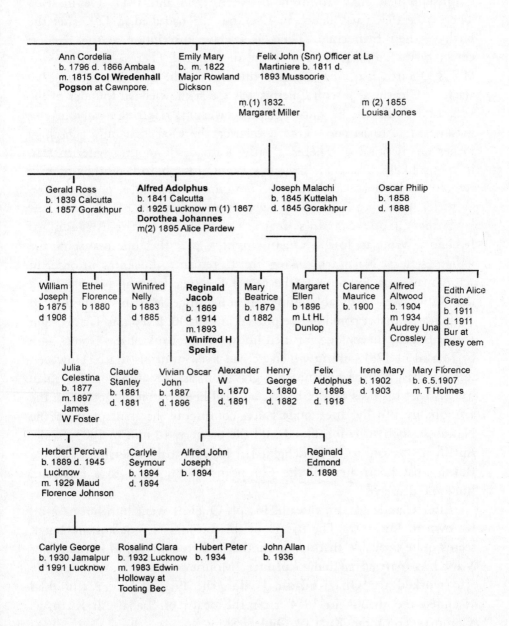

Ann Cordelia
b. 1796 d. 1866 Ambala
m. 1815 **Col Wredenhall**
Pogson at Cawnpore.

Emily Mary
b. m. 1822
Major Rowland
Dickson

Felix John (Snr) Officer at La
Martiniere b. 1811 d.
1893 Mussoorie

m.(1) 1832.
Margaret Miller

m (2) 1855
Louisa Jones

Gerald Ross
b. 1839 Calcutta
d. 1857 Gorakhpur

Alfred Adolphus
b. 1841 Calcutta
d. 1925 Lucknow m (1) 1867
Dorothea Johannes
m(2) 1895 Alice Pardew

Joseph Malachi
b. 1845 Kuttelah
d. 1845 Gorakhpur

Oscar Philip
b. 1858
d. 1888

William
Joseph
b 1875
d 1908

Ethel
Florence
b 1880

Winifred
Nelly
b 1883
d 1885

Reginald
Jacob
b. 1869
d 1914
m.1893
Winifred H
Speirs

Mary
Beatrice
b. 1879
d 1882

Margaret
Ellen
b 1896
m Lt HL
Dunlop

Clarence
Maurice
b. 1900

Alfred
Altwood
b. 1904
m 1934
Audrey Una
Crossley

Edith Alice
Grace
b. 1911
d. 1911
Bur at
Resy cem

Julia
Celestina
b. 1877
m.1897
James
W Foster

Claude
Stanley
b. 1881
d. 1881

Vivian Oscar
John
b. 1887
d. 1896

Alexander
W
b. 1870
d. 1891

Henry
George
b. 1880
d. 1882

Felix
Adolphus
b. 1898
d. 1918

Irene Mary
b. 1902
d. 1903

Mary Florence
b. 6.5.1907
m. T Holmes

Herbert Percival
b. 1889 d. 1945
Lucknow
m. 1929 Maud
Florence Johnson

Carlyle
Seymour
b. 1894
d. 1894

Alfred John
Joseph
b. 1894

Reginald
Edmond
b. 1898

Carlyle George
b. 1930 Jamalpur
d 1991 Lucknow

Rosalind Clara
b. 1932 Lucknow
m. 1983 Edwin
Holloway at
Tooting Bec

Hubert Peter
b. 1934

John Allan
b. 1936

Martin Queiros. Joseph was also named as an Executor and Administrator to Claude Martin's will—again indicating a bond between the two men unlike the usual relationship shared between employer and employee.

Joseph had eight children, between 1788 and 1811. He married Theresa Le Blanc at Calcutta in 1783, but she had died in 1790 after the birth of their fifth child. There is a grave inscription at the Kacheri cemetery in Kanpur, ' Sacred to the memory of Theresa Queiros, wife of Jos Queiros Esq who departed this life on the 17th December 1790 aged...'[5] Clearly, as Joseph Queiros was the acknowledged founder of the dynasty in India, the likelihood of this gravestone referring to anyone else is too remote to be considered. However, the Queiros family genealogy makes no mention of Theresa's early death or of another wife. In fact, it seems likely that after Theresa's death, Joseph had another partner (whom he did not marry) and who bore him his last three children, Ann Cordelia, Emily and Felix John who were illegitimate.[6]

After Claude Martin's death, Colonel Scott, the Resident of Lucknow, wrote to Joseph Queiros (who was at the time managing the indigo estate at Najafgarh) asking him to return to Lucknow in order to act as managing Executor to the General's estate.[7] Joseph complied and the duties were probably quite onerous since Martin's will was so complicated that it could not be proved until 1840. Joseph, in fact, bought Farhat Buksh, the unique fortified house on the bank of the Gomti built by Martin in 1781, and in which he had lived until his death. However, this purchase caused him much aggravation, as Nawab Saadat Ali Khan had also set his eyes on the house, but had been outbid by Joseph in the auction. Eventually, after undergoing continuous harassment from the Nawab, Joseph succumbed and sold the property to him in 1803. Saadat Ali Khan was said to be so delighted at his eventual ownership of Farhat Buksh, that he treated all the Europeans in Lucknow to a feast and firework display.[8]

After Claude Martin's death, Joseph Queiros went into business on his own in Lucknow. The nature of this business is not known, but it seems quite probable that it was another indigo concern, as his daughter Mary had married an indigo planter (Monsieur Peter de Verinne). He also worked for Ghazi-ud-din-Hyder, the Nawab Vizier who had ascended the throne in 1814, after the death of Saadat Ali Khan, as 'Commander of the King of Oude's Ships'.[9]

Although Joseph Queiros had become wealthy on account of his business ventures, by the time of his death in January 1822 the tide of fortune had turned sharply against him and he was declared insolvent, to the extent that he owed twenty-seven lakhs of rupees.[10] It appears that most of this debt had accumulated from loans taken out at an extortionate interest rate with native bankers who had refused to settle with him for anything less than the full sum owed. Now Joseph had managed to separately accumulate one lakh and thirty thousand rupees, which he wished to leave as an inheritance for his children. But clearly, if he had simply left this sum to his children by will, they would have received nothing as his creditors had first claim on his estate. So, 'he placed it in the hands of the late King of Oude and requested his late Majesty to grant it as a donation from himself, in order to prevent it being claimed by his (the late Mr Queiros Senior's) creditors; for, being deeply insolvent he knew that he could not make a Will. He, therefore, requested his late Majesty to affix his signature to a Document called the Hookam-Namah—so as to render it ostensibly a donation or grant from the King, while it was in reality the late Mr Queiros' last Will'.[10]

King Ghazi-ud-din Hyder had readily agreed to the proposal and signed a Royal Furmaun on 29 December 1821 (only nine days before Joseph Queiros' death) granting the 130,000 rupees to Joseph Queiros' children. But almost immediately after his death, three of his children became engaged in a bitter, acrimonious feud over the precise distribution of the money. The dispute occurred over whether or not Joseph Queiros had produced the Hookum-Namah to be signed by the King, stating his intentions for the exact distribution of the money.

Joseph's daughter Theresa was married to Captain Nesbitt, and she swore that her father had dictated a will to her, under which she and her husband were to be his Executors and their children were to receive Rs 50,000. She said that her father wanted to wait for Captain Nesbitt before signing the document—but had died before the latter's arrival at Lucknow a few days later.

Another daughter, Ann Cordelia, was married to Captain Wredenhall Pogson, and the couple claimed that they had seen the will (as dictated to Theresa Nesbitt) and that they were to receive Rs 30,000 under its provisions, with a further Rs 20,000 being provided for Ann's sister Emily and a similar sum for her young brother, Felix John. Wredenhall Pogson confirmed that this document (written in Persian) had been passed to the Acting Resident of Lucknow, Major Raper, for transmission to the King of Awadh one week after Joseph Queiros' death. Major Raper did not at first take any action over the Persian document, as he realised it had not been signed or witnessed. But later, on being pressed by Captain Pogson, he informed the government that he had submitted the 'will' to King Ghazi-ud-din Hyder.[11]

The reader can probably imagine the jealousies caused by Joseph Queiros' 'will', with Rs 70,000 being provided for three illegitimate children and Rs 50,000 for a legitimate daughter – leaving only Rs 10,000 to be shared by his four other legitimate children. Joseph Queiros' eldest son, Joseph (junior), evidently took great exception to it. As a result, he placed seals over his late father's documents and produced his own proposal for the division of the bequest, under which each of the children were to receive 15,000 rupees and all grand-children 2000 rupees. Joseph (junior) said that he had produced this document in the absence of any valid will made by his father. Strictly, of course, he was correct, as a will is not valid unless signed by the Testator and witnessed. But, as Captain Nesbitt pointed out,

> Understanding by good authority from Calcutta, that the Will I delivered to you of the late Mr Queiros is good in either the English or Mahomedan Law, provided the Writer of it can make oath that it was dictated by the Testator, or bring any witness of his being employed to make his Will, I beg leave to inform you that Mrs Nesbitt can declare on Oath that this Will was dictated by her Father, and that she can bring a confidential Servant of her Father to prove that she was so employed by him to write it.[12]

From the correspondence, it seems that Ghazi-ud-din Hyder preferred a more equitable distribution, so he decided to adopt a compromise along the lines proposed by Joseph Queiros (junior). This compromise was soon accepted by all of the family, except Wredenhall and Ann Pogson. They still held out for the distribution given in the dictated will, but found themselves isolated as, with the disappearance of that document, they had no means of substantiating their claim. They also complained bitterly to the Resident that Joseph Queiros (junior) had effectively forced Ann Pogson's mother out of a house known as Mahl

Serai and had appropriated the title deeds to that and another property. In her letter, Ann Pogson added that 'Mr Queiros' people have apprised her that he intends selling both her houses—both these houses being bought for her and in her name, by my late father. There is abundant proof, both written and verbal, notwithstanding Mr Queiros has taken forcible possession of the papers of the deceased. I therefore entreat, that you will have the goodness to mention the Subject to the King, soliciting that her claim to these houses may be taken into His M's consideration.'[13]

Although Joseph (junior) assured the Resident that he had only taken charge of the Mahl Serai 'until the proprietary right to it shall be regularly established', he certainly seems to have acted highly vindictively towards his step-mother. It is not clear whether Ann Pogson's mother managed to re-claim her houses. However, Joseph (junior) definitely won the dispute over the distribution of bequests, although he evidently did recognise that his father had dictated the will, but as he considered that his father had not 'done it according to my conceptions of the Law' he felt justified in producing his own distribution of bequests. However, this distribution itself strongly suggests that Joseph (senior) actually favoured his unmarried partner and his illegitimate children over his legitimate ones. The distribution also shows that Felix Queiros, his illegitimate final son, already possessed a house valued at Rs 10,000 unlike any of his other children. (In his distribution, Joseph (junior) makes allowance for the value of this house as part of the bequest to him).

There are also sound reasons for assuming that Ann and Wredenhall Pogson were telling the truth. Firstly, the latter was still campaigning for reimbursement of ten years after Joseph Queiros' death (not the action of someone who has made up a story to gain a quick profit). Secondly, Wredenhall Pogson confirmed that 'when the late Mr Queiros Senior's papers were examined after his death, your Memorialist saw the original Hookm Namah with a X affixed to it—similar to that which was his late Majesty's sign Manual—and your Memorialist has every reason to believe it to have been actually and truly signed by the late King'.[14] But the new King of Awadh, Nasir-ud-din Hyder, was not prepared to repay his father's debt. Nor, when Wredenhall Pogson explained that a dowry of Rs 10,000 sent by Ghazi-ud-din Hyder as a wedding present for Ann Pogson had never been received by her, but had been taken by her father, was he prepared to send the couple a similar sum. However, on being presented by Wredenhall Pogson with a copy of his book *The Economy of Human Life*, Nasir-ud-din Hyder gave him a Khillut of shawls, worth approximately Rs 1,000. Now, officers in the Company's service were normally strictly prohibited from keeping any Khilluts given to them at Native Courts (Khilluts would be handed to the British Resident, who sold them and credited the proceeds to the Company's account). But, as this Khillut had been presented as a means of encouraging literature, Captain Pogson was allowed to keep the present as an exception.[15]

The Pogson family has quite an interesting history, so I will here divert the reader's attention to Wredenhall Pogson and his family. Wredenhall came from an English family that had settled on the Caribbean Island of St Christopher (commonly known as St Kitts). St Kitts was under British and French occupation since 1624. The main produce of the island was sugar, which in those days was grown on large plantations employing bonded labour. The Pogson family had settled there after the arrival of Wredenhall's ancestor, Captain John Pogson, in 1677. He had been a Lieutenant in Charles II's independent army, probably fighting for the future king in the third English Civil war of 1651. After the restoration in 1660, when Charles II was eventually proclaimed king, he repaid similar acts of loyalty by granting large tracts of land in the new colonies, and in this manner Captain John Pogson was granted two hundred acres on the island of St Kitts in 1677.[16] His son, another John Pogson had turned a farmer, the tenant of a Mr William Freeman, on Dieppe Bay Estate, the most Northerly area of St Kitts.

One day in September 1706, John Pogson II was invited to dinner by Mr Kimberson. Also present at the dinner was John Johnson, the Lieutenant Governor of the nearby island of Nevis. During the meal there was an angry exchange of words between Pogson and Johnson, who had become rivals after William Freeman had been dispossessed of an estate by the Governor, Christopher Codrington.

Freeman had felt badly treated by Codrington, and John Pogson had taken his landlord's side. In April 1704 this animosity was further fuelled when Johnson was tricked into passing illegal legislation on St Christopher and was wrongly accused, by Pogson, of accepting a bribe to do the same. Johnson, on discovering the lie, had removed Pogson from the Council of St Christopher. Pogson felt he had been wronged and sought revenge.

According to contemporary trial accounts, as Johnson left dinner at Kimberson's, John Pogson followed him out. Riding home, Johnson stopped to tie his breeches and was caught by Pogson, who drew a pistol and shot him. According to Col Richard Payne, who witnessed the event, Johnson said, 'I am barbarously murdered', dismounted his horse and lay down on his back. Payne was sure that there had not been a duel and, in his statement, confirmed this by saying that Johnson was unarmed.

By 2 October 1706, Pogson had been captured and was in Fort Charles in St Christopher, awaiting trial. By the end of October, Pogson was free, having been unanimously acquitted of murder by a jury of his fellow islanders, leaving even the new Governor, Parke, (who was known to be highly biased against both Johnson and Codrington) to complain of an unfair trial:

...had not my instructions tyed me up to the contrary, I would have turned out all the twelve justices.

In November, Pogson's wife Sarah petitioned the Council of St Christopher on behalf of her husband, who had fled to England after Parke had threatened to charge him on a lesser account of stabbing Johnson. However, by 1707, he had returned to Nevis and was triumphantly elected to the Assembly of St Christopher after Queen Anne had ordered him turned out of the Office of the Council.[17]

Wredenhall Robert Pogson (who has been previously mentioned in this chapter) was the great-great grandson of John Pogson II. His father, Bedingfield Pogson, was born in St Kitts and possessed land there, but he had settled in England and evidently became prosperous, having estates at Sutton in Surrey, Daunsal Hall in Essex and at Lavenham in Suffolk. He married Elizabeth Philadelphia Pearce Hall. Wredenhall Robert was their fourth son, born at the family home in Sutton in 1787. Wredenhall had been admitted to the Honorable Company's army as a cadet in 1803, and after training in England, had travelled to India as an Ensign in the Bengal army in 1805 (coincidentally, the author's great-great grandfather Alexander Speirs had applied to the Company and arrived in India during the same year).

Wredenhall was appointed to the 24th Regiment of Native Infantry (subsequently renamed as the 47th NI) which he served for almost his entire military career. He married Ann Cordelia Queiros at Kanpur in

March 1815, when he was a Lieutenant. The couple stayed at Lucknow for some time, as it is clear that they lived with the Queiros family in Lucknow at the time of the dispute over Joseph Queiros' estate. Shortly after their marriage, Wredenhall had been promoted as Interpreter and Quarter Master for the Regiment. A letter from his grandmother congratulating him on the forthcoming appointment still survives. [19]

It is not, however, for his military career that Wredenhall Pogson is chiefly remembered but more for his literary pursuits. He seems to have acquired sufficient fluency in Persian to undertake the translation of at least two books—a *History of Jounpoor*, and a strangely titled book *The Economy of Human Life* (a copy of which he presented to King Nazir-ud-din Hyder of Awadh). He also later penned *The History of the Boondelas* in 1824—a work which has often been quoted by historians. His literary leanings are probably best summed up by the statement, 'He was a man of learning, and author of some rather eccentric writings'.[20]

Like so many other British officers in the Honourable Company's service, Wredenhall suffered heavily when the failure of Palmer and Company in 1830 precipitated the collapse of several Calcutta banking houses. During this time, he had been helping his younger sister Henrietta who was in the process of suing her husband, Sir John Miles Winnington, for divorce on the grounds of adultery. But, by June 1833 Wredenhall's personal losses meant that he could no longer support his sister's legal proceedings.[21] Wredenhall lived on for another ten years, dying as Lieutenant Colonel of his Regiment at Benares in August 1843. His burial place is somewhat unusual—he is buried in a mango tope on the parade ground at Benares. Apparently, his dying wish was that he should be buried within the sound of his Regiment's bugles. And this wish seems to have been satisfied, as the mango tope was later selected by the bandmaster as a suitable spot for buglers to practice.[22]

Wredenhall and Ann Pogson had twelve children, including eight sons, of whom three sons and a daughter died young. He also had two illegitimate children, a son born before his marriage, and a daughter born in 1820—although in neither case is the name of the mother recorded. Three of Wredenhall's sons followed him into military service, two serving in his own Regiment (the 47th Native Infantry). Both of them, Wredenhall Queiros Pogson and John Frederick Pogson, saw active service in the actions against the Sikh army in Punjab near the Sutlej River in December 1845—and both were subsequently wounded in the engagements at Moodkee and Ferozepur. Wredenhall Queiros Pogson retired to England as a Major General and died at Brighton in 1891, whereas his brother John Frederick stayed on in India, dying at Kotgarh in 1890. Their younger brother, Edward Reynell Pogson, was the third son who joined the army, but he died at the tender age of twenty-eight.

John Frederick Pogson seems to have taken after his father in literary pursuits. He was a keen gardener, putting this knowledge to good use when he published his *Manual for Agriculture in India* in 1883. On another occasion, he presented a paper to the Royal Horticultural Society of India, consisting of proposals for the extensive cultivation of the Singhara nut throughout India, to alleviate periods of famine. He evidently had an inquiring mind, having invented a new type of mortar cement as a twenty-five year old Lieutenant. Luckily, he was given ample time to test his new discovery in a new building construction, whilst still being officially considered 'on duty'.[23] Later, he apparently invented a 'pill' which would instantly convert kerosene non-flammable and in 1882 he also applied for a patent on the technique.[24] Like his father (who was reprimanded for the 'tone and tenor' of his remarks to the Resident when making his claim to the Estate of Joseph Queiros senior), John Frederick was inclined to be short-tempered. After being severely wounded in the right arm at Mudkee in the Sutlej campaign, he had been withdrawn from active service and was placed on the 'invalid establishment'. He was eventually employed as a supervisor during the construction of the 'Hindoostan to Thibet Road'. However, within a few months, he ended in a serious dispute with his superior officer, for having made unjustified excuses to take leave at Simla and then having greatly exceeded the period granted. These were referred to the government, as a result of which he was dismissed from his appointment despite his pleas that suspension would lead to his financial ruin.[25] Whilst his claim of financial ruin was obviously an exaggeration, the loss of this appointment was significant to him considering he had recently married and built a house at Simla—which was on the route of the new road.

Military service in the East India Company was clearly a traditional choice of occupation for the Pogson family. Wredenhall Robert Pogson also had an uncle, Thomas Pogson, who became a Colonel in the Madras army (Colonel Thomas Pogson retired to live at Kesgrove House, in the

POGSON FAMILY TREE
(From information kindly given by Cherry Armstrong)

NOTE: Characters shown in bold type also appear in other trees.

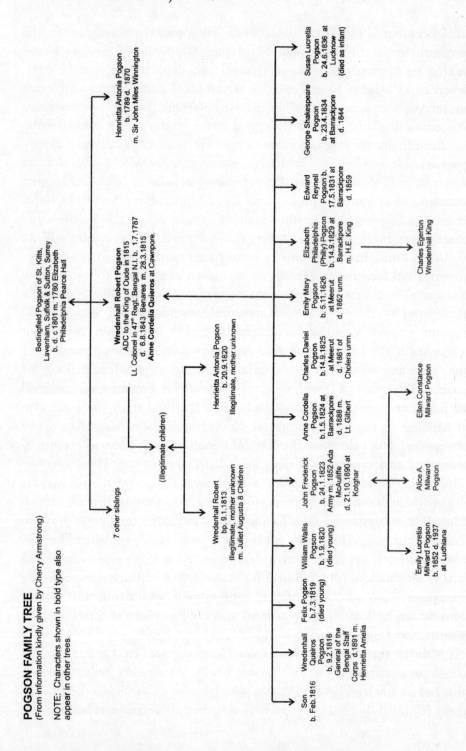

Bedingfield Pogson of St. Kitts, Lavenham, Suffolk & Sutton, Surrey
b. d. c 1801 m. 1780 Elizabeth Philadelphia Pearce Hall

Henrietta Antonia Pogson
b. 1789 d. 1870
m. Sir John Miles Winnington

Wredenhall Robert Pogson
ADC to the King of Oude in 1815
Lt. Colonel in 47th Regt. Bengal N.I. b. 1.7.1787
d. 6.8.1843 Benares m. 28.3.1815
Anne Cordelia Quieros at Cawnpore.

7 other siblings

(Illegitimate children)

Henrietta Antonia Pogson
b. 20.9.1820
Illegitimate, mother unknown

Wredenhall Robert
bp. 9.1.1813
Illegitimate, mother unknown
m. Juliet Augusta 8 Children

Son
b. Feb.1816

Wredenhall Queiros Pogson
b. 9.2.1816
General of the Bengal Staff Corps d.1891 m. Henrietta Amelia

Felix Pogson
b.7.3.1819
(died young)

William Wallis Pogson
b. 1.9.1820
(died young)

John Frederick Pogson
b. 24.1.1823
Army m. 1852 Ada McAuliffe
d. 21.10.1890 at Kotghar

Anne Cordelia Pogson
b.1.5.1824 at Barrackpore
d. 1888 m. Lt. Gilbert

Charles Daniel Pogson
b.14.9.1825 at Meerut
d. 1861 of Cholera unm.

Emily Mary Pogson
b. 5.11.1826 at Meerut
d. 1862 unm.

Elizabeth Philadelphia (Philly) Pogson
b. 14.9.1829 at Barrackpore
m. H.E. King

Edward Reynell Pogson b. 17.5.1831 at Barrackpore d. 1859

George Shakespeare Pogson
b. 23.4.1834 at Barrackpore d. 1844

Susan Lucretia Pogson
b. 24.6.1836 at Lucknow (died as infant)

Emily Lucretia Milward Pogson
b. 1852 d. 1937 at Ludhiana

Alice A. Milward Pogson

Ellen Constance Milward Pogson

Charles Egerton Wredenhall King

village of Kesgrave, near Ipswich). Three of Thomas' sons (i.e. Wredenhall Robert's cousins), George Thomas, John and William Waldegrave, also joined the Honourable Company's service. The latter served in HM's 8th Regiment of Foot and died a few days after being severely wounded at the siege of Delhi on 17 September 1857.

Let us now return to the Queiros family of Lucknow—picking up the threads of the story from where we left it, with Joseph Queiros (junior) having succeeded in getting his proposed 'equal shares' distribution of his late father's bequest accepted. I will however now backtrack slightly to tell the story of Joseph (junior)'s life in brief since he himself did not live long to enjoy his share of the bequest, dying at Lucknow a mere two years after his father's death.

Joseph (junior) had a varied career. He started by enrolling as an Ensign with the Company's Bengal army, but resigned after only four years' service to join his father's business at Lucknow around 1818. Later, he was employed by King Ghazi-ud-din Hyder as 'Superintendent of His Majesty's stud' on a handsome salary of Rs 1000 per month.[26] It seems that both Joseph and his father enjoyed the favour of the King. In his will, Joseph requests 'that the fine oil painting of His Majesty done by Rt Home Esqre and given to my late Father and subsequently on his demise confirmed to me may be returned to His said Majesty the King of Oude with a communication on my part expressive of the very high estimation in which I ever held it and my grateful sense of the many favors which he was graciously pleased to confer on me during the period I had the pleasure of being in his service'.[27]

In 1816, he married Rozalie Vrignon, at the ancient Portuguese Church of Nossa Senhora di Rozario at Bandel, forty-eight km north of Calcutta. Rozalie belonged to a French family who had lived at Chandernagore, the independent French colony established in 1673. Her father, Gabriel, was born there in 1737 and was a ship-builder and merchant, who had left Chandernagore and settled in Calcutta in 1763. This move was mainly triggered by the fact that Chandernagore had been captured from the French in 1757 by Robert Clive, following which many houses had been demolished leaving the town of secondary importance as compared to Calcutta. Gabriel Vrignon had died just a year before his youngest daughter's marriage, but he left each of his nine children well-provided for in his will. Like her siblings, Rozalie inherited a house in Church Lane, Calcutta together with a dowry of Rs 25,000, as well as a collection of silver plate worth Rs 5000.[28] However, the couple only had eight years together, before Joseph's untimely demise in March 1824.

The items listed in the inventory of Joseph's estate indicate a man of considerable wealth, who clearly entertained on a grand scale. The following are just a selection from the sixty-six 'items' listed under china and crockery:

> 46 Queensware soup-plates; 46 Queensware plates; 17 Queensware beefstake [sic] plates; 30 hotwater plates; 4 curry dishes with covers...

Claude Martin Queiros was Joseph (senior)'s second son, named after his illustrious godparent, Claude Martin. He became a merchant at Calcutta, but he also lived and worked in Singapore as an agent of Palmer and Co, the Calcutta banking house that eventually collapsed in 1830. Claude's name occurs in several extant documents: in February 1824 he was a juror at a Coroner's inquest into the deaths of the Captain and a seaman of the *Brig Philotax*;[30] he also bought a house there, but later discovered that it had been built on reserved land due to which he was forced to allow the building to be demolished, receiving 3000 dollars in compensation.[31] Claude and his wife, Mary, had four children, two sons (both of whom joined the Indian Navy), and two daughters. Their eldest son, Palmer Hayes Queiros, was accidentally drowned while traversing the surf at Madras in order to join or leave his ship. Claude himself died at Calcutta on 2 August 1843 and was buried at the Park Street cemetery.

It was Joseph (senior)'s youngest son, Felix John, who was to eventually establish the family's presence in Lucknow. At the time of his father's death, Felix was only eleven years old and was at school in England. On his return to India, he seems to have initially settled in Calcutta, probably staying there with his brother Claude. He later confirmed that he had spent a year in Singapore probably assisting Claude in his agency business there. In 1832, he married Margaret Miller, a widow and the daughter of Joseph Malachi Lyons of St John's Wood in London.[32] Over the next twelve years, the couple had six children, five of whom were baptised in Calcutta. Sadly, though, Margaret seems to have died during the birth of their last child, Joseph Malachi Queiros who was named after his maternal grandfather.

In 1842, two years before Margaret's death Felix had bought a large grant of jungle wasteland at Bansi near Gorakhpur and, over the years, had organised the clearance of the jungle together with the establishment of numerous villages on the land.[33] It was here that Margaret died and, to add to Felix's misfortune, his youngest son too died fifteen months later.

Like his father, Felix converted most of the land into an indigo plantation and factory, known as the Kutthela Grant Factory. Felix stayed on at the Kutthela Factory for another ten years before remarrying in 1855. His second marriage, to a seventeen year old Mary Jones, took place at St Paul's Cathedral in Calcutta. However, only two years later, a double tragedy befell the family. The first heartbreak occurred just before the outbreak of the mutiny, at 4 pm on 26 April 1857, when Felix's son, Gerald Ross, accidentally shot himself in his right arm above the wrist at the Kutthela Grant Factory. He was brought to Gorakhpur by his brother, Edward, for medical treatment, but he later died there from loss of blood.[34] The second tragedy was simply an economic failure, caused mainly by lawlessness during the mutiny. Up to then, Felix had not been making a profit at the factory as the rents he received barely covered the costs of land clearance and taxes paid to the government. He had expected this situation to improve within a few years as the land became more fertile through constant cultivation. He had even established a subsidiary to produce railway sleepers as a by-product of the continual jungle clearance forming a partnership with George Wallace. The mutiny and the prolonged disturbance that followed caused considerable damage to his property; the land too suffered neglect and he received no income. Eventually, he was forced to declare himself insolvent, as he was unable to meet his obligations under a contract worth five lakhs of rupees to supply wood for sleepers to the East Indian Railway Company. Realising that 'the existing state of the Country leaves little or no prospect, even after the re-establishing of quiet, of any immediate occupation or resort to business of any sort' he finally surrendered all his land at Gorakhpur to the Insolvency Court for a nominal sum of Rs 5,700 in order to satisfy his creditors, even though he had paid Rs 50,000 for the property.[35]

Having lost heavily on this business, Felix was now desperate to find some other means of livelihood. Moving to Park Street, Calcutta, he wrote in January 1858 to the government, offering his services to the army of 9000 men that had been assembled by Jung Bahadur, the Maharajah of Nepal, and which was then marching towards Gorakhpur. Felix hoped to offer valuable information and assistance to the army, from his detailed knowledge of the area, but he was too late since by the time he wrote, Jung Bahadur had already driven the rebels out of Gorakhpur, thereby allowing the British Civil administration to resume their work there. As a result, the government declined Felix's request to be assigned to Jung Bahadur's army nor did they take up his offer to act 'as a Settlement Officer to converge & collect local intelligence, or for the procurement of supplies &c'. In the same letter, Felix mentioned an offer of assistance by the Relief Fund Officer, so it seems that, like Mary Duhan and so many others, he was destitute whilst in Calcutta, dependent on the Relief Fund until the troubles had subsided and he could find some alternative employment.[35]

Felix probably did briefly work for the government at Calcutta since at his last son's baptism the following year, he listed his occupation as 'late of the home department' (rather than a merchant). However, he later reverted to his usual occupation as a merchant, staying at various addresses in Calcutta.

It was probably in the mid 1860s that Felix and his family moved to Lucknow, where he took up an appointment as the Superintendent of the late Claude Martin's estate at La Martiniere, which he held until his retirement. His second wife, Mary, separated from him in about 1876 and went to live at Howrah, near Calcutta, leaving her estate to her 'dear friend William Edward Green', a driver on the East Indian Railway, when she died in 1896.[36] Felix had died before her from diarrhoea at Mussoorie at the age of eighty-two in 1893.

As mentioned earlier, two of Felix's sons had died while at Gorakhpur; the fate of his last son, Oscar, is not known, but his other three sons all stayed on in Lucknow. His eldest son, also called Felix John, worked as a clerk at the Chief Commissioner's Office in Lucknow for many years, right from the inception of that office after the annexation of Awadh in 1856. Then, from about 1878 onwards, he held a more prestigious position as Superintendent of the Wasika Office. Felix John (junior) married Catherine Braganca at Lucknow in 1850. She was probably the daughter of D. Braganca, who was listed as a piano-tuner in directories of the period. They had five sons and a daughter. But Catherine died in 1872 and Felix re-married seven years later to a widow, Emily Rebertest, who bore him two more children. Three of Felix's sons went to La Martiniere School and went on to work for the Awadh & Rohilkhand Railway, which had its headquarters at Lucknow.

It was Felix's next son, Edward Arthur, who formed the first connection with the Short family, when he married Joseph Short's daughter Nelly in 1860. The couple went on to have fourteen (!) children over the next twenty-seven years, although four of them died as infants. Nelly obviously had a strong constitution, as she survived all of these childbirths, only dying in 1906 aged sixty-four. Edward joined the Lucknow Police in the early 1860s, as an Inspector of Police. The job was however not well paid and Edward generally earned about one third less than his other brothers, in the civil service.

The next surviving son, Alfred Augustus Queiros, followed his elder brother Felix John's example, working at the Chief Commissioner's Office for many years, starting in 1860 at the young age of nineteen. He progressed steadily, starting as a copyist and finally ending up as Record Keeper. When Allahabad took over from Lucknow as the Capital of Awadh in 1878, Alfred, like many others working for the government, shifted to Allahabad. In 1867, Alfred married Dorothea Johannes, the young half-sister of Joseph Johannes, and daughter of the merchant Jacob Johannes by his second wife. The couple had three sons and a daughter, their eldest son Reginald eventually marrying my great-aunt Winifred Speirs. This was however not a happy marriage, ending in divorce and with Winifred living 'in sin' with a Muslim man.

Dorothea died in 1890 and Alfred got remarried a few years later to Alice Mary Pardew. Subsequently, the couple had seven children. Alfred lived on to the ripe age of eighty-three, dying at Lucknow in 1925 of general debility. He is buried in the Nishat Ganj cemetery along with his widow, Alice Mary.

I should point out here that the three sons of Felix John Senior I have just mentioned had entered the Residency and fought alongside the soldiers of the garrison during the prolonged siege of Lucknow in 1857. Felix John (junior) served in Sago's Garrison with William Sangster and Edward Duhan, Joseph Short's son-in-law who had died later due to failing health as a result of the seige. Felix John had been one of the

several people who had replied to Mary Duhan's request to testify to
the arduous conditions suffered by her late husband. Edward Arthur and
Alfred Augustus Queiros also assisted in the defence of the Residency
although I do not know whether they too served in Sago's Garrison. All
three of them received 'India Medals' and 'Defence of Lucknow' clasps
for their services during the siege, although Alfred's medals went astray
and were only finally delivered to him in 1863.[37] As survivors of the siege,
both Felix and Edward were buried in the Residency cemetery. It is not
clear why Arthur wasn't buried there. A probable answer is that the
Residency graveyard was closed when he died, twenty-five years after his
brother.

I could easily continue with the story of the Queiros family who lived
in Lucknow, as a further three generations lived there after Felix John
(junior), Edward and Alfred. I shall desist, however, simply because it
would become too confusing for the reader, as the family was so prolific!
Felix, Edward and Alfred between them had thirty-three children and
even after eliminating those who had died as infants, we are still left with
twenty-five. And, to add to the confusion, there was a wide age-gap—
Felix's eldest son being fifty-eight years old by the time Alfred's wife
gave birth to her last daughter in 1911.

La Martiniere College became the favourite choice for the boys;
although later, after the opening of St Francis' School in 1885, a number
of Queiros boys were sent there too. In fact, three of Edward Arthur
Queiros' great-grandsons attended St Francis School in the 1940s. Most
of the boys went to McConaghy's School, the infant school close to
Christ Church, before entering either La Martiniere or St Francis. In
their later life, working for the railways was certainly the most popular
occupation for the Queiros men. Alban Augustus, Edward Queiros'
eldest son, worked for many years in the audit office of the O&R Railway
at Lucknow besides several other Queiros family members who worked
either as platform inspectors, carriage inspectors, drivers, guards or
clerks for the O&R Railway. It seems though that gradually their jobs
caused most of them to migrate from Lucknow, so that only a few
members were living there by the 1940s.

The last members of the Queiros family left in Lucknow belonged
to the family of Herbert Percival Aday Queiros, grandson of Edward
Queiros, the Police Inspector. Living at 3, Barrow Road, it was Percival

who sent his three sons to St Francis School, although he did not survive to see his sons complete their education, dying suddenly of a fever early in 1945. He was buried at Nishat Ganj cemetery, and within a few months his elder brother too followed him there. His widow, Maud Florence Queiros lived on at Lucknow until her death in 1968. One of their sons, Carlyle, remained at Lucknow and was buried there in 1991. His sister was there until at least 1988 and may still be living there...

THE JOHANNES, BOURBON AND LAFRENAIS FAMILIES

WE ENCOUNTERED JOSEPH JOHANNES AND HIS FATHER JACOB FIRST IN Chapter 3. The reader may recall that Jacob Johannes was the prosperous Armenian merchant who had converted a large house in Golaganj into a shop, from where he used to sell European goods to the populace for twenty years. He had also served the Kings of Awadh for forty-two years, having started his military service in 1814 under Ghazi-ud-din Haidar, serving as a Lieutenant in Captain Magness' Regiment, which was renamed as the 7th Oude Infantry after the annexation in 1856. Like many of his regiment, Jacob was discharged after the annexation with a pension of hundred rupees a month, half of his previous salary.[1] It seems in fact that Jacob's duties in his regiment had been very nominal. When he wrote to General Outram, the Chief Commissioner of Awadh, shortly after annexation he confirmed that 'at the suggestion of the Durbar I was stationed at Lucknow to carry out its orders. As Captn Magness is always out in the district with his Corps, he frequently writes to me to ascertain the wishes of the authorities, I would therefore feel extremely thankful by being informed whatever may be your orders on the subject that I may communicate the same to him for his information and guidance'.[2] Jacob's military duties clearly did not affect his business, and seem to have been merely a sinecure. In the latter years, he also, however, served

JOHANNES FAMILY TREE

NOTE: Characters shown in bold type also appear in other trees.

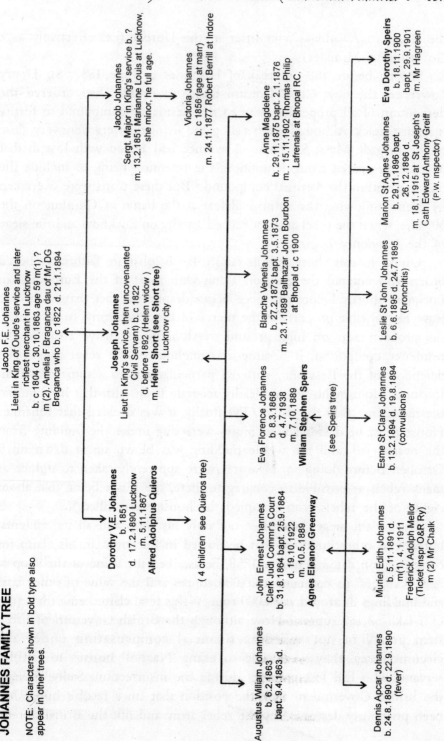

Jacob F.E. Johannes
Lieut in King of Oude's service and later richest merchant in Lucknow
b. c 1804 d. 30.10.1863 age 59 m(1) ?
m (2). Amelia F Braganca dau of Mr DG Braganca who b. c 1822 d. 21.1.1894

Jacob Johannes
Sergt. Major in King's service b. ?
m. 13.2.1851 Marianne Louis at Lucknow, she minor, he full age.

Victoria Johannes
b. c 1856 (age at marr)
m. 24.11.1877 Robert Berrill at Indore

Joseph Johannes
Lieut in King's service, then uncovenanted Civil Servant) b. c 1822
d. before 1892 (Helen widow)
m. **Helen Short (see Short tree)**
l. Lucknow city

Anne Magdelene
b. 29.11.1875 bapt. 2.1.1876
m. 15.11.1902 Thomas Philip Lafrenais at Bhopal RC.

Eva Dorothy Speirs
b. 18.11.1900
bapt. 29.9.1901
m. Mr Hagreen

Dorothy V.E. Johannes
b. 1851
d. 17.2.1890 Lucknow
m. 5.11.1867
Alfred Adolphus Quieros

Blanche Venetia Johannes
b. 27.2.1873 bapt. 3.5.1873
m. 23.1.1889 Balthazar John Bourbon at Bhopal d. c 1900

Marion St Agnes Johannes
b. 29.11.1896 bapt. 26.12.1896 d.
m. 18.1.1915 at St Joseph's Cath Edward Anthony Greiff (P.w. inspector)

(4 children see Quieros tree)

Eva Florence Johannes
b. 8.3.1868
d. 4.7.1938
m. 7.10.1889
William Stephen Speirs

Leslie St John Johannes
b. 6.6.1895 d. 24.7.1895 (bronchitis)

(see Speirs tree)

Augustus William Johannes
b. 6.2.1863
bapt. 9.4.1863 d.

John Ernest Johannes
Clerk Judl Commr's Court
b. 31.8.1864 bapt. 25.9.1864
d. 19.10.1922
m. 10.5.1889
Agnes Eleanor Greenway

Esme St Clare Johannes
b. 13.2.1894 d. 19.8.1894 (convulsions)

Muriel Edith Johannes
b. 5.11.1891 d.
m(1). 4.1.1911
Frederick Adolph Mellor (Ticket inspr O&R Ry)
m (2) Mr Chalk

Dennis Apcar Johannes
b. 24.8.1890 d. 22.9.1890 (fever)

the Kings of Awadh as a courtier in the Durbar (i.e. effectively as a Government Minister).

Shortly before the outbreak of hostilities in June 1857, Sir Henry Lawrence, the new Chief Commissioner of Awadh, had ordered the demolition of all properties close to the Residency compound to fortify it against attack. Although Jacob's shop and living quarters were very close to the Brigade Mess, Sir Henry Lawrence had agreed with Joseph that it could be spared from demolition, the intention being to include the building within the fortified compound.[3] But these plans were overtaken by events following the surprise defeat at the battle of Chinhut on the 30 June, when the rebel army advanced rapidly on Lucknow and the siege of the Residency began.

Unlike Joseph Short and his family, Jacob Johannes faithfully obeyed orders and entered the garrison along with most of the Europeans in Lucknow shortly before the siege began despite the fact that he had to leave his valuable property at the mercy of the rebel army. In fact, since the property was on high ground overlooking extensive areas of the residency compound, it became a stronghold of the rebel army. The defenders of the Residency suffered particularly from a sniper based in Johannes House who was so deadly accurate in his aim that he acquired the nickname 'Bob the nailer'. Eventually, it was decided that Johannes House must be destroyed, so mines were dug under the building from the nearby jail, and the whole building was blown up at dawn on 5 October. Before doing so, measures were apparently taken to induce as many rebels as possible to congregate there, the result being that about eighty of the rebels who occupied the house were killed.[4]

During the siege, Jacob lost not only his shop and all its contents, but several other buildings that he owned in Lucknow. In his claim for compensation dated February 1858, he ascribed the value of the shop at 32,000 rupees, its contents at 20,000 rupees and the value of other land and buildings destroyed at 35,000 rupees—his total claim being for a sum of 1 lakh 53,180 rupees.[5] Now, although the British Government had a firm policy of not awarding financial compensation under any circumstances, they were able to grant 'Nazool' houses to faithful servants who had lost property during the insurrection. Sadly, though, the British Government took the position that since Jacob's house had been previously destroyed by the rebel army and not the British forces, they need not compensate for it. Even though Jacob rightly argued that the house had been bombarded by the garrison and was still standing and capable of holding more than eighty rebels when it was blown up, the government refused to alter its stance. Jacob produced several testimonials, including one from Mr Martin, the Deputy Commissioner, who confirmed that his house was a very fine one, worth at least 30,000 rupees. Major General Sir John Inglis, under whom Jacob had served during the siege, testified (as did many others) that Jacob was a highly respectable man and had been a very heavy loser as a result of the siege. In fact, it was suggested that he had probably lost more than anyone else in Lucknow.[6] Nevertheless, Jacob's petitions fell on deaf ears and he was left high and dry to rebuild his life as best he could, without any compensation.

Later, though, when the British government was forming the new cantonments at Dilkusha, Jacob received some compensation for a piece of land he owned there, which he described as:

A garden of 6 beegahs situated in Bhadawun and adjacent to Captain Magness's estate. This garden is also studed [sic] with beautiful fruit grafts and I have been twice to the expense of putting it into first rate order, first prior to annexation, and next after the rebellion. It contains a garden house with some out-offices, a pukka chubootra and 2 pukka wells cost Rs 5000.

In this case Jacob was granted an alternative piece of land at Jia Lall Bagh.[7] Little is known about Jacob's subsequent life but judging by the entries in the annual Bengal directories, he does seem to have recovered somewhat and to have started some new business ventures. The entries for 1859 and 1860 show him as 'merchant and ice contractor', but by 1860 he had evidently started a 'horse-dawk' business, carrying passengers between Kanpur and Lucknow. This business seems to have lasted only two years, and his main occupation was listed in 1862 as 'proprietor of the Oude Gazette'. This, however, was his final venture, as he died the following year—the certificate showing paralysis as the cause of death.

It was Jacob's son, Joseph Johannes, who formed the association with the protagonist of this book, through his marriage to Joseph Short's daughter Helen. As described already, Joseph Johannes had remained outside the Residency during the siege and had been captured along with

Joseph Short. After their release, he apparently assisted in effecting the release of Madeleine Orr and the other 'English Captives of Oudh'.

Joseph fared somewhat better than his father regarding compensation for his losses during the siege. He had previously owned a house in Golaganj close to Gubbins battery and not far from his father's shop, which had been destroyed during the demolition work by the British Military Engineers to make the city safe against further insurgency. Joseph was eventually awarded 'Galib Junge's' house, which was valued at 3,000 rupees, and later was allowed to buy five adjacent shops for the princely sum of 200 rupees.[8]

Like his father, Joseph had served in the King of Awadh's army before annexation, for eighteen years as a Lieutenant in the King's Body Guard. He too had been discharged from service on pension shortly after annexation. Besides being a soldier, he was also a talented artist and in 1856 (the year of annexation) his name appears as 'painter to the King of Oudh', whilst in 1857 although his royal patronage had ended, he still listed his occupation as 'portrait painter'.[9] Evidently though, he could not earn a living from art immediately after the mutiny, when most of the citizens of Lucknow were suffering hardship, having lost their homes, and were attempting to start their lives afresh. Hence, for several years Joseph appears to have worked with his father as a merchant and ice-contractor. In those days, before the advent of refrigeration in India, ice was a highly sought-after commodity. The usual method of collection was quite painstaking—peasants would go into the fields at dawn on cold winter mornings, meticulously collecting ice-crystals formed from the dew, which were then quickly transferred to large underground chambers, well-insulated with straw. As contractors, Joseph and Jacob Johannes would buy the stocks of ice from each village in the summer and transport them to the city, where it fetched a high price.

Joseph was however keen to utilise his artistic talents, having already made the transition from portrait painting to photography. Eventually, in 1863 he set up a photographic studio in Lucknow which he ran for a number of years, including briefly being in partnership with Mr H.S. Clarke. However, his name does not appear in the records after 1870, from which it might be presumed that he retired in that year. His death has also not been covered in the indexes returned to Britain, but according to his son, he died 'some time in 1890'.[10] Joseph's widow,

Helen (or Ellen as she was commonly called) lived on until the winter of 1910, actually dying on Christmas Day of heart failure.

Joseph had one brother, named Jacob, but very little is known about him. The only surviving record that mentions him is his marriage certificate, which shows that he married Marianne Louis at Lucknow in February 1851. At the time he was a Sergeant-Major in the King of Awadh's 6th Cavalry and was 'of full age'. Like Joseph, he must have been born to Jacob Johannes' first wife, whose name is not known. They also had a half-sister, Victoria Johannes, born to Jacob's second wife, Amelia.

It is at this point that we begin to notice the strange intermingling of the established European families of Lucknow. In 1867, Victoria Johannes was married to Alfred Adolphus Queiros—the younger brother of Edward Arthur Queiros, who had married Nelly Short. And twenty-five years later, their eldest son, Reginald Queiros married my great aunt, Winifred Speirs. Further examples of the complicated links between the Johannes, Queiros, Short and Speirs families will be revealed later!

Joseph and Ellen had five children—two sons followed by three daughters. I have found no records of their eldest son apart from his baptism details in 1863 which makes me suspect that he died relatively young. It was their second son, Joey, who was well-known by our family—but unfortunately he leaves behind him quite a mystery about his real full name!

'Joey' was born on 31 August 1864 and baptised under the full name of John Joseph Jacob Johannes. And when he married Agnes Eleanor Greenway, he only used his first name but it is clear that he is the same person, as he gave his full name for one of his children's baptisms. Now at each of his children's baptisms, his occupation is given as 'Clerk, Judicial Commissioner's office'. However, the records of the Judicial Commissioner's office show him as J.E. Johannes. This at first seemed just a typographical error, until I found his mother's two warisnamas each naming her only surviving son as J.E. Johannes. His death certificate however mentions his name as John Ernest Johannes. I can only conclude that for some reason he changed his middle names to Ernest, but for church records he felt obliged to use the names under which he had been baptised.

However, for our family he was always 'Joey'. Hence, that is the name that I will use for him. Joey joined the La Martiniere College as

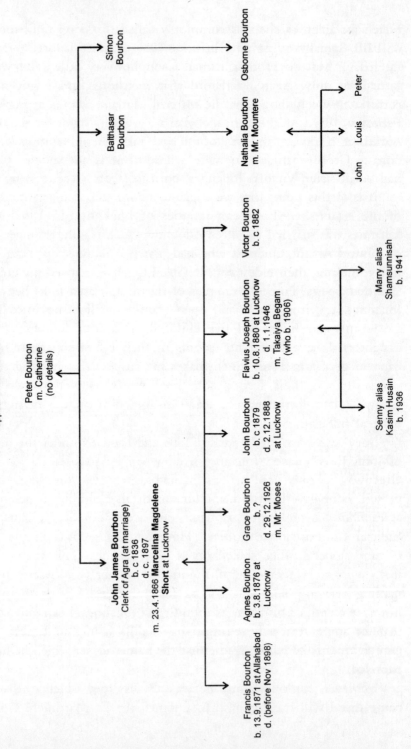

BOURBON FAMILY TREE

NOTE: Characters shown in bold type also appear in other trees.

Peter Bourbon
m. Catherine
(no details)

Simon Bourbon

Osborne Bourbon

Balthasar Bourbon

Nathalia Bourbon
m. Mr. Mountere

John   Louis   Peter

John James Bourbon
Clerk of Agra (at marriage)
b. c 1836
d. c. 1897
m. 23.4.1866 **Marcelina Magdelene
Short at Lucknow**

Francis Bourbon
b. 13.9.1871 at Allahabad
d. (before Nov 1898)

Agnes Bourbon
b. 3.8.1876 at
Lucknow

Grace Bourbon
b. ?
d. 29.12.1926
m. Mr. Moses

John Bourbon
b. c 1879
d. 2.12.1888
at Lucknow

Flavius Joseph Bourbon
b. 10.8.1880 at Lucknow
d. 1.1.1946
m. Takaiya Begam
(who b. 1906)

Victor Bourbon
b. c 1882

Senny alias
Kasim Husain
b. 1936

Marry alias
Shamsunnisah
b. 1941

a day-scholar in 1878, the same year that my great-uncles Alexander and William Speirs and several of the sons of Edward Arthur Queiros entered.[11] These boys were all cousins and soon William and Joey became particularly close friends. After school, they both started work in 1893 as clerks in the Judicial Commissioner's Office at Lucknow—initially on a salary of fifty rupees per month. For the next fourteen years, they both worked as clerks in the same office. In 1889, when Joey married Agnes Eleanor Greenway, the daughter of Thomas Greenway, William Speirs was one of the witnesses to the marriage. Later, William became the godparent to three of their five children. William later married Joey's younger sister, Eva Johannes further cementing the strong bond between the two families.[12]

Unfortunately though, in the early 1900s something happened which scarred their relationship forever. It was the affair between William Speirs and Joey's wife Eleanor. And when William's wife Eva realised what was happening and walked out on him in disgust, Eleanor simply moved in with William and they began cohabiting as man and wife. This had a terrible effect on Joey, as vividly described by the Wasika Officer when an application was made to withhold his wasika in his own interest:

Mr Johannes is not a lunatic and I have known him for the last twenty five years when he was working for the Judicial Commissioner's Office whence he retired on an invalid pension (reduced) which was due to the fact of his wife's infidelity who has been living in open immorality with his brother-in-law (sister's husband) for the last twenty years or so. The brother-in-law above mentioned is Mr Speirs who is working in the Judl. Commr's Office. This calamity has turned his head and he talks like an idiot but does not harm or injure anyone, but before he reaches home he gives away his wasika to anyone who flatters him.[13]

The application was made in 1917 by Eleanor Quieros, the wife of Joey Johannes' cousin, Alban Augustus Quieros who had been looking after Joey for a number of years. However, five years later Joey found peace at last when he died at Lucknow in October 1922, the cause of death being given as 'stricture of the urethra'.

Joey had three sisters, Eva, Blanche and Annie and I will deal with Blanche first, as it was she who formed the next connection to the Bourbon family. The reader may recall from Chapter 3, that when Joseph Short's daughter Rachel married John Speirs, it was a joint wedding with Rachel's half-sister Marcelina, who married John James Bourbon. John and Marcelina Bourbon remained at Lucknow while their family were growing up but it seems that they later moved to Bhopal sometime in the late 1880s since they had many Bourbon relatives living there. Presumably, it was through her Bourbon relatives of Lucknow that Blanche had met Balthazar Bourbon, a jaghirdar of Bhopal. The couple were married at the Roman Catholic Church in Bhopal in January 1889.[14]

Balthazar Bourbon and his two brothers and sister were heirs to the Bhopal Estate, a large estate in Bhopal with a rental value of Rs 12,000 a year. The estate had been granted to his great-great-grandfather, Salvador Bourbon in 1812, in grateful recognition of his valuable services to the town of Bhopal when the town had been besieged for six months by the Mahratta armies of Scindia and the Bhonsla Rajah of Nagpur. Salvador had previously been appointed by the Minister of Bhopal as Commander of forces, and it was through his efforts that his small force of 3,000 men had resisted the combined Mahratta force of 82,000 men— aided by every able-bodied citizen of the town. Later, when Maharajah Scindia ordered a second invasion of Bhopal and it was realised that they could no longer resist, Salvador was sent to meet the invading General Fanthome in order to buy time for the city. He succeeded in obtaining a temporary reprieve. This was all that was needed, as the British Government, who had been asked to intervene, did so and the city was saved.[15]

Like John James Bourbon, Balthazar was also a direct descendent of Jean Philippe de Bourbon, a member of the French Royal family who had left France and arrived in India in 1560. He and Blanche had three children—Napoleon, Joanna and Anton, born between 1893 and 1898. The family subsequently settled in Bhopal, but Blanche herself died in about 1900 aged only twenty-seven.

About two years before she died, Blanche was caught up in a controversy when Marcelina Bourbon died on a visit to her daughter, Grace Moses, in Bhopal. Marcelina, whose husband John had died the previous year, had brought with her on the trip her two younger sons,

Flavious and Victor. However, after her death the boys were held captive in Bhopal, as described by their aunt, Mary Duhan:

> I have tried to have the children brought to Lucknow but cannot do so. The Roman Catholic Priest has informed Mrs Blanch Bourbon that the 2 children are kept locked up in one room of the house belonging to a Sowar in the service of the Begum of Bhopul, whose name is Mozuffur Jung. The Sowar on being asked by Mrs B. Bourbon to make over the 2 boys by name Victor and Flavius Bourbon refused to do so, stating the mother had died as a Mahomedan and her two children had embraced the Mahomedan faith—the motive for saying this (which is a falsehood—and at any rate cannot affect the boys who are sons of Christian parents and are too young to legally change their religion) is that the girl named Grace Moses who is a widow and is living with Mozuffur Jung the Sowar mentioned in the preceding part of my letter and it is their desire to secure possession of the person of the two boys and appropriate their shares of the Wusseeka of their late mother to the uses of herself, Mrs Moses.[16]

Mary Duhan later confirmed to the Wasika Officer that all the Bourbon relatives wanted the two boys to continue being brought up as Roman Catholics. She also asked the Wasika Officer to write officially to the Resident asking the Begum of Bhopal to intervene. It seems that this deadlock persisted for over six weeks when finally in February 1899 the boys returned to Lucknow and were placed under the guardianship of their uncle, Edward Arthur Queiros (Nelly Short's husband), who lived at Lall Bagh. At this stage, the Reverend Father Bartholomew, Principal of St Francis College, Lucknow, offered to take the boys under his care, and to educate them at his college as he had done in the case of William Short. However, it seems that this offer was not taken up since there is no record of the boys entering St Francis College.[17]

It seems doubtful whether the family's attempts to ensure that Flavius and Victor Bourbon remained Roman Catholics were successful. Grace evidently drew Flavius' wasika on his behalf until he reached the age of majority. When he died in 1946, Flavius left a widow named Takaiya Begam and a son and daughter with 'aliases' Kasim Husain and

Shamsunniss, surely indicating that the family had adopted Islam in favour of Christianity.

Let us now turn to Annie Johannes, Joey's youngest sister, who formed the connection with the Lafrenais family through her marriage to Thomas Lafrenais in 1902. Thomas was born at Quilon in South India, the son of another Thomas Lafrenais. Thomas (senior) was a Superintendent of Police at Quilon, eventually rising to become a sub-magistrate and finally a Judge. The Lafrenais family were of French origin, the first settler probably being Joseph Lafrenais, a Sergeant in the French garrison at Mahe, originally from Anjou in France who married at Mahe in 1745.[18] The family seems to have lived in the coastal towns along the Malabar Coast for several generations typically at Cannanore, Cochin, Quilon and Trivandrum.

Thomas Lafrenais, who worked as a Permanent Way Inspector for the East Indian Railway Company, was twice widowed before his marriage to Annie Johannes. I have not found the record of his first marriage, but the second is interesting—it took place at St Joseph's Church, Lucknow in 1899, when he married Ellen Clarke, the marriage being witnessed by Joey Johannes. It is clear that this marriage involved a connection with the Johannes family, particularly as Eva Speirs (nee Johannes) acted as the godparent to their second child, born in 1901. In fact, the most likely explanation is that Ellen Clarke was Annie Johannes' niece! This can be assumed because Ellen Johannes listed 'Ella Clarke—grand-daughter' on her warisnamas issued between 1888 and 1893. And, on Ellen Johannes' death, her nephew Alan Queiros certified on oath in 1911 that 'Ella Clarke died over 10 years ago. I cannot say how many children she left... Ella Clarke was Mrs Ellen Johannes' daughter's daughter.'[19]

This compels us to believe that Joseph and Ellen Johannes had one more daughter (name unknown), probably born before the insurrection of 1857, which would account for the fact that no record of her baptism exists (the church records were all lost at the end of the siege when the padre forgot to take them with him on the evacuation of the Residency compound). Evidently, this daughter had married a Mr Clarke and Ellen (or Ella) was their daughter. And, although it seems strange that Annie Johannes should marry her late niece's husband, she and Ella were probably of similar age, as Annie was the last child, born to Joseph and Ellen Johannes in 1875.

Annie and Thomas Lafrenais were married at the Roman Catholic Church in Bhopal where Annie's sister Blanche had been married thirteen years before. At the time, Thomas was working at Sehore, a few miles west of Bhopal. Soon they were joined there by Annie's sister, Eva Speirs, who had walked out on her husband when she learned about his infidelity with Joey Johannes' wife, Eleanor. Eva Speirs never divorced her husband and seems to have lived for the rest of her life with Annie and Thomas. At some point, their mother Ellen Johannes joined them as well, and was living with them at Thomas' new station of Narsinghpur, near Jabalpur when she died on Christmas Day, 1910.

Annie and Thomas had two daughters, Florence and Evelyn, born in about 1913 and 1916. Florence married a Mr Dyce and Evelyn married a Mr R. Wal d'Eremao. Both of Annie's daughters were living at Evelyn Lodge, off Station Road, Lucknow when Annie herself died of heatstroke in June 1947, the year of India's independence.

10

JOHN ALPINE SPEIRS

IN THE PRECEDING CHAPTERS I HAVE COVERED IN SOME DEPTH THE lives of Murium Begum, her brother Joseph Short and his offspring, including the Duhan, Queiros and Johannes families who had married three of his daughters. My own family's connection with the Short family came, of course, through my great-grandfather, John Speirs, who had married Joseph Short's daughter, Rachel, at Lucknow in 1866.

John Speirs was the youngest son of Colonel Alex Speirs—to whom the reader was introduced in the prologue. A few months before John's birth, Alex Speirs was appointed as the Political Agent at Nimach and his duties involved a considerable amount of travel, as he was also responsible for the state of Sirohi and two or three other minor states. It is not clear as to where John was actually born since his father was in the middle of a two month-long tour of these states at the time of his birth although it is unlikely that Alex would have brought his heavily pregnant mistress along with him on this round trip of 442 miles over rough terrain. Most probably 'Bibi Bunnoo' (as Alex affectionately called his mistress) remained at the Residency in Nimach, where some medical aid was available, for her last confinement.

From the information passed down to me by my grandfather, I know that John and his three elder brothers had all been educated in England, before returning to India to take up their chosen careers. Besides that, I have had limited success in tracing their exact movements and following

SPEIRS FAMILY TREE

NOTE: Characters shown in bold type also appear in other trees.

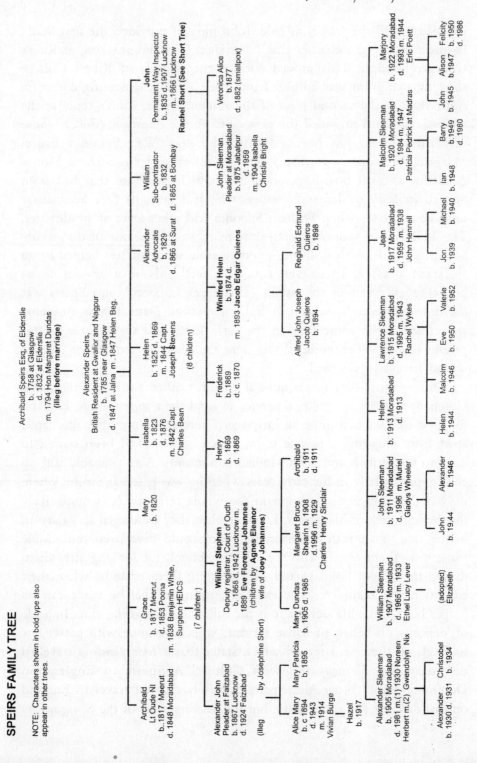

Archibald Speirs Esq, of Elderslie
b. 1758 at Glasgow
d. 1832 at Elderslie
m. 1794 Hon Margaret Dundas
(illeg before marriage)

Alexander Speirs,
British Resident at Gwalior and Nagpur
b. 1785 near Glasgow
d. 1847 at Jalna m. 1847 Helen Beg.

John
Permanent Way Inspector
b. 1835 d. 1907 Lucknow
m. 1866 Lucknow
Rachel Short (See Short Tree)

William
Sub-contractor
b. 1832
d. 1865 at Bombay

Alexander
Advocate
b. 1829
d. 1866 at Surat

Helen
b. 1825 d. 1869
m. 1844 Capt.
Joseph Stevens
(8 children)

Isabella
b. 1823
d. 1876
m. 1842 Capt.
Charles Bean

Mary
b. 1820

Grace
b. 1817 Meerut
d. 1853 Poona
m. 1838 Benjamin White,
Surgeon HEICS

Archibald
Lt Oude NI
b. 1817 Meerut
d. 1848 Moradabad

(7 children)

Veronica Alice
b.1877
d. 1882 (smallpox)

John Sleeman
Pleader at Moradabad
b.1875 Jabalpur
d. 1959
m. 1904 Isabella
Christie Bright

Winifred Helen
b. 1874 d.
m. 1893 **Jacob Edgar Quieros**

Frederick
b. 1869
d. c. 1870

Henry
b. 1869
d. 1869

William Stephen
Deputy registrar, Court of Oudh
b. 1868 d.1942 Lucknow m.
1889 **Eve Florence Johannes**
(children by **Agnes Eleanor**
wife of **Joey Johannes**)

Alexander John
Pleader at Faizabad
b. 1867 Lucknow
d. 1924 Faizabad

(illeg   by Josephine Short)

Reginald Edmund
Quieros
b. 1898

Alfred John Joseph
Jacob Quieros
b. 1894

Archibald
b. 1911
d. 1911

Margaret Bruce
Shearin b. 1908
d.1996 m. 1929
Charles Henry Sinclair

Mary Dundas
b. 1905 d. 1985

Mary Patricia
b. 1895

Alice Mary
b. c 1894
d. 1943
m. 1914
Vivian Burge

Hazel
b. 1917

Marjory
b. 1922 Moradabad
d. 1993 m. 1944
Eric Poett

Felicity
b. 1950
d. 1986

Alison
b.1947

John
b. 1945

Malcolm Sleeman
b. 1920 Moradabad
d. 1984 m. 1947
Patricia Pedrick at Madras

Barry
b.1949
d. 1980

Ian
b. 1948

Jean
b. 1917 Moradabad
d. 1959 m. 1938
John Hennell

Michael
b. 1940

Jon
b. 1939

Lawrence Sleeman
b. 1915 Moradabad
d. 1995 m. 1943
Rachel Wykes

Valerie
b. 1952

Eve
b. 1950

Malcolm
b. 1946

Helen
b. 1913 Moradabad
d. 1913

Helen
b. 1944

John Sleeman
b. 1911 Moradabad
d. 1996 m. Muriel
Gladys Wheeler

Alexander
b. 1946

John
b. 19.44

William Sleeman
b. 1907 Moradabad
d. 1965 m. 1933
Ethel Lucy Lever

(adopted)
Elizabeth

Alexander Sleeman
b. 1905 Moradabad
d. 1981 m.(1) 1930 Noreen
Herbert m.(2) Gwendolyn Nix

Christobel b. 1934

Alexander
b. 1930 d. 1931

up 'leads' until the trail runs cold. John himself provided the first 'lead', having told my grandfather that he studied Civil Engineering at King's College, London. This proved correct, the records of King's College showing that John was admitted into their Civil Engineering course in April 1856 in the second term of the academic year. John's reply in the admission record provided the next clue. To the question, 'under whose care the student has been educated' he says 'W.L. Spooner Esqre, Margate'.[1] It turns out that John was referring to the Dane House Academy, a small boarding school for boys in Margate that had been opened in 1830 by James Newlove, who had been its first headmaster until about 1848, when William Spooner had taken over as headmaster. The 1851 census indicates that John Speirs was there, one of the twenty boarding pupils, with William Spooner as the schoolmaster helped by an assistant master, three servants and with his mother acting as housekeeper. Most of the pupils came from London; John Speirs was the only one who was born in India. However, Dane House Academy was closed down some time in the early 1850s and the records of this private school which could throw light on when he entered or left the school have not survived.

During those days it was quite normal for officers in the Honourable Company's armies or political service to send their sons back to England for their education at quite an early age. There was often little alternative apart from engaging a private tutor, as few schools had been started to cater to the British and Anglo-Indian community. Alex probably had no choice, particularly in his early years when he was based at Sirohi, where he was the only British person in the whole territory. It is quite likely that he sent each of his sons to England when they were aged six or seven, in the care of an ayah or governess, who would have been responsible for getting them enrolled in the selected school, for looking after them during the school holidays and for returning them to India when their education was complete. The exact arrangements that he made can no longer be traced, although there is the following intriguing clue. In a file of 'deposits on behalf of native servants who have gone with passengers to England' there is a record which states that a Mrs Gosling travelled on board the *Seringapatam* with Colonel A. Speirs to England in December 1839.[2] Now Alex Speirs definitely did not travel to England on that date (or any other date), but the passenger list of the *Seringapatam* includes 'two master Speirs', implying that Mrs Gosling travelled with his sons to arrange for their education. I cannot be certain which of Alex's sons travelled on that date as their names are not given, but it is reasonable to assume that it was his two youngest sons. If so, John Speirs would have been just under five when he left India.

Another minor breakthrough in my research came from a letter written to the Wasika Office at Lucknow following John Speirs' death in 1907. The Wasika Office had asked what religion he had followed, to which my great-uncle William replied, 'my father, the late Mr John Speirs has died, as he lived, a member of the Church of England. He was baptised as such in St Jude's, Chelsea, England.'[3]

Naturally, this comment caused me to pay a visit to the London Metropolitan Archives, where a check on the baptism registers for St Jude's Church revealed to my delight, not only the baptism of John Speirs in January 1848, but also of his brothers William and Alexander in the following two months. A question of course arises over why all three of them got baptised at nearly the same time. My guess is that it was not a case of sudden religious fervour in the teenage boys. The more likely motive seems to be that they needed some proof of identity following their father's death the previous year, in order to establish that they were still alive and hence eventually claim their bequests under his will on attaining the age of twenty-one. In fact, the day after Alexander was baptised, he and William were on board the ship *Essex* at Gravesend, ready to sail for Bombay—surely conclusive proof of their ulterior motive for getting baptised. Alexander and William were aged eighteen and sixteen respectively, so they presumably had finished their education but John was only thirteen. Therefore, he stayed on at the school in Margate.

Presumably, John left this school some time after his sixteenth birthday, but I have no knowledge of his movements for the next five years, until he was admitted as a student at King's College, London, in the department of Applied Sciences. In 1856 there were fifty-nine students taking this course, which lasted a minimum of three years, but without leading to a degree. John had evidently missed the first term of the academic year which started in October, so accompanying his application form he made payment for only two terms' fees, totalling £29-1-6. The application form also asked the student to state the name and address of his parent or guardian and this is how we discover that John was living with his widowed elder sister, Isabella Bean, in Paddington[4] at that time. Isabella was twelve years older than John and had been widowed in 1853 after twelve years of marriage. After winding up her affairs in India, she had sailed to England in the spring of 1854 and settled in Paddington.

It seems that John did not complete the course, as we find him the following year in India, when he is listed in the Bombay Almanac of 1858 as an inspector working for Bray and Co's Railway Works at Barsi. The data for these annual almanacs was collected a year before publishing, so the implication is that John must have returned to India some time in 1857, probably during the mutiny (which would accord with family tradition that he was working as an engineer on the railways during the mutiny). We can only assume that he cut short his engineering course either because Bray and Co had already offered him this job or because he was anxious to join the rest of his family in India.

Railway construction in India had commenced only a few years before John joined Bray and Co. It all started in March 1849, when the East India Company agreed on terms with the Great Indian Peninsular Railway (GIPR) and the East Indian Railway (EIR) whereby the government provided the right of way and the companies were guaranteed a five percent return on their investment in constructing the railway—this agreement being ratified by formal contracts in August that year. Such guaranteed terms were the necessary inducement to release British capital for building the railways, and the following year survey work began on the first two contracts, awarded to the GIPR and EIR. The former involved the construction of a thirty-five mile long railway line from Bombay to Kalyan at the foot of the Western Ghats while the latter was a 121 mile line from Howrah (near Calcutta) to the small town of Raniganj. This initial 'race' was won by GIPR, who not only made an earlier start (the first sod being turned on 31 October 1850, in front of a large crowd), but also opened the first ever section of a railway in the sub-continent when a train with fourteen railway carriages carrying four hundred guests departed from Bombay's Boree Bunder terminus at 3:35 pm on 16 April 1853 on the twenty mile historic journey to Thane, taking just seventy-five minutes.[5] Boree Bunder, the first terminus at Bombay, was merely an old shack, with a single pair of tracks and without even a platform. The majestic Victoria Terminus, known and admired by countless millions, was only completed in 1888.

The railway contracts granted to the GIPR, the EIR and other railway companies were generally divided into a series of smaller contracts that were awarded to local contractors—a number of whom lost money and failed to complete their sections. When John returned to India in 1857, there were only five such contractors listed in the Bombay Almanac, and he was fortunate enough to join one of the more successful ones, run by Joseph Bray.

John's first assignment was on the Pune to Sholapur line, which was being constructed by Bray and Co for the GIPR. He evidently worked there, based at Barsi, until 1859. This section was opened to the public in 1861, but by then John had moved to an unidentified location (Bhend, Nullah) and then to work on the Nagpur line for three years, being based in 1862 at Nandurah, sixty miles East of Bhusawal.

It was while John was in this region that he had a narrow escape. At the time of this incident, he was with a party surveying the line that was being laid from Bombay to Nagpur. One night his party had camped near Bhusawal, and he was asleep in his tent when some disturbance outside woke him up. Now it was John's habit to keep the money for the men's wages in a locked trunk under his bed, and in order to safeguard this money he always kept two loaded pistols beside his pillow. So, he lit a candle and just as he reached for the pistols, two men armed with tulwars rushed into his tent and attacked him. He managed to shoot and kill both of his attackers, but not before receiving a severe wound across the face from one of these sabre-like swords. Apparently, he grew a beard thereafter, which he wore for the rest of his life, in order to hide the scar from this wound.

On another occasion however he was not quite so lucky. While he was surveying and plate-laying, he contracted blackwater fever. When he recovered from his delirium, he discovered that the trunk under his bed had disappeared alongwith not only the labourers' wages, but also his own savings!

John worked as an inspector for Joseph Bray's company for at least six years, but in 1864 he disappears from the records only to reappear the following year as an Inspector of Police at Lucknow. I am not quite sure why he made such a drastic change of career at this stage. My guess is that romance featured heavily in his decision to opt for a more settled life. The records do not show exactly when John entered the Police force, just that he was already a serving Deputy Inspector of Police (grade 1) at Lucknow on 1 April 1866, on a monthly salary of sixty-five rupees.[6] Even before this he gave his occupation as police inspector when, on 19 December 1865, he took the unusual step of being baptised for a second time. The reason for this was that although he had previously been baptised into the Church of England, he was now adopting the Roman Catholic faith—the same faith as practised by his fiancee, Rachael Short. Despite my earlier disparaging remarks about Joseph Short's lack of obvious commitment to the Roman Catholic faith, it appears that the Short family took it very seriously. In fact, it seems that the change of religious faith was set as a pre-condition for the alliance. However, since John Speirs' son later wrote that his father had lived and died as a member of the Church of England, it seems that John's second baptism was just a matter of pragmatic convenience rather than a case of a true conversion.

John and Rachel were married at St Paul's Church, Lucknow, on 28 April 1866 in a joint ceremony which also marked the marriage of Rachel's half-sister, Marcellina Short to John James Bourbon. As mentioned in an earlier chapter, two of the original wedding invitations have survived, and they show that after the service the guests were invited to Joseph Short's house, near Neil's gate (one of the former entrances to the Kaisar Bagh palace), to 'partake of cake and wine' and to a dinner party at 7:30 pm on the same evening.

After the wedding, John and Rachel settled down in Lucknow and soon started a family. Their first son, Alexander, was born in March 1867, their next, William, was born in September 1868 and in the following June, Rachel gave birth to twin boys, named Frederick and Henry. However, neither of the twins appears to have survived long. Henry's death, at the tender age of four months of a cough and fever is recorded in October 1869 and, although no record has been found of Frederick's death, he probably also died as an infant. He had certainly died before October 1882, as otherwise his name would have been included in a wasika distribution on that date.

John and Rachel's first four children were all baptised at St Paul's Church, Dilkusha which had been built by Father Gleeson shortly after the mutiny to serve the Roman Catholic soldiers in the cantonments, being consecrated in 1862. Until the mutiny, the only Catholic church in

Lucknow was a small chapel built by Father Adeodatus on land granted in Golaganj for the purpose.[7] But this church was levelled to the ground during the insurrection with the small RC cemetery at Kaisar Pasand (where Murium Begum is buried) being the only surviving remnant of the previous Catholic Mission in Golaganj. St Paul's is now the oldest surviving church of Lucknow.

John continued his new job as Inspector of Police at least until June 1869, when he decided to revert to his original vocation, as a Civil Engineer working on railway construction. One of the reasons behind this turnaround could be the low pay he received whilst working for the Police (his salary as an Inspector of Police was merely sixty-five rupees a month) which was less than half of what he could make in the railways. He therefore, took up a post as a platelayer with the East Indian Railway in July 1870, on an initial salary of 150 rupees a month. The duties of a platelayer involved surveying and setting out lines and levels for the railway and supervising the preparation of the base and actual laying of the railway sleepers and lines.

We are all aware of the distinction made between Indians and British during the reign of the East India Company. Here I will expand on some comments I made in the prologue about prejudice against the Anglo-Indians. Throughout his career, John is described in official registers as 'East Indian', which was the existing term for an Anglo-Indian. It is a matter of fact that in those days only certain jobs were available to Anglo-Indians, including working on the railways, in the police force, post, telegraph offices etc. Not only did they have very little prospect of promotion, but they were also forced to work at the same level in similar low-paid jobs throughout their lives. This was certainly true for my great-grandfather, who later became an Assistant Inspector on a salary of 200 rupees a month and eventually a Permanent Way Inspector on 250 rupees a month, his salary remaining at this level until his retirement. Just a simple comparison with his own father, Colonel Alex Speirs, who earned 1200 rupees per month when he took up his first post as a Political Agent and 4500 rupees per month in his final post as Resident at Nagpur, shows the drastic effect that skin-colour had upon a man's career prospects in India in those days. Now obviously, the jobs carried out by father and son are not directly comparable, but there is no question that John's post as Civil Engineer was a technically demanding job and so the fact that he was earning such a small fraction of his father's income seems to reinforce the impression that Anglo-Indians were simply treated as a 'commodity' to be exploited.

Just before John took up his new appointment, the family's finances had improved slightly following the death of Joseph Short in February 1870 (Rachel, being one of his fifteen children and being named in his warisnama, duly succeeded to her share of his wasika, inheriting the sum of Rs 41-10-8 per month). At the same time, her mother had been awarded the monthly sum of Rs 50 which she had contested and (as mentioned in Chapter 4) had spent the next seventeen years and a vast sum of money challenging the decision, eventually being awarded her full right of one-third of her late husband's wasika. In fact, from an early stage, John had assisted his mother-in-law and I will return later to deal with his involvement in her battle with the wasika authorities.

Getting back to John's professional life, his new job inevitably involved spending long periods away from their home in Lucknow. For the next few years, he worked as a platelayer on the new line being constructed between Allahabad and Jabalpur. In 1870, he was shown as being at 'Surrowl', which is probably Sohawal, a town roughly half-way between Allahabad and Jabalpur. The following year he was working at Manikpur, a town closer to Lucknow, and just within the boundaries of Uttar Pradesh; and during 1872 and 1873 he was at Shemabad, an unidentified location. Then, from 1874 to 1878 he was based at Sleemanabad—a town only forty miles from Jabalpur, which had been named after the famous Major General W.H. Sleeman who became well-known for his discovery and virtual elimination of the practice of 'Thuggee'.

It was during this period that John and Rachel's last three children were born—two daughters, Winifred and Veronica (born at Lucknow in February 1874 and July 1877 respectively), and my grandfather, John Sleeman Speirs (born at Jabalpur in May 1875). Evidently, although their permanent home was in Lucknow, John and Rachel lived for some time in Jabalpur, as shown by Sleeman Speirs' baptism certificate. However, the question that I find more fascinating is: Why was my grandfather given the unusual Christian name of Sleeman? Although he would almost certainly have been told the reason, unfortunately this has not been passed on and so I am left to draw my own conclusions. Obviously, the name could have been given simply in honour of the great W.H. Sleeman, but I think it more likely to indicate that Sleeman had been a close friend of Colonel Alex. Whilst no personal correspondence has survived to corroborate this theory, they had similar status on the 'political ladder' and the HEIC political correspondence files show that they frequently wrote to each other in an official capacity. Therefore, it is entirely feasible that they also did so on a personal level. In any event, my grandfather himself was always known by his second Christian name of Sleeman, and he was proud enough of this name to give it in turn to each of his sons (as their last Christian name).

In July 1878 John was promoted to the post of Assistant Permanent Way Inspector, where his duties involved the inspection of completed track in the region and supervision of any necessary maintenance work. For this post, John was transferred to the railway station at Bolpur, a small town about eighty miles from Calcutta. He was to remain at Bolpur for the next nine years, being upgraded to the full rank of Inspector in December 1880. Initially, he received a miserly increase in salary of only twenty-five rupees a month, with a further similar increase in 1882. Finally, in December 1887 he was transferred to Fatwah, a small town about thirty miles east of Patna, where he seems to have remained as an Inspector until his retirement in about 1893 (when his name disappears from the lists of employees of the East Indian Railway).

Now I must go back to the autumn of 1882, when two terrible blows hit John's family. The first occurred when Rachel caught dysentery, which was a common cause of death in the unhealthy climate of northern India. Tragically, Rachel died from this disease on 10 October 1882 at the age of thirty-six, and was buried the same day in the Nishat Ganj cemetery on the north side of the Gomti River, which had only just been opened. Her grave, one of the first plots in this cemetery, carries the following inscription:

> In memory of Rachael, the dearly loved wife of John Speirs and devoted daughter of Joseph and Amelia Short. Born 16th Dec 1846, died 10th Oct 1882. Deeply regretted by her seven children and relatives.

Then, scarcely two months later, John's youngest daughter, Veronica Alice, died of smallpox and was buried next to her mother's grave although no inscription has been found to help positively identify her grave.

Whilst it is hard to imagine the depths of John's despair at this double tragedy, sudden deaths occurred only too frequently in nineteenth century India, and, like so many others, John too could only accept and adapt to the cruel turn of fate. He was unable to leave his job with the East Indian Railway, as the family needed his salary to make ends meet. So, whilst he remained in his post at Bolpaur, his mother-in-law, Amelia Short, looked after his children at their home in Lucknow following Rachel's death.

I would here recount a strange circumstance: my father and his siblings only met their two uncles, Alexander and William, and were never told about their aunt Winifred or of the fact that their grandfather had three other children who had died as infants, my finding of Rachel's grave and reading the inscription during a trip to India in 1978 being the first time that my father realised that his grandmother had born seven children. Now whilst not being told about the deaths of the infants is not so surprising, it is surely strange not to have been told that they had an aunt who lived in Lucknow, close to their uncle William. The answer, I am sure, is the one that I revealed in Chapter 4.

Whilst Amelia Short was looking after his children in Lucknow, in his spare time John was assisting her in her legal battle with the government for repayment of arrears of her wasika (as mentioned in Chapter 4). John had evidently taken a keen interest in his mother-in-law's case from a very early stage, having written separately to the former Advocate General of Bengal, J.H. Cowie, shortly after Amelia had commissioned him to give his opinion of the merits of her case in January 1871. Since Amelia was too impoverished to continue fighting her case, as she was already Rs 9,500 in debt to native bankers (who charged high interest rates), she gave John a general Power of Attorney over her affairs. From then on, he took over the correspondence and appeals to the government that had formerly been carried out by Amelia's solicitor, Justinian Watkins of Calcutta.

Amelia's solicitors had advised her that she should not submit any petition to the government for the payment of the outstanding wasika arrears until after the last possible date for any appeals to be heard against the award of one-third of Joseph's wasika to her. Some of Joseph's children had in fact submitted appeals, and the final date for all such appeals to be heard only occurred in July 1883. So John waited till then, and composed a petition to the Viceroy, the Marquis of Ripon, which was duly submitted to the government early in February 1884.[8] The government's deliberations took some time—the first response from the Supreme Government in Calcutta being to the effect that the petition should first be submitted through the government of the North West Provinces for their comments. Eventually, after John had done so and chased the progress of the petition, Lord Ripon decided that there was considerable merit in the case as presented. Privately, the Supreme Government accepted that Amelia had lost substantially due to errors made by the NWP Government and the Wasika Office, particularly by paying Joseph Short's wasika to his children without setting aside the one-third portion claimed by Amelia when they were aware that this was likely to be contested. But it was decided that, though the NWP Government had been extremely negligent, they had acted in 'good faith' and accordingly the Viceroy decided to offer arbitrarily half the sum claimed, as a matter of grace, without of course admitting any liability.

This offer was made to Amelia in July 1885 but, before accepting it, she decided to make one further appeal through her Solicitor who appealed on her behalf in July 1886 for the full amount. However, the government was no longer prepared to reconsider the case and their response to this and a subsequent appeal made by John in January 1887 was the same—that their offer was final and if not accepted would eventually be withdrawn. And this is where the trail of correspondence 'goes cold', so one can only assume that Amelia finally accepted the offer of Rs 7,426, which was half the amount claimed.

At this point, sadly, I must draw this short chapter to a close as I have no family records to show how John spent the rest of his life. He certainly lived in Lucknow after his retirement and must have seen his first grandchildren, William's two daughters, born in 1901 and 1905; and also Sleeman's first child, my uncle Alec, born in December 1905. But, as he died in June 1907, none of my father's brothers had any recollection of their grandfather. In death, too, John Speirs remains an elusive man—no trace having been found of his grave. And, more sadly, two very good studio photographs, a lovely picture of John Speirs and another of his wife Rachel, wearing a full Victorian dress, which always hung in

Sleeman's study at Fairlawns, seem to have disappeared without trace. The photograph of John apparently showed him with a full beard, which he had worn since receiving the sabre wound at Bhusaval.

11

SLEEMAN SPEIRS AND HIS BROTHERS

In the last chapter I had mentioned that Sleeman Speirs was born in May 1875 at Jabalpur, where the family lived while John Speirs was working in that region during construction of the Allahabad to Jabalpur railway line. But this was only a temporary interlude in their life at Lucknow, where Rachel had shortly returned with her young family. In February 1878, Sleeman's elder brothers, Alexander and William, were both admitted to La Martiniere—the famous school in Lucknow designed and built by the French entrepreneur Claude Martin. Initially he had constructed it as a grand house for himself, named Constantia. But unfortunately Martin died in 1800 before the palatial building could be completed, and decreed in his will that the building should become a school. This was eventually accomplished some years before the mutiny, the building being re-named as 'La Martiniere' in honour of its founder[1].

La Martiniere was a very popular school for boys from the European and Anglo-Indian families of Lucknow (in those days Indian nationals were not admitted). At least three of Joseph Short's sons (Martin, George and Benjamin Joseph Short) attended it together with numerous boys from the Quieros family. Another boy who entered the school at the same time as Alexander and William Speirs was John Johannes, popularly known as 'Joey' Johannes[2]. He became a firm friend of both William and Sleeman Speirs, and later he and William worked together as clerks in the Judicial Commissioner's office. He also later became a photographer and set up his own studio in Lucknow in the late nineteenth century. As a grandson of Joseph Short (and his first wife, Jane), he was in fact a 'half-cousin' of Alex, William and Sleeman Speirs, who were also descended from Joseph Short, but by his second wife, Rachel.

Like most boys from Lucknow, Alexander, William (and later Sleeman) and their friend Joey Johannes attended the school as day scholars. However, many students came from far-off places such as Allahabad, Jhansi, Orai, Agra and even Nagpur. They of course tended to be boarders unless they had relations living in Lucknow. Sleeman, who was considerably younger than Alec or William, also went to La Martiniere though the exact dates of his attendance cannot be found, as the Admissions Register for that period is missing. The family almost certainly lived fairly close to La Martiniere, as Sleeman told his sons that although he generally went to school by pony-trap, he would occasionally walk to school.

I have already described how Sleeman represented his brothers and other relatives in a Court Hearing in 1896 (in chapter 4) to determine the succession to his uncle Benjamin Short's wasika. He did so at the tender age of twenty-one, making very pertinent points in his cross-examination of a Barrister thereby leading to a decision in his favour. I am sure that this early success must have whetted his appetite for Law as a career. Another probable reason was that one of his close friends Edwin Manuel, had also followed his father, Augustus Manuel and become a pleader in Lucknow in the 1890s (Edwin was nine years older than Sleeman, being born in 1866, but he had attended La Martiniere at the same time as William and Alexander Speirs).

At this point I had intended to give an account of how Alexander was the first of his brothers to train and become a pleader ('pleader' being a term used in India for an advocate), first practicing in Lucknow and then shifting base to Faizabad. The account, related to me by my father, went on to describe how Alexander had encouraged his youngest brother, Sleeman, to follow his example and, as a practicing lawyer himself, had helped and coached Sleeman when he was studying at Allahabad for his pleader exams. But unfortunately, it seems that my father used to embellish the stories he had been told occasionally! Certainly both of the brothers became pleaders, Alexander having a very successful practice at Faizabad, and Sleeman an equally successful one at Moradabad. But when I tried searching the official records, I discovered quite a different story!

In reality, there is no record of Alexander having practiced as a pleader at Lucknow, and his name first appears on the records as an assistant master at Allahabad Boys' High School in the 1895 edition of Thacker's Directory. Then, from 1896 to 1902 Thacker's shows that he was an assistant master at the East Indian Railway School in Mussourie. Meanwhile, Thacker's shows Sleeman's name first appearing in 1895 as an employee of J.C. O'Connor, civil and military tailors of Lucknow. He is again shown as being in Lucknow in 1896; then he next appears in 1898 and 1899 as an Assistant Master at the same school that his brother Alexander started at—the High School in Allahabad.

But the real surprise came during a visit to Allahabad in 2001 when I searched through old 'Oudh Gazetteers' to trace the records of candidates for the annual pleader exams (having first satisfied myself that neither of the brothers had attended the Law Department at Allahabad University). The records showed that both Alexander and Sleeman had sat their first pleader examination together on the 13 December 1899 at the Muir Central College in Allahabad but that only Sleeman had passed at the first sitting, being notified of his success in February 1900. Meanwhile, Alexander took a further two attempts at the exam, before finally passing it in December 1901.

So apparently, the two brothers studied privately for the exams whilst they were employed as schoolmasters and it was Sleeman who tasted early success. And so, having dealt with that minor 'hiccup', let us now continue with my father's account of Sleeman's later life and career with a few additions from my subsequent research.

Passing his 'pleader' exams at his first attempt was much to Sleeman's credit as law exams were pretty tough in those days, lawyers being expected to be fluent in both Persian and Urdu. (In the course of his training, Sleeman also learned to speak the Urdu of the Court, the most eloquent dialect of that language.) However, he could not immediately capitalise on his exam success, as lawyers needed considerable financial resources in order to set up a law practice. So, at first he took up a post as tutor to the sons of the Raja Rikh of Tajpur, a small town about thirty miles North West of Moradabad. Evidently, Sleeman actually lived in Moradabad whilst working for the Raja, probably in the latter's house. He was accompanied by his bearer (or valet), who had been with him since his childhood and who spoke English fairly well. Whilst working as a tutor, his bearer continually reminded him that he must make an effort to begin his professional life as a lawyer. Eventually in 1902, after working roughly two years as a tutor, Sleeman felt that he had saved up enough money to set up a practice and to sustain both of them for a while. So he took a month's unpaid leave from his tutoring, at the same time informing his employer of his intentions and that he might not return. The Raja kindly wished him good luck and added that if things did not work out satisfactorily, he could return to his post.

Having already lived for two years in Moradabad, Sleeman apparently decided that this would be a reasonable place to start his legal career. Moradabad was at the centre of a large district. It had a district magistrate, a judge as well as a city magistrate and occasionally an additional judge too. The Collector and an Assistant Collector were also based there. So, as an important legal centre, there was already a thriving bar at Moradabad.

I should here point out to the readers that the legal system in India differed from the English legal system in that the intermediaries such as solicitors were not used between advocates and their clients. Instead, the clients would be introduced directly to the advocate through a clerk, who would also arrange for the fees to be paid by the client. Hence, it was desirable though not essential, to maintain an office for the clerk close to the courts.

On leaving the Raja's employ, Sleeman rented a house near the courts for a month and spread word through his bearer that he was available to accept briefs in the criminal courts. At that time there was already an English advocate in Moradabad named Gasper and it soon became apparent that all the work was already being offered to Gasper. Although Sleeman did not know this at the time, it was common knowledge that Gasper was a rather testy old man who tended to abuse his clients at the slightest excuse.

As the month drew to a close, Sleeman dejectedly said to his bearer, 'I think we will have to pack up as my money has nearly run out and, if we stay any longer, I won't be able to pay you your wages'. But the bearer who was more of a friend and adviser than a servant, replied saying, 'Don't bother about my wages; I can get by on my own savings. But you simply must hang on and I will redouble my efforts to obtain work for you'. So somewhat in desperation, they stayed on for another week. Then, one evening, a number of well-dressed Muslims approached

Sleeman and asked for his advice on a matter saying that they had already asked 'Gasper Sahib', but that he had been so rude to them that they had walked out on him. Sleeman promptly and courteously gave them the requested advice whereupon they said: 'You realize that you have given us all the advice we requested without even stating your charges. This was quite an omission. We could now leave you and, using your free advice, obtain a cheap lawyer to take the case to court. But we are so impressed with your advice and your openness that we will now appoint you to be our advocate in the matter'.

That marked the beginning of his splendid legal career. Thereafter it soon became known that the new lawyer in Moradabad treated his clients far better than Gasper did and that his legal knowledge was excellent. Consequently, he very soon built up a thriving practice. The Muslims who became Sleeman's first clients were local butchers. They maintained a warm relationship with him thereafter, using him as their advocate for the next thirty-five years; anytime they needed advice, they would simply get in a tonga and turn up at his house or office.

Life for Sleeman was not all work though and he rapidly made friends with other young men of his age. They were keen on motorcycles and Sleeman soon bought the most popular type, the 'Indian', made at Springfield, Massachusetts, USA, his machine also having a side-car. This was a 7 HP motorbike, one of the most powerful available in those days. He used to ride around at great speed on the local roads which were either 'kutcha' (unlayered) or 'pukka' (solid but with only a rammed limestone surface rather than tarmac). Bullocks frequently used to cause pot-holes in these roads, and consequently motorcycling was quite hazardous. Several times Sleeman came off his motorbike and twice he was picked up unconscious after a particularly bad fall.

One particular friend, Fred Murcott, known to his friends as 'young Murcott' was keen on duck-shooting. He encouraged Sleeman to join him in this sport, visiting the jheels (shallow lakes much favoured by the migrating duck) around ten to twenty miles from Moradabad on the Meerut road. They would shoot at these jheels during the winter months, when ducks migrated there from Siberia. But young Murcott eventually came to a tragic end. He also used to go tiger shooting and on this occasion had set up a machaan with a goat tethered below as bait. As soon as the tiger approached the goat, Murcott shot it. He then called the shikaris and climbed down to inspect the kill, approaching cautiously in case the tiger was shamming dead. It was! Once within reach, the tiger grabbed at the muzzle of his gun, leaving Murcott unable to shoot. So he yelled to a shikari who was now behind him and was carrying his other gun, to shoot the tiger. The shikari did so, but missed and hit young Murcott behind the knee. The shikaris then rushed to tell Murcott's wife, who ran two miles to fetch him but he died from loss of blood before they could get him to a hospital.

Another close friend was John Gordon, and I believe that the two had met originally in Lucknow. He later became the headmaster of the high school at Moradabad, located near the bridge over the Ram Gange. He married the sister of Mrs Embleton (whom I will refer to later in this chapter), a very pleasant woman. They had children and the family lived in a lovely house. Both families visited each other regularly. In fact, Sleeman kept in touch with the Gordons for over fifty years, visiting John Gordon at his home in Oakfield Grove, Clifton, Bristol for two or three days in 1947 and still writing to him at the age of eighty in 1955.

In those days, it was not easy for single English men to find a match simply because there was a shortage of eligible young ladies! Sleeman accordingly followed the usual practice by starting to write to young ladies from England who advertised in a 'Lonely Hearts' journal. After corresponding with Isabella Christie Bright for some time, they both felt a growing attachment for each other. Eventually, she came out to India to see Sleeman and they both met in Bombay. They obviously liked each other as much on meeting as they had while corresponding because their wedding took place within two weeks of her arrival! I have a record of their marriage, which took place at the Bowen Memorial Methodist Episcopal Church in Bombay on 23 December 1904. The marriage certificate gives the bride's maiden name as Isabella Christie Smith, the daughter of Henry Smith. This caused my father considerable trouble in tracing her family, because it turned out that her true maiden surname was Bright and that Henry Smith was really her stepfather! Her real father was Walter Bright.

At this point I ought to introduce my grandmother more fully. Isabella Christie Bright was the daughter of Walter Bright, a Scottish brass worker and Janet Bright (nee' Porteous). She was born on 12 September 1885 at their home, 50 Castle Street East in Marylebone. Hereafter, I will refer to her as Chris, since this is the name by which Sleeman always knew her throughout their married life.

Chris's parents were married on 12 August 1886 when they were living in Osnaburgh Street which is just off Albany Road, near Regents Park. Walter Bright's father, Edward Bright, was also a brass worker whereas Janet Porteous's father, David Porteous, was deceased, but had been a coach painter. This accords with what Chris had told Lawrence that she had an uncle and a cousin called Mckechnie who worked for a firm called Coopers and looked after the Queen's carriages. Also, that they were Heraldic Painters, a trade that ran in the family. She had told Lawrence that her uncle was the foreman and on one occasion he had sat her in the glass coach (or the gold coach which had glass partitions surrounding it). Her uncle teased her saying that 'You will now be able to say that you have sat where the Queens of England sit on state occasions'.

Chris was named 'Isabella Christie' after her grandmother, Isabella Christie, who had married David Porteous and had lived in Edinburgh. She disliked her father because he was a drunkard who had made their lives very miserable, and had only been prepared to marry Janet a year after Chris was born. As a result, neither she nor her mother missed him when he died. Her mother Janet then married Henry Smith, a widower with children, who was a cooper (ie a barrel-maker). Chris considered Henry Smith to be a good man in contrast to her father. So it was probably not surprising that she subsequently assumed his surname while giving her maiden name for her marriage certificate.

After their marriage, Janet and Henry Smith lived in a street near The Angel in Islington. Two of her step-sisters were called Florence and Katherine. They were once photographed with Chris and this photograph was kept by Chris and was later hung in her married home where it was seen by all of their children. We believe that Florence died young, at the age of thirteen. Chris had another sister (or step-sister, we are not sure) called Rose. There were also two step-brothers (one of whom was called Arthur) both of whom later fought in the First World War. Chris said that they had a very bad time at the front and that one or both of them were sent in the expeditionary force to Russia where they suffered great hardship in the retreat in the depths of the Russian winter.

After leaving school, Chris worked for a florist and was trained both in flower arrangement and in making bouquets, nosegays and button-holes. For a few years, she kept up a correspondence with Sleeman Speirs and as she was really curious about India, he suggested that she visit at his expense. She however decided to get there under her own steam and she had her passage to Bombay paid by an English lady who was returning to India, in return for her services as a companion and as a nurse to the lady's children.

On hearing of her plans, one of her Porteous uncles, who owned several ships said that she could have gone out free on one of his ships if he had known of her intentions. Anyway, she travelled with the English lady and was met at Bombay by Sleeman Speirs. After an engagement of two weeks, they were married as described previously. Let us now return to the subsequent married life of Sleeman and Chris Speirs in northern India.

Once Sleeman found his feet in the legal corridors of Moradabad, he extended the short rental period on his accommodation. The property was a thatched bungalow standing in pleasant grounds of about three acres, close to Meston Park and immediately adjacent to the courts. It was therefore ideally situated for him professionally. This house became his and Chris's first married home. For a month or so after their marriage, they were joined there by Sleeman's father, John Speirs, who then returned to his home in Lucknow.

As they both liked this house, Sleeman shortly negotiated with the landlords to sell it to him. The house had been passed down to Mr Thomas Hill and his two sisters by their father, Mr Roland Hill of Moradabad but they were happy to sell it as they no longer wished to live there. So Sleeman bought the house, then known as 'bungalow number 33', for a sum of Rs 4500, the purchase being completed on 5 May 1906.

Meanwhile, the couple had started a family, their first two sons, Alec and Bill, being born in 1905 and 1907 respectively. With a growing family and a high income from his law practice, Sleeman decided that it was time to expand their living accommodation. But he was not content to simply extend the bungalow. Besides, an extension would in any case have been difficult to achieve without removing the steeply pitched thatched roof. So the thatched house was demolished and he organised the construction of a very large, impressive house which he promptly called 'Houston House' after the Speirs family home at Houston in Scotland that had been bought by his great-great-grandfather, Alexander Speirs of Elderslie. This grand house was built by a Master Mason named Abdul Haq, a devout Muslim who had built many beautiful buildings.

Whilst they lived at Houston House, they had four more children—John, Helen Rachel, Lawrence and Jean being born at regular two yearly intervals between 1911 and 1917. But a sad event occurred in the autumn of 1913 when their fourth child, Helen Rachel, died at the age of only two months. At the time of Helen's birth, Chris had been very ill with typhoid and consequently was unable to feed her. Although a wet-nurse was engaged, Helen did not receive adequate sustenance and wasted away. She was buried in the civil cemetery and her epitaph reads:

Helen Rachel, Darling baby of John Sleeman and Isabella Christie Speirs, Fell asleep 18th October 1913, Aged two months

Probably to help her get over this loss, Sleeman took Chris on holiday to England in the summer of 1914, just before the outbreak of the First World War, bringing their three sons with them. It seems that they must have had relatives or friends at Margate, as they left Alec, Bill and John there, before starting a hectic six-week sightseeing tour of England and Scotland. Writing to his brother William near the end of their tour, Sleeman said that the incessant travelling had been too much for Chris, who was still in delicate health. She had been continuously ill on the sea-voyage and had not recovered properly until they reached Scotland, where they toured for three weeks. He loved Scotland, the dramatic scenery, the mountains, the lochs and particularly the city of Edinburgh. Glasgow, though, was a disappointment, being simply a business town so they only stayed there for a morning, and then visited Elderslie village. During his tour of Scotland, he had managed to see Houston House, the current Speirs family home, and had evidently intended to see their first ancestral home, Elderslie House, near Renfrew but had run out of time as they were returning to London that evening. Little did he know that he had missed his last chance to see that magnificent mansion, which was pulled down only a few years later.

Sleeman was writing from Brighton on 17 August, barely two weeks after Britain had entered the First World War following Germany's invasion of Belgium. He noted that:

> Evidences of the war are all over. Soldiers guard every inch of the lines, bridges & stations. The Military control the running of the railways. Paper money is used by Act of Parliament. £1 notes & Postal Orders are issued by all the Great daily papers. The ordinary life of the people does not seem greatly upset by the war. The places of amusement etc are going on just the same but for all that the war is the one topic of conversation. People realize it's going to be a bigger thing than anything we have had in this way, but all are hopeful of ultimate success.

However, as a fall-out of the war he was unable to easily collect the boys since coastal train services had been suspended. So he had to take a train to London and another out again to Margate in order to pick up Alec, Bill and John. He was very concerned at the time as he had run out of money and needed to return to India quickly since being on holiday on the South coast of England with a young family was hardly appropriate in the circumstances! Fortunately, his elder brother Alec sent Sleeman £100 and they were then able to organise their return journey. This though was not without incident. A German U-boat was sighted when they were in the Mediterranean Sea, leading to an extensive diversion. However, they arrived back in India safely.

Ever since her arrival, Chris used to regularly receive long letters from her mother. But one day in about 1917, she was found crying on receipt of a letter from England—the letter informing her of the death of her mother. Her mother's death effectively ended Chris's chief connection with England, and this probably led to her decision many years later to make India her final retirement place (even though her husband and four of her children had settled in England by then).

In 1918 Sleeman became involved in a famous case where a large number of Muslims and Hindus had been arrested and charged with rioting. The disturbances had started one evening when a Hindu bania heard a rumour that the Muslims had arisen and were attacking the Hindu shrines. The Hindus then massed together and in a short time a violent riot ensued in which several people were killed, others having their heads cracked open with lathis. The riot had occurred in Saharanpur and it soon became evident that Sleeman would need to move there for the duration of the trial and the pre-trial preparation of the defence (he had been engaged to defend the Hindus). So the family moved to Saharanpur, staying at the house of a senior lawyer for a few months.

A trial of this proportion and significance needed massive legal resources. Hence, Sleeman was shortly asked to obtain the best defence lawyer available regardless of the expense. He soon confirmed that the man required was Eardley Norton, a Madras High Court Lawyer with impeccable credentials. Sleeman's next task was to engage him. Arriving in Madras, he visited Eardley Norton at his home, Holmcroft, in Harrington Street and outlined the case to him. Norton expressed interest but replied saying, 'Yes, I'll come, Speirs but I've another trial on at the moment'. So Sleeman had to wait there patiently for that trial to finish before he could return to Saharanpur with Eardley Norton.

Eardley Norton's fee was indeed quite impressive—Rs 3000 a day for himself and Rs 100 a day for his clerk. Besides, he also required the use of a special train for himself together with an all expenses-paid shopping trip in Calcutta en route. This special train had to wait there for nearly a week whilst he was shopping!

Apparently, Mrs Norton was not too keen on the climate in India, so she lived in Switzerland. Presumably with his high fees, Eardley Norton was easily able to afford to keep homes in two countries and to regularly visit his wife in Switzerland! For this trial though, he lived in the house next door to that occupied by Sleeman's family.

Some time ago I found (amongst Sleeman's effects) the photograph which has been signed by Eardley Norton. The photograph almost certainly depicts the defence lawyers in the case, Eardley Norton obviously being the central figure, and Sleeman being at the right hand end of the back row. Besides this impressive team of defence lawyers, the case also had a panel of judges appointed specifically for the trial!

Despite all the perks, Eardley Norton did not stay long as the case for the Hindus was fairly hopeless, there being ample evidence that guns had been hoarded in preparation for the riot and that the weapons had been used freely without provocation. So in order to protect his reputation, Mr Norton beat a hasty retreat as did Chris, who was having a terrible time controlling her sons who had very little to do there.

Sleeman also left as soon as he could, but he had to remain in Saharanpur for a further three months or so.

Another interesting trial, this time at Moradabad, that Sleeman told Lawrence about was one in which a moneylender (bania) was prosecuting a client for not repaying the money lent by the bania.

In this case, Sleeman was acting as Defence Council. The Indian who had been charged told Sleeman that he had definitely repaid all of the money including interest over a period of time. In fact, he had seen the bania entering the repayments into his books on each occasion and at the time the bania had never informed him that he owed any more. It was only after he had completed all the repayments and each time seen them entered in the books that the bania had backtracked. Subsequently, the bania had shown him the books without any record of the repayments.

Of course it was fairly evident that the bania had two sets of books, one in which he entered up repayments in front of his client and the other for official display, showing none of the repayments (this was a very common practice!). But the problem lay in getting hold of the first set of books. Sleeman however realised that this was probably not the first time that the bania had used this scam so he had him watched to see when he tried it again. He did not have to wait long because on one of the days of the trial, the bania was spotted carrying out his trade within the confines of the court and with both sets of books!

So Sleeman conferred with the judge, telling him that the truth would emerge if they could restrain the bania immediately. The judge ordered the court buildings to be sealed and soon the bania himself was in court trying to explain the discrepancies between the two sets of books.

However, although an amusing case, this was not a typical one for Sleeman, who prospered on the frequent cases of murder, the lawyers' fees for these more serious cases being correspondingly higher.

One particularly sad murder case involved Abdul Haq, the Muslim builder who had built Houston House for Sleeman. Abdul Haq had become a friend of the family and although not a servant, he lived on the premises in one of the servants' quarters. Whenever he saw young Mac, he would pick him up and ask if he was keeping well. Then he would toss him high above his head and catch him expertly, setting him gently down on the ground and then stand with his arms folded, staring into space. He used to visit Sleeman and Chris for an hour or so regularly, though never more than twice a week. On one occasion, Sleeman saw him lift a bag of cement and toss it aside as though it was feather-light. After a few words with Abdul Haq, Sleeman happily invited some of his friends over to dinner that night. During the meal they discussed the feats of a well-known strong man, named Sandow. Julian Manuel,[1] a close family friend and himself a very powerful man, was of the opinion that no other man could equal Sandow's feats. As the evening wore on, Sleeman prolonged the discussion suggesting that a man might exist who could equal and perhaps exceed even the great Sandow. Julian wouldn't accept that, so shortly bets were placed and then Abdul Haq who had been waiting patiently in the kitchen was summoned. When Julian had finished putting Abdul Haq to the test, all of those present were dumbfounded at his strength and Sleeman cheerfully collected his winnings. Abdul Haq had proved to be even stronger than Sleeman had thought him to be, and for a while Julian and other of Sleeman's friends enjoyed themselves winning small amounts on bets placed on Abdul Haq who whenever asked by Sleeman gladly provided the entertainment. However, when Abdul Haq finally realised that money was changing hands and that he was being used to win bets, he declined to have anything more to do with this entertainment being a devout Moslem and no amount of cajoling would move him. Sleeman did not press the point as Abdul Haq was a valuable workman and he respected his principles. It was shortly after this incident that Abdul Haq's life as a master mason was turned upside down.

Every morning, long before sunrise, Abdul Haq would set off on a long run, returning around 7 am, when Sleeman would generally be out in his rose garden inspecting his new plants imported from the UK or planning some new beds of flowers or examining the tennis court. Abdul would join him and they would chat as old friends and then each of them would go about his day's business. One morning, though, Abdul Haq

---

[1] Julian Manuel was one of the sons of Edwin Manuel, pleader of Lucknow, and the grandson of Augustus Manuel, also a pleader of Lucknow. Augustus Manuel had married Mary Bourbon, a descendant of the French Royal family and relative of John Bourbon, who had married Joseph Short's daughter, Marcelina. The close family ties that existed between European families in Lucknow is again demonstrated by the fact that one of Julian's aunts had married William Sangster, the father of Augustus Sangster, who married Alice Short and whose troubled life is described in Chapter 5.

failed to keep his regular appointment with Sleeman. Although a bit put out, Sleeman was not unduly perturbed and was preparing to go to Court after breakfasting when the City Station Police Officer arrived and informed him that he had arrested Abdul Haq on a charge of murder. So Sleeman at once went to the Police Station, where he learnt from Abdul Haq that in the morning, when he was running along the footpath adjacent to the main road leading out of town, a Thakur riding on a horse had ridden up from behind him and while passing had struck him with his whip and had abused him, calling him a pig. Abdul Haq had sprinted forward and seized the horse by the bridle, whereupon the Thakur had leaned forward and again struck him with his whip across his face. Abdul Haq had then hit the Thakur with the back of his hand, the force of the blow flinging the Thakur from his horse and breaking his neck, thus killing him instantly. He had then tied the horse to a nearby tree and gone straight to the police station, where he was now incarcerated. In the absence of any witnesses, the station officer was obliged to charge Abdul Haq with murder.

When the news spread, there was a tremendous outcry from the Hindu population and it was found expedient to try Abdul Haq for murder. Sleeman defended him and he was eventually convicted of manslaughter. Punishment in those days was severe, and taking account of the tremendous outcry from the Hindus, the prosecutor asked for a maximum sentence as a deterrent to other strong men. He was sentenced to a number of years' imprisonment and, serving them as a model prisoner, was eventually paroled. But he never returned to Sleeman's house, living instead in one of the Muslim communes within the city. From then onwards Abdul Haq lived on the money he had saved and on the charity of his friends, being unable to obtain work again. He visited the family from time to time, but mostly just stood in the road outside the house, doing and saying nothing. His life had evidently been destroyed and he could not understand how justice had failed him so.

In the years up to 1918, Sleeman's practice was thriving and he had become quite prosperous. But he wanted to give his sons the best possible education which involved sending them to English public schools, obviously at considerable expense as it would involve not only the school fees but also the cost of the sea travel and providing for their keep during school holidays.

Unfortunately, the length of his stay at Saharanpur resulted in a significant reduction in business at Moradabad, even though his faithful munshi remained there trying to keep the business thriving. So in order to fund school fees for Alec and Bill, he decided to sell Houston House and live in rented accommodation for a while. (He had in fact already bought two other properties, one named Fairlawns and the house next to it. But he was renting these out, and needed the rents to supplement his income.) So he sold Houston House in 1920, and the following year Alec and Bill were sent to England to attend at Westminster school where they became boarders, staying in Rigaud's House. Sleeman had made arrangements with a clergyman whose son was also at Westminster School, to look after Alec and Bill during the school holidays. (Westminster has for many years been a popular school for the clever sons of impoverished clergymen who aimed to become 'Queen's Scholars', by passing an extremely difficult exam known appropriately as 'The Challenge' with the benefits of greatly reduced fees and exalted status within the school.)

Meanwhile, the family moved to a rented house called Eagerness on a road at the far end of Meston Park from Houston House. Malcolm was born there in August 1920. After the family left Eagerness, that property was bought by a lawyer friend of Sleeman's, named Kidar Nath. Then in about 1921, they moved to the house next to Eagerness, a charming Indian style house called Ashfaq Manzil, where their last child, Marjory, was born in December 1922.

Whilst they lived at Eagerness, Sleeman and Chris took pity on a family in distress, named Embleton (it was Mrs Embleton whose sister had married Sleeman's good friend, John Gordon). Alec, Bill and John occasionally used to play with the Embleton boys, Gavin and Bob, and their sister, Tootsie at their home in Moradabad. Mr Embleton, an Engineer working on the railways, had caught flue in 1920 and died. After being asked to vacate their railway accommodation, Sleeman had offered to let them stay at Eagerness until Mrs Embleton could make other arrangements. So for a few months, the two families occupied the same house.

Alec and Bill unfortunately did not make much use of their expensive education at Westminster School. With his income from his legal practice diminishing, Sleeman decided that he would not send any more of his children to England for schooling as there were several good schools with substantially lesser fees not far from Moradabad. This decision also meant that he could now afford to live in the house that he had previously been renting out.

As mentioned earlier, this house was called Fairlawns. It was situated on the outskirts of Moradabad and was a large thatched bungalow in grounds of about five acres, adjacent to the Collector's house on one side and the Superintendent of Police's house on the other. The gardens had numerous fruit trees of mango, guava, and a huge tamarind tree near the gate. There was a tube-well near the boundary, with a pump-house nearby. Often during the summer, the pump would be running continuously for days on end in the everlasting battle to keep the grass from parching. Sleeman always loved roses and he used to send for rose plants from England. These would arrive looking very dried out and lifeless but he followed the instructions, leaving them in wet moss for a fortnight before transferring them to pots indoors to gain strength before planting them out. Surprisingly, they were very successful in that hot climate.

Sleeman also planted numerous orange trees in a half-acre plot but he gave up in despair when he realised that there was no means of keeping them watered. However, this was where Lawrence showed his practicality and rescued the orange trees. He started by excavating a conduit for the water from the pump-house to the orchard, the earth sides being lined with pieces of tile and guttering to prevent massive leakage. In fact, although there were frequent bursts in the sides of the conduit, it achieved the objective of keeping the orchard watered. Despite all the efforts, the crop of oranges was disappointing, probably because of the climate.

Although it was a nice property and the family kept it longer than any other, Fairlawns did not have the same attraction as Houston House and was certainly not as conveniently situated. Sleeman now generally had to take a tonga or his car to the courts. He had bought his first car, a Ford, in 1921 and was either chauffeured by his driver or by Alec or John to the courts in it, avoiding driving himself.

Sleeman used to go to work after the mid-morning meal which was supposed to be ready by 10 am, so that he could get to the courts by 10.30. However, sometimes the meal wasn't actually ready until about 11am. Since he would insist on eating before going to work, this delay caused great annoyance to him. He would never, though, dream of showing his displeasure as he believed in treating his servants well and was in turn rewarded by faithful service over many years. In particular, his malis (gardeners) came from one family and three generations served Sleeman's family, the last generation being the brothers Maith, Pouran and Kinairian. The family always had a khansama (cook), whose job was to prepare meals in the kitchen and place them in the hot food containers fifty yards away for serving by the bearer. But the count of other servants would vary according to the number of children at home.

With his income from his legal practice still at a reduced level, Sleeman decided to set up a business in about 1925. With two partners, Oswald Mossley (who worked for the Railways, at a fairly high level) and Miss Johnstone (a doctor who practiced in the city), Sleeman purchased a mill in Moradabad, with himself as the major shareholder. The mill was intended for milling flour and rice and producing linseed oil although they never actually used it for rice. It was situated on the outskirts of the city but in a very unpleasant location, close to an abattoir. As a result, there were often unpleasant odours in the air besides vultures circling or waiting in the trees nearby.

Unfortunately, none of the three shareholders had any experience of such work and Sleeman, though a very scholarly man was not at all practical. So he had to rely totally on the experience of whoever was left in charge of the mill, not a very good recipe for success in business.

At first, after advertising for the position of manager, he employed a young English engineer, who was given a house very close to the mill. But this engineer had no experience with mills and in an effort to increase the oil extraction rate from the grain, he increased the pressure on the crusher mandrels too much. The result was that these mandrels, which were made from high-grade tool-steel and were expensive to form, kept breaking at an alarming rate. Eventually, a director of the manufacturers, Franz Smulders & Co, had to actually come from Holland to find out what was going wrong.

In fact, the pulp from which most of the oil had been extracted was being re-fed into the mill for a second crushing to increase the yield. This was the main cause of the problem. There was a simpler means of achieving this, and it is interesting to note that it was Chris, who worked out the solution, being quite a practical woman herself. One day she visited the mill and asked for a good-sized sample of the pulp, which she brought home in an oil drum. She then added water to the pulp and tried slowly heating it on the kitchen stove. As she had expected, the heating had the effect of bringing the oil out of the pulp. Being lighter than water, the oil floated to the surface after the heat was removed, from where it could easily be skimmed off.

When he learned of the young engineer's mistakes, Sleeman decided that he must be replaced. Knowing that Alec was at home without a job, it seemed a good idea to install Alec as the manager of the mill. Unfortunately, this proved to be a disaster! Although he had good intentions, Alec was not a person who could stick at any task for a long period. He also didn't like getting up early and the mill had to open at 7 am in order to be in production for sufficient hours to compete with the banias. Whilst he started off his duties in a promising way, he soon reverted to getting up at 10 am or later and casually going to the mill around mid-day. But since he held the keys to the mill, the mill-workers would be left standing outside until Alec eventually arrived to open it up!

It soon became clear that flour, which was the main product of this mill, only gave a marginal profit as it could not be sold at any higher a price than the hand-ground flour produced by the banias in the chauk. But to compound Sleeman's problems, the banias realising that they could be driven out of the market if this enterprise succeeded, reduced their prices drastically knowing that their combined strength could force Sleeman out. Eventually, Sleeman bowed to the inevitable and decided to withdraw from flour production. This left the linseed oil production as the only viable source of revenue. But by then the mill had already suffered heavy losses and Sleeman's partners decided to withdraw from the venture, accepting that they had lost their stakes. However, Sleeman still felt that it was possible to make a profit from linseed oil production, so in about 1927 he bought another mill near the Himalayan foothills at Ramnagar and arranged to have the oil expeller plant transferred there. (This plant was run by a 50 HP diesel engine which had an enormous flywheel.)

But Sleeman had yet not realised that Alec had been opening the mill late, so he again left Alec in charge, giving him a flat nearby together with a servant. Thus, with Alec living by the second mill and only infrequent visits by Sleeman, it was a long time before Sleeman realised why the venture wasn't making any money. In fact, he struggled on with Alec running the second mill for about two years before finally conceding defeat in 1929. By then Sleeman had made huge losses on this enterprise. And to add to his woes, this was the year of the great world Stockmarket crash. Sleeman had a large portfolio of shares and he lost very heavily on shares that were presumably intended to provide income for his retirement. Many years later, his son Mac abandoned two large trunks, full of his worthless share certificates.

Though by then Sleeman's income from his legal practice had reduced, he had already been acknowledged as the most prominent lawyer in Moradabad. Being an important legal centre, there were between thirty and forty lawyers at Moradabad. The other lawyers always chose Sleeman to act as their representative in any important dealings with the judges. He was also elected the Secretary of the bar library besides holding the post of Chairman of the Bar Association year after year because as an Englishman and an outsider, he was the only lawyer who was deemed completely impartial in disputes between Hindus and Muslims. By then, there were two distinct groups of lawyers at Moradabad—the older group of prominent lawyers headed by Sleeman (who all spoke 'Court' Urdu and took the major cases) and a group of younger lawyers (who did not have the same training in Urdu and could only take the minor cases). These younger lawyers were assisted by the Clerk of the Court in presenting their cases in this difficult language.

Two particular lawyer friends of Sleeman were Shanti Prasad Agarwal and Murli Manoher. Shanti was a Hindu lawyer of about the same age as Sleeman. He was a nice chap, always the soul of the party, prone to making up 'tall' stories although few people ever believed them! Murli was also a Hindu (or possibly a Brahmin), but quite a bit younger. He had a quick wit, an equally quick tongue and was always cracking jokes. He got on well with everyone and Sleeman particularly liked him. In fact, Sleeman kept in close contact with both of them after he retired to Mussoorie and wrote to them for many years even after leaving India in 1945.

I know little about Sleeman's life in India after 1937 for the simple reason that Lawrence and John, who described the family's life to me, had both left India by 1937. All that I gathered is that Sleeman eventually sold Fairlawns after retiring in about 1940. He subsequently moved to a house in Happy Valley, Mussourie called Silverwood. Jean was already married by then and Malcolm had joined the army in 1940 so I am sure that only Sleeman, Chris and Marjory lived at Mussourie. Then Marjory got married in May 1944, so all of Sleeman's children had left home by the time that he and Chris finally left India just before the end of the Second World War, arriving in England in May 1945.

I do not intend to relate here the story of my grandfather's subsequent life in England; it will suffice to say that he had a peaceful, serene life living mainly with my parents and taking great delight in his grandchildren until he finally passed away on 4 May 1959, just before his 84th birthday. But I would be doing him a grave injustice if I did not mention how much he was loved and respected both by his family as well as by his friends. Sadly, he died of a stroke on hearing about the death of his daughter Jean. It is surely a mark of the man that he cared so much for his family that this news was more than he could bear. At the same time, I know how much his children cared for and loved their father, from the many letters that he left behind on his death. My cousin Alison tells me that the only time she ever saw her mother weeping uncontrollably was when she was told of Sleeman's death. However, I will leave the last word on the subject to his lawyer friend, Kidar Nath, who wrote in a letter to my father:

> My dear Lawrence, Your heart-rending news-letter to Shanti Pershad was a blow to us all. Your late father was dearly loved by us all. His qualities of head & heart and his brotherly affection we can never forget.
> You will see from the resolution of condolence passed under my chairmanship today, that one and all the members of the Bar Association were deeply grieved. Jean's premature demise broke his heart. His memory we will always cherish. May He grant you peace to the departed soul & fortitude to you & John to withstand the blow.

> Yours sincerely
> Kidar Nath

I will now turn to Sleeman's eldest brother, Alexander, and say a bit more about his life after we left him having finally passed his pleader exams in December 1901.

To his nephew Lawrence, he always seemed a somewhat austere, learned gentleman of impeccable conduct and with a commanding presence. This is certainly the impression we gain from his photograph. But we all know that looks can be deceptive! Further research indicates that his conduct was not always so impeccable! Alexander never married but when he was living in Lucknow, he had an affair with a girl called Shahzadi. Subsequently, he lived with her as his mistress for several years. I have already introduced Shahzadi in Chapter 5 as the daughter of Edwin Short's mistress, Amina Begum by another man.

The true facts about Alexander Speirs' affair with Shahzadi began to emerge in 1917 when Edwin attempted to change his warisnama in favour of Shahzadi. Witnesses confirmed that Alexander had lived with Shahzadi as his mistress for some considerable time. During this period, Shahzadi had borne him two daughters; the first who was born in Golaganj had died as a child. She was called Mary Patricia Speirs and appears to have lived until at least 1906, when she was baptised at St Joseph's Church, Lucknow with a stated date of birth of November 1895. The second, Alice Mary Speirs, but commonly known as Pultan, was born at Balrumpur hospital in Golaganj.

Alexander's affair with Shahzadi seems to have ended shortly after Alice Mary's birth. In fact he joined as assistant master at Oak Grove School in Mussourie in June 1895, and that school's records show that he had just left a similar post at Allahabad High School. Clearly, it is very unlikely that he could have brought his mistress and illegitimate children with him for either post, as he was living on the school premises. For this reason, the stated year of birth of his first daughter appears incorrect; a more likely year being 1893. After the breakdown of their affair, Shahzadi converted to Islam and married a Muslim, going to live in Malihabad. It seems though that she left her daughters in Lucknow to be brought up by Edwin Short and his mistress Amina Begum (who was of course their grandmother).

Alexander did not shirk his responsibility for Alice Mary and for many years sent eight rupees every month through the Alliance Bank to provide for her upkeep and schooling. The money was initially sent via Eva Speirs (his brother William's wife) to Edwin Short. But Eva Speirs left her husband in 1902, so thereafter Alexander used to send this maintenance money through Edwin Manuel, a family friend and a pleader of Lucknow. He was however ashamed of his relationship with Shahzadi and does not appear to have told even his younger brother Sleeman about the existence of his daughter Alice. Apparently, sometime around 1911 Amina Begum threatened to expose the details of the affair, whereupon he stopped sending the maintenance money. In the words of his aunt, Margaret Snell, 'on account of this threat he used to stop payment, continue again, again stop it. As Alexander Spears felt ashamed so Pultan was not brought before him. He wanted that it should not be known Pultan was born from him'.[3] However, when Alice was married to Vivian Morris Burge in December 1914, Alexander sent a wedding gift of Rs 50 although he did not attend their wedding.[2]

He continued to work as an assistant master at Oak Grove School until June 1901, teaching the fifth standard for most of his time there. He seems to have satisfied the Principal, Lt Col Chapman, who reported after Alexander had been there just over a year that he was steadily improving and should become a good class master. By then, Sleeman had joined his elder brother at Oak Grove School, but Mr Chapman was scathing about his abilities, commenting: 'It seems to me very doubtful whether Mr S. Speirs will make a good teacher; at present his methods are very crude, and his ideas on the subject nil.'[4] To be fair to my grandfather, however, it should be remembered that he was studying for his law exams at this time and presumably had

---

[2] Alice's husband, Vivian Burge, worked as a clerk at the Traffic Manager's Office in Lucknow. He was the son of Samuel Burge, a train driver working for the Oude & Rohilcund Railway, and Dorcas Burge, a lady Doctor. Alice and Vivian had one daughter, Hazel Lorna Burge, whom they sent to La Martiniere Girls' school in 1924. But Hazel died of tuberculosis in 1935, aged only sixteen, and was buried in Nishat Ganj cemetery. Vivian Burge himself seems to have died young, because when Alice remarried in 1929, the register records that she was a widow. Her second husband, Francis Jones, was a telegraphist at Lucknow. They had two or three more children but according to a witness, they had all predeceased Alice, who died in August 1943. The witness, Mr A.J. Fanthome, said that Alice was a family friend, as his mother had brought her up since childhood and that she rented a house from him in Lalbagh for many years. In fact it appears that one of her later children did survive her, as there is a record of John Henry Jones, son of Mrs A. Jones of B.M. Ghai Road, Lalbagh, entering St Francis College in January 1943. Clearly the mother is almost certainly Alice, and this record actually shows that John Henry Jones (born in April 1931) left the college in Grade V in 1947 after Mr Fanthome made his statement. So possibly at least one grandson of Alexander Speirs may still be alive today.

no ambition to remain in the teaching profession once he had qualified as a barrister.

Alexander started his legal career in about 1903. He was very successful and lived a comfortable bachelor life at Faizabad, having a large house with an enormous wooded garden and numerous servants. During his years as a lawyer, Alexander collected coins of the Mughal era and built up a very valuable collection of gold Mohurs of the various reigns. Apparently, he would often accept gold Mohurs in lieu of his legal fees, if they happened to be the ones that he needed for his collection!

Although Alexander did not marry, he had at one time been engaged to an English woman, a Miss Emily Lack. But she broke off the engagement and eventually married a Mr Cole. Evidently though, he still retained a deep attachment for her, as he left his house to her in his will. He died on 9 December 1924 after having a stroke and collapsing whilst he was arguing a case in court at Faizabad. It appears that he was taken back to his house and laid down on a table, but he expired shortly afterwards. An urgent telegram was then sent to Sleeman, notifying him of the tragic circumstances. He immediately set out for Faizabad, arriving there on 10 December. Unfortunately, he was too late to preserve most of his brother's assets, the servants having vanished after ransacking the house and stealing most of his personal effects, including the valuable coin collection. Sleeman arrived there to find his brother's body lying on the table, surrounded by utter chaos.

Alexander was buried at the Faizabad cemetery on the following day. Then, because Mrs Cole wanted to sell the property straight away, Sleeman had to immediately remove his late brother's furniture and personal effects which had been left to him. A rather unseemly haste at the end of a life!

And finally turning to Sleeman's other brother, William, I can only offer the following snapshot of his life:

William was seven years older than Sleeman but he did not have such a distinguished career nor was he ever as prosperous as either Alexander or Sleeman. Having been a Civil Servant for most of his life, he rose to become the deputy Registrar at the Judicial Commissioner's Court in Lucknow. He was generally very shabbily dressed, his clothes seeming to come from a long extinct fashion! He was however a charming person to talk to and Lawrence and his brothers were very fond of him.

I mentioned previously that John (or 'Joey') Johannes had been a good friend of William Speirs, working alongside him as clerk in the Judicial Commissioner's office. In fact, the intertwining between their families became very complicated, and apparently incestuous (bearing in mind that they were 'half-cousins', both having Joseph Short as a grandfather) but I will try to describe it as best I can!

In October 1889 at the age of twenty-one, William married Joey's younger sister, Eva Florence Johannes (whom Sleeman always described as being very refined and ladylike). Only five months earlier, William had been a witness at Joey's marriage to Agnes Eleanor Greenway, the daughter of Thomas Greenway, an indigo merchant from Texas, USA. Interestingly, on his marriage certificate, Joey describes himself as a 'photographer', indicating that he had probably already set up his photographic studio in Lucknow whilst still being employed as a clerk.

William and Eva do not seem to have had any children but they both acted as godparents at the baptisms of three of Joey's six children, born to Agnes Eleanor over the next eleven years. The last of these children, who was born in November 1900, was given the Christian name, Eva Dorothy Speirs, surely indicating an intimate bond between the two families.

And this is where the plot thickens! Whilst Joey Johannes was working alongside William in the Commissioner's Office, William had started a relationship with Agnes Eleanor in about 1900. Eva apparently learned about the affair and left her husband in 1902. She subsequently went to stay with her sister Annie Johannes who had married Thomas LaFrenais and was living at Bina in Saugor district. After Eva's departure, William and Agnes openly started living together, apparently as husband and wife, having two daughters, Mary (born in May 1905) and Margaret (born in 1908) as well as a son Archibald (born in 1911) who only survived a few days.

William's exact relationship with Agnes Eleanor (who was always known as Ellie) was kept as a closely guarded secret from my father and his brothers although they certainly suspected that their uncle was not married to their aunt. Whilst nowadays 'living together' seems to be just as acceptable and equally popular as marriage, in those days the phrase was 'living in sin' and the facts were left shrouded in the delicate mists of Victorian prudery!

Unfortunately, William's affair with Ellie had a devastating effect on his erstwhile friend, Joey Johannes. He began to talk idiotically and soon had to retire from his post at the Judicial Commissioner's Office. Although harmless, he became incapable of looking after himself and was known to simply give away his wasika to anyone who flattered him. One can only imagine that William Speirs' guilt-ridden appearance was caused by grief over the effects of his affair on his former friend.

The full names that William gave to his daughters (Mary Dundas Rachel Amelia and Margaret Bruce Shearin) are quite interesting because they strongly suggest a detailed knowledge of his Scottish ancestors. Now the names Rachel and Amelia are very likely derived from his mother's and grandmother's Christian names, and the name Shearin was almost certainly chosen after Ellie's mother, whose maiden name was Emilie Shearin. So this leaves us with Mary Dundas and Margaret Bruce. Now I am sure that it is no coincidence since Dundas was the maiden surname of Archibald Speirs' wife, and Margaret Bruce was the name of one of Archibald Speirs' daughters.

My father, on realising this, made the assumption that William's brother Alexander, as a wealthy lawyer, had arranged for their Scottish ancestry to be researched. However, I think this is unlikely, particularly bearing in mind that William named his first daughter in May 1905, not long after Alexander had started his legal career. I believe that the truth is far more simple; this information had been handed down to them by their grandfather, Colonel Alexander Speirs who had kept up a surprisingly close relationship with his half-brothers and sisters.

William's job as a Civil Servant was naturally not as well paid as his brothers but he seemed to like to emphasise and wallow in his comparative poverty. He would walk for two miles to get to work everyday, giving the impression that he couldn't afford transport which was very cheap in India. Since he lived in a small one-roomed flat without a garden and with no servants, his living expenses could not have been that high! He also had a pathetically humble demeanour, typically standing slightly stooped whereas his brothers Sleeman and Alexander always stood erect. In fact, he always looked and behaved like an old man, older and more care-ridden than his actual age. He had also become very much of a loner, seeming to prefer solitude to having company. The boys were aware of these traits which seemed to them to be artificial, and which consequently led them to tease him gently. When the boys later guessed that William was 'living in sin' they also concluded that William's mannerisms were his way of atoning for his sins. I would tend to agree with their conclusion.

William occasionally came to stay at Moradabad but always by himself. Possibly because of his Civil Service career, he tended to be over-cautious and a bit of a 'fuss-pot'. He hated to miss a train so much that he once set off from his house on the short trip to the station at 10:30 am when the train was only due at 4:00 pm. He wasn't going to miss that train! On other occasions when he visited the family, he would be seen restlessly pacing the veranda and urging them to take him to the station several hours before the train was due. His nephews would say 'but there's plenty of time', to which he would reply 'Oh yes, my boy, but it pays to be ready!'

When they went as a family to visit William and Ellie, the boys naturally took a back seat in any conversation. By the time Lawrence and his brothers knew their aunt Ellie, she was a cripple and remained permanently either in bed or in a wheelchair. Apparently, Ellie had dislocated her hip one day when she tripped over her granddaughter Pamela Hagreen, who had been standing behind her whilst she watered the pot-plants on the veranda of their flat at Jehangirabad mansions in Hazratganj. But Ellie was a stubborn woman and instead of going to hospital to have the hip-joint attended to, she simply took to a wheelchair. So from that day onwards she was unable to walk and needed constant attention from her family and servants.[5]

When the boys were at school in Lucknow, Mary, who was an extremely good-looking girl, was living in a separate flat above William and Ellie's. She was being kept by a wealthy Indian who was thought to be a Raja's son. However, the boys did not know William's other daughter Margaret Shearin.

There is a reference to William in the book *Armenians in India from the Earliest Times to the Present Day* by Mesrovb J. Seth M.R.A.S. published in 1937. The following is an extract from page 564 of that book, in which the author talks about Murium Begum:

In December, 1926, when we visited Lucknow a second time to attend the annual meeting of the Indian Historical Records Commission, we met an elderly resident of Lucknow, one Mr William Stephen Speirs, a Government Servant, and one of the descendants of Joseph Short, who very kindly took us to the old Christian cemetery where the Armenian queen, Mariam Bebum Saheba, was laid to rest on the 5th April, 1849.

Mr Speirs told the present writer that both his mother and maternal grandmother, in accordance with the time-honoured Armenian custom, used to burn candles and incense over the grave of Mariam Begum Saheba, on the anniversary of her death.

Aunt Ellie died in December 1939 and was buried in the Nishat Ganj cemetery in Lucknow, with a fine tombstone erected by her daughter Mary. William only survived another thirty months, apparently collapsing on the pavement and dying quite suddenly from heatstroke whilst out for one of his long walks. He was buried in the same cemetery, but has only a simple grave with a row of bricks at ground level and a tiny plaque bearing his name.

12

SLEEMAN SPEIRS' CHILDREN

I WROTE THE FIRST DRAFT OF THIS CHAPTER IN 1994, AFTER SPENDING many hours with my father, Lawrence, tape-recording his childhood memories. By then my father had been suffering from Alzheimer's disease for over three years and I had come to realise that if any permanent record was to be made of his life in India, and of the research that he had carried out into our family history, I needed to take the initiative. I am sure that my father would have liked to write about his life and about our ancestors, but he simply left it too late. In fact, when I started tape-recording my father, I often felt that I had also left it too late. The memories were very difficult to extract, and it took a lot of perseverance to achieve coherent stories. Sometimes he would repeat the same story several times, without realising that we had just heard that tale. And on more than one occasion he would look at me, his son, without a trace of recognition, and say, 'I'm not telling you that—it's a personal family matter!' However, I kept going and, although I am sure that a few years earlier I would have achieved far more, as Lawrence had a very keen memory before the Alzheimer's 'fog' descended, I think the results are impressive in the circumstances.

Later that year I visited my uncle Malcolm's widow, Patty, in South Africa and she gave me much useful data about his life, including several of Malcolm's written memories of life in Moradabad, which of course I have included in this chapter. And on another trip I met my uncle John in Australia and repeated the exercise. But, although he was then in good health, he did not remember as many childhood incidents as Lawrence had. Nevertheless, he did corroborate most of what my father had already said, and gave me some useful pen-pictures of the Speirs boys, which I will now share with the readers by way of introduction, starting with Bill...

Bill was always the most studious member of the younger generation of the family—very intelligent and a bit of a book-worm. In that aspect he probably most closely resembled Sleeman. In fact, as an adult, Bill was treated by Sleeman as a friend, since they both shared common interests and loved to engage in intellectual conversation. However, Bill did not share Sleeman's thoughtfulness and consideration for others, but tended to be rather selfish, not prepared to share anything and somewhat self-centred. He was particularly concerned about his stomach, so a constant refrain from Bill when he was eagerly watching the serving dishes at mealtimes would be: 'Hold on, Alec! There are others to come!' Often the rest of the family used to deliberately bait Bill by ensuring that the dishes were passed to him last.

Bill was the only boy who always had the ear of his parents and could apparently do no wrong in their eyes. However in practice, he was generally at the centre of any rascality that the boys got up to, but was always adept at standing back when any blame was being apportioned! If the finger was being pointed at him, he would talk 'nineteen to the dozen', giving his alibi or excuses until eventually Sleeman would give up trying to get Bill to accept responsibility and would select an easier scapegoat. Conversely, Alec in particular tended to take the blame for any incident without bothering to give any excuses and so he was always regarded as the naughty son.

Turning now to Alec; his attitude of his simply accepting the blame (and of course the corresponding punishment) for any naughtiness unfortunately had serious repercussions for him. His early reputation as the naughty son led him to being chosen automatically as the chief suspect in any wrongdoing; his sullenness and the lack of denials merely seemed to confirm his guilt in Sleeman's eyes. But clearly he must have felt increasingly bitter at always accepting responsibility. So gradually he began to withdraw from the family, became pig-headed, refused to obey family rules and consequently got into even more trouble. Sleeman simply didn't understand his eldest son, slapping him and using force when a more subtle approach was needed. Eventually, Alec kept away from the family, alienating himself from his parents. He had brought himself into a 'state of war' with his family and eventually with the world.

This 'state of war' was most clearly depicted by the fact that as an adult he seemed to be incapable of holding a job for any length of time. He would simply not turn up for work and then would be surprised when his employers wouldn't tolerate his attitude. By then, Sleeman had mellowed and he tried to regain Alec's affection and to help him by giving him work. Unfortunately he was too late; Alec continued in the groove that he had created for himself. The young man had been destroyed.

John however had a quite different temperament and outlook, partly shaped by an early illness. In about 1918, while the family was still living in Houston House, John became very ill with enteric fever (nowadays better known as typhoid). Chris nursed John at home, supported by a lady doctor who attended quite frequently. But John had a relapse, following which he had a close brush with death. It took John years to fully get over this double dose of typhoid. As a result, he became very skinny, remaining thin ever since. and rightfully earning the nick-name 'Johnny thin'. However, there were some advantages to be exploited too; he was now regarded as the family weakling and so was always given special privileges and concessions due to his frailty.

Also, although he was several years younger than both Alec and Bill, he was generally not only included in their games but also acted as the undisputed 'elder brother' to Lawrence, Jean, Malcolm and Marjory. This was particularly the case when Alec and Bill left to go to Westminster School. He was now in charge and he effectively remained so, since Alec and Bill were no longer boys but young men when they returned. So John had an easier time than Alec. He had the advantage of being able to learn from the mistakes of his elder brothers and also the special status his parents gave him after his illness.

The result was that John matured early, taking both his responsibilities as elder brother and his education seriously. Apart from when he was quite young, he rarely got involved in much of the general mischief of his brothers.

Lawrence had quite a different character. Being ten years younger than Alec and four years younger than John, he was scarcely tolerated by his elder brothers, who simply regarded him as the baby. So he became fairly independent of them, mostly keeping his own company and finding his own ways of amusing himself. However, he would often be 'hanging around', observing his elder brothers and hoping to be allowed to join in their games (possibly this was what led to his developing an extraordinarily vivid memory, being able to recall numerous of his brothers' exploits, even seventy years after the event). He was very fond of his sister Jean and would often take her out with him to events in Moradabad.

Like Bill and John, he was quite a studious boy and would often be found engrossed in a book by the window-sill. Sometimes, at meal-times he would exasperate the other boys by asking a question that no one knew the answer to unless they happened to be reading the same book that he had just put down! But his interest in so many diverse subjects did lead to his development of both an encyclopaedic knowledge and a very enquiring mind. At the same time, not being shouldered with the same 'elder brother' responsibilities as John, he was not averse to getting involved in rascality!

And here I must leave my pen-pictures. I regret that I have so little information about the early days of Jean and Marjory that I cannot reliably recreate either of their childhoods. So on with the memories...

Let us first turn to an incident that occurred in 1918 when the family had moved to stay in a house in Saharanpur while Sleeman was acting as a defence lawyer in the riot trial (mentioned in chapter 11).

At that house, the bath-water used to be heated in an old kerosene tin which was supported on a few bricks and heated by a twig fire just outside the house. The tin used was labelled 'The Standard Oil Company of New York'. Alec and Bill were playing outside with a rifle and, in his usual way, Bill suggested to Alec that he should take a shot at the tin whilst the water was heating. My father, Lawrence, was standing nearby, but being much younger than Alec or Bill, he did not then join in their fun. Lawrence recalls Alec expressing some reservations about the wisdom of this act but Bill kept egging him on saying, 'Go on Alec; go on Alec'. Eventually, Alec knelt and took aim for the shot succumbing to the temptation and to Bill's urgings. But just as he pulled the trigger, the Rolls Royce that had been lent to their father for the trial came out of the garage. The shot ricocheted off the wall and then went straight through the windscreen, just missing the startled chauffeur!

Needless to say, this incident was reported to their father. But, true to his usual form, Bill's involvement in the act was never mentioned and Alec had to take the full blame. Fortunately, the Muslim owner of the car took the attitude that these things just happen, so the car was repaired without too much fuss.

The family had gone to Saharanpur during the school holidays and the boys were effectively running wild there since Sleeman was very busy with the trial preparation and Chris had her hands full with the domestic arrangements and with baby Jean, who was only a year old. The garden there was more like a forest and the boys, having nothing to do, were up to all sorts of mischief and silly games such as riding bicycles backwards. Chris was particularly worried because Eardley Norton, the senior lawyer on the case, was living next door. She didn't want the boys causing a nuisance or trespassing. Eventually, the strain 'got' to Chris, who persuaded Sleeman that she and the children should return to their home, Houston house in Moradabad, even though the trial was only just beginning.

Houston house wasn't as well insulated as the thatched house it replaced. In the summer, the bedrooms would become uncomfortably hot at night and so the family followed the usual custom of sleeping out on the flat roof. One morning as the family was waking up on the roof, Chris said to Lawrence, 'Go downstairs and fetch me a handkerchief, there's a good boy!' But four-year old Lawrence didn't show any inclination to follow his mother's edict until she repeated the instruction, 'Go on, do as your mother says. The handkerchief is in one of the little drawers of my dressing-table'.

So down Lawrence went, cocking his leg over the bannister and sliding down in his usual way. But he couldn't find one, saying on his return, 'There aren't any hankies there.' 'Of course there are', said Chris. 'Go and look again properly.' 'But there isn't one there', said Lawrence, almost in tears. 'What on earth do you mean? There are always plenty in the drawer!' 'But there aren't any drawers in the dressing-table!' 'What do you mean?', said Chris, more baffled than ever. 'Well, the drawers are lying outside', stated Lawrence, who was simply reporting facts as he observed them. So finally Chris got up to investigate why Lawrence was being so obstructive, which was when the truth was revealed—they had been robbed during the night! Lawrence had in fact been strictly accurate in his replies but was too young to realise what had happened.

Fortunately, very little had been taken by the thieves who had missed a large sum of money that Chris had left in a drawer to pay the servants the next day. This drawer was very stiff, requiring quite a technique to open it, and the thieves had evidently not tried too hard. They were lucky that this was the only attempted theft, as Chris used to be very careless with money, leaving large sums lying around. Often she would ask Jean: 'Jean, go and fetch my bag; it's in the second drawer down.' But while the bag was where Chris said, Jean would invariably find large sums of money just lying around on top of the dressing table.

Although he was only four when Houston House was sold, Lawrence clearly remembers living there. He particularly recalls that there was a grapevine trained over some canes and forming a bower in the garden under which he used to play. Also, if his parents were calling for him and he didn't feel like answering, he would quickly crawl under these vines and hide until he eventually felt like appearing. He also used to love sitting by the bush and eating the grapes to his heart's content which frequently meant that he over-indulged himself resulting in messing his pants!

The following year the family had moved to a rented house named Eagerness. And not long after they moved to Eagerness, a family called Embleton came and stayed with them. The reason was rather sad. Sleeman had been friendly with Mr Embleton, who was an engineer on the railways, his job involving inspecting the track, often at distant locations. He had incidentally become quite deaf, which of course posed quite a problem when working on the railway; he had to have extra assistants to ensure that he realised when a train was coming. Once when he had left Moradabad on one of his tours of inspection, he caught flu (this was during the world flu epidemic of 1920). He seemed to get better and the doctor had advised him to sit out in the sun. This was fatal advice, because he then had a relapse and died suddenly. Meanwhile, he had left a widow and three children in his railway accommodation at Moradabad. But the East Indian Railway didn't seem to exude compassion, as they immediately turned the family out of this house.

So Sleeman offered Mrs Embleton part of the house until she had found somewhere to live. She came with her daughter, Tootsie, and her sons, Gavin and Bob, who were then aged about fifteen and fourteen, and who had become friends of Alec, Bill and John.

Like many houses in India, Eagerness had a flat concrete roof, which was accessed via a staircase leading to a roof-level room with two doors out to the roof. Just as they did at Houston House, the family would generally have their beds out on the roof in summer and sleep there, as it was much cooler at night than inside the house.

Often, before they went to England to go to Westminster School, Alec and Bill used to go up to this roof-level room with Gavin and Bob to smoke cigarettes, and John would also join them. But Lawrence was considered too young for such things, although he always wanted to join in. So he would go up there, only to have the door shut firmly in his face. He would then lift his leg over the bannister, slide down and loudly call out 'Mo-o-ther, those boys are smo-o-king', at which there would be shouts from above of: 'shut up you little sneak!' In fact, Sleeman and Chris were well aware that the older boys used to smoke, although it wasn't officially allowed.

One day when Lawrence went up there, knowing his elder brothers were in the room, he was surprised to be invited in. And when Alec and Bill said to him, 'Why not come out onto the roof with us?' Lawrence was delighted to be allowed to join in. They then suggested that he should get into a large wicker basket, which was lying around on the roof and to which they had attached a rope. So Lawrence got in and before he could stop them, his elder brothers lifted the basket out over the parapet and started slowly lowering him down to the ground using the rope! One of his parents, probably Chris, came out at that moment and, seeing what was going on, shouted, 'What on earth do you think you're doing?' At this the elder boys decided to speed up the procedure so that they could escape! As a result, Lawrence descended the last few feet very rapidly indeed!

Lawrence was five years old in February 1920, when the family was still at Eagerness, and he had already seen an air-gun in the shops that he wanted but couldn't afford. So he asked his father for fifteen rupees to buy the air-gun. He had already told the servants that he would be getting a gun for his birthday, so when the day came and he had bought the gun, he proudly showed it to them. (He couldn't show it to his brothers, who were by then away at school). But one servant, who was not a regular but actually a barber who used to visit occasionally, was rather disparaging about Lawrence's purchase saying, 'Oh Sahib, that is a rubbishy gun!' This annoyed Lawrence, and he retorted saying, 'Well, we'll soon see whether it's so rubbishy'. He then promptly took aim and fired at the servant! Fortunately, the servant had already turned, so he was just hit on the back of his head but despite that the air-pellet stung him and he went away yelling. Of course Sleeman got to hear about this event and he confiscated the air-gun for a few days from Lawrence. Needless to say, the servant never made another disparaging remark about Lawrence's gun!

Lawrence occasionally saw his uncle Alec, the rather solemn and imposing-looking lawyer whom I introduced in the last chapter. Once uncle Alec gave Lawrence a gold Mohur, a small but very valuable coin from the Mughal era. But Lawrence didn't appreciate it, saying to Chris, 'Mother, look what Uncle Alec's given me—just a paise!' But Chris recognised the coin, telling Lawrence, 'No, it's a Mohur—you'd better give it to me!' So Lawrence learnt an early lesson that you shouldn't always confide in your parents!

During the school holidays, the boys tended to run wild around the streets of Moradabad. Being the sons of a respected lawyer certainly helped. Once, the Kotwal stopped John and some of the other Speirs boys, who were riding around Moradabad with one of them sitting on the handlebars of the bike and another balancing on the pin. He was just starting to take down details, after telling them, 'This is a serious offence. Riding with three on a bike is breaking the law'. By then he had evidently decided to make an official report, when he casually asked, 'and what is your name?' On being told that it was Speirs, he suddenly dropped his note-book and said, 'Oh, in that case—you can go!' And they heard no more of it.

Alec, Bill, John and the Embleton boys would often invade the fields of sugarcane on their bikes, cycling into the well-guarded fields and grabbing sticks of sugarcane in front of the guards. There was no real reason for this, apart from simply making mischief. As soon as they were spotted, the guards would shout and chase after them with their lathis. But the boys were too nimble and would always escape with their treasure which was often promptly discarded! There were two main types of sugarcane: the thin cane which had to be pressed to extract the sugar and also the thicker cane, which was about 1 1/2" in diameter and which could be eaten direct after peeling back the outer layers. Naturally, it was this second type that the boys were interested in.

The family had a dog at Eagerness, which Sleeman insisted should be left outside at night to guard the place (particularly as the Embleton boys were sleeping in a tent at night). One morning however there was no sign of the dog. During the day though, the horrible truth emerged when bits of the dog were found in trees in the garden. Clearly, it had been killed by some wild animal. Then someone told them that a hyena had recently been seen in the neighbourhood. It was then that the boys decided that they would stay out that night and keep a watch for the hyena. Gavin, being the eldest and in charge of the operation, opted to take the first watch of the night. But after twenty minutes a sheepish-looking Gavin came back inside with the excuse, 'It's getting a bit cold out there!' And the others were relieved too that it was too cold out there! So the hyena watch was quietly abandoned.

Later in 1920, Alec and Bill left India to go to Westminster School and then the Embleton family also departed. So peace reigned for a while. Then the family moved next door, to a house called Asfaq Manzil, where they stayed for about a year, before making their final move to 'Fairlawns', the house that became the family home for the next eighteen years or so. Sleeman had in fact owned Fairlawns for several years, but had not been able to move there when he sold Houston House as a tenant (being a woman working as a Government Education Officer, whose duties involved inspecting schools in the district) was occupying it.

In ways, Fairlawns became more of a 'home' than Houston House ever did. This was because there were real challenges in trying to transform the rather unkempt grounds into a presentable garden, whilst at Houston House the gardens were already mature. I have already described how Lawrence helped Sleeman save his newly planted orange orchard. John also helped, taking control of operations to install a decent water supply to the house. Previously, there had been an ordinary well there, which was totally inadequate to supply the house as well as watering the five acres of gardens. So Sleeman arranged for a tube well to be installed, with an electric pump and a water tank on a little brick tower. Then John supervised and helped the gardener, Pooran, and his brother to lay the galvanised pipes for hundred yards from the tank to the kitchen and the connections to each of the five bathrooms. The success of these endeavours made the family appreciate the house even more.

When the family had been at Fairlawns for about a year, the Indian Railway held a sports day for their employees. Lawrence took Jean to this event, with the princely sum of one rupee as spending money. Soon they came to a tombola stall and Jean's eyes lit up when she saw the beautiful teddy-bear that was one of the star prizes. A lot of other people had been trying unsuccessfully to win this prize for their children, but by then they were mostly drifting away. Jean kept pestering Lawrence to get it for her, but Lawrence had seen that each try cost one rupee— all the money that he had! Eventually, Lawrence gave in, but he explained that they only had the one chance. This time, one try was all that they needed as a few minutes later an ecstatic Jean came away clutching the teddy!

But now Lawrence had no money left, so he then entered a free race for which the first prize was three rupees. Before the start of the race, all of the children had to take off their shoes. Each pair was then tied together by the laces and put in some large sacks at one end of the track. The race involved running fifty yards barefoot to the sacks, finding, untying and putting on their shoes and then running back to the finish line.

By the time Lawrence got to the sacks, he didn't seem to have much of a chance, because he couldn't even get near them. But the children who got there first were desperately flinging shoes out of the sacks whilst searching for their own. Soon Lawrence saw his shoes flying through the air and they were quite unmistakable as they were so scruffy. Moreover, they were very easy to get into because he never used to put them on properly, but had flattened the heels by wearing them like slippers. So he only had to undo the laces and he was in them in a second! He then sprinted back to the other end and was announced as the winner (although strictly speaking he wasn't, because half-way down the track one of the shoes came off and he later had to return for it but he wasn't going to argue!). So, having spent all of his money to win the prize that Jean wanted, he now had more than he actually came in with! The rest of his money was then spent on a train that he had been pestering his mother to buy him for some time without success and on some sweets for Jean. It was certainly a memorable day for him!

Another incident involving Lawrence and Jean occurred shortly after one of them had been ill. The local doctors were renowned for always hedging their bets and never giving positive advice. So most Europeans preferred to read medical dictionaries and discuss causes, symptoms and treatments for illnesses between themselves rather than involving the doctor. In this instance, Sleeman and Chris had obviously decided that the cause of the current illness was calcium deficiency and they had impressed on the children the importance of sufficient calcium in their diet. So, more as a way of attracting their parents' attention than from a genuine desire to follow their advice, Lawrence and Jean started licking the walls in one of the rooms at Fairlawns. When Chris reprimanded them, 'What on earth do you think you're doing, licking the walls? Stop it right away! That's a disgusting thing to do!' Lawrence calmly replied, 'Mother, you said it's important that we get enough calcium. So we're just doing what you said. We're getting extra calcium from the white-wash!' And strictly speaking, he was quite right because the main ingredient of the white-wash on the walls was lime, a form of calcium-carbonate!

At Fairlawns, the family kept white bull-terriers as pets and Chris was particularly keen on them. She bred several litters from their two bitches, named Judy and Jilly, although in one case two whole litters died when one of the mothers contracted a disease and wasn't separated quickly enough from the puppies. On one occasion, Chris took Judy and Jilly all the way to Lahore so that they could be mated with a pedigree bull-terrier named Don. Later, one of the family's favourite dogs was called Don, who was white with a black patch around one eye. Probably this Don was one of the puppies from the mating in Lahore. One of these litters was raised in a spare bathroom! (There were five bathrooms at Fairlawns) However, one evening when the family was sitting out on the veranda, they heard a yelping noise. On rushing inside, they found that Jilly had disappeared and she wasn't seen ever again. The family assumed that one of the servants had heard about the pedigree mating and thought that Judy and Jilly were very valuable. Loose talk with the servant's friends could have resulted in this blatant theft.

Once one of the dogs was suspected to have picked up rabies and the whole family, except Sleeman and Lawrence had to be driven to Calcutta for injections. The reason why Sleeman and Lawrence were exempt from these precautions was that they were both very fastidious about cleanliness and had never allowed the dogs to lick them. After that, one of the dogs needed to be put to sleep and Sleeman had asked Lawrence to shoot the dog. However, Lawrence naturally hated the idea of shooting a family pet so he was most relieved when a family friend turned up at that moment and was prepared to carry out the unpleasant task.

Let me now briefly mention the cars and other vehicles that the family owned while they lived at Fairlawns. The boys were probably more interested than Sleeman in cars because Alec and John soon learned to drive whereas Sleeman never did, wisely having given up the idea after his early experiences on motorbikes. Although he did actually own another motorbike, which he had won as a prize in a raffle in Calcutta that he often used to enter. This motorbike was sent to Fairlawns, where it remained unused on the veranda for ages.

The first car that the family owned was an old Overland, which had gas lamps. But they didn't keep this long, the first 'real' family car being a brand new Ford that Sleeman bought in Delhi in 1921. This car was very practical for use on the rough roads around Moradabad. After the Ford, Sleeman bought a Chrysler station-wagon for Alec to use when he was managing the mill at Ramnagar. When the mill enterprise finally collapsed, the station-wagon was brought back to Fairlawns for the boys to use, but they reckoned that they didn't really want a station-wagon and so they decided to turn it into a car! But first they needed a car bodyshell.

Lawrence told them of a suitable abandoned donor car belonging to Kidarnath, a Hindu lawyer friend of Sleeman's who had bought Eagerness shortly after the family lived there. He was quite happy to let them have it, so Alec, Bill and John stripped the body from this donor car and used it to convert the Chrysler into a car. This was actually simpler than it sounds, because in those days car bodies were bolted to a separate chassis. So the job merely involved undoing the bolts and man-handling the body from one chassis to the other. But to their consternation they found that the car bodyshell was shorter than the station-wagon and so it didn't fit properly, ending up slightly too high at the rear. Nevertheless, they now had the car they wanted.

While Alec and John had learned to drive at the age of about thirteen and were enthusiastic about cars, Lawrence never showed the same inclinations. He was given some driving lessons, but he evidently had difficulty in concentrating solely on the driving. One day he was at the wheel, with the whole family in the car, when he passed his friend, Harry Thompson.

'Oh, hullo Harry!' shouted Lawrence, taking his hands completely off the steering wheel and waving proudly to his friend. Meanwhile, the car ran completely out of control until one of the other boys managed to grab the steering wheel and correct its course! Needless to say, the family lost any confidence they might have had in Lawrence's driving ability after that incident. His driving tuition thus came to an abrupt end!

One of the boys' major interests was shooting game, each of them having at least one gun. Between them they had two twelve-bore rifles, two twenty two bore rifles and a .303 rifle. They mainly shot birds and rabbits, but were interested in shooting any game and Alec several times went on leopard shoots at Raniket. They actually knew Jim Corbett, who was a very scruffily dressed person but a brilliant shikari. He often went on a tiger shoot with just three cartridges; such was his confidence in his ability. When you consider that it normally takes two cartridges to stop or kill a tiger, he clearly wasn't allowing for any mis-shots!

From Fairlawns they could see the distant foothills of the Himalayas, at the base of which the big game was to be found. But they mainly concentrated on duck shoots and knew the locations of all the local jheels. In summer, these would be very small but after the rains each jheel would cover several acres and there would be ample opportunities for duck shoots.

Alec, Bill and John favoured number four twelve-bore rifles, which they used particularly for duck shoots. Due to the scatter of the shot, often two or three ducks would be hit when they fired into a flock of ducks, although some might only be wounded. Lawrence however felt that this was too much like murder so he tended to use air-rifles, although later he too started using the twelve-bore rifles. Even Sleeman had weapons but by the time the boys used to go out on shoots, he and Chris were content to merely come along and watch. Chris actually took little interest in the sport, contenting herself with picnic arrangements etc.

Sometimes whilst the boys were on duck shoots, they would watch and marvel at the way Indians caught ducks with their bare hands. The Indian would come to the jheel with a gourd from which he had scooped out the inside and in which he had cut holes for his nose and eyes. He would then saunter up to the edge of the jheel, always keeping at least hundred yards from the ducks, who would naturally be watching and prepared to take off if anyone approached too close to them. The Indian would then very slowly edge into the water, having put the gourd over his head, gradually getting deeper and deeper in. Soon of course all that could be seen on the surface was a gourd, which just seemed to drift near to the ducks. The ducks would often be quite interested and might even approach the gourd for food. Then, when a sufficiently large duck was close enough, the Indian would simply grab its legs and hold it under the surface until it had drowned!

When they went shooting for bigger game, they mostly went to the Terai forest below Nainital, taking with them rifles with at least a 450 diameter barrel. They generally took a 500/550 Express rifle, which was double-barreled and was a good rifle for any size of deer. Once when John was using this rifle, he put two cartridges in, but when he pressed the front trigger, both barrels actually fired. The impulse sent him flying! Alec was very successful at shooting leopards and tigers; he must have killed at least a dozen leopards and about three tigers. He hunted them when he was in charge of the mill at Ramnagar. His servants would come out with him in mid-afternoon and help to set up a machaan in the branches of a tree. A goat would be brought as bait and tethered nearby. Then at about 4:30 pm Alec would climb up to the machaan, armed with a 575/500 double barreled smooth-bore rifle and often a shot gun as well. (The shot-gun could be quite effective at close range, provided that it was loaded either with ball or large-grain shot). John once accompanied him on one of these tiger shoots. However, they were late planting the goat that was being used as bait and later still getting into the machaan. So it was very dark when the tiger eventually turned up, with a great deal of growling. John only managed to get a fleeting shot at it from about fifty yards away, but he missed, and the tiger left after more loud growling.

Usually at about dusk the leopard or tiger would make its presence known, either by the terrorised squeals of the goat or from the sound of cracking branches and disturbed undergrowth. It was important to get a good shot at the leopard and to be sure that it was dead before making any move. The most dangerous situation was when the animal was just wounded—the rule being that you should not then move from the machaan until the morning, after a search party had come to meet you making a loud noise as they did so and thereby ensuring that the prey would keep away.

Although not strictly sport, another important use for their guns was shooting at snakes, which occasionally got into the house and were often found in the garden. Sleeman had installed a shower at Fairlawns, which he particularly liked, although most of the rest of the family tended to use the bath. The shower had a raised edge to contain the water and a drainage hole, through which snakes occasionally made their way into the house. Once, on seeing a snake in the bathroom, Lawrence blasted it with his shot-gun but this was considered a rather extreme action as it caused a lot of damage to the shower!

Snakes appeared most frequently during the monsoon period. In the first week or so of this season there would be alternate heavy downpours followed by dry weather. The grass in the orchards which was previously withered and only just surviving would then suddenly turn green and grow very rapidly. Local natives would then ask to be allowed to cut this grass for their animals, but there would be so many snakes around that it was often necessary for Lawrence or one of his brothers to stand guard with a shot-gun while the grass was being cleared.

The servants were under strict instructions not to attempt to kill any snakes they came across but always to call a member of the family who would either use a shot-gun or a long stick of rattan cane to kill the snake. This rule was for the servants' own protection as they tended to have little idea of normal safety precautions when dealing with snakes. They would tend to follow a snake much too closely, so that if it turned to attack they would have no time to get away. Or, if using a stick, they would choose one only about a foot long, which involved the same danger of getting too close to the snake. Occasionally, though, a servant was bitten by a snake when someone would suck out as much of the poison as possible and they would then drive the servant to the local hospital for an injection of the antidote serum. When servants did break the rule and got bitten while trying to kill a snake, they were told that they had been very close to death but they generally knew when anyone was bluffing!

The boys soon got to know which snakes were relatively harmless and which were deadly—the krait and the cobra being the most deadly.

The krait is only about 12" long and as thin as a boot-lace, but its venom can kill within minutes unless it is sucked out immediately. When using a stick, the object is to break the snake's back, so that it can be picked up and chucked out. But as a precaution, it was always made sure that snakes were dead before being thrown away.

One family friend of the boys was Leo Bonney, who also lived in Moradabad. Leo was quite a character, probably most accurately described as a con-man, always involved in some dubious activity, but a firm friend of the family. Lawrence recalls that Sleeman once lent Leo a book about the survivors of the Indian mutiny which was of great interest to our family, who had been at Lucknow throughout the period of the mutiny. Typically, though, when Leo was asked to return the book he would say, 'Oh, sorry, I forgot it. I'll bring it next time I come'. However, he would then avoid coming for a few weeks until the book was forgotten about. (Leo Bonney later came to live close to Alec in Norwood in the late 1960s, so they often met and talked about old times in India. Another family friend who lived near Alec in Norwood was Julian Manuel, the son of Sleeman's lawyer friend, Edwin Manuel, pleader of Lucknow.) Another prized book that was lost in this way to a friend was an original edition of Fanny Parks' wonderfully evocative *Wanderings of a Pilgrim in Search of the Picturesque*. This was a sad loss to the family, as Sleeman must have gone to some trouble to locate this rare book, which includes vivid description of the Awadh court at the time of Murium Begum, and also gives details of encounters with Colonel William Linnaeus Gardner, with whom the family was distantly related through Benjamin Joseph Short's wife, Susan (nee Gardner).

I believe it was the year 1933 when the whole family was present on Christmas Day and although they didn't know it at the time, this was to be their last Christmas together. After a wonderful lunch they were sitting on the front verandah steps of Fairlawns, joking and chatting and looking down the long drive out on to the road which led through the park into the city. Besides the family, there were at least a dozen friends and neighbours present. They were discussing a game of rounders and then someone suggested a game of hockey. As there was no agreement, they continued to chat and joke and were shortly joined by a few more friends who had dropped in to give Christmas greetings. It was at about 4 o'clock when they noticed three men dressed much like hill men, with a mixture of Pathan dress, indicating that they were definitely from some other region, advancing down the drive towards them. Behind them was a young Indian girl of about ten years of age. When they drew closer, they halted and their spokesman greeted the family, saying in Hindustani, 'We are makers of magic. We will show you only one trick. What will you pay?' So John, who was a budding magician at the time, questioned the men, who explained that the girl would be put into a basket carried by one of the men and made to disappear—that everything would be done on the lawn in front of them, and that it was real magic they were about to witness. Much laughter ensued and eventually a sum of five rupees was agreed upon. In those days, it was a princely sum of money.

The little group moved back onto the heart-shaped lawn in front of the house. The wicker basket which was shaped like an urn, was set down on the lawn—the leader turning it sideways so that the family could check that it was empty. John then strolled across and examined it and was satisfied that it was just a plain basket. The girl was then picked up by one of the men and lowered into it and a lid was placed on top. A thin cloth was then thrown over the basket and the leader then proceeded to push swords into the basket, at the same time inviting the family to join him. Several family members then joined in sticking swords into the basket, until it resembled a pin-cushion! They returned to their seats on the verandah steps and the leader then withdrew the swords, removed the cloth from the basket, opened the lid and turned the basket upside down. It was empty! The family was, to say the least, more than a little surprised and to add to their astonishment, the leader then called the girl, who appeared from the rear of the house. Their leader came forward, salaamed, received his five rupees and within a few minutes the group had gone. No one present had any idea how this trick was accomplished!

So far in this story you could be forgiven for thinking that the children were always at home or at least at play. However, they all went to school from about the age of five. But with such a difference in ages, at any one time they were all either in different schools or in very different classes. So it was only when they were on holiday in the winter months that they were together. (Most boarding schools in India were in the hill-stations, the idea being to keep children out of the oppressive heat of the plains. So the academic year consisted of just one nine-month long term from

March to December in order to make the maximum use of the mild climate in the hill-stations.)

The first school that John and Lawrence attended was the Railway School in Moradabad, where they went from the age of about five. Almost certainly, Alec and Bill had also been there before them. This school was run by a lady of German descent named Miss Stahl with an assistant called Miss Nash. Miss Stahl was rather an aggressive, domineering woman, whilst Miss Nash was very sweet and evidently loved children. Although the school was primarily for children of employees of the East Indian Railway, they often accepted children of other Europeans.

Both John and Lawrence enjoyed the time they spent at this little school. Life was quite opulent for the Speirs children, particularly in comparison with the children of the railway employees. John especially remembers the fuss that his parents made of him, always arranging for the bearer to come to the school each lunch-time with a picnic lunch. He and Lawrence used to go there each day on their pony, accompanied by the syce (groom), who often had to run when accompanying Lawrence as he would whip the pony to a trot! John stayed there for only a year until he was just over five, before going to St Mary's Convent at Nainital, where he stayed for about four months. Lawrence also went to St Mary's Convent when he was seven, staying there for a year before returning to the Railway School until he was ten.

One day on the way to the Railway School, Lawrence saw a tube-well being sunk and, being something rather unusual, he diverted his pony and syce to go and watch the process of sinking the tubes. This is done by engaging a clutch on the engine, thereby causing a heavy weight to be pulled to the top of a tripod over the tubes. When the clutch is released, the weight drops onto a mandrel, which in turn hammers the tube into the ground. The soil is extracted by jetting with water down the tubes. Obviously, this was a very exciting process for a young boy to watch! He recalls talking to the English engineer in charge, who gave Lawrence a lemonade and then explained what they were doing. He was also interested to hear about Lawrence's school.

Neither Lawrence nor John was keen on St Mary's Convent, which was mainly for girls, with a few boys in the infant classes. One of the teachers, Miss Haloran, was excessively severe. For a minor misdemeanor, she once gave John a hard smack and forced him to lie on his bed all day. This was a big insult to his dignity.

In 1918, when John was seven, he was sent to the school where each of the Speirs boys received most of their secondary education (although they attended it at different times)—St Joseph's College at Nainital. While he may not have liked St Mary's Convent, this move was definitely a case of 'out of the frying-pan, into the fire' because the regime at St Joseph's was very harsh. It was a Roman Catholic school, run by the Christian brothers. They were undoubtedly well-intentioned, but they used corporal punishment and fear as the primary means of maintaining discipline and instilling learning into the boys. The children there lived in fear since the slightest offence was punished by a strapping on the hand. During study periods, an old man was left in charge. Any boy caught fooling around would be sent to stand outside the room for the rest of the session, when they would generally also be given the strap. Not surprisingly, very little mischief used to occur because punishments were so severe.

There were about six or seven classes at St Joseph's, with about twelve teachers. One of the teachers was a pure disciplinarian, his job being to know and look after every boy. Being a Catholic school, attendance at chapel was of course a requirement for all of the boys.

Although John intensely disliked the school, he actually learned a lot there, the strap being always handy to help instill knowledge. He stayed there for ten years until he was about seventeen, when he was planning to go to university. In fact, he wanted to go to a British university, as the Indian Universities weren't of a comparable standard. But Sleeman had found out that the Senior Cambridge Certificate exams which pupils at Indian schools took before leaving wasn't acceptable for entry to British universities. So John needed to take a preliminary degree at Lucknow university. The entrance exam for Indian universities took place in December, when schools were closed, so John had to go to Bareilly, a town about sixty miles from Moradabad, for this exam. He went there with four other pupils from his class. But one day they missed a paper that they hadn't been told about, and therefore they had to be judged solely on their marks from the other papers. John's results on the other papers weren't quite good enough to be able to ignore this paper, so he was sent to La Martiniere School at Lucknow for a short time. Eventually, after a month or so he passed the exam and was accepted to the Lucknow University.

Once there, John was allowed to stay rent-free in a building belonging to La Martiniere School, which was about three miles from the university. Now, after his childhood illness, John had always been a somewhat sickly youth and this journey would have been very exhausting for him (or at least this was the argument that he used when presenting his case to Sleeman). So Sleeman agreed to buy him a second-hand Triumph motor-bike to use for his daily journeys.

By this time, Bill had returned from England without having achieved much academically even though he was considered the most academic and 'book-wormish' among the lot. Subsequently, Bill decided to take an arts degree from Lucknow University at the same time as John and naturally they shared the same accommodation. Bill benefited considerably from John's motor-bike, either riding as a pillion passenger or holding on to John's shoulders and getting a tow on his own cycle. (In those days this was a common practice and the police rarely took any notice).

John stayed at Lucknow University for two years, eventually emerging in 1934 with a BSc in Maths, Physics and Chemistry. After a while, the rent-free room at La Martiniere was no longer available and he stayed in a private hotel, with his own servant. The woman who ran this hotel made excellent meals and treated him very well. During John's last year there, Lawrence too joined him, as he was also taking a Physics degree at Lucknow university.

Although John was aware that his Lucknow degree was inferior in comparison to a British university degree, it served its required purpose of gaining him admission to a British university. So, armed with his Lucknow degree, John gained admission to Trinity College, Dublin. He preferred the idea of going to this small but renowned single college university rather than Oxford or Cambridge, whose size was intimidating and not conducive for being able to 'stand out from the crowd'.

In 1925, Lawrence was also sent to St Joseph's School as a boarder. He too didn't like it there since it imposed a very harsh life on the pupils. The food was almost inedible and never in sufficient quantity, so that the boys were permanently hungry, and the school's discipline was unnecessarily severe. In order to relieve the pangs of hunger, the boys needed to get good value for money when they bought food from the local stores. They often bought 'pouri-tak', which was pouri with a helping of curry (ie. tur-kari). To get the biggest helping of curry, they always ordered less in the beginning. So they would ask for two pouri-taks when they actually wanted four. When the storeman dished out the curry, they would complain at the quantity until he eventually gave them much more than normal. As soon as they had got as much as possible, they simply repeated the order and the bargaining process! The local curry was very tasty, being well-seasoned.

Another means of supplementing their meagre and inedible diet was the time-honoured pastime of scrumping fruit! The boys used to regularly visit the Government House grounds, always enquiring from the last lot who had visited about how ripe the fruit was. On one occasion, Lawrence had been informed that the delicious pears there were nearly ripe; this was certainly good news for them! So Lawrence and two or three other boys went in to the junior boys' dormitory and removed a couple of pillow-cases to use as sacks. They then went to the big playground and sneaked behind the row of toilets. Behind these toilets there was a narrow way leading to the Government House grounds. They had just filled their pillow-cases with the luscious pears when suddenly four guards came up, intending to corner them. Being 'street-wise' they all dispersed in different directions to avoid capture, but Lawrence was pursued and he had one of the full sacks of pears. Reluctantly, he ditched the pears to avoid capture and made good his escape. Unfortunately though, the pillow-cases were all individually labelled. The groundsmen evidently made a formal complaint because that evening the Principal announced at dinner that Albert Murphy's pillow-case had been found by the guards after the raid. So Albert Murphy was asked to step forward, confirm his involvement and identify the other culprits. Of course Lawrence could not allow this innocent boy to take the blame, so he had to confess his involvement. The principal said that Lawrence would have to pay compensation, to which Lawrence's reaction was, 'fine, but where's the money going to come from?' He was more anxious lest Sleeman should get to know about the incident but luckily in the end no compensation was demanded!

Kite-flying was a favourite pastime at St Joseph's but kites were not always flown just for innocent pleasure! Some of the boys had kites with 'manja' thread. Manja was a cotton thread treated with adhesive and then passed through powdered glass. One of these boys would lie in wait until a kite went up and he would then send up his kite (with the manja thread) on an attacking course. The boy who had sent up the original kite would then frantically try to reel his kite in, but all too often the attacker kite would cross threads with the first kite and sever the first kite's thread. There would then be a race to collect the fallen kite as it floated back to earth, the rule being that the first person to reach it could claim it as his. The kites were invariably home-made, consisting of very light tissue-paper on a frame made of split cane. They were so light that they would fly in almost still air, and would often soar to a height of about 2000 ft. Typically, the boys would add a small weight to one side, so that the kite would fly to that side when the string was pulled.

Later on at St Joseph's, Lawrence joined the army cadet force. Like others who did so, he was not attracted to the cadet force just for the military life but more for the mercenary reason (cadets aged eighteen and over were paid a monthly allowance of sixty-five rupees, which was quite a princely sum!). But the first problem was to convince them that he was eighteen which was not easy as he was only about fourteen at the time besides being small for his age.

Lawrence joined the cadets when they were holding a preliminary parade for the King's birthday. But in the line-up, his small size was all too apparent. As a result he got noticed and the officer approached him saying that he was too young and too small to continue in the cadets. However, Lawrence somehow managed to convince him that he was not only eighteen but that he had already been accepted. He was then duly accepted into the cadet corps thereby becoming eligible for the monthly allowance.

At the end of each term, there was a problem period when all of the cadets had to account for their kit. Naturally, if anyone was missing a piece of kit, the simple solution was to pinch someone else's rather than having to pay for a replacement. At one such parade, Lawrence found that someone had pinched his shorts. So to save himself he immediately grabbed the first pair that he could find and presented his complete kit for inspection. He recalls not being able to look the inspecting officer in the eyes when the officer held up these shorts, which were only half his size, and asked how Lawrence managed to fit into them!

Lawrence did not really enjoy his time at St Joseph's and at the end of the academic year in 1930, he persuaded Sleeman to let him leave. When Sleeman asked where Lawrence wanted to go instead and he said he liked La Martiniere School at Lucknow. So Lawrence went to La Martiniere School until he was nearly eighteen, when he entered Lucknow University for a physics degree course. Whilst he was there, he stayed at a house where Sleeman had rented some of the rooms for the boys whilst they were in Lucknow. At various times during his stay, Alec, John and Bill also stayed in the house. Lawrence occasionally visited his uncle William who also lived in Lucknow. He liked his uncle William, but avoided going to his house too frequently as Lawrence knew that William was hard-up, but would always provide hospitality which he couldn't really afford.

Lawrence obtained his physics degree at Lucknow in 1936, after which he returned to Moradabad, nominally to study for entry to the Indian Civil Service. But he wasn't really interested in it and he wanted to gain higher qualifications in physics, which was only possible in Britain. However by this time, after the disastrous losses from his mill ventures, Sleeman needed to eke out his money and so Lawrence had to wait until John had completed his degree course at Dublin in 1937 before his further education could be paid for. Lawrence also chose Trinity College, Dublin to take a British Degree in physics. Consequently, Lawrence left India in the summer of 1937 to take a shortened two-year degree course.

So far in this chapter I have made just a few references to Alec and Bill, who led a somewhat different life than their younger brothers. So let us now turn our attention to them and follow their adventures (and mis-adventures!)...

Almost certainly they started at the same school that their younger brothers attended, the Railway School at Moradabad From there they went on first to Philander Smith School followed by St Joseph's College, both at Nainital. But Sleeman had higher ambitions for them and he had gained admission for them to Westminster School. So late in 1920, they were withdrawn from St Joseph's to be sent on the long sea voyage to England. Sleeman had arranged for them to stay with a clergyman and his family during the school holidays as return to India by ship was clearly impractical. I imagine that this clergyman probably met the two boys at the docks and that they stayed with him over the Christmas holidays.

They entered Westminster School in January 1921 as boarders in one of the school-houses named Rigauds. By then, however, Alec in particular was too old for normal admission, as he was fifteen compared to the normal admission age of twelve or thirteen. So presumably, he was placed in a higher form. They both stayed at Westminster only until December 1922.

However, it has to be said that in Alec's case, all of the expense incurred by his father on his education seemed to produce little in return. Alec left Westminster school in late 1922 without having achieved much academically and not wanting to go on to University as his father had wished. On the contrary, he decided to become a Mechanical Engineer since he always had a practical nature. So it was soon agreed that Alec would become a gentleman's apprentice at the English Electric Company, learning mechanical engineering whilst he worked there. Soon, he joined them at their Preston office. But although Alec certainly had the ability to become a good engineer, he never took his work seriously enough. In this first job like the string of others that followed, he simply did not apply himself to his work, spending more time with his girlfriend than at work, coming in late etc. Eventually, the company had to write to Sleeman saying that it was becoming pointless for Alec to stay on with them.

So in 1926, Alec left the English Electric Company and returned to India with Bill (who had been studying at a crammers meanwhile). This was when Alec was put in charge of the mill at Moradabad and later the mill at Ramnagar, with the disastrous results as mentioned in the last chapter. Alec was actually very lonely at the mill at Ramnagar, as there were no other Europeans around. So Lawrence and John both visited him there at different times to keep him company (although on one visit, John felt that he had to remonstrate with his elder brother, who had evidently entertained a prostitute there the previous night).

Even before this, Alec had been causing problems for the family. When he first returned to Moradabad from England, he had little to do, not having the inclination to look for a job. So he used to spend quite a bit of time socialising and drinking although unfortunately he couldn't hold his drink! On one occasion he went to a dance at the Railway Institute in Moradabad where he became rowdy, having obviously consumed too much, and was consequently given a ticking off by the most senior Railway

Official at the function. At which, emboldened by the drink, Alec demanded, 'Who the heck do you think you are, talking to me like that?' and promptly slapped the official's face. Following this when two big men were called in to restrain Alec, he fought them back until he was eventually overpowered and thrown out of the premises. Afterwards, Alec was banned from returning to the institute. This incident caused a great deal of embarrassment to the family, particularly in view of Sleeman's position as an eminent lawyer in the town. Sleeman himself was given a lecture by the local magistrate for having a son creating so much trouble, to which he could only reply sheepishly, 'Yes sir, that's very true'. Thereafter, although only Alec had been banned, no one from the family felt that they could attend functions there. Now, although the Railway Institute was not a very impressive place, it was the only place in town where Europeans used to gather at functions and so Alec's stupid action had a huge impact on socialising for the rest of the family.

After the failure of the second mill at Ramnagar, when he eventually realised how little his son had been doing, Sleeman finally lost his patience with Alec, telling him to pack his bags, leave home and get a job. Even at this point, it was Sleeman who arranged a job for Alec in a small motor repair works at Agra. So Alec moved to Agra and started working at the garage. All went well for a while, until the owner, a Mr Hotz, decided to go on holiday to Switzerland, leaving Alec as manager, in charge of the other employees. True to his past form, Alec paid no attention to work once his boss had left, using the garage sprayer to paint tables, going out motor-racing and doing other irresponsible things. So, despite Chris's intervention on his behalf, when the owner returned Alec was immediately fired. Mr Hotz added that he would not allow Alec to return under any circumstances.

While he was working in Agra, Alec met and married Noreen Herbert who had lived in Agra all her life. Her father worked in the Government Telegraph department there. They were married at St Patrick's Church in Agra in March 1930 although no one else from the Speirs family attended. On 11 December 1930 their first child, Alexander John Victor, was born and he was later baptised at the RC Cathedral in Agra on Boxing Day (also Alec's birthday). I assume that it was at this critical juncture that Alec was fired from his job because he immediately returned to Moradabad with his wife and young baby. Naturally, faced with this situation, Sleeman and Chris felt that they had to support their eldest son, no matter what he had done. So they installed him in a rented house on the far side of the maidan (an open area outside the town where carnivals and similar events are held).

However, a tragic event occurred only two weeks later. One day when she was alone at home, Noreen realised that baby Alexander was choking and was starting to turn blue. Having failed to dislodge whatever was obstructing his windpipe, she started to run across the maidan with the baby in her arms to get help. Their driver had been out on an errand and he met her halfway across the maidan on his return. Noreen and the baby got in the car and the driver rushed them to Fairlawns. But she was too late; baby Alexander was already dead by the time they got there.

Lawrence remembers arranging for the funeral service and burial at the local cemetery in Moradabad. The vicar, very inappropriately, took the opportunity to lecture Lawrence on the fact that Sleeman did not regularly attend services there but Lawrence rightly retorted saying that such criticism at a sad time like that was totally uncalled for.

Alec and Noreen's next child, Christabel, was born on 23 January 1934 and I particularly mention her because she was Sleeman's and Chris's first granddaughter and she spent her first few childhood years at Fairlawns with them. Alec and Noreen, on the other hand, were divorced in the late 1930s and that is an appropriate point to draw Alec's story to a close.

And finally I will turn to Mac, who was the fifth and youngest son of Sleeman and Chris Speirs, born when Sleeman was forty-five years old. Mac always felt that his parents paid little attention to him and his younger sister Marjory during their childhood. The two of them used to play together, wandering around the streets of Moradabad without their parents ever knowing their whereabouts. There may well be some truth in this, as their parents were by then middle-aged and had already spent twenty years bringing up their other five children. So it would not be very surprising if they had become a bit casual by that stage.

I know little about Mac's childhood, apart from the fact that, like his other brothers, he went to St Mary's Convent at about the age of five and then to St Joseph's College in Nainital at the age of seven. Unlike his brothers, he enjoyed his time there. He was an excellent sportsman, being quickly chosen to play soccer in local matches between civilians and the military. He left Nainital in December 1937 having passed his School Certificate with credit in six subjects including Urdu.

Before he left St Joseph's, Mac met a woman who was to haunt his dreams for several years afterwards. Her name was Theo and she was a friend of Jean's (they both attended the same teachers' training college). Mac had met Theo on a visit to Jean. She was a very attractive, fair-haired girl. At the time, Mac wasn't generally interested in meeting or talking to girls, so he was surprised to find that he immediately got on well with her. In fact, on later visits, Jean felt ignored as they used to be immersed in talking to each other.

As Theo was older than him, Mac didn't presume to ask her out on a date and a year passed after their initial meetings. Then, during the long winter holiday, Jean invited Theo to stay at their home in Moradabad. As soon as they met again, Mac's previous reticence melted away. But he still wasn't sure that Theo was serious about him when she asked him to kiss her that evening. It was only when she admitted that she had been attracted to Mac from the moment that they met and wasn't in the least worried about their age difference that Mac realised she was as entranced by him as he was by her.

They parted two months later but kept in constant touch over the next two years. However, suddenly there was complete silence from Theo. Mac never heard from her again, although she was constantly on his mind.

After leaving school, Mac had expected to go to university, but apparently Sleeman suggested that he might find something else to do. So Mac enrolled on a science course at the local college although he actually felt himself more suited for an arts course. While he was there, he met a strange young man called Reggie Young and the two of them instantly became close friends. Reggie was half Chinese. He introduced Mac to the martial arts and to the secrets of mysticism.

It took a while before Reggie would speak freely but when he did, Mac was introduced to a totally different world—a world of complete secrecy where he was taught to hunt, shoot, fight and to kill by hand, knife and gun. Mac came to believe in Karma and in Kismet. He developed the ability to see into the future of most people whom he came in touch with. This training was of little practical use for most occupations but it turned out to be vitally useful to Mac during the war when he fought behind the enemy lines in Burma.

During the Christmas holidays in 1939, when Mac was still at the local college, he joined a group of friends going carol-singing around Moradabad. During the carol-singing, they were invited into a house where Mac exchanged glances with a startlingly attractive girl named Pat Pedrick. The attraction was evidently mutual and shortly Mac began to visit the Pedrick household frequently. Their friendship grew and Mac would pop in to see Pat on his way to college each morning, often bringing roses from Sleeman's treasured rose garden at Fairlawns, unknown to Sleeman!

Pat's parents had an entertainment room at their home in Moradabad where Pat and her friends played indoor games and generally fooled around with music in the background. Her father believed that she should bring home any friends and not go wandering around to meet them. So naturally, their home became the stamping ground for the young folk.

One evening, Mac had called in on the pretext of teaching Pat how to throw darts. Having successfully managed to clear the room of all the other young folk, it wasn't long before he started making moves on Pat, lifting her hair away from her neck and kissing her. And Pat certainly wasn't resisting the attentions of this handsome young man. So he grew bolder, turned her round, switched off the light and smothered Pat with kisses. If this was love, Pat liked it! And it was from that moment onwards that their friendship developed into love.

Mac and Patty (as she has always been known) didn't actually get married until after the war, as Mac shortly enlisted in the army and eventually served in Burma with great distinction during the war. But we'll leave that tale to another day. I will now draw this chapter to a close, having given a brief flavour of the lives of most of Sleeman's children in India. (Sadly, I have too little information about the childhood of either Jean or Marjory to attempt a narrative of their lives.)

EPILOGUE

THE READER, HAVING PERSEVERED TO THE FINAL CHAPTER, MAY WELL BE intrigued to know what became of Sleeman Speirs and his children. So I will here give a brief outline of their lives from when I left them in the last two chapters, starting with Alec.

The responsibilities of marriage and starting a family did finally cause Alec to settle in a job, and throughout the 1930s he worked for a firm of Civil Engineering Contractors, supervising bridge construction at various locations whilst Noreen stayed at Fairlawns bringing up their daughter Christobel, until she and Alec separated in about 1939 (their divorce came in about 1944). During the war, Alec enlisted as a private in the King's Regiment in February 1943 but as he had the qualifications of an officer, he was discharged in September that year, only to be re-appointed two days later on an emergency commission as a Second Lieutenant in the Royal Engineers. He served in various Indian Infantry Companies for the next three years, mainly in Burma.

On being demobbed in October 1946, Alec finally left India and came to England, staying initially with Sleeman in Oxford. Then, on being offered a job as Resident Engineer by a firm of Civil Engineering Consultants, he moved to Budleigh Salterton in Devon to supervise the construction of a sewage treatment works. It was here that he met Gwendolyn Nix, the youngest of a large family (whose elder sisters were treating her as a servant) originally from Arnold, Notts. They were married in about 1948 and eventually bought a large house in pleasant grounds called 'Ravenswood' at Woodford Green in Essex, moving there in July 1949.

Around a year after they had bought Ravenswood, Alec's daughter Christobel came to live with them (she had been living with her mother in Lahore until then). But father and daughter both had hot tempers, and when the suitability of her current boyfriend was questioned, Christobel stormed out in a blazing row, never to meet her father again. Meanwhile, Alec continued working for consultants, again mostly supervising the construction and operation of sewage works but he gradually slipped back into his old ways which naturally meant that few companies were prepared to employ him. So by 1955 he could no longer afford to pay the mortgage on Ravenswood. Although he briefly worked again, at a sewage farm in Bracknell, Berks, he then effectively retired, the couple from then onwards eking out a frugal existence in a flat in Tulse Hill, Surrey on his wasika and a small inheritance left to Gwen. He died in January 1981 having led a sadly unfulfilled and wasted life.

Briefly turning to Bill (and the reason for the brevity is simply that when he started work, he became quite a loner, scarcely keeping in contact with his brothers and sisters), he took a degree at Lucknow University in about 1930 after which he applied to the Indian Civil Service and obtained a job at Meerut in the Military Finance Department. In 1933 he married Lucy Lever, an older woman, whom Chris later described (presumably with an element of exaggeration), as a 'white-haired old lady'. In 1935 he was in Quetta, being there at the time of the violent earthquake, which killed many people. The quake occurred late one night and Bill woke to find the house shaking violently around him. He dashed out just in time, turning round to see the house collapse behind him.

After the war, Bill worked in Cyprus, again I believe as an accountant. By then Lucy and he had adopted a daughter, Elizabeth, as they had been unable to start a family. The next fleeting contact that he had with the family was in January and February of 1949, when he stayed with Alec whilst he was in between jobs, presumably intending to settle in England. However, he eventually obtained a job in Lagos, Nigeria, working for the Nigerian Electricity Corporation, from where he briefly wrote to his brother John in 1951. There was then total silence from him, but Sleeman only became concerned when he wrote to Bill in 1954, and his letter was returned with a note 'left Nigeria'. Eventually, someone must have contacted Bill and it emerged that he was now working in Bulawayo, Rhodesia. And the next event, sadly, was when Jean wrote to Sleeman, letting him know that a local paper in Rhodesia had reported his death. This occurred in September 1956, and unfortunately the news caused Sleeman to have a crippling stroke, leaving him unable to speak and with one side of his body paralysed.

Next we come to John, whose story I left at the time he left India in 1934 to attend at Trinity College, Dublin University. John gained an honours degree in Physics there, and also thoroughly enjoyed his student life. On leaving in 1937, he went to London and briefly joined Siemens but did not like the work there; so left to join Baird, who were attempting to design a projection TV with a screen large enough for viewing by a cinema audience. John in fact helped to show that it was possible to build one but that the tubes had such a limited life that the concept was not practical.

He then joined Cossor, and with the outbreak of the Second World War, most of their work was devoted to producing valves used in radar. But in practice the work was hampered by the secrecy, the 'man from the Ministry' not being prepared to give exact specifications in case anyone realised what they were working on! It was then that John met and fell in love with Muriel Wheeler, a nurse working at a casualty station near John's digs. They were married quietly in Sydenham and for a while lived nearby. But this area was subject to intense bombing during the war and so they moved to Highbury in North London, which was less prone to bombing raids and was also close to Cossor's factory. Towards the end of the war, and with a baby expected, John and Muriel decided that they needed a house, so they eventually bought one in Farnaby Road, Bromley. Their two sons, John and Alec, were born in June 1944 and March 1946 respectively while they lived there.

Soon after that, John decided on a change of career and obtained a job with the Ministry of Housing which needed people with technical skills to help deal with the massive post-war housing crisis. Unfortunately, though, this job turned out to be an active man's nightmare rather than a pen-pusher's dream! However, now that he was a Civil Servant, there were plenty of other opportunities available and John soon obtained a post at Farnborough, working on the design of guided missiles. This was far more appropriate and John continued in this job for the rest of his career, moving to a lovely house in Farnborough named Quinneys.

When he retired in 1970, John and Muriel sold Quinneys and moved to a brand-new house in Fleet. But in 1981, Muriel fell ill and the doctors eventually diagnosed cranial arteritis, a cancer-like condition where the blood-vessels going to the brain become inflamed. Nothing could be done to relieve the condition and Muriel died after about three weeks in bed. A few months later John decided that he could not bear to live alone in a house full of family memories, so he wound up his affairs in England and moved to Sydney, where he bought a flat and lived comfortably until his death in 1996.

Like his elder brother John, my father Lawrence also went to Trinity College, Dublin where he obtained a 1st Class honours degree in Physics in 1939 and then spent a further year obtaining an MSc. On graduating, Lawrence also went to London and joined Cossor like his brother. At the time, they were having trouble meeting the War Ministry's specifications for valves and needed a 'trouble-shooter' to help solve their problems. Lawrence however did not stay long at Cossor because the Admiralty were looking for first-rate physicists with a practical flair and had been told of his abilities. In February 1940, he was called for an interview and was shortly offered a job with their research unit based at Birmingham University. The work was top-secret as it involved the practical development of radar which was of course crucial to the war effort.

So Lawrence joined one of two teams at Birmingham University under Professor Oliphant. His team, headed by Randall, was investigating the use of the magnetron for 10cm radar which at the time was considered the less likely option than the klystron being investigated by the second team. In fact it was one of Lawrence's colleagues, Sayers, who made the discovery that the power generated by the magnetron increases dramatically if the anodes are strapped this being the vital missing link that made practical radar a reality. But Lawrence found that he did not get on well with Professor Oliphant, so he asked to be posted to another team and was subsequently transferred to Oxford University to continue the radar work and also to take a Doctorate in Physics.

It was while he was at Oxford, and also giving lectures on radio to young undergraduates, that he met and married Rachel Wykes, a Physics student who had been taking the radio course as a potential WAAF candidate. They were married in September 1943 and stayed on in a flat in Oxford while Lawrence continued with his radar research and completed his doctorate. Whilst there, they had two children, my sister Helen in 1944 and myself in 1946.

With the war over, Lawrence decided on a lecturing career, starting his first post as Physics lecturer at Exeter University shortly after my birth. Then in 1948 he was attracted by a vacancy for a Professor of Physics at Baghdad University, for which he was duly selected. But he did not find this post satisfactory so he returned to England the following year to take up a comparatively mediocre post as Senior Physics Lecturer at the Regents Street Polytechnic in London. Later that year he and Rachel bought a very large house called 'The Mount' in Kenley, Surrey, standing in 4¼ acres of gardens. This was to become home to myself, Helen, and our two other sisters Eve and Valerie, who were born there in 1950 and 1952 respectively. In 1962 Lawrence joined Enfield College of Technology, where he remained until his retirement in 1975. Meanwhile, in 1971 he and Rachel sold 'The Mount' and bought their final retirement home, a farmhouse in Suffolk called 'Jillings' and it was while he lived there, that Lawrence died in 1995.

Turning now to Jean (about whose early life in India I know very little) I can at least relate that she went to school as a boarder at the Ramnee Convent in Nainital, and later to All Saints' College, also in Nainital. After that, she enrolled for a teacher training course. From notes left by her brother Mac, I believe that this was also in Nainital, probably at All Saints College. She completed her teaching course in 1937 and then moved to Karachi for her first teaching job which I think involved acting as a tutor to the children of several English families there, rather than working in a school. While she was working there, she occasionally met a young flight engineer, Jack Hennell, who frequently came to Karachi as a member of the flight crew on Imperial Airways flights (in those days Karachi was a main stop-over point for flights from England to Australia, where passengers would transfer from Imperial Airways to Qantas planes for the second half of the journey).

Jack and Jean fell in love and he shortly proposed to her. They came to Moradabad for their wedding, which took place at St Paul's Church in front of Jean's family and witnessed by Sleeman's lawyer friend, Kedar Nath. After the marriage, Jean and Jack came to England, shortly buying a new house at Cheylesmore, Coventry, where they lived for the next eight years. While they lived there, their two sons, Jon (in January 1939) and Mike (in September 1940) were born.

During the war, Jack gave up his job with Imperial Airways and worked for Armstrong Whitworth Aircraft, who were based in Coventry. His work there involved secret research, development and testing of jet engines.

After the war, the couple feeling depressed by the post-war austerity and rationing in England, decided to emigrate to Rhodesia. However, they soon found that all ship passages had been booked for about a year ahead, as many others had similar ideas. Rather than wait, they decided to make the whole journey overland! Once official permission had been given for the trip, they bought a Chevrolet four-wheel drive truck, which was to become their home as well as their transport for almost five months. After selling their Coventry home, they arrived at the docks at Dover on 6 January 1947, only to discover that they had left their passports behind! Nevertheless, they still managed to sail the next day after a frantic dash back to Coventry! They travelled through Belgium and France, crossing the Mediterranean at Marseilles and landing at Algiers before facing a 9,000 mile journey across Africa, including a long diversion just in order to see the Victoria Falls. They finally arrived at their destination, Salisbury, on 22 May.

Once there, they settled into a mud-walled house but soon found that this was a bit primitive and unsuitable for entertaining. So Jean was relieved when in October 1949 they moved to a new house set in two acres of grounds on a large estate outside Salisbury, known as Marlborough Township. But Jean's relief was shortlived, as she had no car and was consequently stranded for long periods when Jack was away from home. She wanted to return to teaching, but found that there were no openings for married women. So she took up writing short stories, but after many unsuccessful attempts at getting them published with dwindling finances, she eventually took up typing jobs in Salisbury still finding transport into town a major problem.

Meanwhile, Jean's health was steadily deteriorating. She had started developing nervous symptoms not long after their arrival in Rhodesia, and had a nervous breakdown in 1948. Soon she found that she needed to take sleeping pills or sedatives every night in order to sleep. She began to think more and more of emigrating, either to Australia or back to

England and eventually returned to England in the summer of 1957, along with Jon and Mike, leaving Jack behind in Rhodesia.

With very limited finances, she bought a caravan, where they lived at Goffs Oak in Hertfordshire. Jean took up a teaching job while the boys attended courses at the Northern Polytechnic. But in the spring of 1959, Jean's health finally gave way, probably due to her constant use of sedatives over many years. She was admitted to Hammersmith hospital for urgent treatment when she had begun to haemorrhage badly. The doctors could do nothing, however, and a blood transfusion actually made matters worse. She died on 20 March 1959.

In the final chapter, I left Mac as he was about to enter the army during the war. In fact like Alec, he too was first conscripted as a private, serving in the second Battalion of the Royal Berkshire Regiment. In 1942 though, he was released as he was not liable for conscription in the British Army. This enabled him to take an officer's training course in Bangalore, on passing which he was commissioned as a 2nd Lieutenant in the Hyderabad Regiment. Not long afterwards, he was selected for 'V' Force, a highly secretive guerrilla unit operating in Japanese controlled areas of Burma. Here, the lessons that Mac had received from his friend Reggie in the martial arts were of real value and he was shortly given intensive training in guerrilla warfare by Colonel Ord at a camp in Shillong, making him efficient in the use of weapons, knives, explosives, living off the land, reading maps and other essentials for a guerrilla force.

During the next two years, Mac was mentioned in despatches three times for bravery, but his most valiant act went un-rewarded. He had been selected to lead a patrol deep into enemy territory in the Pegu Yoma to ascertain their precise strength and whereabouts for a proposed massive ambush. He did so, penetrating close enough to be able to report back accurate numbers of men, weaponry and their exact movements. This operation was so hazardous that he and his men could not sleep for three straight weeks to avoid being exposed. The information that they provided was so precise that the eventual 'battle of the breakthrough' (as it became known) was the most sensational victory over the Japanese 18th army, who lost eleven thousand men, whilst the British only sustained seventy-five casualties. Mac's superiors and his intelligence liaison officer, who formed their battle plan based on his information, were all given decorations including the OBE and the DSO but in the excitement the officer who had carried out the work was forgotten. An embarrassed Colonel subsequently had to admit that they had used up their quota of decorations and the only award available was the DSO for which he was too junior in rank. So Mac was offered an immediate promotion from Captain to Lieutenant Colonel as a consolation but he refused this, saying he would rather hold out for the award which all acknowledged he should have received. Sadly, though, despite eventual appeals to Sir Winston Churchill and H.M. King George VI, Mac never received an award.

Mac left 'V' Force as a Major and 2nd in command of his unit after the Japanese surrender, and served as station Commander of Kenttung State on the triple border between Burma, China and Thailand for the next year, after which he was seconded to the Burma Police until his eventual return to India early in 1947. When Mac arrived in India, he was posted to Madras, but his first action on arriving there was to contact Patty, whose family had arrived in Hyderabad, being due to leave India and return to England. Patty's family had been keeping a trunk of Mac's possessions, so he asked if he could stay with them for a few days and collect his trunk. The real reason of course was to be reunited with Patty and to prevent her from going to England, which he swiftly achieved by offering her his hand in marriage.

Mac and Patty were married at Madras in May 1947. Shortly afterwards Mac resigned his army commission, in order to join the Indian Police Force. Mac was initially sent to his home town of Moradabad where there was a large Police training camp for initial training. His first posting was at Agra, where the couple stayed for the next two years, during which time their two sons were born, Ian in 1948 and Barry in 1949. He spent the next two years at Jalaun, moving to Rae Bareli for the next three years and thereafter to Lucknow until 1957. In 1958 he was promoted to Senior Superintendent of Police at Agra, a very prestigious post, with high responsibility and where he incidentally met many visiting VIPs including the Duke of Edinburgh, Lord and Lady Mountbatten, Yuri Gagarin (the first man in space) and many other dignitaries, whose overall safety was his direct responsibility. Then in 1960 he was transferred in the same rank to Lucknow where he stayed until he finally resigned and left India in 1962, when it had become clear that further promotion was not possible for him, not being an Indian national.

Mac and his family then settled in Durban, South Africa, where he eventually became a manager of a hotel. Some time during the late 1970s the family moved to Roodeport, near Johannesburg, where Mac became a hotel owner (and later became joint partner in two hotels). They were however devastated a few years later when their younger son, Barry, was beaten to death by a local gang on Christmas Day 1980. Sadly, though, Mac himself was to suffer a similar fate, only four years later in June 1984, when a drunken customer, who had just been evicted from his hotel in Johannesberg, returned and shot Mac at point-blank range in the hotel bar.

As I said in the final chapter, unfortunately I know little about Marjory's childhood simply because she was much younger than Lawrence or his brother John, who did not include her in any of their childhood memories. As she grew, she was not only very attractive (apparently looking much like her mother at the same age), but also very considerate. She became a real companion to Chris, who enjoyed her friendship, good advice and pleasant disposition. Mother and daughter seemed to like to do the same things. Marjory dressed her mother and helped her to make the most of herself, even designing and fitting frocks for her.

But then, one spring day in 1944, a young RAAF flying officer, Eric Poett, came to Mussourie whilst on leave from a flying mission. He met Marjory at a dance and they were immediately attracted to each other, the marriage proposal following almost the next day. They were married three weeks later in Mussourie Methodist Church on 16 May 1944. Needless to say, although Chris was sad to lose her daughter and friend, she gave her up gladly for Eric, for it was plain to see how much in love the two were.

The couple sailed to Australia about a month later on the American ship *General Butner*, which landed at Melbourne. But Eric, as a serving officer in the RAAF, was immediately posted to duty with the 11th Squadron, Catalina Flying Boats. So he arranged for Marjory to fly to Western Australia to stay with his parents, William and Naomi Poett. This was quite a daunting prospect for the new bride, particularly when she shortly realised that she was pregnant! Her first child, John, was born in February 1945 while Eric was still away but he eventually returned in about October that year.

Eric and Marjory soon bought a farm at Katanning, about 200 miles south of Perth, which became their home for the next five years. Whilst they lived there, their two daughters, Alison (in January 1947), and Felicity (in September 1950) were born. Then, in 1951, Eric bought a farm of about three hundred and fifteen acres called 'Oakleigh' near Kendenup. Over the years though he bought further parcels of land until this sheep farm was eventually 3000 acres—all the land starting off as virgin scrub and needing to be cleared and fenced before it was serviceable. Somewhat amazingly (considering her sheltered upbringing) Marjory was a tower of strength, working on the farm all day as well as maintaining the household and bringing up the children. There was no job that she couldn't do on the farm. She helped with hay carting, tractor driving, fencing, droving sheep and all other sundry chores which have to be dealt with in farm life.

In 1981, Marjory developed breast cancer but recovered well after surgery, allowing her a further ten years of pain-free life, during which period she and Eric travelled extensively. But in 1990 Marjory developed bowel cancer which she again fought with great determination. She and Eric then had another three precious years of togetherness, before it returned and eventually claimed her life. Her last battle ended on September 1993 and she was very deeply missed by all of her family.

And now I will at last turn to Sleeman, who, as the reader will recall, finally left India with Chris at the end of the Second World War. They arrived in England in May 1945 and travelled to Coventry to stay with Jean and her sons (Jack at the time being in Palestine). But Chris was by now suffering from some nervous disorder which made her become overwrought over trifling matters and insanely jealous. Jean could only tolerate her for about three weeks, so they moved to Oxford renting a flat near Lawrence. Again, though, Chris's disorder led to a major row with Lawrence. Sleeman was obviously feeling the strain too, because when Alec returned from India in October 1946, he moved with Alec to Buddleigh Salterton, leaving Chris at the flat in Oxford.

Sleeman stayed with Alec for the next five years, mostly occupying himself with reading and translating Persian books and poetry, going for walks and keeping in close contact with the rest of his family. But he became very lonely, as Alec and Gwen had no children to keep him company. Eventually in May 1951 he came to live with my father,

Lawrence, settling in to his usual quiet routines, but now with four grandchildren to keep him occupied. He seems to have thoroughly enjoyed his old age living peacefully with us and although he often contemplated joining Jean in Rhodesia or Marjory in Australia, he never finalised any arrangements.

As previously mentioned, the news of Bill's death in 1956 was such a shock to this gentle, family-loving man that he suffered a severe stroke which left him unable to walk or speak for many months. However, over a period of about eighteen months he gradually recovered, and was even able to write letters again or go for short walks. But undoubtedly it was the news of Jean's sad demise in March 1959 that caused him to have a final fatal stroke six weeks later. He died on 4 May 1959 and was buried alongside his daughter Jean.

Meanwhile, Chris had decided that she had no wish to stay on in England, so she returned to India in the autumn of 1948, staying with Mac at Agra. But her stay in India was brief and she shortly travelled to Western Australia to join Marjory at Katanning some time in 1949. Unfortunately, though, her nervous disorder now made her impossible to live with, and Marjory and Eric were soon at their wits' end. After about six months, when the strain became too much, Chris moved to Perth, where she worked as a Cottage Mother with Swan Homes to keep herself. Eventually, she decided that the only place where she had really been happy was India, so in about April 1954 she returned once again to India and joined Mac, who was by then living at Lucknow. But the same problem persisted, with Chris being rude and abusive to Mac and Patty, causing many scenes and generally making life unbearable for them. Within a year they were forced to break off all communication with her, although she continued to live with them. Finally, after Sleeman's death, each of the brothers started sending a regular allowance to their mother to give her some independence, but she still stayed with Mac until he finally left India in 1962. Then Chris went to Mussourie where she took a flat in the annexe to the Methodist Church. She died there in February 1965 bringing to an end almost one hundred and sixty years in which our family made India their home, she being the last member of our family for whom India was the final resting place.

Appendix

NAI Gen B June 1862 No 45

To
The Right Honorable the Earl of Elgin
and Kincardine K.J. G.C.B
Viceroy and Governor General of India
Fort William

The Memorial of Joseph Short of Lucknow

Humbly Sheweth,

That in 1859 Your Lordhip's Memorialist returned from Calcutta to Lucknow when he found that his two large Pucca Houses valued at Rupees 25,000 was under demolition by the Engineer Department for the alleged purpose of improvement and clearance in a certain locality now a plain. On this Your Memorialist, as indiscriminate demolition was the order of the day, represented the matter to the Civil Authorities as in similar cases other Christians and Natives whose houses were similarly demolished by Government were compensated by getting other Nazool Houses in lieu of theirs thus demolished. Your Memorialist's case was enquired into fully and his claim established and a house given him which also after 3 days occupation was accordingly demolished this left Your Memorialist again houselefs and deprived of his domicile by the Executive Government. Your memorialist again petitioned and other houses in fact 3 Native huts were offered him of small value in the aggregate in lieu of his established claim of Rupees 7,500 these huts Your humble Memorialist was precluded from accepting which Your Lordship will be pleased to consider as inevitable owing to the nature of the accommodation they afforded. As the last resource Your Memorialist appealed his grievances to the Chief Commifsioner of Oudh, who called on the Civil Executive Officers for a report as to whether the circumstances of Your Memorialist were such, as would entitle him to receive at the hands of Government reparation by way of getting another house in lieu of the two demolished by the said Government. However the Deputy Commifsioner of Lucknow submitted his report on Your Memorialist's circumstances, the pith of which was to the effect, that Your Petitioner was a Wuseekadar of the Oudh Government drawing so much per Memsem that he pursued no trade, and that he was given to keeping Pigeons (fancy ones) and moreover was in the habit of taking doses of Opium, hence Your Memorialist was not a fit object of consideration. Your Memorialist humbly begs to state that in regard to his being a Wuseekadar (Pensioner) of the Oudh Government there is no doubt, that Your Memorialist has on his farm yard a few Pigeons as many Noblemen and Gentlemen of respectability in India, yea even in England have for their use and amusement—and as regards Opium eating Your Memorialist begs humbly to ignore the use of that drug. This Your Memorialist can establish by reference to most of the respectable Christian and Native Community who have been acquainted with Your Memorialist prior to British Rule in Oudh and up to the present period. The above are arguments brought forward, as Your Lordship will observe, to set aside Your memorialist's established claim duly investigated into and admitted by the Executive Officers of the State. Your Memorialist applied for a copy of the above decision but was denied it and now Your Memorialist will not tax much upon Your Lordship's time by again entering into a full detail of his case, but humbly begs to append a copy of his appeal to the Chief Commifsioner together with that Officer's final orders in the case from which the whole course of the proceedings will be clearly seen and Your humble Memorialist lays his case before Your Lordship for Your Lordship's favorable consideration and just decision such as Your Lordship is wont to defseminate to the rich and poor alike. If Your Lordship will direct the Chief Commifsioner to call for the District File of the case the allegations Your Memorialist herein and in his copy of appeal stated, will be clearly set forth and that functionary will then after a review of the proceedings which he has not as yet done, be fully made aware of the injustice done Your Memorialist by depending simply on the reports of the Executive Officers which through some misunderstanding have been entirely wrongly, represented. This will clear up Your Memorialist's case and afford Memorialist ultimate justice.

Lucknow
The 10th of May 1862

To,
G.U. Yule Esquire C.B.
Chief Commisfsioner of Oudh

Sir,

I humbly beg to appeal against the orders of the Commifsioner of Lucknow communicated to me in his docket No 123 dated 31 January 1862, and the letter therein alluded to, to the addrefs of the Deputy Commifsioner in which Colonel Abbot throw *[sic]* out my claim. The facts of the case are as follows.

On the 29th July 1859 I applied to Coll Abbott as Commifsioner for compensation for my two houses valued at 25,000 situated in Golagunge which had come under the Engineer Demolitions, on this the Commifsioner referred my application to the Deputy Commifsioner Mr Carnegy which Officer desired Mr Elliott the then Nazool Officer to institute enquiries from the city Magistrates Mr Wood which was done and that Gentleman reported on the 4th August/59 that the said houses were actually demolished by the Engineer Department and estimated at Rupees 7,500, on which Mr Elliott ordered Moonshee Ramdyal to select a house for me, several small houses were shewn me in which a Christian could not think of living in fact they were more to be clafsed with huts than houses which might be made habitable for any respectable person and as those houses did not suit me nor would they have been of any use to me especially as I had no place where to lay my head in with my large family who were likewise suffering the same inconveniences as myself from want of accommodation, I was compelled to rent a house in the suburbs of the city. These proceedings occupied the interval till 13th February 1860 when I again petitioned Coll Abbott and was again referred to the Deputy Commifsioner Mr Carnegy which Officer I addrefsed on the 14th February /60 and again on the 26th April /60 on which the Deputy Commifsioner ordered that I should get a house of the estimated value by Mr Wood Rupees 7,500. I then found that the case was again delayed and accordingly addressed Mr Berkeley on the 27th September/60. On which that Officer directed the Nazool Darogah to select a proper house for me this occupied the space of time till the 14th December/60. On which date I petitioned Mr Lindsay the Nazool Officer for the disposal of my case and grant of a house that Officer ordered a house to be given to me and the Nazool Darogah offered me a house valued in the Nazool Register to Rupees 550, whereas my established claim was for 7,500. This I was, you will admit Sir, necefsitated to refuse taking, and on the 18th February/61 I again petitioned Mr Lindsey asking him to give me either of the three house valued far below my claim as will be seen in the margin*—but that Officer was removed and the case again over until the 26th of February /61 when I petitioned Mr Wyllie who was then appointed as Nuzool Officer and that Gentleman took up my case and

on the 27th February 1861 ordered the Darogah to give me a house or houses valued
, at Rupees 7,000 and I was accordingly put in pofsefsion of Oomrao Begum's house
situated near the Kaisur Pufsund and had commenced clearing the premises of the
accumulated filth &ca. I had not been in pofsefsion for 3 days when an Official of
the Engineer Department came and told me that the house was to be demolished
on the 5th of March 1861. I addrefsed Mr Wyllie and that Officer ordered a report
to be sent to [the] Commifsioner to confirm the grant of the house on me, but
before this was done, the house was razed to the ground and I was left without a
house again. Having met with so many disappointments as you will see Sir
extending from July 1859 to March 1861, a period of nearly two years and having
already petitioned the various Official over and over on no lefs than 10 occasions
and without any final result of my established claim, I was at last obliged to hold
my peace till the 6th of September 1861, when I heard that some of the Nazool
houses were offered for sale and Sufder Bagh was amongst them at an upset price
of Rupees 6,000. I then addrefsed the Commifsioner Coll Abbott to grant me this
house and lands attached thereto and stated that as it was valued by the Nuzool
Engineer at 6,000 I would accept of it though my established claim was that of 7,500
and cited a precedence in which Mr Jacob Johannes received a Nuzool house
which was about being sold, in compensation for similar lofses. On this the
Comifsioner ordered that he could not suspend the sale of the house (not sold to
this day) but directed the Deputy Commifsioner to report on my claim. On the
14th October 1861 the Deputy Commifsioner reported and forwarded Mr Lang's
decision or report in the case. That Officer (Mr Lang) in his report stated that Mr
Lindsay had dismifsed my claim. On this the Commifsioner in his letter of the 17th
October /61 ruled that as Mr Lindsay had dismifsed my claim he would also throw
it out which order was communicated to me in Commifsioners No 123 of 31st
January/62 to my addrefs on my petitioning him again on the 23rd Idem. Permit me
Sir most humbly to observe that had Mr Lindsay dismifsed my claim on the 18th
February /61 how could he have offered me a house valued at 550 and how could
Mr Wyllie have subsequently taken up the case on the 27th February 1861 and
ordered me to be put in pofsefsion of Oomra Begum's house, which was I have
before stated demolished after my being in pofsefsion for about 3 days, this Sir, will
itself prove that my Claim was not dismifsed but put off from time to time until
it has arrived at this crisis. Had Mr Lindsay dismifsed my claim Sir, I beg to observe

---

* Safdar Bagh	5,000
Bahar Eunuch's	6,000
Kumrooddeen's	5,000

that that Officer would have recorded an order to that effect and I would have been informed of it in due course of proceedings and then could have taken steps to appeal the case, but as such an event never occurred I was as a matter of course not required to appeal but await the time and pleasure of the Authorities to dispose of my long outstanding claim which I was well aware would be finally settled as time and work would permit for my claim was not the only one that was to be attended to, there must have been several other cases of a more important nature than mine, hence I was patient on the subject, but now I find that my case has afsumed quite another feature which induces me to lay before you Sir, the Ruler of Oudh, my case in all its true colors and stages through which it has pafsed. My claim has been established by the City Magistrate Mr Wood from his demolition register and also by Mr Wyllie the then Nazool Officer, as also by Mr Berkeley, Moonshee Ramdyal, Mr Lindsay, and lastly Mr Lang himself was made aware of the facts by a report of the Nazool Darogah on a report framed from the Demolition Register as well as from the Proceedings in the case. It is true Sir I applied for the Sufdur Bagh being fully aware that that house was of lefs value than my established claim and more especially as it was for Sale I though there could be no question of settling my claim to Rupees 7,500 by granting me the house in question valued at 6000 only. The delay in the disposal of my case does not rest with me Sir, and I do not perceive why [I]should be the poor unfortunate that should be the sufferer.

Now after having gone through the entire case Sir I leave it to you Sir, to judge whether I am at all in the wrong the whole case has been evidently misrepresented to Mr Lang and that Office[r] has therefore based his notes accordingly this Sir your far searching disposition and abilities will at a glance reveal to you the actual features of the case which when cleared up to your satisfaction, I am sanguine that justice will be the ultimate result which can only be looked for to you by those who are cast, from whatever reason be it, in the Courts subordinate to yourself.

As the Sufder Bagh is not as yet sold nor is there any likelihood of its fetching so much as Rupees 7,500, were it to be sold, I humbly beg that it with its grounds, may be granted to me in satisfaction of my claim which has been established. My case is not a singular one—many Christians and even Natives have had similar claims which gave been satisfied by the grant of houses to them in lieu of theirs demolished by the State. If Sir it is impracticable to grant me Safdur Bagh for reasons other than I may be aware of I hope you will be so kind as to order me another respectable house of equivalent value to my established claim and thus dispose of my long outstanding case and enable me to have a house in lieu of the two appropriated by Government so as I may with my family be placed in circumstances to lay our heads in and be grateful for the remaining portion of our short lives to the donor. Owing to my old age and infirmities I have suffered long and much from the want of a dwelling place and you Sir can now relieve my sufferings finally.

Lucknow		I am Sir,
Fakeer Mahomed		Your Most Obedt. Servant
Khan's Hatta	/ signed /	J Short'
The 10th of February 1862		

NAI Fin A' Jan 1863 Nos 25-29 &KW

THE WILL OF SULTAN MURRIUM BEGUM

That whereas the Mortality of body known to all that it is appointed unto all men once to die and all must taste the flavour of death and see the face of the Angel of Death, therefore it is most necessary for every human being to make arrangement of his transactions for the future and to make out his last Will for his Relatives and Dependants as directed in the religious tenets for the guidance on consideration that it may come to pass that no dispute or enmity should take place after his death amongst the Relatives and dependants, and in conformity to the instructions laid down in the articles of the Treaty held between the both Governments, that is the British Government and the King of Oude, on the 1st Mohurrum 1241Hijree corresponding with the 17th August 1825 AD the conditions of which articles having been settled thus in Article 2nd 'This loan is made in perpetuity The Sovereign of the Kingdom of Oude shall never have the power to take it back nor shall they exercise any interference with its interest'—Article 3rd 'The British Government guarantees that it will pay for ever the monthly sums hereafter mentioned out of the interest of the above loan to the persons set down in this instrument in the current coin of the place where they may reside without any diminution whatever' Article 4th 'The Honorable Company will always protect the honor of the stipendiaries who will be paid out of this fund, and it will be the protector of their possessions such as houses, and gardens (whether bestowed by the King of Oude or purchased or built by themselves) from the hands of the Sovereign and their enemies and in whatever city or country they may be, their allowance will be paid to them there' and it is further inserted in the said Instrument that 'after her demise one third of the allowance will be paid to any person or for any purpose she may will it will be allowed'. Being of perfect mind health and memory I do make and ordain this my Last Will and place it under the immediate protection of the authorities of the Honorable Company that after my death conforming to the instructions laid down in this my Last Will may be carried into effect. My monthly allowance is Rupees (2500) two thousand five hundred and under the said Treaty of the both Governments the one third of which is Rupees (833-5-4) eight hundred and thirty three five annas and four English pie. I fix and ordain monthly allowance for my youngest brother Joseph Short (whom from his infancy I brought up under my care and protection like my own son) and for other dependants (in privilege of their fidelities to me) according to which the authorities of the Honorable Company shall regularly pay their monthly allowance in perpetuity to all my Legatees as hereafter particularized without any deduction whatever and in what City or Country they may be their allowance will be paid to them there that they should provide themselves suitably without seeking for and from any one else. That during my life time or after my demise in case of any of my Legatees' death his allowance is to be continued and distributed to his heirs in conformity to the tenets of the Law. In case if he has no heir his allowance will be paid to any person according to his will. It happens that he makes no will in that case, the Resident should distribute his allowance to his heirs according to the Tenets of the Law. Except this my last Will and Testament no other documents or Will should be considered valid and nothing shall be admitted to eradicate the claim of my Legatees specified in this my Last Will and orders when they choose may be given to them to proceed in what country they like and regarding their proceeding no other should be allowed to interfere in their affairs. May Holy God perfume the tomb of blessed memory His late Majesty Ghaz eeooddeen Hyder who has placed me under the immediate protection of the Honorable Company and conformably to the Treaty held between the both Governments I always have been given privileges from Government I place all my Relatives and dependants under the immediate protection of the Government and trusting that my Legatees will also be treated the like manner as myself and the allowance Rupees 833-5-4 I settled on them from my allowance will regularly continue on them Vizt: Rupees 800-0-0

My brother Joseph Short (as my own son). This allowance for my brother's expences and to give maintenance and clothing to my other brother John Short (who is insane) and my youngest sister Eliza (who is attacked with severe palpitation also) in case of her husband and son will not support her under such circumstance my said Brother will also give her food and clothing Rupees 750 and also to be disbursed by my Brother's own hands and direction and after my Brother's demise to be acted in the same manner by his heirs. In repairs illuminations and charity of the Roman Catholic Churches Rs 50 Vizt Lucknow 20 Rupees and Cawnpore 50 Rupees.

Hakeem Mahomed Ally in recompense due by me to his duties as Physician
15-0-0
Moosummat Cheotee Khannum daughter of Mirza Noor Begum recompence
of her fidelity and good services   18-5-4
833-5-4

Regarding the arrangements of my funeral and burial obsequies in whatever
place I may be and whatever time it may happen all the requisites shall be
performed by my brother Joseph Short. I have recorded in the Residency office
an original and Duplicate of this my last Will agreeably to the particularized
monthly allowances fixed by me for the Legatees to be regularly paid to them in
perpetuity by their own seals and receipts and those of their heirs' seals and
receipts. Should it chance that my death take place here in Lucknow my funeral
ceremonies and the tomb may be erected by my said brother Joseph short's
discretion and after my demise my said brother will be sole proprietor of all my
household property including jewels cash Booneead Munzil premises as well as
all and every property of mine and after my demise the male and female slaves
and abyssinian females who are left my brother has full power over them either
to keep them or let them free and no other person has liberty to interfere
respecting them. I have already examined and adjusted all my accounts from the
Legatees and none owe me a fraction. Therefore the representatives of the
Honorable Company will not allow anyone to claim any thing from them. I have
made out and set my seal upon this my original Last Will and Testament as also
a duplicate has been recorded into the Resident's office. I have as well delivered
copies of this my Last Will, one to my Brother, second to Hukeem Mahomed
Ally otherwise Nubba Physician and third to Moosummat Chotee Kannum
daughter of Asoor Beg for rendering good services. Exclusive of this my Last Will
should any of my dimissed servants or those in the service produce any other
documents deed of gift or Last Will it ought to be considered false and forged
and proper for the authorities of the Honorable Company to seize the person and
destroy the forged document. I have also executed a separate Will exclusive for
the purpose of my funeral and burial performances dated 1st July 1838 AD
corresponding with the 7th Rubbee oos surree 1264 Hijree which I have made
and set my seal upon and delivered to my Brother who will produce the same
and Government will assist him to carry it out into effect Dated 23rd Mohurrum
1260 Hijree corresponding with the 13th February 1844 AD.'

NAI Finance: A: Jan 1863 Nos 25 –29 & KW(Joseph Short's petition to be paid his pension in full)

To His Excellency
The Viceroy and Governor General of India in Council

The humble Petition of Joseph Short of Lucknow

Sheweth,

That on or about the seventeenth day of August one thousand eight hundred and twenty five an Agreement or treaty was entered into between Mordaunt Ricketts Esquire Resident at the Court of the King of Oude on the part of the British Government by virtue of the powers vested in him by the Right Honorable William Pitt Lord of Amherst Governor General of India in Council and His then Majesty Abool Moozuffer Moizooddeen Ghazeeooddeen Hyder Shah King of Oude as follows.

Agreement between His Majesty Abool Moozuffur Moozooddeen Ghazeeooddeen Hyder Shah King of Oude and the British Government on account of a sum which the former has given as a loan to the Honorable Company settled by His Majesty on his part and Mordaunt Ricketts Esquire Resident at the Court of the King of Oude on part of British Government in virtue of full powers vested in him by the Right Honorable William Pitt Lord Amherst Governor General in council &ca &ca.

Article 1st

His Majesty the King of Oude has given as a loan forever to the Honorable Company One Crore of Rupees the interest whereof being five Lacs of Rupees per annum, will be paid from the 1st Mohurrum 1241 Hijree to the persons hereafter particularized by monthly instalments and the Interest of this sum will always remain at Five per Cent per annum though the British Government may reduce their interest below or raise it above the aforesaid rates.

Article 2nd

This loan is made in perpetuity The Sovereigns of the Kingdom of Oude shall never have the power to take it back nor shall they exercise any interference with its interest.

Article 3rd

The British Government guarantees that it will pay for ever the monthly sums hereafter mentioned out of the interest of the above loan to the persons set down in this instrument in the current coin of the place where they may reside without any diminution whatever.

Article 4th

The British Government will always protect the Honor of the stipendiaries who will be paid out of this fund, and it will be the protector of their possessions such as Houses and gardens (whether bestowed by the King of Oude or purchased or built by themselves) from the hands of the Sovereigns and their enemies and in whatever City or country they may be their allowance will be paid to them there.

Article 5th

This agreement having been settled by His Majesty the King of Oude for himself and by Mordaunt Ricketts Resident at the Court of Lucknow on the part of the British Government the Resident at Lucknow has delivered one copy thereof in Persian and English signed and sealed by him to His Majesty the King of Oude from whom he has received a counterpart also duly executed by His Majesty, the Resident engages to procure and deliver to his Majesty the King of Oude a copy of the same under the seal and signature of the Right Honorable the Governor General in Council, when that executed by the Resident will be returned.

Interest Rupees Five Lacs per annum by solar years twelve months at per month Rupees forty one thousand six hundred and sixty six, Ten annas and eight English pice (Rs 41,666-10-8)

To the persons attached to the new Imambarrah called Imambara Nujuf Ushruf according to a separate detail Rupees one thousand one hundred and thirty seven Ten annas and eight Pie (Rs 1137-10-8)

This sum will be paid forever to the persons who will be appointed to the charge of the Imambarah through the King and its Amlah or officers will be kept or discharged at the pleasure of the Superintendent.

Nawab Mobaruck Mahul Rupees ten thousand (Rs 10,000)

This allowance will be paid to the Begum Nawab Mobaruck Mahul during her life time and after her demise one third of the allowance will be paid to any person or purpose she may will. The remaining two thirds and whatever may be the saving of the one third agreeably to the will which will be an addition to the two thirds, or in case of her not making a will, the whole allowance is to be divided into two equal parts one half to be given to the Nujuf Ushruf and the other half for Kurballa to the high Priest Meyawurs (or persons who have its charge) on the part of the said King, that His Majesty may thereby draw its benefit.

Sultan Murrium Begum rupees two thousand five hundred (Rs 2,500)

To be given to Sooltan Murrium Begum as to Nawab Mobaruck Mahul and after death to be appropriated in the same manner.

Moomtaz Muhul Rupees one thousand one hundred (Rs 1,100) as the foregoing

Surfuraz Mahul Rupees one thousand (Rs 1,000) ditto ditto

The servants and dependants of Surfuraz Mahul as per separate list Rupees nine hundred and twenty nine (Rs 929)

To be paid in perpetuity as per separate statement.

The allowance of persons dying without heirs to be added to the sums for Nujuf Ushruf and Kurbulla.

Nawab Maotumudood Dowlah Bahadur Rupees twenty thousand (Rs 20,000)

This allowance is to be paid in perpetuity to the Nawab and his heirs. It will be paid in perpetuity after his demise agreeably to his will to his sons daughters and wives and other dependants. If it happens that he makes no will, in that case the allowance is to be given to his lawful heirs according to the laws of inheritance in conformity with the tracts of the Sheeas. The allowance which are assigned to his wife one son and a daughter from this fund as specified below are also to be continued in perpetuity separately and whatever the Nawab may bequeath to them out of the above allowance is to be given to them in perpetuity separately and in like manner if a will be not made shares are to be given to these three persons from the Nawab's allowance according to Law.

Nawab Begum the wife of Nawab Maotumud ood Dowlah Rupees two thousand (Rs 2,000)

This allowance is to be paid to her during her life time and after her death to be paid to her lawful heirs in perpetuity according to the laws of inheritance in conformity to the tenets of the Sheeas.

Nawab Auleea Begum the daughter of the said Nawab Rupees one thousand (Rs 1,000)

According to the foregoing rate.

Ameenood dowlah Bahadur son of the Nawab Rupees two thousand (Rs 2,000) Ditto ditto ditto

Done at Lucknow the 1st Mohurrum 1241 Hijree corresponding with the 17th August 1825.

(signed) M Ricketts
Resident
(signed) Amherst
Harington
W.B. Bayley

Ratified by the Right Honorable the Governor General in Council Fort William in Bengal the thirteenth day of September one thousand eight hundred and twenty five AD.

(signed) G. Swinton
Secy to Government
(True Copy)
Compared Signed Mordaunt Ricketts
(signed) F Hare Resident
(True copy from the English Writing)

That your petitioner's sister Sooltan Murrium Begum continued up to the time of her death which happened on or about the fifth April one thousand eight hundred and forty nine to receive the said sum of Rupees two thousand and five hundred per month from the British Government in pursuance of the said Articles.

That on or about the thirteenth day of February one thousand eight hundred and forty four your petitioner's said sister executed her last will and testament in duplicate translation of which is as follows.

That whereas the Mortality of body known to all that it is appointed unto all men once to die and all must taste the flavour of death and see the face of the Angel of Death. Wherefore it is most necessary for every human being to make arrangement of his transactions for the future and to make out his last Will for his Relatives and Dependants as directed in the religious tenets for the guidance on consideration that it may come to pass that no dispute or enmity should take place after his death amongst the Relatives and dependants . And in conformity to the instructions laid down in the articles of the Treaty held between the both Governments (British Government and the King of Oude) on the 1st Mohurrum 1241Hijree corresponding with the 17th August 1825 AD. the conditions of which articles having been settled thus in Article 2nd This loan is made in perpetuity The Sovereign of the Kingdom of Oude shall never have the power to take it back nor shall they exercise any interference with its interest'—Article 3rd The British Government guarantees that it will pay for ever the monthly sums hereafter mentioned out of the interest of the above loan to the persons set down in this instrument in the current coin of the place where they may reside without any diminution whatever' Article 4th The Honorable Company will always protect the honor of the stipendiaries who will be paid out of this fund, and it will be the protector of their possessions such as houses, and gardens (whether bestowed by the King of Oude or purchased or built by themselves) from the hands of the Sovereign and their enemies and in whatever city or country they may be, their allowance will be paid to them there', and it is further inserted in the said Instrument that after her demise one third of the allowance will be paid to any

person or for any purpose she may will it will be allowed'. Being of perfect mind health and memory I do make and ordain this my Last Will and place it under the immediate protection of the authorities of the Honorable Company that after my death conforming to the instructions laid down in this my Last Will may be carried into effect. My monthly allowance is Rupees (2500) two thousand five hundred and under the said Treaty of the both Governments the one third of which is Rupees (833-5-4) eight hundred and thirty three five annas and four English pie. I fix and ordain monthly allowance for my youngest brother Joseph Short (whom from his infancy I brought up under my care and protection like my own son) and for other dependants (in privilege of their fidelities to me) according to which the authorities of the Honorable Company shall regularly pay their monthly allowance in perpetuity to all my Legatees as hereafter particularized without any deduction whatever and in what City or Country they may be their allowance will be paid to them there that they should provide themselves suitably without seeking for and from any one else. That during my life time or after my demise in case of any of my Legatees' death his allowance is to be continued and distributed to his heirs in conformity to the tenets of the Law. In case if he has no heir his allowance will be paid to any person according to his will. It happens that he makes no will in that case, the Resident should distribute his allowance to his heirs according to the Tenets of the Law. Except this my last Will and Testament no other documents or Will should be considered valid and true and be admitted to eradicate the claim of my Legatees specified in this my Last Will and orders when they choose may be given to them to proceed in what country they like and regarding their proceeding no other should be allowed to interfere in their affairs. May Holy God perfume the tomb of blessed memory His late Majesty Ghaz eeooddeen Hyder who has placed me under the immediate protection of the Honorable Company and conformably to the Treaty held between the both Governments I always have been given privileges from Government I place all my Relatives and dependants under the immediate protection of the Government and trusting that my Legatees will also be treated the like manner as myself and the allowance Rupees 833-5-4 I settled on them from my allowance will regularly continue on them Vizt: Rupees 800-0-0

My brother Joseph Short (as my own son). This allowance for my brother's expences and to give maintenance and clothing to my other brother John Short (who is insane) and my youngest sister Eliza (who is attacked with severe palpitation also) in case of her husband and son will not support her under such circumstance my said Brother will also give her sustenance and clothing Rupees 750 and also to be disbursed by my Brother's own hands and direction and after my Brother's demise to be acted in the same manner by his heirs. In repairs illuminations and charity of the Roman Catholic Churches Rs 50 Vizt Lucknow 20 Rupees and Cawnpore 50 Rupees.

Hakeem Mahomed Ally in recompense due by me to his duties as Physician
15-0-0

Moosummat Cheotee Khannum daughter of Mirza Noor Begum recompence of her fidelity and good services 18-5-4

833-5-4

Regarding the arrangements of my funeral and burial obsequies in whatever place I may be and whatever time it may happen all the requisites shall be performed by my brother Joseph Short. I have recorded in the Residency office and original and Duplicate of this my last Will agreeably to the particularized monthly allowances fixed by me for the Legatees to be regularly paid to them in perpetuity by their own seals and receipts and those of their heirs' seals and receipts. Should it chance that my death take place here in Lucknow my funeral ceremonies and the tomb may be erected by my said brother Joseph short's discretion and after my demise my said brother will be sole proprietor of all my household property including jewels cash Booneead Munzil premises as well as all and every property of mine and after my demise the male and female slaves and abyssinian females who are left my brother has full power over them either to keep them or let them free and no other person has liberty to interfere respecting them. I have already examined and adjusted all my accounts from the Legatees and none owe me a fraction. Therefore the representatives of the Honorable Company will not allow anyone to claim any thing from them. I have made out and set my seal upon this my original Last Will and Testament as also a duplicate has been recorded into the Resident's office. I have as well delivered copies of this my Last Will, one to my Brother, second to Hukeem Mahomed Ally otherwise Nubba Physician and third to Moosummat Chotee Kannum daughter of Asoor Beg for rendering good services. Exclusive of this my Last Will should any of my dimissed servants or those in the service produce any other documents deed of gift or Last Will it ought to be considered false and forged and proper for the authorities of the Honorable Company to seize the person and destroy the forged document. I have also executed a separate Will exclusive for the purpose of my funeral and burial performances dated 1st July 1838 AD. corresponding with the 7th Rubbee oos surree 1264 Hijree which I have made and set my seal upon and delivered to my Brother who will produce the same and Government will assist him to carry it out into effect Dated 23rd Mohurrum 1260 Hijree corresponding with the 13th February 1844 AD.

Seal of Sooltan Murrium Begum

That during the life time of the said Sooltan Murrium Begum both copies of the said Will were delivered to the then Resident of Lucknow with a request that one copy might be submitted to the Government of India and that the other might be recorded in the Residency records of the city of Lucknow with the view to the recognition or confirmation of the Will in her life time and the Will was accordingly so recognised.

That immediately on the death of your Petitioner's said sister Sooltan Murrium Begum Colonel Sleeman the then Resident of Lucknow locked up and sealed the whole of the deceased's property and made a report to the Government respecting it and on obtaining orders from the Government all the moveable and immoveable property of the Testator was made over to your Petitioner as directed by her Will.

That soon after the death of your Petitioner's said sister the Reverend Father Adeodatus the pastor of the Roman Catholic church at Lucknow made application for the Rupees twenty directed by the said Will to be expended by your Petitioner in repairs illuminations and charities of the Chapel at Lucknow to be paid direct to him but such application was not complied with and your petitioner accordingly from the fifth day of April one Thousand eight hundred and forty nine the date of the death of the Testatrix up to the month of October One thousand eight hundred and fifty five duly received monthly the full Waseeka allowance or sum of Rupees eight hundred bequeathed him by the said Will as aforesaid and thereout your petitioner duly paid and expended monthly during such period as last mentioned the sum of Rupees fifty as follows Viz: Rupees twenty in repairs illuminations and charity of the Roman Catholic Church at Lucknow and Rupees thirty in repairs Illuminations and charity of the Roman Catholic church at Cawnpore as directed by the said Will.

That subsequently the Reverend Father Adeodatus again represented to the then Resident of Lucknow General Outram that your petitioner's sister the Sooltan Murrium Begum had left in her Will Rupees fifty per month for him but that your Petitioner had refuted it and did not wish to pay him where the said Resident who was unconscious of the exact terms of the will of the said Testatrix or that the claim previously preferred by the same Reverend Gentleman to Colonel Sleeman the former Resident had been rejected directed in November one thousand eight hundred and fifty five that the monthly Waseeka allowance of Rupees eight hundred should be detained and before any proper enquiry or investigation was made as to the said claim the then Resident went to Calcutta and returned to Lucknow in February one thousand eight hundred and fifty six as Chief Commissioner when the Kingdom of Oude was annexed.

In consequence of your petitioner's allowance being so detained your petitioner repeatedly applied to Captain Hayes the Secretary to the Chief Commissioner to have the matter of the alleged claim decided but owing to the laborious duties then imposed upon the Commissioner consequent on the recent annexation of Oude he was unable to investigate it but desired your petitioner to draw the arrears of his Waseeka allowance at the rate of Rupees seven hundred and fifty per month and to leave the disputed amount in the Treasury on deposit until the claimant's right had been proved or disallowed. Your petitioner accordingly from November one thousand eight hundred and fifty five to May one thousand eight hundred and fifty seven gave receipts for the full Rupees eight hundred per month but in fact only received Rupees seven hundred and fifty and your petitioner afterwards on Mr Jackson being appointed Chief Commissioner discovered that the whole accumulated deposit at the rate of Rupees fifty per month for the same period of one year and seven months had been paid over to the Reverend Father Adeodatus by General Outram previous to his departure for Calcutta without any regular decision having been come to or the Will properly examined.

That during the time that Sir Henry Lawrence was Chief Commissioner of Oude your Petitioner repeatedly solicited the Secretary Captain Hayes to bring his case to the notice of the Chief Commissioner who held out hopes of speedily investigating them when unfortunately the mutiny broke out.

In one thousand eight hundred and fifty eight when Oude was re-conquered by the British Government Report was made to the Government for the sanction of the payment of your Petitioner's full Waseeka allowance of Rupees eight hundred per month and the following letters were received from G.F. Edmonstone Esquire Secretary to the Government of India by the Chief Commissioner of Oude as follows.

No 1200

From G.F. Edmonstone Esquire
To the Chief Commissioner

Oude

Dated Allahabad 12th July 1858

Sir,

In reply to your Secretary's letter No 227 dated 7th Ultimo I have the honor to inform you that the Right Honorable the Governor General is pleased to sanction the admission of the claim of Mr Joseph Short to a Waseeka of Rupees 9600 per annum and the payment of the Interest on the Government Notes as recommended by you.

I have &ca
(signed) G.F. Edmonstone
Secretary to the Govt of India
With the Govr General
(True copy)

In accordance with this letter your petitioner received the arrears of his Waseeka allowance at Rupees eight hundred per month from June one thousand eight hundred and fifty seven ......unpaid and continued to receive the full sum of Rupees eight hundred to the end of July one thousand eight hundred and fifty nine when the Reverend Father Gleeson the Chaplain of Lucknow there being then no chapel at Lucknow or Cawnpore made application for the Rupees fifty per month out of the Rupees eight hundred to be paid to him and notwithstanding an explanation was given by your Petitioner to Lieutenant MacAndrew the Secretary to the then Chief Commissioner Mr Wingfield the Rupees fifty per month were directed to be deducted and paid to the Reverend Father Gleeson and that sum was accordingly deducted from your Petitioner's Waseeka of Rupees eight hundred per month from August one thousand eight hundred and fifty nine to November one thousand eight hundred and sixty a period of one year and four months and paid to the said Reverend Father Gleeson. From December one thousand eight hundred and sixty up to April one thousand eight hundred and sixty one your petitioner again received his full allowance of Rupees eight hundred per month less Rupees thirty two per month for income tax and forwarded to the Reverend W Gleeson the sum of Rupees forty eight per month being the Rupees fifty less Rupees two for income tax for the purposes of expenditure as directed by the Will and for which your Petitioner holds receipts.

The Reverend W Gleeson in April one thousand eight hundred and sixty one claimed from your Petitioner the sum of Rupees one thousand and five hundred for arrears stated to be due in respect of the Rupees fifty per month of the Lucknow and Cawnpore churches during the period of the late Mutiny and stated that he would receive the Rupees fifty per month direct from the Treasury and on application being made by your petitioner in July one thousand eight hundred and sixty one to G.W. Yuile Esquire C.B. The officiating Chief Commissioner that the express directions of the Testatrix might be carried out your petitioner was officially informed that as it appeared he had made an arrangement with the priest no order was required thereon. Since May one thousand eight hundred and sixty one up to the present time your Petitioner has received no portion of his Waseeka allowance he declining to receive a portion of it without the whole as he has ascertained that from the first June one thousand eight hundred and fifty nine up to November one thousand eight hundred and sixty no portion of the Rupees thirty a month has ever been received by the Chaplain of Cawnpore for the purposes directed by the said Will although the full Rupees fifty were paid monthly direct to the Reverend Father Gleeson the Chaplain of Lucknow in direct opposition to the Will of the said Testatrix.

That the following is a copy of the certificate of the Reverend Fr Alphonsus the Chaplain of Cawnpore.

Cawnpore 4. 9. 1861

I the undersigned do declare upon my honor that since I have been at Cawnpore from the 1st June 1859 I never either heard or received any money from Miss Short's bequest of 50 Rs a month for this chapel nor I have authorized any person at Lucknow to draw the amount nor I had heard anything about it except this day from Mr F Menzies.

F Alphonsus
C Chaplain

P.S. I prefer to draw the money from Mr Short direct than through any other person.

From the facts above stated it therefore appears that your petitioner from fifth April one thousand eight hundred and forty nine to October one thousand eight hundred and fifty five received his full monthly Waseeka allowance of Rupees eight hundred.

That from November one thousand eight hundred and fifty five to May one thousand eight hundred and fifty seven without any sufficient reason and contrary to the express stipulation contained in the said agreement of the seventeenth August one thousand eight hundred and twenty five and to the directions in the Will of the said Testatrix Rupees fifty per month portion of the Rupees eight hundred for the last mentioned period amounting to Rupees nine hundred and fifty were deducted at the Treasury at Lucknow and paid over to the Reverend Father Adeodatus.

That no portion of these Rupees fifty has ever been applied by the said recipient from June one thousand eight hundred and fifty nine to November one thousand eight hundred and sixty for the purposes of the chapel or worship &ca at Cawnpore.

Your petitioner therefore humbly submits that he should receive direct from the Treasury his full Waseeka allowance of Rupees eight hundred from May one thousand eight hundred and sixty one up to the present time and so continue to receive the same without any deduction whatsoever as directed by the said Will of his said sister and for the following reasons.

That by the said agreement of the seventeenth August one thousand eight hundred and twenty five article 3rd The British Government guaranteed that it would pay forever the monthly sums thereafter mentioned out of the interest of the loan therein referred to, to the personnel down in that instrument in the current coin of the place where they might reside without any deduction whatever and by the same agreement it is stipulated that after the death of the said Sooltan Murrium Begum one third of the allowance will be paid to any person or for any purpose she may will.

That by the said Will there was an express bequest of the Rupees eight hundred per month to your Petitioner for certain purposes with an express direction that the Rupees thirty and Rupees twenty be disbursed by your Petitioner's own hands and direction and that after your Petitioner's demise to be acted in the same manner by his heirs in repairs &ca of the Roman Catholic Churches.

This amounted to an express bequest to your Petitioner by Will which your petitioner submits cannot be varied and that even if the pastors or other custodians of the Roman Catholic Churches at Lucknow or Cawnpore have good ground of complaint (but which it is humbly submitted is not the case here) that the funds directed to be expended for the benefit of such churches have not been so expended your petitioner is quite ready and willing to pay the said two sums of Rupees thirty and Rupees twenty less any deduction for Income Tax direct to such pastors respectively so that your petitioner may be sure that they are expended as directed by the said Will and which he is bound to do.

Your Petitioner also humbly submits that the mode that has been adopted as above stated of at different times paying the said monthly sum of Rupees fifty to the Lucknow Chaplain has in a measure deprived the Cawnpore Church as above mentioned.

That such pensions and Waseeka independently of any express directions contained in the documents creating them, are specially exempted even from seizure by a Creditor who has obtained judgment and it has already been decided by Government that no process of any Court could attack the stipend of any Waseequadar and that the full sum of each stipendiary must be paid to that stipendiary direct by the Treasury officer and it is submitted that the Government would be still more zealous of in any way withholding payment of a Waseeka allowance ... complaint of misappropriation by the stipendiary has been made out.

Your Petitioner therefore humbly prays your Excellency that your Excellency will cause an order to be passed directing payment to your Petitioner of the arrears of his full Waseeka allowance of Rupees eight hundred according to the directions contained in the said Will of his sister the Sooltan Murrium Begum deceased and for the regular payment to your Petitioner in future of such full allowance without any deduction being made or without any interference of third parties.

And your Petitioner will ever pray &ca
Joseph Short by his constituted Attorney
John U ... 6th March 1862

Wasika Office—File 3 of 1874

(John Alpine Speirs' petition to the Chief Commissioner of Oude
on behalf of Amelia Short)

East Indian Railway,
Jubbulpore Extension,
Manickpore Station,
9th October 1870

To
R.H. Davies Esq., C.I.S.
Chief Commissioner Oude,
Simla

Sir,

1. I beg to bring to your notice the unusually harsh measures which have been used in the case of Mrs Short.

2. Allow me to lay the facts of the case as briefly as possible before you.

3. A short time previous to your proceeding on leave, Mr Joseph Short died—he was the holder of a Government Annuity,—a Wasikadar.

4. Some years prior to the death of Mr Short, he was called upon by the Junior Secretary of your predecessor, Sir Charles Wingfield, to furnish the Administration of Oude with a List of his heirs. This was duly done by the late Mr Short and the document was duly filed in the Wusseeka Office. Unfortunately Mr Short omitted to assign or particularize any specific amount as the sum he desired to be distributed to each of his heirs.

5. On Mr Short's demise a question appears to have arisen as to how the Wusseeka should be divided, there being illegitimate and legitimate children—Mr Murray your junior Secretary was directed to obtain the opinion of the Offg Judicial Commissioner. That officer, after some months' delay, decided that the Wusseeka should be divided equally among Mr Short's children, legitimate or illegitimate—reinstating one James Short whose father had disinherited (by the list of heirs furnished as above stated) but deciding at the same time that the widow of the late Mr Short was not entitled to any share in the Wusseeka—although her name was first on the list of heirs furnished to Government by Mr Short.

6. A month's time was allowed to the children to prove or disprove the marriage of their Grandmother Mrs Short with one Dr Short, the father of the late Mr Short. Now on the other hand, no intimation was given to the poor widow—neither was she called on to show cause why she should not be excluded from all right to inherit a share in the Wusseeka—Although the Counsel (Mr Arrathoon) who appeared for her forwarded to the Judicial Commissioner a letter received by him from his client (Mrs Short) soliciting the favour of his asking the Judicial Commissioner what was to be the Widow's share in the Wusseeka.

7 The decision of the Judicial Commissioner was in substance upheld by Genl Barrow your locum tenens, although he ordered that the sum of Rupees fifty a month should be allowed to the Widow for life—thus reducing the position of a lawful married wife of a Christian to a lower status than the offspring of a slave-woman, such offspring having the right of bequest and the widow being denied it.

8. The Judicial Commissioner's decision with regard to the widow is based apparently on two points—

1st when describing the manner in which her Wusseeka should be divided, the testatrix Miss Short alias Sultan Murrium Begum makes use of the phrase Nuslan baad Nuslan or butnan baad butnan' this phrase being translated as heirs of the body. I would ask you Sir, who must be well versed in Oriental Law terms and literature whether the term Nuslan baad Nuslan has not the same and identical meaning with the conjoint phrase. I am informed by learned Maulvis and others that the real signification of the term Nuslan bad Nuslan is male heirs and Butnan bad Butnan is female heirs and the two phrases when used conjointly are only intended to intensify the meaning of the Testatrix which was that should her Wusseeka be escheated to Government by the failure of direct heirs and is by no means intended to exclude the participation of the widow in the Wusseeka and one phrase cannot be held to debar the claim of the widow more than the other—also I would beg to draw your attention to the fact that the Testatrix used the phrase (Nuslan baad Nuslan or Khaladun va Mohholadun may Gafta Bashund) in describing the manner in which according to the Treaty her Wusseeka is to be distributed. Further the Testatrix in the Will speaks of the heirs of Mr Short as (Warid)—Moreover there is no direct proof that it was the direct aim or set purpose of the testatrix to exclude the widow of her brother in the event of there being one from all participation in the wusseeka—it is susceptible of proof on the other hand that the Testatrix never treated the then wife of Mr Short her Brother with any other than the greatest courtesy.

2nd The Judicial Commissioner stated that there is no evidence to prove the fact of there being any existing Christian usages in the family of which Miss Short alias Sooltan Murriam Begam was a member. This view of the question is strangely at variance with the facts of the case, for it could have been proved that one sister of Miss Short was during her life-time married to one, a merchant (Christian) at Lucknow, that her younger sister Eliza was married to one Capt Besant of the Hon'ble East India Co's Service, that one of her nieces, a daughter of her brother Mr Joseph Short was during the life time of the Testatrix married to one, a Mr Duhan one of a firm of merchants at Cawnpore by Father Adeodatus a Roman Catholic Priest. Mr Short's first wife was not as stated by the Judicial Commissioner a girl sent from Lucknow and married to Mr Short at Cawnpore but the person whom Mr Short married publicly was the daughter of a soldier in one of Her Majesty's Regiments of Horse then laying at Cawnpore. This I trust you will consider disposes of the fact adduced by the Judicial Commissioner Viz: the total absence of any Christian usages, marriages &c in the Short's family. I might also add that all Mr Short's daughters have been duly married by the rites of the Roman Catholic Church and that the rite of Baptism has been duly administered to his children.

9. During the life-time of the Testatrix the sister of one of her legatees (by name Chotee Khanum) was declared the inheritor of the Wusseeka willed to Chotee Khanum by Miss Short. The Testatrix was also well aware of the impossibility of either of the dependants to whom she left a Wusseeka having any

offspring —Besides all this there are some 40 or more precedents in the Wusseeka Office to prove that the widows of Wusseekadars have inherited their legal share of their deceased husband's Wusseeka when the Wusseeka papers have been drawn up in similar terms (Nuslan bad nuslan) to the Will of the late Sooltan Murrium Begam.

10. Mrs Short is the lawful wife of the late Mr Joseph Short, was married to him by the rites of the Roman Catholic Church, having been first converted and baptised into that faith and it is indeed against all law and precedent that the legal and acknowledged wife of a Christian should have a lower status and less privileges than that of a Pagan Hindoo or misguided and Polygamous Mahomedan.

11. There is yet a more curious and salient feature in this case than I have hitherto touched on—Sooltan Murrium Begam in her Will makes provision that in case of any of her legatees dying intestate his portion should be distributed by what is termed in the Will Shurriat Ghurrah'—it was clearly proved in the Court of the Judicial Commissioner that at the time the will in question was drawn up Sooltan Murrium Begam was a Christian and as Prima Facie evidence the testatrix left a sum of Rs 50 per mensem for the Roman Catholic Churches at Cawnpore and Lucknow. It was also proved that the testatrix frequently received the Blessed sacrament at the hands of the then Roman Catholic Priest of Lucknow. In face of these proofs of Christianity and those recited in Part 2 of Para 8 there appears to be still a doubt in the mind of the Judicial Commissr as to whether Miss Short was or was not a Christian. Even if Shurriah Ghurrah means the Bright Law as translated by the Judicial Commissioner, still I say what brighter law could be conceived by one who was truly repentant of the fault committed by her in her youth. I hardly think it admits of contradiction that it is evident Miss Short alias Sooltan Murrium Begam evidently deeply repented of her former course of life and there can be but little doubt that she was sincerely a Christian—moreover she made particular arrangements for her sepulture in Christian or rather consecrated ground, (even going to the length of leaving a separate deed which is alluded in her will) relative to this matter, so great was her horror of being laid in other than consecrated ground and having her corpse exposed to the profanity of other rites and ceremonies than the religion to which she belonged, i.e. the Roman Catholic Church.

12. I would now conclude my letter to you with the following remarks:
1st I affirm that great injustice has been done by setting aside the document which Mr Short filed as his list of heirs as in it he clearly showed that his wife was lawfully married to him and seven of his children who were born from his wives were legitimate and five sons who were the offspring of slave women

were his illegitimate children, and Mr Short was also under the certain impression that he had provided for his wife and under this impression for a series of years making no effort to provide for her in her old age—and I can personally aver that the late Mr Short was fully under the impression that come what might his wife would receive 1/3 of his Wusseeka as her share being his lawful and acknowledged wife.

2nd The terms of the Will in question used by a common Moonshee unaccustomed to draw up documents and those for a female who had no acquaintance whatever with law have been construed and translated with more than literal exactness although, as I have had occasion to state, some forty or more precedents are to be seen in your Wusseeka Office where the term Nuslan bad Nuslan has been used and yet the widow has received her legal rights.

3rd I can state that a grave injustice has been done in not permitting the widow to show cause why she should not be allowed to inherit her legal share of the Wusseeka and this Sir lays with you the cry of the widow defrauded of her rights as it is still in your power to do it and you Sir being for some time in the Station knows much more about the Wusseeka cases than any other man.

4th Equity, or as the Judicial Commissr terms it 'Natural Law' may have been applied fairly in the case of the legitimate and illegitimate children but as there were no other wives of the late Mr Short other than this poor widow equity is not required in her case for she being the sole lawful wife of Mr Short is entitled to 1/3 of the Wusseeka.

5th On the first day of the trial of this case, the Judicial Commissioner said orally in an Open Court that the three children of Mrs Amelia Short (widow) are become legitimate by the subsequent new marriage but I was astonished when I saw that he, the Judicial Commissioner, has written a different thing in his opinion.

6th Now I state that it having been clearly proved that the sacrament of Matrimony and the sacrament of Baptism was the rule and not the exception in the family to which Sooltan Murriam Begum belonged and that the rights of Christian Sepulture had been in every case accorded to the adult members of the family, it is impossible to draw any other inference than that the family was a Christian family.

In conclusion I beg you will not see so great an injustice done to a defenceless widow for she has suffered many wrongs and I also beg you will excuse any hasty remarks I have made.

Again trusting you will give my letter to you the benefit of your most favourable construction, seeing that it is not for myself but for my widowed mother-in-law who has hitherto been brought up and bred in what is called easy circumstances that I am pleading,

I am Sir,

Your[s] most obediently,

John A. Speirs

P. Way Inspector

P.S. I might add that Mr Short died in debt, that he has left no provision for his widow other than her share of his Wusseeka – that all the children of Mr Short with the exception of three are step-children of Mrs Short (widow) and that almost all have been well-educated and the daughters and one son married—that the widow of Mr Short has to support on few Rupees a month herself and a boy and girl children of Mr Short who are still of tender years—10 and 12 respectively. The daughters of Mr Short who are married are in good circumstances, the sons are also educated & some employed—whereas the widow has no-one to look to but the annuity to which she believed, with her late husband, she was entitled to.

NAI Fin B: Sep 1871 Nos 12-14 (Amelia Short's Petition to the Viceroy of India)

To the Right Honorable
Earl Mayo K.J.G.C.S.J
Viceroy and Governor General of India
The humble Memorial of Amelia Short
Widow of Joseph Short deceased late of Lucknow

Sheweth

That on the 3rd April 1844 one Sooltan Murriam Begum, (one of the Stipendiaries under the treaty between His Majesty Ghazeeooddeen Hyder Shah of Oudh and Her Majesty's Government, dated the 17th of August 1825) made her Will in accordance with the law a translation whereof is in the words following

The Mortality of body known to all that it is appointed unto all men once to die and all must taste the flavour of death and see the face of the Angel of Death. Wherefore it is most necessary for every human being to make arrangement of his transactions for the future and to make out his last Will for his Relatives and Dependants as directed in the religious tenets for the guidance on consideration that it may come to pass that no dispute or enmity should take place after his death amongst the Relatives and dependants. And in conformity to the instructions laid down in the articles of the Treaty held between the both Governments (British

Government and the King of Oude) on the 1st Mohurrum 1241Hijree corresponding with the 17th August 1825 AD. the conditions of which articles having been settled thus in Article 2nd This loan is made in perpetuity The Sovereign of the Kingdom of Oude shall never have the power to take it back nor shall they exercise any interference with its interest'—Article 3rd The British Government guarantees that it will pay for ever the monthly sums hereafter mentioned out of the interest of the above loan to the persons set down in this instrument in the current coin of the place where they may reside without any diminution whatever' Article 4th The Honorable Company will always protect the honor of the stipendiaries who will be paid out of this fund, and it will be the protector of their possessions such as houses, and gardens (whether bestowed by the King of Oude or purchased or built by themselves) from the hands of the Sovereign and their enemies and in whatever city or country they may be, their allowance will be paid to them there' and it is further inserted in the said Instrument that after her demise one third of the allowance will be paid to any person or for any purpose she may will it will be allowed'. Being of perfect mind health and memory I do make and ordain this my Last Will and place it under the immediate protection of the authorities of the Honorable Company that after my death conforming to the instructions laid down in this my Last Will may be carried into effect. My monthly allowance is Rupees (2500) two thousand five hundred and under the said Treaty of the both Governments the one third of which is Rupees (833-5-4) eight hundred and thirty three five annas and four English pie. I fix and ordain monthly allowance for my youngest brother Joseph Short (whom from his infancy I brought up under my care and protection like my own son) and for other dependants (in privilege of their fidelities to me) according to which the authorities of the Honorable Company shall regularly pay their monthly allowance generation by generation & womb by womb in perpetuity for ever [Nuslim bad Nuslim wo Butrim bad Butrim wo Khaladun Mukhaldun]to all my Legatees as hereafter particularized without any deduction whatever and in what City or Country they may be their allowance will be paid to them there that they should provide themselves suitably without seeking for and from any one else. That during my life time or after my demise in case of any of my Legatees' death his allowance is to be continued and distributed to his heirs in conformity to Divine Law. [Furaiz Ullah] In case if he has no heir his allowance will be paid to any person according to his will. It happens that he makes no will in that case, the Resident should distribute his allowance to his heirs according to the Bright Law [Shurijut Ghuera]. Except this my last Will and Testament no other documents or Will should be considered valid ... and be admitted to eradicate the claim of my Legatees specified in this my Last Will and orders when they choose may.be given to them to proceed in what country they like and regarding their proceeding no other should be allowed to interfere in their affairs. May Holy God perfume the tomb of blessed memory (His late Majesty Ghaz eeooddeen Hyder who has placed me under the immediate protection of the Honorable Company and conformably to the Treaty held between the both Governments I always have been given privileges from Government I place all my Relatives and dependants under the immediate protection of the Government and trusting that my Legatees will also be treated the like manner as myself and the allowance Rupees 833-5-4 I settled on them from my allowance will regularly continue on them Vizt: Rupees 800-0-0

My brother Joseph Short (as my own son). This allowance for my brother's expences and to give maintenance and clothing to my other brother John Short (who is insane) and my youngest sister Eliza (who is attacked with severe palpitation also) in case of her husband and son will not support her under such circumstance my said Brother will also give her maintenance and clothing Rupees 750 and also to be disbursed by my Brother's own hands and discretion and after my Brother's demise to be acted in the same manner by his heirs in repairs illuminations and charity of the Roman Catholic Churches Rs 50 Vizt Lucknow 20 Rupees and Cawnpore 30 Rupees.

Hakeem Mahomed Ally in recompense due by me to his duties as Physician

15-0-0

Moosummat Cheotee Khannum daughter of Mirza Noor Begum recompence of her fidelity and good services 18-5-4

833-5-4

Regarding the arrangements of my funeral and burial obsequies in whatever place I may be and whatever time it may happen all the requisites shall be performed by my brother Joseph Short. I have recorded in the Residency office and original and Duplicate of this my last Will agreeably to the particularized monthly allowances fixed by me for the Legatees to be regularly paid to them in perpetuity by their own seals and receipts and those of their heirs' seals and receipts. Should it chance that my death take place here in Lucknow my funeral ceremonies and the tomb may be erected by my said brother Joseph short's discretion and after my demise my said brother will be sole proprietor of all my household property including jewels cash Booneead Munzil premises as well as all and every property of mine and after my demise the male and female slaves and Abyssinian females who are left my brother has full power over them either to keep them or let them free and no other person has liberty to interfere respecting them. I have already examined and adjusted all my accounts from the Legatees and none owe me a fraction. Therefore the representatives of the Honorable Company will not allow anyone to claim any thing from them. I have made out and set my seal upon this my original Last Will and Testament as also a duplicate has been recorded into the Resident's office. I have as well delivered copies of this my Last Will, one to my

Brother, second to Hukeem Mahomed Ally otherwise Nubba Physician and third to Moosummat Chotee Kannum daughter of Asoor Beg for rendering good services. Exclusive of this my Last Will should any of my dismissed servants or those in the service produce any other documents deed of gift or Last Will it ought to be considered false and forged and proper for the authorities of the Honorable Company to seize the person and destroy the forged document. I have also executed a separate Will exclusive for the purpose of my funeral and burial performances dated 1st July 1838 AD. corresponding with the 7th Rubbee oos surree 1264 Hijree which I have made and set my seal upon and delivered to my Brother who will produce the same and Government will assist him to carry it out into effect Dated 23rd Mohurrum 1260 Hijree corresponding with the 13th February 1844 AD.

Seal of Sooltan Murrium Begum

Second	That the said Sooltan Murrium Begum was the sister of your Memorialist and was during her life time a Waseekadar and received the monthly stipend of Rupees 2500—
Third	The said Sooltan Murrium Begum died on the 5th April 1849 without altering her said Will.
Fourth	That under the said Will of the said Sooltan Murrium Begum your Memorialist's said husband the said Joseph Short became entitled to the monthly sum of Rupees 750 out of the monthly stipend of Rupees 2500 of the said Sooltan Murrium Begum according to the terms of the original Will *Nuslun bad Nuslum wo Butum Bad Butum wo Khaludun Mukhaldun'* i.e. offspring by offspring womb by womb in perpetuity for ever'
Fifth	That on the 25th of January 1863 the said Joseph Short in accordance with the terms of a notification ifsued from the Wuseeka Department dated the 5th January 1863 filed in the Wuseeka office at Luknow a list of his heirs of which the following is a correct translation—

That on the 25th February 1863 a memo of my heirs had been filed in the Wuseeka office as the names of my heirs were written in Persian and were not clear enough to read the English names in Persian. Therefore I beg to submit another copy of the same in Persian and the names of my heirs also written in English by which the names of my heirs will be clearly known.

The children by the wombs of the lawful married Christian wives vizt.

Four daughters by the first married Wife the deceased:	Second lawful married wife and three children by her vizt:
1. Mrs Mary Duhan 31 years' age	Mrs Amelia Short wife of 38 years of age

2. Mrs Ellen Johannes of 25 years' age — Mifs Rachael Short daughter of 15 years' age
3. Mrs Nelly Queiros of 21 years' age — Benjamin Short son of 8 years' age
4. Mifs Marcelia Short of 16 years' age — Mifs Anna Margaret daughter of 5 years' age

The children born by Mahomedan Slave Girls vizt:

By Mufsummat Illaheejan slave girl

Macdonald Short son of 21 years' age — (As his conduct if very bad therefore I had repudiated him from my heart)

Martin Short son of

By Mufsummut Seotee slave girl vizt;

George Short son of 12 years' age

Isabella Short daughter of 4 years' age — (That as the said Seotee had deserted to Calcutta with her daughter therefore I had repudiated this daughter also from my heirs)

By Mufst Muhboobjan slave girl vizt:

Emma Short daughter of 4 years' age — (That as the said Muhboob deserted to
Georgiana Short — Calcutta with her both daughters therefore I had repudiated them from my heirs)

By Mufsummutat Nourozee slave girl vizt:

Isaac Short son of 6 years' age

By Mufsummat Peearee slave girl vizt;

Edwin Short son of 6 years' age

Seal of Joseph Short

Sixth — That under the treaty between Ghazeeooddeen Hyder and the British Government of the 17th August 1825 (which is set out at P166 Vol II of Aicheson's Treaties) the monthly allowance of Rupees 2500 was payable to Sultan Murrium Begum during her life and after her demise one third of the allowance was to be paid to any person or for any purpose she might will.

Seventh — That the then resident of Lucknow continued to pay the said stipend to the said Joseph Short from the time of the death of the said Sooltan Murrium Begum till Mr Short's death on the 26th of February 1870.

Eighth — That the said Joseph Short left him surviving your Memorialist, his widow and three children by her and he also left four daughters by his first wife and several children by slave girls.

Ninth — That after the death of the said Joseph Short disputes arose amongst the several members of his family as to the division of the stipend and claims were filed by the parties in the Wuseeka Department – The children by Joseph Short's first wife basing their claims upon the fact that their parents were Christians and that they should inherit to the exclusion of the children by the slave girls and the latter claiming on the ground that the testator was a Mahomedan and the case should be decided according to the Mahomedan Law.

Tenth   That your Memorialist took no part in these proceedings which took place before the Chief Commissioner of Oudh.

Eleventh   That the said Chief Commifsioner of Oudh referred the following questions to the Judicial Commifsioner of Oudh for his opinion.

1.   What was the intention of Sooltan Murrium Begum as exprefsed in her Will.

2.   Is the Wufseeka to be divided according to the Mahomedan or Christian law.

3.   If by Christian law does the subsequent marriage of Amelia Short (your Memorialist)make her children legitimate or not.

Twelfth   That the said Judicial commifsioner therefore held an investigation without summoning or calling for any explanation from your Memorialist (who was the widow of the Testator and the head Member of the family) and so far as your Memorialist is concerned the case was heard ex-parte.

Thirteenth   That the following is a copy of the opinion of the Judicial Commifsioner of Oudh.

No 654

Court of the Judicial Commisfsioner of Oudh

Dated Lucknow the 12th August 1870

Minute with reference to the Secretary to the Chief Commifsioner's letter No 5 dated 12th May 1870 regarding claim to Wuseeka Pension of the late Joseph Short

This enquiry was instituted in consequence of the receipt of officiating Junior Secretary's No 75 of 12th May 1870.

The questions asked are:

1st   What was the intention of the Sultan Murrium Begum as exprefsed in her will?

2nd   Is the Wuseeqa to be divided according to the Mahomedan or

3rd   If by Christian Law, does the subsequent marriage of Amelia Short make her children legitimate or not?

To determine these points a prolonged enquiry was found necefsary – evidence has been taken on oath here and elsewhere registers have been searched. Counsel have been heard for the several parties on more than one occasion.

I find that by an agreement or treaty between Ghazeeooddeen Hyder Shah King of Oudh and the British Government done on 17th August 1825 the British Government is bound to pay in perpetuity to certain persons set down the interest on a loan then given to the Honorable East India Company by the King generally known as the 3rd Loan.

Among those persons is one Sultan Murrium Begum to whom a power of appointment was given over a monthly sum of Rupees 833-5-4 to be paid to any person or for any purpose she may will.

That power she exercised by her will dated 13th February 1844 AD whereby she bequeathed a sum of Rs 800 monthly to her brother Joseph Short for the following purposes.

For his own expenses and those of an imbecile brother and sister   Rs 750
For the repairs lighting and charities of Roman Catholic Chapels at

Lucknow Rs 20
Cawnpore Rs 30
Total Rupees 800

If Joseph Short should have no heirs he was allowed to bequeath his allowance to whomsoever he pleased, but if he had heirs he had no such power.

The bequest is to him that he may receive it generation by generation and womb by womb (nuslim bad nuslim wo butuen bad butuen) and that after his death it may be divided among his heirs according to Divine law (Bar Warseh O mowafik Faraiz Ullah) there is a further provision that should he die intestate and without ifsue then the resident at the Court of Oudh for the time being shall divide it according to the Bright Law among his heirs (hasbi Shareij Ghurra Mushaherah wo bar Wursehash taksim Sazand).

As the words Faraiz Ullah' and Shariyat Gharra' are employed by Mahomedan writers to exprefs the law of Islam it is contended on the part of the children of Joseph Short born out of wedlock that the intention of the Testatrix was that the division should be according to that law.

Whilst the children born in Wedlock with a Christian woman deny this and would exclude from the succefsion all illegitimate children according to the existing English law of marriage.

But the words really only mean Divine Law' and Bright Law' and words immediately applicable to this case owing to Joseph Short leaving ifsue only mean Divine Law.

If it were established that Sultan Murrium Begum at the time of execution profefsed Islam no doubt the Law of the Koran would be the law referred to—But there is no reliable evidence to shew that even during the life time of Ghazeeooddeen Hyder she profefsed Mahomedan faith. The weight of what testimony there is shew that she did not and that after his death, during the reign of his son and succefsor Nufseerooddeen Hyder, she must more or lefs have openly received visits from a Christian Priest and this will is dated 7 years after the death of Nufseerooddeen Hyder when Testatrix was middle-aged, and as concubine of a King who had reigned two succefsions back was probably lefs noticed by and lefs under the restraint of the Authorities of the Royal Harem than previously.

It is proved that at that time Joseph Short himself had a Christian wife, that he never openly profefsed Islam though for the most part living after the fashion of the Mahomedan gentry. I hold it proved that the Testatrix in her separate will referred to requested Christian burial and after consulting several Authorities I exprefsed my conclusion in the language of Sir W Muir it would be inconsistent with the profefsion of Testatrix and position of the parties to construe the term in an exclusively Mahomedan view. The words (Faraiz Ullah) Divine Law in the mouth of a person during Christian burial and making afsignment for Christian purposes could hardly be taken as implying an exclusively Mahomedan meaning. My opinion is that the intention of the Testatrix was not that the succefsion should be according to Mahomedan Law: but that it should be regulated by some other law of which the resident was a fitter exponent than the Mahomedan High Priest.

It remains to see what law should be applied. To ascertain this all pofsible enquiry has been made into the antecedents of the family their domicile and creed or religious persuasion.

Sultan Murrium Begum was at the time of her death domiciled in Lucknow. At that time owing to the sovereignty of the Oudh rulers there was no *Lex loci* of the Province in which she was domiciled and the law applicable to her depended on her personal status which mainly again depended on her religion and though as a general rule the succefsion of an East Indian Christian in the Bengal Presidency would be regulated by English law, yet in every case for the purpose of determining the status personalis regard must be had to the mode of life and habits of individuals and to the usage of the clafs or family to which he belonged. If no specific rule could be ascertained to be applicable to the case, then the Judge must act according to justice equity and good conscience.

This Mary Short is shewn to have been an Armenian by birth and by religion, who Doctor Short was cannot be ascertained. The tradition that he was English is probably correct but whether he was English proper Scotch or Irish Protestant or Roman Catholic, no-one can say positively and in a case turning on marriage this is important especially ... ... which is probably from Joseph Short having been married by the Protestant Chaplain at Cawnpore.

Stephens Commentaries Book III of 1860

I cannot say that Lord Brougham's marriage act might not affect Doctor Short's marriage, if marriage there were, as I have failed to procure a copy of that act, but I see no reason to doubt that his marriage to be valid must have been so solemnized by a Minister in Holy Orders and according to the rites and ceremonies of the English Church or in the house of an Ambafsador or Resident Minister or the Chaplain of a British factory abroad or the house of any British subject residing at such factory or by a Chaplain or other person officiating by authority within the lines of a British army abroad.

And it is neither proved or afserted in this case that Doctor Short's marriage was performed by such clergyman or minister of the English church or officiating by authority with a British Army.

If therefore we believe the witnefs Gabriel whose mother was God-daughter to this Mary Short, she was not married to Doctor Short.

If we believe Mrs Moses then he was married at Patna according to the Armenian creed in a ceremony by an Armenian Bishop and such a marriage was by the then law of England void. I think it clear that Mary Short had been previously married to a Mr Carapiet an Armenian for not only does Gabriel afsert his but the Witnefs Bibi Catherine herself baptized by an Armenian priest at the instance of Mary Short says that Mary Short told her that her husband had died in his own city Bagdad some years ago.

Doctor Short's origin is therefore unknown a valid marriage is not shewn and if the evidence to marriage be true then the marriage is void and the children are illegitimate. Sooltan Murrium Begum therefore being illegitimate can belong to no family no custom can be applied and the law of England would not regulate her succefsion.

As to Sooltan Murrium Begum herself we first find her as a child with her mother at Agra, Doctor Short having then died or deserted his family. Thence she was brought to Lucknow and at a very tender age was by her mother given as a concubine to the Mahomedan King of Oudh.

It is not likely that she had received any firm imprefsions of the Christian religion from a mother who consigned her to such a fate for marriage undoubtedly there was none and although I hold that she never profefsed Islam which is confirmed by her being known by the distinguishing name of Willaitee Begum it is certain that she would not during the King's lifetime have opportunities to learn more of the Christian tenets and indeed none of the witnefses who are worthy of credit speak to any open acts shewing a Christian profefsion till long after that King's death.

She brought up her brother Joseph Short as a nominal Christian and caused him and a girl profefsing Christianity to be sent to Cawnpore to be married by the Protestant Chaplain and that they were so married appears from the certified extract from the Registers.

But at the same time up to the date of making her Will she lived according to customs of Mahomedans. Joseph Short did the same up to a much later date. At the time her Will was made Joseph Short had ifsue by this Christian wife as well as by the present Amelia Short then a Mufsulman and unmarried and Sooltan Murrium Begum herself presented him with a slave girl as concubine.

I think it very clear that the Testatrix regarded the ceremony of Marriage as of small importance, illegitimate and unmarried herself she lived in a state whence had she born children to the King they would have been illegitimate, and I cannot but think that her intention was that all heirs of the body of Joseph Short according to the law of nature were to be considered his heirs.

It is abundantly evident that Joseph Short deceased recognised all his children as his children making no difference between them – at one time he was angry with Macdonald Short and wished to deprive him of his Wuseeqa inheritance – but it is abundantly evident that there was subsequent reconciliation and as shewn below Joseph Short had no power of bequest and could not alter the devolution of property under the Will of Sooltan Murrium Begum. I think the terms of that Will limiting the inheritance to what may be conveniently called heirs of the body excludes widows or others not children or ifsue from participation in the Wuseeqa.

I submit therefore the following answers to the questions of the Chief Commifsioner:

1. The intention of Sooltan Murrium Begum was that should Joseph Short have children the allowance was to be divided among them according to the law of nature.

2. That neither Mahomedan or Christian law regulates the division, if by Christian law is meant the law of England.

3. That any how the subsequent marriage of Amelia Short would not legitimize children otherwise illegitimate.

And I further submit that the Wuseeqa falls to be divided among all the recognized children of Joseph Short whether male or female in equal shares with reservation of the special afsignments to the Roman Catholic chapels of Lucknow and Cawnpore.

The enclosures of the former Secretary's two letters as well as various documents filed here will be forwarded with this.

The evidence taken in this Court or by commifsion from this Court may be retained.

W. Capper
Offg Judicial Commr of Oudh

It may be as well to add that the succefsion under the treaty and the devolution of the estate of Joseph Short are distinct questions and would be dealt with differently.

(True copy)
Roopchund
Superintendent

Fourteenth That on the 7th of September 1870 General Barrow the Officiating
Chief Commifsioner of Oudh pafsed an order based upon the opinion
of the Judicial Commifsioner amongst other things declaring that your
Memorialist was equitably entitled to maintenance for her lifetime and
that she would draw Rs 50 a month from the said Wuseeka. The
following is a copy of his order.

The heirs of Mr Short claim a Wuseeka pension amounting to 800
Rupees per mensem or after deducting the undisputed item of 50
Rupees for repairs to Roman Catholic Chapels, the said amount is
reduced to 750 Rupees.

Three points were referred to the officiating Judicial Commifsioner
which are detailed in his minute and he has recorded his reply.

Mr Capper does not think that either Mahomedan or Christian law
should regulate the division of this Wuseeka and has given as his
opinion that all the recognised children of Joseph Short whether male
or female should participate in equal shares. Concurring in this view
the Pension will be divided accordingly and a list of the sons and
daughters will be filed with this order. The following reservation is
made in favor of the widow who is equitably entitled to maintenance
for her life-time. She (the widow of the late Joseph Short) will draw
from the 750 Rupees the sum of 50 Rupees per mensem.

Lucknow Wuseeka Office)   sd Barrow
The 7th September 1870)   Offg Chief Commr Oudh

Fifteenth   That your Memorialist finding her interest had been disposed of
behind her back presented to the Chief Commifsioner of Oudh a
Petition a translation of which is hereto annexed and marked A.

Sixteenth   That upon this Petition the following orders were pafsed by the Chief
Commifsioner on the 6th of September and 18th November 1870
respectively—

By order of the Officiating Chief Commifsioner all further Petitions
in this case are to be filed and rejected .

F Barrow
Offg Junr Secy to the Chief Commr
Of Oudh in charge of Wa office 6th 9. 70

The Chief Commifsioner declines to alter the orders given in this case.

R H Davies, Chief Commr of Oudh
18th Novr 1870

Seventeenth That your Memorialist being thus deprived as she submits contrary to
all law and precedent of her one third share of the said monthly

allowance of Rs 750 has no recourse but to place her case before your Excellency with the confident hope that justice may be done.

Eighteenth In addition to the facts before stated your Memorialist relies upon the following grounds in support of her claim to one third of the said monthly stipend.

1. That the Judicial Commifsioner was wrong in deciding that the terms Nuslun bad Nuslun wo Butrim' bad Butrim' in the Will of Sooltan Murrium Begum limited the inheritance to the heirs of her body in as much as the said terms are used merely to create an absolute permanent interest and do not create an entail.

2. That the division of the estate of Joseph Short is regulated neither by Mahomedan or Christian Law nor by the law of nature but by the Succefsion Act No X of 1865 under which your Memorialist would be entitled to one third of the stipend absolutely and not by way of maintenance.

3. That in other cases under similar treaties where the same terms have been made use of the husbands or wives of the Wueekadars as well as collateral relatives have inherited as well as the heirs of the body.

Nineteenth In support of the first of these grounds your Memorialist begs to add the following opinion of the late learned Advocate General Mr Cowie given by him on your Memorialist's case on the 10th of April last –

Madam, Calcutta 10th April 1871

I very much regret that in consequence of my numerous engagements I have not until now been able to give attention to the case submitted by you in your communication of 12th January. I have duly received the fee and also a letter on the same subject from your son-in-law Mr Spiers.

It is quite clear in my opinion that the decision (if decision it is to be called) of the Judicial Commifsioner is entirely erroneous. I think the intention of the Testatrix simply was to give her brother Joseph Short not a mere life interest but an absolute and perpetual interest in the Wuseeqa of Rs 750 a month. I am not a Persian scholar but the exprefsions which as I understand, are used in the Persian language where the general object is to create or transfer an absolute permanent interest—such exprefsions do not denote any intention to create descendants—and further it appears to me that what the Will says about the Legatees making a Will &ca is only an unnecefsary reference to what his powers would by law have been under the absolute gift.

The question then simply is who are the persons entitled to succeed to the property of Joseph Short—from such statement of the evidence as is confirmed in the opinion of the Judicial Commissioner. I can only come to the conclusion that Short was the ifsue of a British subject by an Armenian woman, and that prior to his birth his parents were married by an Armenian Bishop or Priest – such a person would I apprehend have been according to English Law as much a Priest in Holy Orders as a Priest of the Anglican or Roman Church, and Joseph Short was consequently a legitimate son. He was neither a Hindoo nor a Mahomedan; most probably he was in point of law a natural born British subject. But whether he was that or not the descent to his property he having been domiciled in British India would be according to the Indian Succefsion Act consequently you as his widow are entitled to one third of the Rs 750 a month.

I advise you to bring a suit in the Civil Court at Lucknow against your late husband's children for a declaration of your right to one third of the Rs 750 a month and having got a decision in your favor to apply to the executive Authorities for payment to you during your life of such one third. I do not consider that there has as yet been any judicial determination of the question.

Yours truly
JH Cowie

Twentieth	In advising your Memorialist to bring a suit the learned Advocate General probably forgot that the Wuseeka Department is under the control of the Political Authorities and that therefore a suit would hardly be a proper course for your Memorialist to adopt to obtain her rights until the highest Authority in all political matters had been petitioned on the subject.
Twenty first	In further support of this ground your Memorialist begs to refer to the case of Her Highnefs Bhow Begum (p.144 Vol 2 of Aitchison's treaties) in that case the words of the Will were precisely the same as in that of Sooltan Marrium Begum
Twenty second	These words in the case now referred to were construed by the then resident as merely tending to create a permanent interest and not an entail. In proof of which the wives and husbands of many of the parties named in her Will and who were to take Nuslun bad Nuslun wo Butrim bad Butrim' now enjoy their portion of the shares of their husbands or wives respectively.
Twenty third	That there are in the precedents under the very Nuseeha (?) (of the 17th of August 1825) in which your Memorialist seeks a share.

1. Newab Begum the wife of Newab Mootarnadowla who was a wuseekadar for Rs 20,000 a month after the death of her husband received a share of her husband's stipend.
2. Newab Anha Begum was also a Wuseekadar after her death her husband received a share of her stipend.

3. Ameenooooddowla Bahadoor son of the last mentioned was also a Wussekadar—his stipend is now divided amongst his widow and children.

4. Newab Begum the wife of the above died childlefs and her allowance was divided amongst her collateral relatives although there were numerous other children of her husband by other wives.

Twenty fourth   In fact in all instances in the said Wuseeka except your Memorialist's wives husbands and collateral relatives have taken their shares in spite of the terms Nuslun bad Nuslun wo Butrim bad Butrim'.having been used & that for a 3rd precedent your Memorialist begs to refer to the Wuseeka of the 1st March 1829 of His Majesty Nufseerooddeen p.169 Vol II of Aitchison's treaties.

Twenty fifth   Of the interest in this loan Rs 6000 a month were afsigned by the said King to his wife Mookudaoolah to be paid to her and her heirs and succefsors Nuslun bad Nuslun wo Butrim bad Butrim'

Twenty sixth   The said wife was the child of a Captain Waters and therefore stood in very much the same position as Sooltan Murrium Begum. On her death her allowance was divided between her step-sister her brother and others.

Twenty seventh   Your Memorialist submits that these precedents conclusively establish that the terms Nuslun bad Nuslun wo Butrim bad Butrim' are not intended to create an entail but are merely words used to create an absolute permanent interest and your Memorialist further submits that it would be a case of the greatest injustice if your Memorialist were decided to be the only one out of all collateral relatives of the Wuseekadars not entitled to have a share in her husband's stipend. This decision would really if upheld decide that a Will can and should be construed in several different ways—a conclusion which your Memorialist feels sure Her Majesty's Government would never adopt.

Twenty eighth   As to the second point your Memorialist submits that the Indian Succession Act is the law regulating the division of the said Joseph Short's Estate.

Twenty ninth   Your Memorialist was legally married to Mr Short according to the rites of the Roman Catholic church and her marriage certificate was submitted to the Chief Commifsioner of Oudh with a Petition filed by her after the order of the 7th September 1870 hereinbefore set out.

Thirtieth	That the said Joseph Short's sister Sooltan Murrium Begum was a Christian is fairly evidenced by the fact that she bequeathed Rs 50 a month to Roman Catholic Chapels: moreover your Memorialist's said husband was buried according to the rites of the Roman Catholic Church and the Administrator General has taken out administration to his estate.
Thirty first	Your Memorialist submits that the opinion of the Judicial Commisfsioner is not a Judicial decision in any way binding upon the Wuseeka Department and that the order of the Chief Commifsioner pafsed (in part) upon that opinion is altogether incorrect, contrary to Law, and productive of great injustice to your Memorialist.
Thirty second	That your Memorialist is in great distrefs and in reduced circumstances owing to her being deprived of her share in the Wuseeka as your Memorialist's husband (under the idea that your Memorialist would recover her proper share of the Wuseeka) failed to make any special provision for her.

Your Memorialist therefore humbly prays that your Excellency may be pleased to set aside the order of the Chief Commifsioner of the 7th of September 1870 and to order that your Memorialist do receive from the said sum of Rs 750 per month her one third share in accordance with the provisions of the Succefsion Act and that she may receive all arrears from the death of her husband.

And your Memorialist shall ever pray &ca
Amelia Short

NAI: Gen A: July 1885 Nos 16–18
(Amelia Short's petition to the Viceroy of Feb 1884, written by my great-grandfather, John Speirs)

To His Excellency the Most Hon'ble the Marquis of Ripon, K.G.P.C., G.M.S.I.
Viceroy and Governor General of India in Council assembled
The humble memorial of Amelia M Short, widow of the late Joseph Short, Wasikadar, residing at Lucknow.

Most respectfully showeth,

Your memorialist is indubitably entitled to receive the sum of fourteen thousand eight hundred and fifty three Rupees, three Annas and three Pies (exclusive of interest) from the Government of Oudh in the Wasika Department, the above-mentioned amount (exclusive of interest) being due to your memorialist, owing to the manner in which the said Government persistently declined to pay your memorialist the sum of Rupees two hundred and fifty per mensem being the amount accruing to your memorialist as the 1/3 of her late husband's wasika, your memorialist being the lawfully married wife of the said Mr Joseph Short and as his widow becoming entitled under section XXVII of Act X of 1865 to 1/3rd share of the said Wasika of Rupees seven hundred and fifty per mensem, immediately on the demise of her husband, which event took place on the 26th February 1870; but after many years of litigation and consequent poverty, your memorialist had succeeded in removing even the shadow of a doubt as to the legality and rightfulness of your memorialist's claim, when on the 14th March 1877 your memorialist received or rather expected to receive the moneys due to her, the officer in charge of the wasika in lieu of paying your memorialist the sum of Rs 21,056-3-10 which (exclusive of interest) was the amount justly due to your memorialist, the sum of Rs 6,113-0-7 only was paid to your memorialist's agent thus leaving an unpaid balance (exclusive of interest) of Rs 14,853-3-3.

2. Your memorialist having now set forth the great injury which has been inflicted on her (a poor widow) would now beg to lay before Your Excellency as succinctly as possible all the main facts connected with your memorialist's case.

3. As before stated your memorialist's late husband enjoyed during his lifetime a wasika allowance of Rs 750 per mensem; this had been left him under the Will of one Sultan Murrium Begam, a stipendiary under the treaty between His Royal Highness the late Gazi-u-din Hyder Shah, King of Oudh, and the Honorable the late East India Company under date 14th August 1825, Aitchison's Treaties and Sunnuds, Vol III.

4. On the demise of your memorialist's husband, Mr J. Short, which occurred on the 26th February 1870, a doubt arose as to the distribution of his wasika allowance, although he (Mr J Short) had in accordance with an intimation from the Junior Secretary to the Chief Commissioner of Oudh in charge of the Wasika Office, dated the 5th January 1863, filed in the Wasika Office a list of his heirs, dated 25th February 1863, which document was duly attested, on the 14th September 1865, before the officer in charge of the Wasika Office, and it had hitherto been the custom of the Wasika Office to distribute the wasika of deceased wasikadars, on similar documents, as can be easily seen by reference to the files of that office.

5. In this instance, however, the Officiating Chief Commissioner of Oudh addressed a letter to the then Officiating Judicial Commissioner of Oudh, dated 25th May 1870, asking that officer's opinion respecting the devolution of Mr J Short's wasika. The Officiating Judicial Commissioner of Oudh held some *quasi-*judicial proceedings, in the course of which all the claimants to a share in your memorialist's late husband's wasika allowance with the exception of your

memorialist appeared either personally or by Counsel and pleaded their claims before the said Officiating Judicial Commissioner. Your memorialist (not having received any summons to appear in Court and in point of fact being unaware that her claim was in any way involved in the proceedings then pending) did not interest herself in the matte; further, your memorialist was led by interested parties to believe that your memorialist's claim was not a matter in dispute before the Officiating Judicial Commissioner.

6. On the 12th August 1870, the Officiating Judicial Commissioner of Oudh gave his opinion in the case intimating *inter alia* he thought your memorialist had no claim wahtever to share in her late husband's wasika allowance.

7. Your memorialist would here beg leave to point out the proceedings before the Officiating Judicial Commissioner were not regular, there being no plaintiff and no defendant, they were therefore informal as your memorialist is advised, and further had the proceedings been of a formal, i.e., regular type, still the proceedings could not be regarded as otherwise than *ex parte* , and as far as your memorialist is concerned were therefore invalid.

8. On the 7th September 1870 the Officiating Judicial Commissioner of Oudh passed an order, in which it was directed by him that the wasika allowance of your memorialist's late husband was to be divided in equal shares amongst the children mentioned in his list of heirs, but made a reservation of Rs 50 per mensem in your memorialist's favor. Your memorialist had, however, prior to the issue of the said order obtained the opinion of Counsel and memorialized the Officiating Chief Commissioner of Oudh, stating that your memorialist's claim was to the 1/3rd share of her late husband's wasika, Viz Rs 250 per mensem, but with no effect; your memorialist however, refused to accept the Rs 50 per mensem as ordered by the Officiating Chief Commissioner of Oudh, despite the fact that the death of her husband deprived your memorialist of all means of support.

9. The Officiating Chief Commissioner of Oudh in spite of your memorialist's protest having passed the order mentioned in preceding paragraph, and the other claimants to her late husband's wasika being in receipt of their wasika allowances awarded them under it, your memorialist proceeded to petition the Chief Commissioner of Oudh on his return from furlough, until orders were passed on the 6th September 1870 that all petitions in the case should be filed and rejected.'

10. Your memorialist was induced to lay her case before the Advocate General of Bengal (in the early part of 1871), who, in his opinion (dated the 10th April 1871) stated the descent of his (Mr Short's) property, he having been domiciled in India, would be according to the Indian Succession Act, and you as his widow are entitled to 1/3rd of the Rs 750 per mensem.

11. In June 1871 your memorialist placed her case, together with the opinion above referred to, in the hands of Mr J. C. Watkins, a Solicitor practicing in

Calcutta, who, on the 21ˢᵗ June 1871, addressed a memorial to His Excellency the then Viceroy and Governor-General of India, the late Earl of Mayo, pointing out the injustice with which your memorialist had been treated, and praying His Lordship to interfere in her behalf; this by a letter No 375-F dated 13th September 1871, from the Secretary to the Government of India, Foreign Department (to the address of the above-mentioned Mr Watkins), His Excellency in Council intimated his inability to do so, stating *this is not a case in which Government can give a decision. Its duty is simply to pay the money to the proper parties, who those proper parties are, must in case of dispute be settled by the Civil Courts'.* Subsequent letters were addressed by Mr Watkins to His Excellency with a view to obtain a reconsideration of this decision; the correspondence however terminated by a letter from the Officiating Under-Secretary to the Government of India, No 127 dated 23rd February 1872, the concluding paragraph of which is as follows: *I am directed to inform you that the orders in question are final'.*

12. On the 4th October 1871, your memorialist petitioned the Officiating Chief Commissioner of Oudh, forwarding a copy of the decision of his Excellency the Viceroy and Governor-General in Council, as intimated in letter No 375-F, under date 13th September 1871 (quoted in the preceding paragraph), together with a copy of the Advocate General of Bengal's opinion, dated 10th April 1871 (referred to in paragraph 10), in which your memorialist might now add that that learned gentleman states his opinion the decision of the Judicial Commissioner of Oudh is entirely erroneous,' and further I do not consider there has been any judicial determination of the question;' acting also on the advice contained in the said document, and being further compelled by reason of not obtaining any reply to your memorialist's repeated petitions to the Chief Commissioner of Oudh, your memorialist proceeded in January 1873 to file a suit for a declamatory decree against the heirs to the wasika allowance of your memorialist's late husband (under the provisions of section 15 of Act VIII of 1859, in the Court of the Civil Judge of Lucknow, filing as an authority (as advised by Counsel) a copy of the Secretary to the Government of India, Foreign Department's letter No 375F dated the 13th September 1871.

13. The case came on for hearing before the Civil Judge, and was by him dismissed on the ground of the Civil Court's want of jurisdiction in cases of wasika allowance.

14. Your memorialist on the 31ˢᵗ July 1873 filed an appeal (against decision above mentioned) in *forma pauperis* (being compelled to do so as your memorialist was unable to borrow money to carry on the case); this appeal was dismissed by the Commissioner of Lucknow, in whose Court it was heard on the ground of the Court's want of jurisdiction; during the course of the proceedings, however, the learned Commissioner stated the only bar to your memorialist's case being

adjudicated on its merits in any Court in Oudh was the want of a certificate such as is contemplated under the provisions of section 6 of Act XXXIII of 1871, the Pension Act.

14A. It might perhaps be as well to state here that in August 1874 your memorialist was informed that some of the children ot her late husband, Mr J Short, had filed an application in the office of Wasika Department, praying that distribution should be made among them of a sum of Rs 7,524 which sum had accumulated in the Wasika Office as the undistributed shares of three children who, though mentioned in the list of Mr Short's heirs (referred to in paragraph 4 of this memorial, but who as was afterwards proved on enquiry had died in their father's lifetime), your memorialist prior to even orders being issued sanctioning such distribution being made, as no decision touching her claim by a Civil Court, as laid down in paragraph 2 of Governor General in Council's letter No 375-F, dated 13th September 1871 (referred to in paragraph 10 of this memorial), had been given, your memorialist's protest was ignored, and the distribution was made by the Wasika Office on the 12th September 1874.

15. Seeing there was no other course left open, your memorialist persistently petitioned the Chief Commissioner of Oudh, and in the early part of 1875, your memorialist received information that her case had been submitted for the orders of the Supreme Government, and hearing this, memorialized His Excellency the Governor-General in Council praying that final orders might not be passed in her case, until an opportunity had been given to lay her case fully before His Excellency. Your memorialist was favored with a reply from the Officiating Under-Secretary to the Government of India, Foreign Department, No 479-G, dated 9th March 1875, intimating that an order had been passed on her memorial to the effect that her case had been left to the Civil Courts, and the Chief Commissioner of Oudh had been requested to grant the necessary certificate under section 6 of Act XXIII of 1871.

16. Your memorialist on the 4th March 1875 received from the Junior Secretary to the Chief Comissioner of Oudh the certificate mentioned in foregoing paragraph, and on the 26th August 1875 her case (a suit for a declaratory decree under Section 15 of Act VIII of 1859) against the children, heirs of her late husband, came on for hearing before the Judge of the Civil Court of Lucknow; the case was decided by him on the 13th April 1876 in your memorialist's favor; the defendants appealed the case to the Court of the Commissioner of Lucknow, who gave a decision adverse to your memorialist's claim; this decision was however reversed in the subsequent appeal made by your memorialist in the Court of the Judicial Commissioner of Oudh, who, on the 27th January 1877, gave a decision in your memorist's favor deciding that your memorialist as the widow of the late Mr Joseph Short, was entitled to a 1/3 share of his wasika allowance, Viz Rs 250 per mensem,

the amount your memorialist originally claimed from the Officiating Chief Commissioner of Oudh in March 1870.

17. The decision of the Judicial Commissioner of Oudh was duly forwarded (as had been in its turn the decision of the Civil Judge of Lucknow) to the Chief Commissioner of Oudh, and in March 1877 your memorialist was paid the sum mentioned in paragraph 1 of this memorial, Viz Rs 6,173-0-7 being the sum of Rs 50 per mensem allotted to your memorialist under the order passed by the Officiating Chief Commissioner of Oudh on 7th September 1870, and against which order your memorialist for a period of nearly seven years had persistently refused to acquiesce in, and to reverse which order had cost your memorialist many thousands of Rupees which your memorialist had been compelled to borrow from native bankers at very high rates of interest, your memorialist was, by reason of the extreme pressure brought to bear on her by the creditors above referred to, compelled to take the sum paid to her by the Wasika Office authorities, though not without protest against the extreme injustice of the manner in which she had been treated. Your memorialist would further add she is yet in doubt as to when the Rs 250 commenced to be credited to her, as it is evident of calculation it could not have been from the date of the decision of the Civil Judge of Lucknow in your memorialist's favor, i.e. from 13th April 1875.

18. Your memorialist would long ere this have memorialised Your Excellency in Council, but very shortly after the Judicial Commissioner of Oudh's decision had been given (on the 27th January 1877) one of the defendents applied to the Wasika Office for a certificate under Section 6 of Act XXIII of 1871, to enable him (the said defendant) to again appeal the case; a fresh certificate was not granted, but the applicant was informed that the certificate already filed in Court was amply sufficient to enable him to bring the case on the file for a re-hearing in appeal, your memorialist was strongly advised to take no further steps in her case until the above-mentioned appeal had been adjudicated; an application for leave to appeal in the Court of the Judicial Commissioner of Oudh was not brought forward until March 1881, this perhaps was owing to the fact that it was not until about that time Mr W Capper (who acted as Officiating Chief Commissioner of Oudh in 1870) and had (as already mentioned in paragraph 6 of the present memorial) given his opinion that your memorialist was not entitled to any share in her late husband's wasika was appointed permanently as Judicial Commissioner of Oudh, however, on the case being brought before that officer for leave to appeal in March 1881, the case was dismissed on the grounds there were no grounds whatever for granting an appeal', your memorialist was still advised not to memorialise Your Excellency until a further period had elapsed, sufficient time in fact to allow all or any one of the defendants to bring their case before the Privy Council in appeal. This period now having passed, and

no such steps having been taken, your memorialist is now induced to lay her case before Your Excellency.

19. It would be futile attempting to point out at any length how utterly opposed to all regular course of legal procedure has been that adopted by the Government of Oudh in your memorialist's case—further that it was only the order of an Officiating Chief Commissioner of Oudh in 1870 - the said order being passed on the opinion of the Judicial Commissioner of Oudh, which opinion was arrived at after what your memorialist trusts has been clearly shown in paragraph 7 of this memorial to be an informal and as far as your memorialist was concerned an entirely *ex parte* course of proceedings held before him, the said Judicial Commissioner of Oudh, in a case, the Supreme Government of India (as shown in paragraph 11 of this memorial) subsequently plainly stated was out of its power to decide, which has caused your memorialist such heavy pecuniary loss, some seven years of absolute penury and grievous mental anxiety. It now remains with your Excellency to decide whether the above mentioned order of an Officiating Chief Commissioner of Oudh in issuing which it would (your memorialist most respectfully submits) appear, the said Officiating Chief Commissioner exercised authority far beyond his powers, shall practically supersede (with regard to the monies, i.e. balance now due your memorialist) what the highest judicial tribunal in the province of Oudh, after a regular course of legal procedure, has decreed to be your memorialist's right, more especially as Your Excellency's illustrious predecessor, the late Earl of Mayo, has in Council laid down (and that too in this very case) what may be shortly termed a rule that only Civil Courts are competant to try rights of succession in disputed wasika cases, your memorialist is advised that a decree under section 15 of Act VIII of 1859, i.e. a declaratory decree without consequent relief, does not create a right to 1/3 share of her late husband's wasika, this being simply your memorialist's inherent right as his widow. That the Judge of the Civil Court of Lucknow, who in April 1876 decided in the court of first instance in favor of your memorialist's claim to a 1/3 share of her late husband's wasika, was of opinion that your memorialist was entitled to this amount from the date of her husband's death, is evident from the following extract from her decision, i.e. the next objection is that it is not open to the Court to give a declaratory decree *** the essence of the condition is that relief could be obtained somewhere or in some other form ** but there is relief which might be granted if prayed for, Viz the recovery of the amount already paid to the defendants by the Wasika Office.

20. It cannot be alleged that the decision of the Chief Commissioner has ever been held to be a final decision in wasika cases, as in any ordinary wasika case, it was quite within the competency of any aggrieved party to appeal by a memorial to His Excellency the Governor-General of India in Council, and the Supreme Government in the exercise of its judgment either upheld or reversed the orders

of the Chief Commissioner of Oudh (and as in the present instance the case being deemed, not even within the power of the Supreme Government to decide, the aid of a regularly constituted court of law was invoked), further, the records of this very wasika allowance when enjoyed by your memorialist's late husband convincingly prove the fact of the Chief Commissioner of Oudh's order in wasika cases not being a final order for as much as *cum cited* 1858,1859 the then Chief Commissioner of Oudh passed an order relative to the manner in which your memorialist's late husband's (Mr J Short) wasika should be paid. The said arrangements were for some reason distasteful to the said Mr J Short, he there and then refused to receive his wasika allowance pending the decision of His Excellency the then Governor General of India who, on being memorialized, reversed the order of the said Chief Commissioner of Oudh, and passed an order that the said wasika allowance should be paid as heretofore, i.e. prior to the order of the Chief Commissioner of Oudh, respecting which Mr J Short had raised an objection and had memorialized His Excellency in Council.

21. In conclusion, your memorialist leaves her case to Your Excellency's merciful consideration, only remarking your memorialist's pecuniary affairs are much embarrassed as owing to the action of the Oudh Government in your memorialist's case, your memorialist has been obliged to contract liabilities in a very onerous extent, to enable her to defray the cost of the various legal proceedings forced on your memorialist, the said liabilities owing to their large amount and to the high rates of interest your memorialist was compelled to contract them at, are by no means liquidated, although your memorialist has been paying and will have to pay for some years to come a very large portion of her wasika allowance before the termination of the said liabilities, unless Your Excellency is graciously pleased to see justice, which is all your memorialist asks at your Excellency's hands, done to your memorialist's claim, your memorialist would however most humbly submit that justice will not be done in her case if it should be ruled that your memorialist is at liberty to sue the parties to whom the Oudh Government has mistakenly paid the monies which as a matter of right and justice were due to your memorialist; further, your memorialist would most humbly submit it will be neither justice or equity to compel her to go through a most protracted and therefore as a matter of necessity a most expensive course of legal procedure to recover (or rather attempt to recover) what has been without any legal grounds withheld from your memorialist, such withholdment not being in any way attributable to any act of deed on the part of your memorialist, but entirely due to the erroneous procedure adopted by the Oudh Government. Your memorialist would further beg permission to state that (to add to other complications, suing the co-sharers in her late husband's wasika would force on your memorialist) wasika allowances cannot be attached by any Court of Law (as they are at present

constituted) in Oudh, as thousands of creditors of wasikadars have found to their cost and sueing the abovenamed parties would be of no pecuniary benefit as the parties in question are, with one or two exceptions, entirely dependent on their several wasika allowances of Rs 41-6 per mensem for their support. In order to point out how void of any pecuniary benefit a successful suit against the other shares in your memorialist's late husband's wasika would inevitably be, your memorialist has not been able to date to realise the costs of the several law-suits decreed against them, during the litigation which has already taken place; your memorialist having now to the best of her limited means laid down before Your Excellency the nature of her claim and also how the claim has arisen, would now pray Your Excellency to cause enquiry to be made into and justice done with regard to the said claim.

And your memorialist will, as in duty bound, ever pray.

Bolpur   Sd Amelia M Short
EI railway loop line
The 9th February 1884

References

Chapter 1

1. Seth, Mesrovb Jacob, *A History of Armenians in India from the Earliest Times to the Present Day*, Calcutta 1937 (published by the author 9 Marsden St, Calcutta).
2. Sheikh Tassaduque Hussain, *Begammat-i-Awadh* (translation from Urdu), Lucknow?, 1896.
3. OIOC P/354/1 p2043 Bombay Military Consultations 1797 June-Dec.
4. OIOC P/354/11 p1405 Bombay Military Consultations 18th Apr – 29th Aug 1800.
5. OIOC P/354/27 p1378 Bombay Military Consultations 1802.
5A. Herefordshire Record Office: Ref: AL/40/8221.
6. OIOC P/354/28 p2070 Bombay Military Consultations 1803.
7. OIOC L/MIL/12/187 Surgeons' papers.
8. PRO Wills granted probate in 1808.
9. NAI FC 23 Jul 1858 No 182.
10. OIOC L/MIL/9/373 f382 (A certificate from a surgeon at the London Hospital, stating that Michael Short had been a pupil there, but discontinued his attendance in April 1820, being unexpectedly obliged to go to the East Indies).
11. NAI Fin:B Sept 1871 Nos 12-14.
12. OIOC L/MAR/B/343A Log of the ship 'Lunjee Family'.

Chapter 2

1. Sheikh Tassaduque Hussain, *Begammat-i-Awadh* (translation from Urdu), Lucknow, 1896.
2. NAI Fin 'B' Sept 1871 Nos 12-14 (Amelia Short's 1st petition to the Viceroy; full text given in the Appendix).

3. Llewellyn-Jones, Dr Rosie, *A Fatal Friendship*, Delhi OUP Press, 1992. pp 211-2.
4. Praveen, Yogesh; *Lucknow Monuments*.
5. Santha, Dr K.S., *Begums of Awadh*, Tara Printers Varanasi, 1980. Chapter V and XI.
5A. Bhatt, Ravi, *The Life and Times of the Nawabs of Lucknow*, Rupa & Co, Delhi, 2006.
6. NAI FC 17 Sep 1858 No 176.
7. Heber, Right Revd Reginald, *Narrative of a Journey through the Upper Provinces of India, from Calcutta to Bombay, 1824 – 1825*, London, 1828. Chapter 15.
8. Hastings, Marquis of, *The Private Journal of the Marquis of Hastings* 2 Vols, 1858.
8A. Fisher, Michael, *A Clash of Cultures; Awadh, the British and the Mughals*, Manohar publications, Delhi, 1988. p109–116.
9. Seth, Mesrovb, *A History of Armenians in India from the Earliest Times to the Present Day*, Calcutta 1937.
9A. Lucknow Wasika Office (LWO): File No 3 of 1874, demise of Joseph Short.
10. NAI FC 6 Mar 1839 No 110.
11. NAI FC 29 Jul 1848 No 59.
12. NAI Fin 'A' Jan 1863 Nos 25-29 &KW A full transcription of Murium Begum's Will—see Appendix (Note: other, slightly different translations of Murium Begum's will exist. Our family also has a translation prepared in 1849 by Andrew Busk, the Assistant Resident at Lucknow).
13. NAI FC 29 Jul 1848 No 66.
14. NAI FC 14 Jul 1849 No 79 (Copy of the original Treaty of 17th August 1825 for 'the Third Oudh Loan' under which Ghazi-ud-din Haidar loaned a Crore of Rupees to the Hon'ble Company in perpetuity).
15. NAI FC 29 Jul 1848 No 60.
16. NAI FC 29 Jul 1848 No 59.
17. NAI FC 29 Jul 1848 No 58.
18. NAI FC 14 Jul 1849 No 78.

Chapter 3

1. NAI Fin 'B' Sept 1871 Nos 12-14 (Amelia Short's 1st petition to the Viceroy – full text given in the Appendix).
1A. Lucknow Wasika Office (LWO): File No 3 of 1874, demise of Joseph Short
2. NAI FC 30 Dec 1859 No 1118.
3. Yalland, Zoe, *A Guide to the Kacheri Cemetery and the Early History of Kanpur*, BACSA, London, 1983.
4. NAI PC 11 Jan 1817 No 137.
5. UPSA Lucknow file No 111 of 1859-60.
6. Sheikh Tussaduque Hussain, *Begammat-i-Awadh* (translation from the original Urdu), Lucknow, 1896.

7.   M Wylie (editor), 'The English Captives of Oudh: an episode in the history of the mutinies of 1857–58': in *Tracts relating to the Indian Mutiny*.
8.   NAI FC 23rd July 1858 No 182.
9.   NAI FC 15th May 1857 Nos 136–139.
10. NAI Fin B: June 1876 Nos 1, 2.
11. NAI FC 31st Dec 1858 No 886.
12. NAI FC 15th May 1857 Nos 136-139.
12A Seth, Mesrovb, *A History of Armenians in India from the Earliest Times to the Present Day*, Calcutta 1937(page 564).
12B Llewellyn Jones, Dr Rosie, *Engaging Scoundrels—True tales of Old Lucknow*, Oxford University Press, New Delhi(p. 99 and note 32, p.123).
13. Map photocopied from Mesrovb Seth's book *A History of Armenians in India from the Earliest Times to the Present Day*, Calcutta 1937.
13A UPSA—Lucknow file 2081 of 1858.
14. NAI FC 30th Dec 1859 No 1118.
15. UPSA—Oude General—File No 2030 (1859-60).
15A. Hay, Miss Sidney, *Historic Lucknow*, first published 1939 (republished 2002 by Rupa).
16. UPSA Lucknow file No 111 of 1859-60.
17. NAI FC 23rd July 1858 No 181.
18. Oldenburg, Veena Talwar: *The Making of Colonial Lucknow*, Oxford University Press, Delhi, 1989.
19. NAI Gen B: June 1862 No 45.
20. NAI Gen B: June 1862 No 44.
21. UPSA Lucknow file No 2654 of 1859.
22. UPSA Lucknow file No 1181 of 1861-62.
23. Information on Jean Philippe de Bourbon kindly given by Jean-Pierre Bourbon.
24. Wedding invitation card reproduced by kind permission of my 2nd Cousin, Mrs A Moriarty.
25. NAI FC 22nd July 1859 Nos 102-110.
25A Lobo, Chevalier Austin Malcolm: *Growth and Development of the Catholic Diocese of Lucknow, 1940–1997*, Lucknow 1998.
26. NAI Fin:A: Jan 1863 Nos 25–29 & KW (Joseph Short's petition to have his wasika paid in full without deduction for the RC churches. The full text of this petition is given in the Appendix).
27. Lobo, Chevalier Austin Malcolm: *Growth and Development of the Catholic Diocese of Lucknow, 1940–1997*, Lucknow 1998.
28. UPSA Lucknow file No 114 of 1858-61.
29. NAI Fin:A: Jan 1863 Nos 25–29 & KW (Joseph Short's petition to have his wasika paid in full without deduction for the RC churches. The full text of this petition is given in the Appendix).
30. PRO: Will of THG Besant 23rd Sept 1874.

31. Norfolk County Record Office: Casebook SAH 268.
32. Norfolk County Record Office: Casebook SAH 306.
33. Norfolk County Record Office: Casebook SAH 268.

Chapter 4

1. NAI Fin B Sep 1871 Nos 12-14 - Amelia Short's 1st petition to the Viceroy [full text given in the Appendix].
1A Lucknow Wasika Office—file of Joseph Short, deceased. (full text given in the Appendix).
2. NAI Fin A Aug 1875 Nos 2-4.
3. NAI Gen B: July 1885 Nos 16-18—Amelia Short's petition to the Viceroy dated 9th Feb 1884– (full text given in the Appendix). This petition was written by my great grandfather, John Speirs, who then held power of Attorney.
4. NAI Gen B: April 1893 Nos 68-93.
5. Lucknow Wasika Office—file of Benjamin Joseph Short, deceased.
6. Saroop, Narindar: *A Squire of Hindoostan*, London, 1983.
7. Details of claim from my grandfather's (almost illegible) notes made in 1956 at the age of 81.
8. The Times, 9th May 1956. (cutting taken by my grandfather).
9. Lucknow Wasika Office—file of John Speirs, deceased.

Chapter 5

1. Lucknow Wasika Office (LWO): file No 7 of 1890, George Short (demise)
2. LWO: File No 22 of 1890, William Short.
3. LWO: File No 10 of 1962, William Short (demise).
4. Llewellyn-Jones, Dr Rosie, *A Fatal Friendship*, Delhi OUP Press, 1992, p27.
5. LWO: File No 7 of 1919, James Macdonald Short (demise).
6. LWO: File No 4 of 1925, Charles Short.
7. UPSA file No 2415 of 1860.
8. LWO: File No 10 of 1939, Frederick Martin Short (demise).
9. LWO: File No 4 of 1944, Alice Jane Sangster (demise).
10. LWO: File No 7 of 1916, Isaac Short.
11. LWO: File No 15 of 1917, Edwin Short.

Chapter 6

1. LWO: File No 3 of 1870, Joseph Short (demise).
2. LWO: File No 4 of 1906, Wahid-un-Nissa Begam.
3. 'Bi Nanna's tale' was written by Syed Badruddin, son of Syed Ainuddin

(Wahidunissa Begum's brother) as an article in the MAO College magazine (Aligarh). I am indebted to Rizwan Rahman for obtaining the article. This translation from the original Urdu was kindly carried out by my third-cousin, Tayyaba Qidwai.

Chapter 7

1. Yalland, Zoe, *Traders & Nabobs, the British in Cawnpore, 1765-1857*, Michael Russell Publishing Ltd, Wilton, Wilts; 1987.
2. IOR/P/131/3 Bengal Criminal & Judicial Cons 19th Sept 1812 No 64.
3. IOR/P/131/3 Bengal Criminal & Judicial Cons 19th Sept 1812 No 67.
4. IOR/P/131/18 Bengal Criminal & Judicial Cons 12th June 1813 No 69.
5. IOR/P/131/18 Bengal Criminal & Judicial Cons 12th June 1813 No 68.
6. IOR/P/131/33 Bengal Criminal & Judicial Cons 12th March 1814 No 52.
7. NAI PC 11 Jan 1817 No 137.
8. IOR/ L/AG/34/29/53 f121-132 Will of James Duhan.
9. A fourth child, Jane Alice Angeline, had been conceived just before her husband's death, but had only survived fourteen months and was buried at the Dissenters' Burial Ground in Calcutta.
10. UPSA—Lucknow file No 111 (1859-60).
11. NAI Genl: B Apr. 1893: Nos 68-93.
12. Information from Caroline Laing (nee Duhan).

Chapter 8

1. Eaton, Natasha, *Excess in the City?: The Consumption of Imported Prints in Colonial Calcutta c 1780–c 1795*: Journal of Material Culture March, 2003 p45–74 (Calcutta Gazette 1784).
1A *Bengal Past & Present—the journal of the Calcutta Historical Society*, Vol XIV pt 1, Jan-Mar 1917 p. 22, 3.
2. Llewellyn Jones, Dr Rosie, *A Very Ingenious Man, Claude Martin in Early Colonial India*, Oxford University Press, Delhi, 1992.
3. *Bengal: Journal of the Calcutta Historical Society*, by Calcutta Historical Society.
4. Llewellyn Jones, Dr Rosie, *A Very Ingenious Man, Claude Martin in Early Colonial India*, Oxford University Press, Delhi, 1992.
5. Yalland, Zoe, *Kacheri Cemetery Kanpur – a complete list of inscriptions with notes on those buried there*, BACSA, London, 1985.
6. OIOC—Bengal Pol Cons 9th Aug 1822 No 23.
7. OIOC—Bengal Pol Cons 2nd Feb 1822 No 25.
8. Llewellyn Jones, Dr Rosie, *A Fatal Friendship, the Nawabs, the British and the City of Lucknow*, Oxford University Press, Delhi, 1985.

9. Bullock, Brigadier H., *Genealogy of the Quieros Family*, presented to the Society of Genealogists 13th Dec 1946. This document describes Joseph Queiros (senior) as 'Commander of the King of Oude's ships' and his son, Felix John Queiros (senior) as 'Indigo planter, Kutthela Grant Factory in the Gorakhpur dist, Bansi'.

10. NAI—FC 20th Feb 1832 No 33 (petition from Capt W.R. Pogson to HM. The King of Oude).

11. OIOC—Bengal Pol Cons 5th July 1822 No 64

12. OIOC—Bengal Pol Cons 5th July 1822 No 65

13. OIOC—Bengal Pol Cons 10th May 1822 No 74

14. NAI—FC 20th Feb 1832 No 33 (petition from Capt W.R. Pogson to HM. The King of Oude).

15. NAI—FC 8th Oct 1832 No 45

16. Information by Cherry Armstrong, a descendent of the Pogson family, who has provided the author with a vast amount of data on her ancestors.

17. Machling, Tessa, *Colonial Fortifications. From Ireland to Nevis: The life of Governor John Johnson*.

18. [not used]

19. Letter dt. 4th Dec 1814 from Elizabeth Philadelphia Pearce Hall (kind permission of Cherry Armstrong).

20. Hodson, Major VCP, *List of the Officers of the Bengal Army 1758–1834*, London, 1946.

21. The Times Jun 24 1833 pg 6.

22. Letter from the Chaplain, Benares to Lt. C. Pogson dated Sep 1913 (kind permission of Cherry Armstrong).

23. OIOC—E/4/797 p1172 & E/4/798 p1200.

24. The Athenaeum and Daily News. Madras. Friday July 28th 1882 (kind permission of Cherry Armstrong).

25. NAI—FC 28th July 1854 Nos 209–211.

26. OIOC—Bengal Pol Cons 9th May 1823 No 50.

27. OIOC—L/AG/34/29/37 f 49-51 (Bengal Wills 1825).

28. LDS FHC Library Film 506838 f.105–122 (with grateful thanks to Rowena Summers for transcribing the Will).

29. OIOC—L/AG/34/27/87 Bengal Inventories Pt 4 1826.

30. Lee, Y.K., *A Short Account of the Coroner in Early Singapore (1819–1869)*, Singapore Med J. 2005; 46 (10); 576.

31. Logan, James Richardson, *The Journal of the Indian Archipelago* 1847 (p454).

32. *Genealogy of the Queiros Family* q.v.

33. NAI—FC 5 Feb 1858 No 202

34. *Genealogy of the Queiros Family* q.v.

35. NAI—FC 5 Feb 1858 No 202 .

36. OIOC—L/AG/35/29/141 Bengal Wills & Administrations 1897 pt 1 f54 Mary Louisa Queiros.

37. NAI Foreign Dept – Mily Poll Desp to Secy of State No 1 of 8 Mar 1864.

Chapter 9

1. OIOC India Pol Cons 15th May1857 No 137 - P/202/25.
2. NAI—FC 18th June 1856 No 321-331.
3. NAI—FC 31 Dec 1858 No 898.
4. Ibid.
5. UPSA—Lucknow File No 2278 of 1858.
6. NAI—FC 31 Dec 1858 No 902, 3.
7. UPSA Oudh Proceedings, General Dept, Home 1871.
8. UPSA Lucknow File No 2654 of 1859, No 2894 & Oudh Abstract Proceedings—Revenue 1859, No 99.
9. New Calcutta Directory, 1856, 7.
10. LWO: 1911 file No 11 of Ellen Johannes.
11. La Martiniere School, Lucknow – Admission register.
12. St Joseph's Cathedral, Lucknow Baptism & Marriage registers.
13. LWO: File No: 21 of 1917 John Johannes.
14. LWO 1911 file No 11 of Ellen Johannes.
15. Kinkaid, W. *The Indian Bourbons*: Vol 3, 1887.
16. LWO: File No: 2 of 1899 Marcelina Bourbon.
17. Ibid.
18. Information from Dr. Lindsay Gethin.
19. LWO: 1911 file No 11 of Ellen Johannes.

Chapter 10

1. King's College London Archives Dept.
2. OIOC—L/MAR/C/888 Register of deposits on account of Native Servants who have gone with Passengers to England.
3. Wasika Office, Lucknow, file of John Speirs (1907).
4. King's College London Archives Dept.
5. Kerr, Ian J., *Building the Railways of the Raj, 1850–1900*, Oxford University Press, Delhi, 1997.
6. OIOC: L/F/10/211 List of uncovenanted Civil Servants in the office of Supt of Police Lucknow on 1st April 1866
7. Lobo, Chev Austin, KSG, *Growth and Development of the Catholic Diocese of Lucknow*, published by Lobo, Lucknow, 1998.
8. NAI Genl:A July1885 No. 17 The full text of John Alpine Speirs' petition is given in the appendix.

Chapter 11

Note: No references are given for the majority of this chapter, which is derived mainly from family memories, related to the author by his late father, Dr Lawrence Speirs.

1. Llewellyn-Jones, Dr Rosie, *A Very Ingenious Man, Claude Martin in Early Colonial India*, Oxford University Press, Delhi, 1992.
2. La Martiniere School, Lucknow—admission registers (by kind permission of the bursar).
3. Lucknow Wasika Office (LWO) file of 1927 (decease of Edwin Short)
4. Oak Grove School, Mussoorie, diary of Lt. Col. A.C. Chapman 1888–1910.
5. Information from Annette Moriarty, William Speirs' grand-daughter.

BIBLIOGRAPHY

Books and printed sources

Anon, *A lady's Diary of the Siege of Lucknow,* London, 1858 (reprinted 1997)

Badruddin, Syed *Bi Nanna's tale* (article in MAO College, Aligarh, magazine)

Bhatt, Ravi, *The Life and Times of the Nawabs of Lucknow,* Delhi, 2006

Bullock, Brigadier H., *Genealogy of the Quieros Family*, 1946

Devine, T.M., *The Tobacco Lords,* Edinburgh, 1975

Eden, Emily, *Up the Country – letters from India,* 1866 & 1872 (reprinted 1983)

Eaton, Natasha *Excess in the City: the Consumption of Imported Prints in Colonial Calcutta c 1780-c 1795* by Journal of Material Culture March, 2003

Fisher, Michael, *A Clash of Cultures; Awadh, the British and the Mughals*, Delhi, 1988.

Hastings, Marquis of, *Private Journal of the Marquis of Hastings KG,* 2 Vols, 1858

Hay, Miss Sidney, *Historic Lucknow*, 1939 (republished 2002)

Heber, Bishop Reginald, *Narrative of a Journey through the Upper Provinces of India,*

Hodson, Major VCP, 'List of the Officers of the Bengal Army 1758-1834', London, 1946

Huddleston, G. CIE, *History of the East Indian Railway*, 1906

Hussain, Sheikh Tussaduque, *Begammat-i-Awadh,* 1896 (Urdu)

Llewellyn-Jones, Dr. Rosie, *A Fatal Friendship – the Nawabs, the British and the City of Lucknow,* Delhi, 1985

Llewellyn-Jones, Dr. Rosie, *A Very Ingenious Man—Claude Martin in Early Colonial India,* Delhi, 1992

Llewellyn Jones, Dr. Rosie, *Engaging Scoundrels—True Tales of Old Lucknow*, Delhi, 2000

Lobo, Chevalier Austin Malcolm: *Growth and Development of the Catholic Diocese of Lucknow, 1940-1997,* Lucknow, 1998

Keene, H.G., *A Handbook for Visitors to Lucknow*, Calcutta, 1875 (reprinted 2000)

Kerr, Ian J., *Building the Railways of the Raj 1850- 1900,* Delhi, 1997
Lee, Y.K., *A Short Account of the Coroner in Early Singapore* (1819-1869) Singapore Med
    J. 2005
Logan, James Richardson, *The Journal of the Indian Archipelago* 1847
Machling, Tessa, *Colonial Fortifications.From Ireland to Nevis: The life of Governor John Johnson*
Meer Hassan Ali, Mrs., *Observations on the Mussulmans of India,* 2 Vols, 1832
Mundy, Captain, *Pen & Pencil Sketches, being the Journal of a Tour of India,* 1833
Oldenburg, Veena Talwar: *The Making of Colonial Lucknow,* Delhi, 1989
Parks, Fanny, *Wanderings of a Pilgrim in Search of the Picturesque,*
Philips, C.H., *The Correspondence of Lord William Cavendish Bentinck* Vol II 1832-1835, 1977.
Pinhey, Lt. Col. A.F., *History of Mewar,* 1909; reprinted 1996, Udaipur
Praveen, Yogesh, *Lucknow Monuments,*
Rao, M.A., *Indian Railways,* Delhi, 1975
Renwick, Robert, *Extracts from the Records of the Burgh of Glasgow, Vol VI-IX 1739-1809*
    Glasgow 1911
Saroop, Narinder *A Squire of Hindoostan,* London, 1983
Santha, Dr K.S., *Begums of Awadh,* Varanasi, 1980
Seth, Mesrovb., *A History of Armenians in India from the Earliest Times to the Present Day,*
    Calcutta, 1937
Wylie, M, *The English Captives of Oudh: An Episode in the History of the Mutinies of 1857-8,*
Yalland, Zoe, *Kacheri Cemetery, Kanpur* London, 1985
Yalland, Zoe, *Traders and Nabobs – The British in Cawnpore 1765-1857,* 1987
Yalland, Zoe, *Boxwallahs -- The British in Cawnpore 1857-1901,* Norwich, 1994

Records and manuscripts

Note: The following abbreviations have been used for these references in each
chapter:

FC   Foreign Consultations
Fin   Finance files
Gen   General files
UPSA   Utttar Pradesh State Archives (Lucknow)
LWO   Lucknow Wasika Office
OIOC   Oriental and India Office Collections, British Library, London
NAI   National Archives of India, Janpath, New Delhi
PC   Political Consultations
PRO   National Archives, Kew (formerly known as the Public Records Office).

British Library – Oriental and India Office Collections (OIOC)

E/4 series   Despatches 1848
L/AG/34/27   series Bengal Inventories 1826

L/AG/34/29	series Bengal Wills 1825, 33, 97
L/F/10/211	List of uncovenanted servants in Lucknow Police, 1866
L/MIL/9 series	Cadet papers 1803
L/MIL/10 series	Military service records 1847
L/MIL/12 series	Surgeons' papers 1807
L/MAR/B series	Ships' log 1803, 1805
P/ series	Bengal Pol Cons 1822-1834
P/ series	India Pol Cons 18340û1847
P/131 series	Bengal Criminal and Judicial Proceedings 1812-14
P/354 series	Bombay Military Consultations 1797-1803

Glasgow City Archives, Mitchell Library, Glasgow

TD/1318 Speirs of Elderslie family records

Houston House, Houston, Renfrewshire

Speirs of Elderslie papers (private collection)

King's College, London, Archives Dept

Enrolment records 1856

La Martiniere School, Lucknow

Admission registers 1858-1958

Library of Virginia

Carey family papers (early records of Alexander Speirs, the tobacco Lord)

Lucknow Wasika Office (LWO)

The most important source of records for this book, with files from 1858-1945
for the following:
Bourbon: Marcellina
Carrol: Grace
Chalk: Muriel
Duhan: Mary, E.M., J.R., J.W.B.
Johannes: Ellen, John
Moses: Grace
Queiros: Alban, E.B., Victoria, Winifred
Saddington: Louisa, Joseph
Sangster: Alice Jane, Augustus
Short: Agnes, Amelia, Benjamin, Charles, Edwin, Eliza, Frederick, George, Isaac,
    James Mcdonald, Joseph, Louisa, Martin, William
Snell: Margaret
Speirs: Alexander, Alice Mary, Eva, John, Rachel, Sleeman, William

National Archives of India, Janpath, New Delhi (NAI)

Foreign Consultations (FC) 1832, 39, 47, 48, 49, 54, 57, 58, 59
Finance (Fin) 1863, 1871, 1875, 1876
General (Gen) 1862, 1885, 1893
Political Consultations (PC) 1817
Military Despatch to Secretary of State 1864

National Archives (Great Britain), Kew (PRO)
Wills 1808, 1874

Norfolk County Record Office
Casebooks SAH series

Oak Grove School, Mussoorie
Diary of Lt Col A.C. Chapman 1888 – 1910.

Uttar Pradesh State Archives, Lucknow (UPSA)
Oude General, 1859-60
Lucknow files, 1859, 1859-60, 1861-62, 1858-61,

GLOSSARY

Abba	Father
Amlah	Indian court official or personnel
Ana	Indian coin worth one-sixteenth of a rupee
Ashrafi	A gold coin [from Arabic]
Atr	traditional muslim incense or perfume
Aumeen	A land-manager, under the Amani system.
Aurang	Factory
Ayah	A maid.
Bacha	Where does this word occur?
Bagh	Garden
Bania	A Hindu shopkeeper; money launderer
Barahdari	A rectangular building with twelve (barah) openings; residence of an eminent office bearer
Bhatta	An allowance to a public servant in addition to his wages. In the East India Company's army, bhatta was paid to all soldiers and officers when on detached duty.
Bazaar	market
Begum	Wife or queen
Bhil	A hill-tribe of Rajasthan
Bigha	A measure of land, varying in extent in different parts of India
Beldar	A labourer involved in digging or excavating.
Burrah sahib	An important person—typically applied to a European official. [literally: 'big person']
Butrim bad butrim	'womb by womb' [from Persian]
Chawkidar	A guard—usually of a house, cemetery, building etc.
Chawkhat	A door or window opening [from Hindi: chau = four khat = timber]
Chabutra	A raised platform

Chaprasi	Peon
Crore	Ten million—usually refers to money : i.e. 'a crore of rupees'
Dacoit	An armed robber
Damum	Reputation
Darogha	A manager or a superintendent, particularly the head of a customs and excise or police post.
Dirham	A coin; currency of Kuwait or countries in the middle-east.
Doli	A type of sedan carriage for ladies
Durbar	King's Court
Durbar Vakil	Ambassador of a Muslim court. In states where the East India Company had a British Resident, the durbar vakil was the intermediary between the King and the Resident for most matters.
Furaiz Ullah	Divine Law [from Persian]
Furlough	A period of extended leave usually applied to officers or civil servants of the East India Company, who were entitled to proceed on furlough for periods of two years after a number of years' service.
Furmaun	Royal edict or order.
Ghat	Level terraces at the bank of a river used for bathing, performing religious rituals etc.
Ghee	Clarified butter
Gomastah	An agent, steward or officer employed by zamindars to collect land-rents
Gora Sahib	A European man. Literally: 'white man'.
Grassia	A hill-tribe of Rajasthan
Gaddi	Literally a cushion but used to signify the royal throne like rajgaddi
Hackerie	A hand-pulled cart.
Hakim	A native doctor
Hazrat Mahal	Honour of the palace.
Hijree	The name of the Mohammedan era, starting from Mohammad's departure from Mecca. Usually applied to the calendar, to distinguish dates as Hijree rather than AD. (Christian calendar).
Hookm namah	A royal decree.
Howdah	A seated enclosure for travelling on an elephant's back.
Hurkarah	A messenger; courier; spy.
Hurrum	A slave-wife.
Idaat	A period fixed after divorce between Muslims, allowing the husband to change his mind.
Imambara	A Shia Muslim building expressly built for the celebration of Mohurrum.

Jagir	An area of land bestowed by a ruler on a subject who is then entitled to receive rents from the land during his lifetime.
Jheel	A lake.
Khansama	A cook.
Khawas	The closest person or confidante.
Khillut	A ceremonial present given to or received from Muslim rulers at court.
Khureeta	A special letter, enclosed in a silk bag for correspondence with Indian royalty. The 'Kharita' is actually the silk-bag, but the term generally implies the contents.
Kothi	A house, usually with its own compound.
Kotwal	Chief of Police.
Kutcha	Incomplete or not properly made. For example a 'kutcha road' is an unsurfaced or unlayered road.
Lakh	One hundred thousand; usually applied to money, as 'a lakh of rupees'.
Machaan	A platform constructed on trees for a hunter, generally overlooking the prey.
Maharaja	An Indian King.
Maharani	Generally the wife of a Maharaja, but may be a ruler in her own right.
Mohammedan	A Muslim.
Mahratta	Warrior tribes of the Central Indian plains.
Mahul	Palace.
Mali	Gardener.
Manja	A special string for kite-flying dipped in a sticky mixture of powdered glass used for breaking the strings of other kites in play.
Manzil	A grand house or residence; segment or portion; destination.
Marpit	A physical fight/tussle.
Maqbara	A Muslim shrine.
Masnud	A throne, literally a cushion.
Maulvi	A Muslim religious leader.
Mohalla	Division, quarter or colony of a city.
Mohur	A small gold coin of the Moghul era.
Moharram	A religious festival of Shia Muslims to commemorate the martyrdom of Imam Hussein.
Mootsuddi	Accounts clerk.
Mubaruck Mahal	Literally 'dignity of the palace'.
Muhaldar	A palace guard.
Mukhtar	An agent, representative or attorney.
Mumtaz Mahal	Literally 'distinguished palace'.
Munshi	A clerk.

Mussamat	An honorific title for a Muslim lady.
Mussulman	A colloquial term for a Muslim.
Mutah	A temporary marriage under Islamic law.
Nawab	Originally a deputy governor under the control of the Muslim emperor of Delhi. The Nawabs of Awadh, however, only paid nominal allegiance to Delhi and actually ruled independently.
Nazool	Government property.
Nikah	A formal marriage ceremony under Islamic law.
Nuslun bad nuslun	Literally 'generation by generation' [from Persian].
Palanquin	A box-like conveyance usually for upper class ladies with poles carried by six to eight bearers to transport a person.
Pice	An English pice was originally 1/64th of a rupee or a quarter of an ana.
Pleader	An advocate.
Pukka	Properly made or done. For example a 'pukka road' is a surfaced road and a 'pukka Sahib' is a proper gentleman.
Purdah	The Muslim system whereby wives and daughters are kept secluded from the eyes of other males. The purdah is literally the curtain behind which the women are shielded from view.
Raja	A King.
Rana	A local ruler.
Rao	A local ruler.
Rupee	The Indian unit of currency.
Sadar	Chief e.g. Sadar Bazaar is the main market and Sadar Darwaza is the main gate.
Sahib	A gentleman. The term was generally applied to all European men of authority.
Shia	A branch of the Islamic faith.
Shikari	An expert native hunter.
Shurriat ghurrah	Literally 'Bright law' [from Persian]
Sowar	An Indian army cavalry rank, equivalent to a trooper.
Sunni	A branch of the Islamic faith.
Taluqdar	A large land-owner.
Terai	The tarai literally 'moist land' is a belt of marshy grasslands, savannas, and forests at the base of the Himalayan range.
Thakur	A local chief or landlord.
Thana	A police post.
Thug	A thief; a member of a gang who practiced thuggee (see below).
Thuggee	A gang, whose members befriended travellers on the road, murdered them and stole their possessions. The practice was eliminated by about 1850 mainly due to the exertions of Major W.H. Sleeman (later Major General).

Tonga	A light horse-drawn carriage.
Tope	A grove of trees (often of mango).
Tika	The red marking applied by Hindus to the forehead.
Talwar	A long curved sword.
Vakil	A lawyer.
Vasiqueh	See under wasika.
Vilayuti	Foreign.
Vizier	A minister, usually the Prime Minister.
Warisnama	A formal list of heirs.
Wasika	A royal pension [derived from the Persian 'Vasiqueh', meaning bond or pledge].
Wasikadar	A pensioner in receipt of a wasika.
Zamindar	A small land-owner.
Zila	A district as in 'Zila Adawlut' or district court.

INDEX